FAIRY TAIL

51

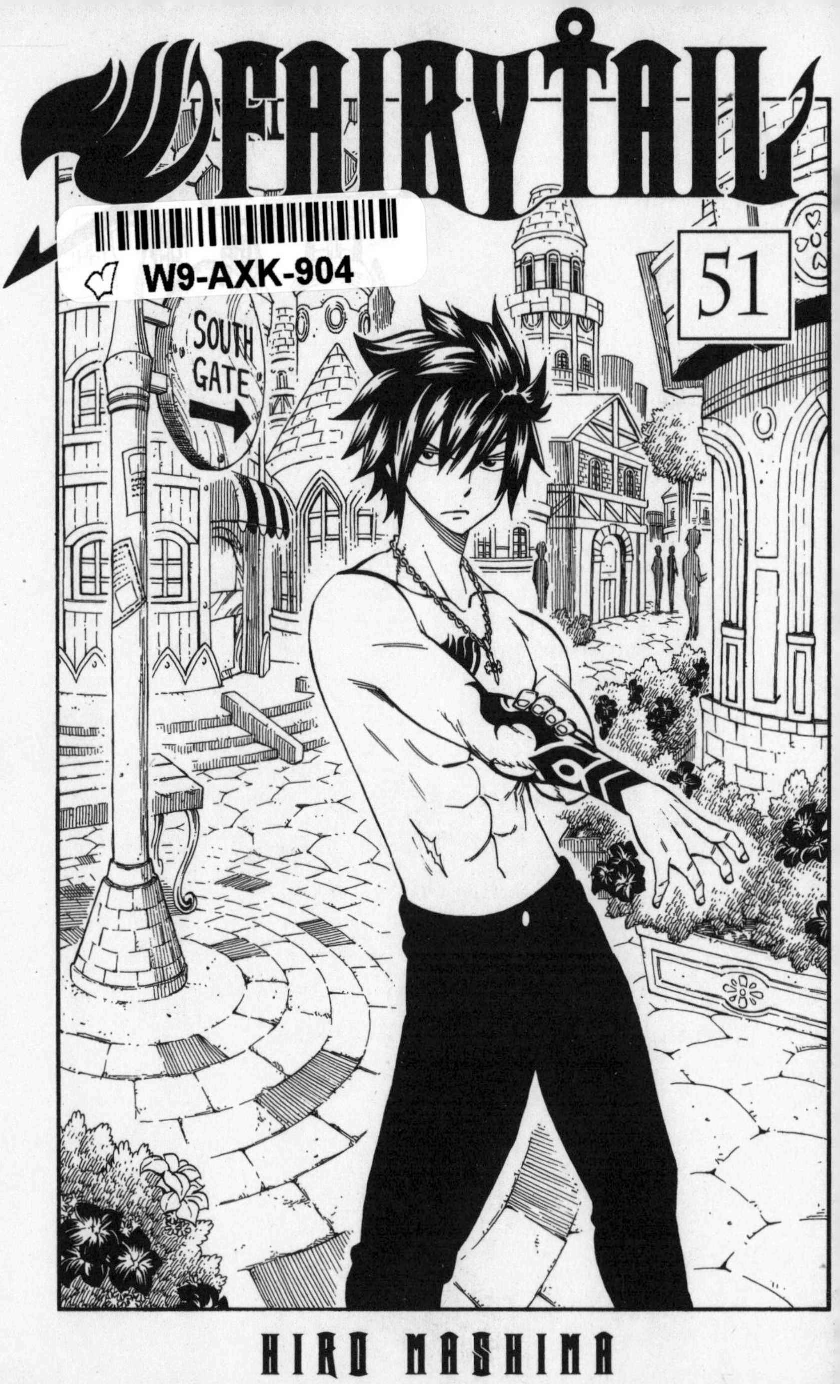
SOUTH GATE

HIRO MASHIMA

FT51
CONTENTS

FAIRY TAIL

フェアリーテイル

Chapter 430: Operation Purify

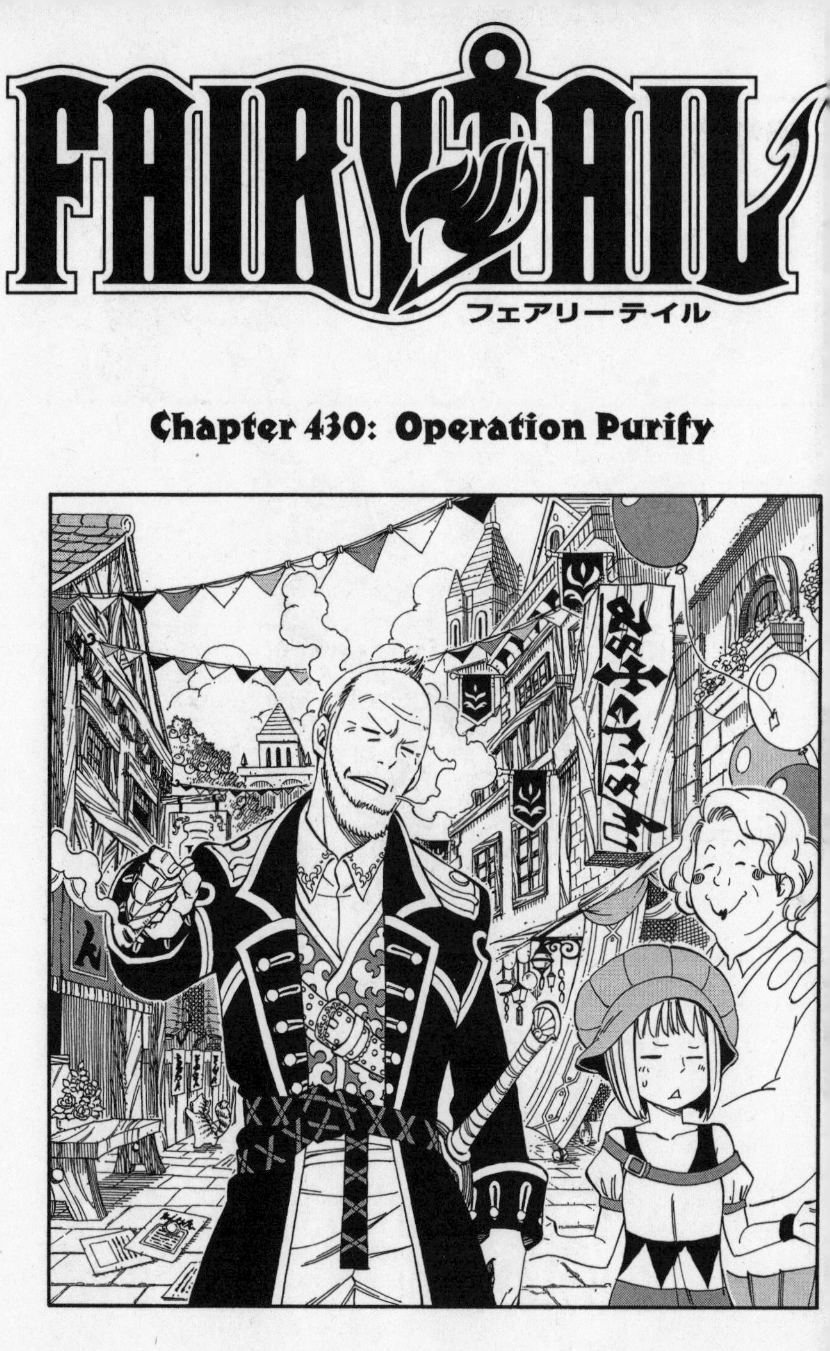

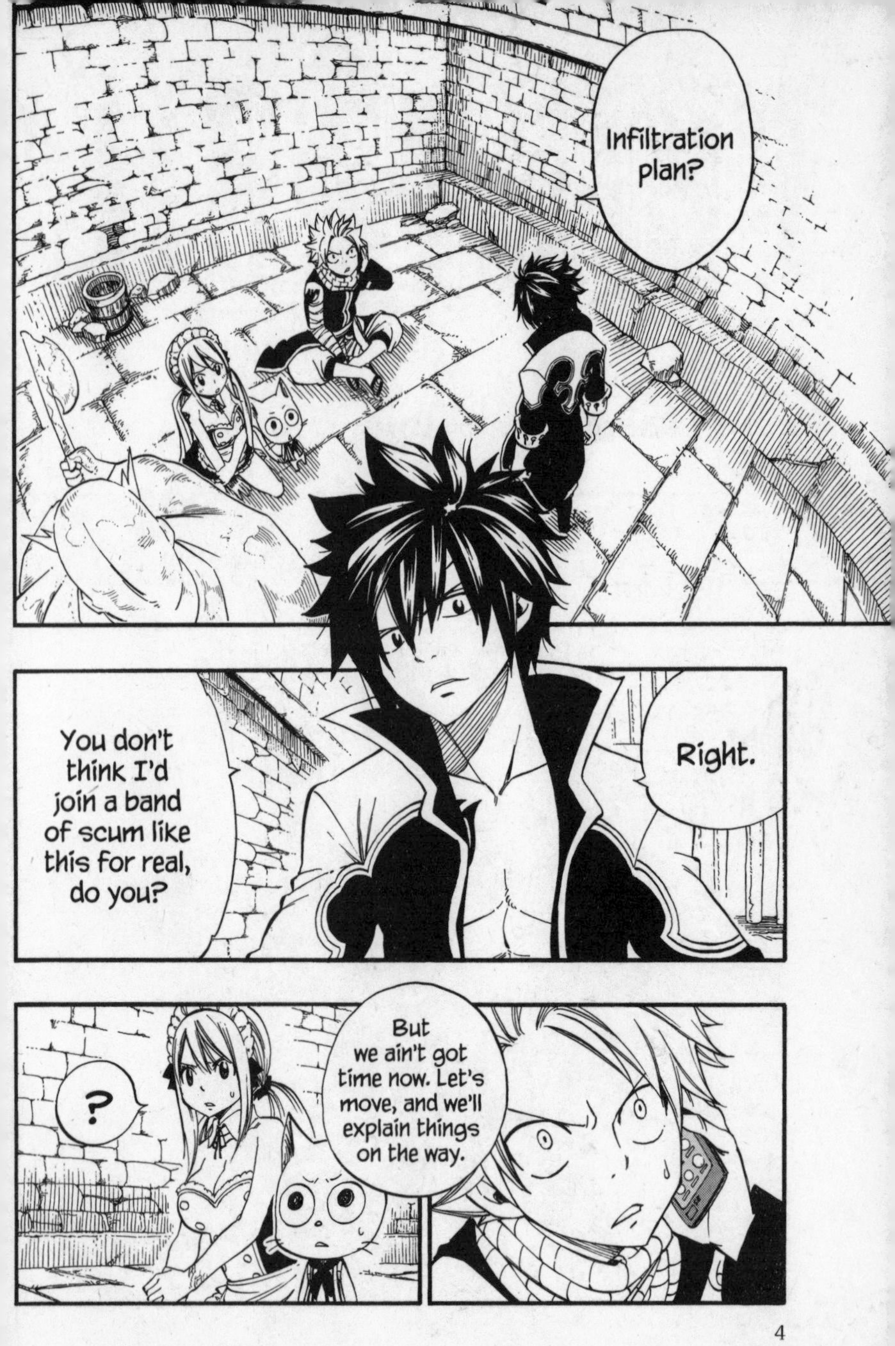
Infiltration plan?
Right.
You don't think I'd join a band of scum like this for real, do you?
But we ain't got time now. Let's move, and we'll explain things on the way.
?

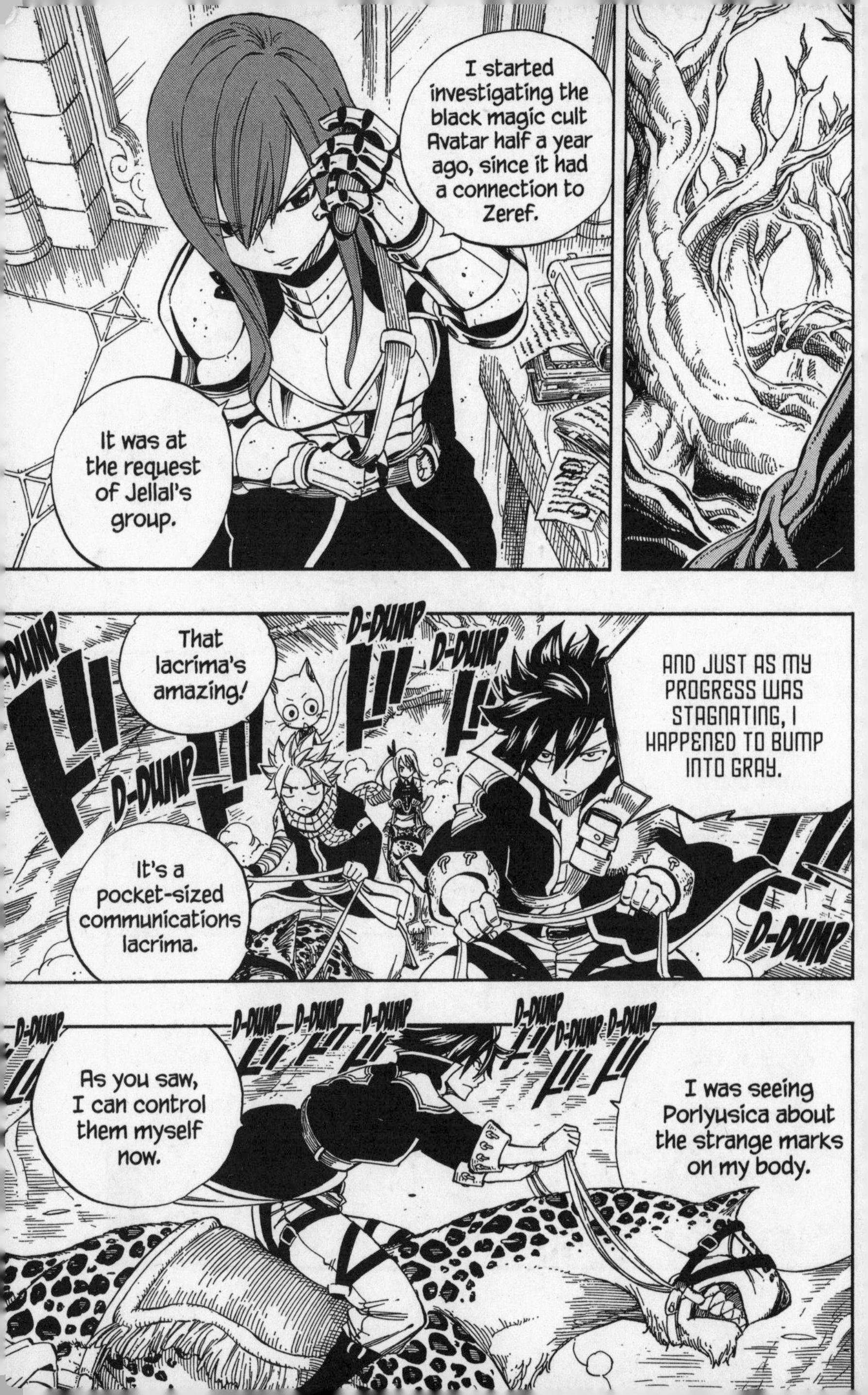
I started investigating the black magic cult Avatar half a year ago, since it had a connection to Zeref.
It was at the request of Jellal's group.
AND JUST AS MY PROGRESS WAS STAGNATING, I HAPPENED TO BUMP INTO GRAY.
D-DUMP
D-DUMP
That lacrima's amazing!
D-DUMP
D-DUMP
It's a pocket-sized communications lacrima.
D-DUMP
D-DUMP
D-DUMP
D-DUMP
D-DUMP
D-DUMP
D-DUMP
D-DUMP
I was seeing Porlyusica about the strange marks on my body.
As you saw, I can control them myself now.

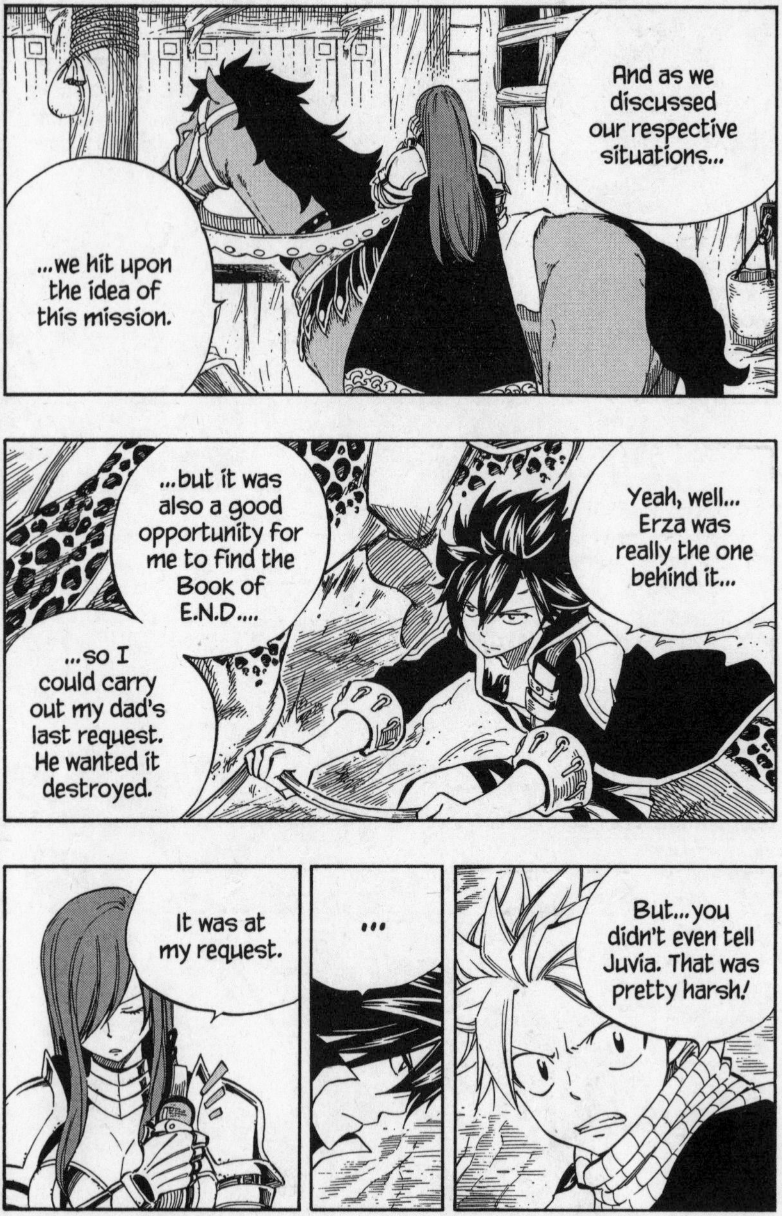
And as we discussed our respective situations...
...we hit upon the idea of this mission.
Yeah, well... Erza was really the one behind it...
...but it was also a good opportunity for me to find the Book of E.N.D....
...so I could carry out my dad's last request. He wanted it destroyed.
But...you didn't even tell Juvia. That was pretty harsh!
...
It was at my request.

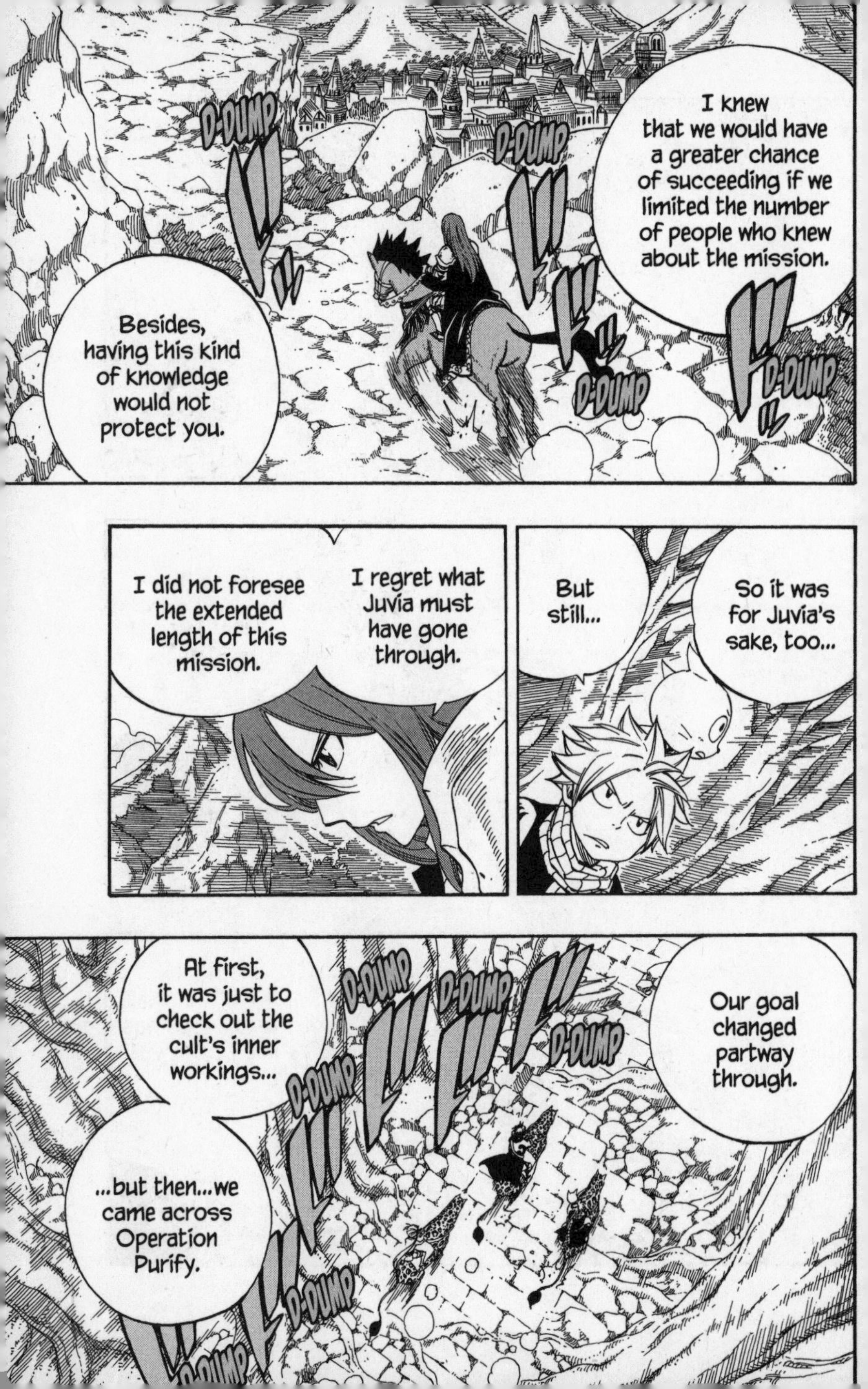
I knew that we would have a greater chance of succeeding if we limited the number of people who knew about the mission.
D-DUMP
D-DUMP
D-DUMP
D-DUMP
Besides, having this kind of knowledge would not protect you.
So it was for Juvia's sake, too...
But still...
I regret what Juvia must have gone through.
I did not foresee the extended length of this mission.
Our goal changed partway through.
D-DUMP
D-DUMP
D-DUMP
D-DUMP
At first, it was just to check out the cult's inner workings...
...but then...we came across Operation Purify.
D-DUMP

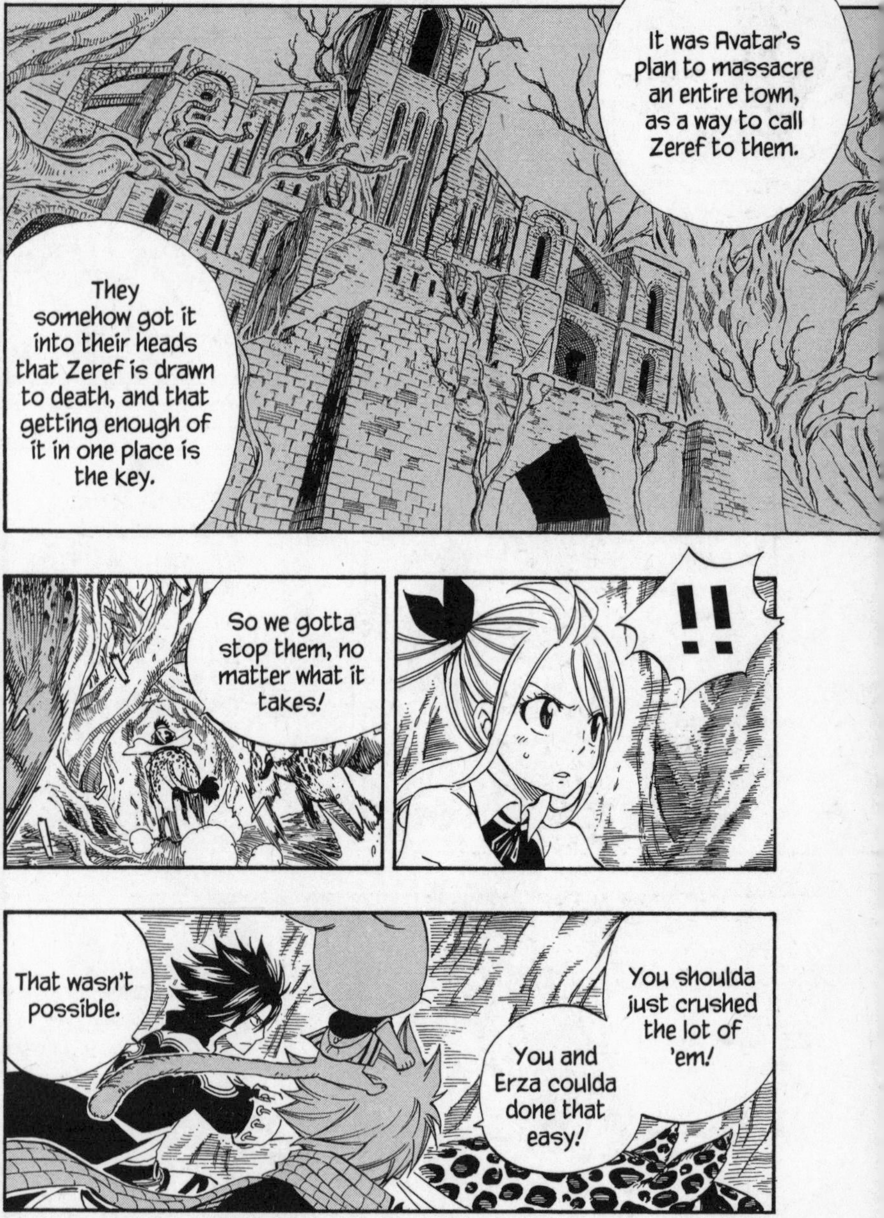
It was Avatar's plan to massacre an entire town, as a way to call Zeref to them.
They somehow got it into their heads that Zeref is drawn to death, and that getting enough of it in one place is the key.
!!
So we gotta stop them, no matter what it takes!
You shoulda just crushed the lot of 'em!
You and Erza coulda done that easy!
That wasn't possible.

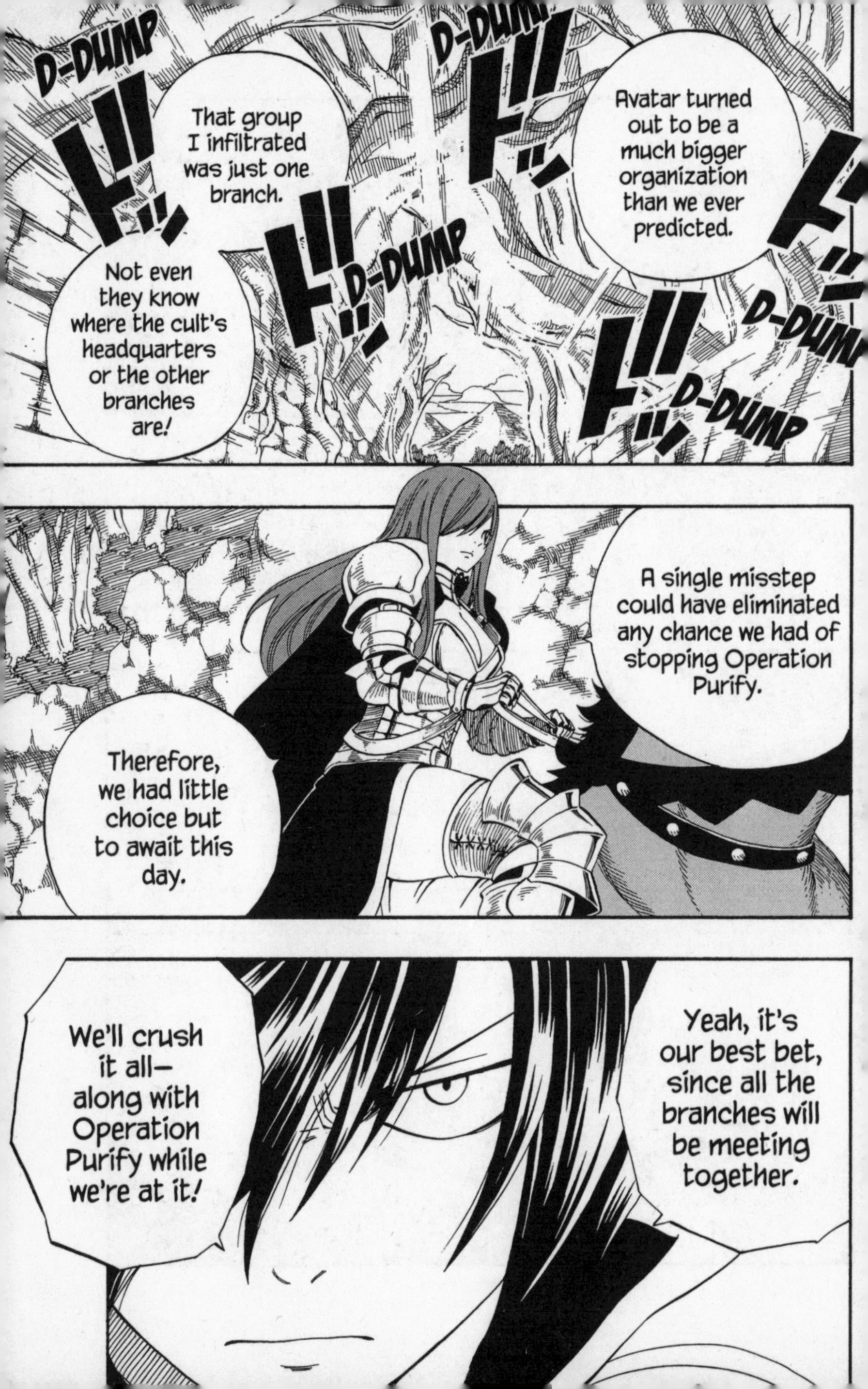
D-DUMP
Avatar turned out to be a much bigger organization than we ever predicted.
D-DUMP
D-DUMP
D-DUMP
That group I infiltrated was just one branch.
D-DUMP
Not even they know where the cult's headquarters or the other branches are!
A single misstep could have eliminated any chance we had of stopping Operation Purify.
Therefore, we had little choice but to await this day.
Yeah, it's our best bet, since all the branches will be meeting together.
We'll crush it all—along with Operation Purify while we're at it!

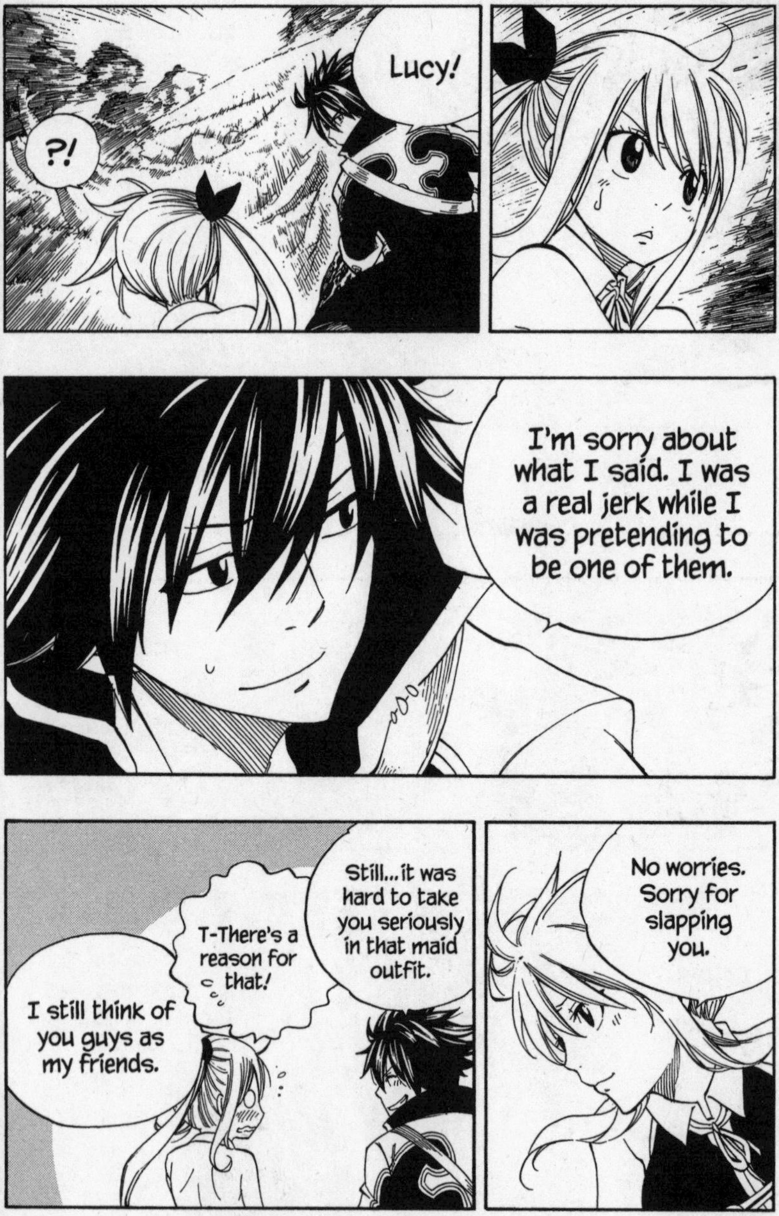
Lucy!
?!
I'm sorry about what I said. I was a real jerk while I was pretending to be one of them.
No worries. Sorry for slapping you.
Still...it was hard to take you seriously in that maid outfit.
T-There's a reason for that!
I still think of you guys as my friends.

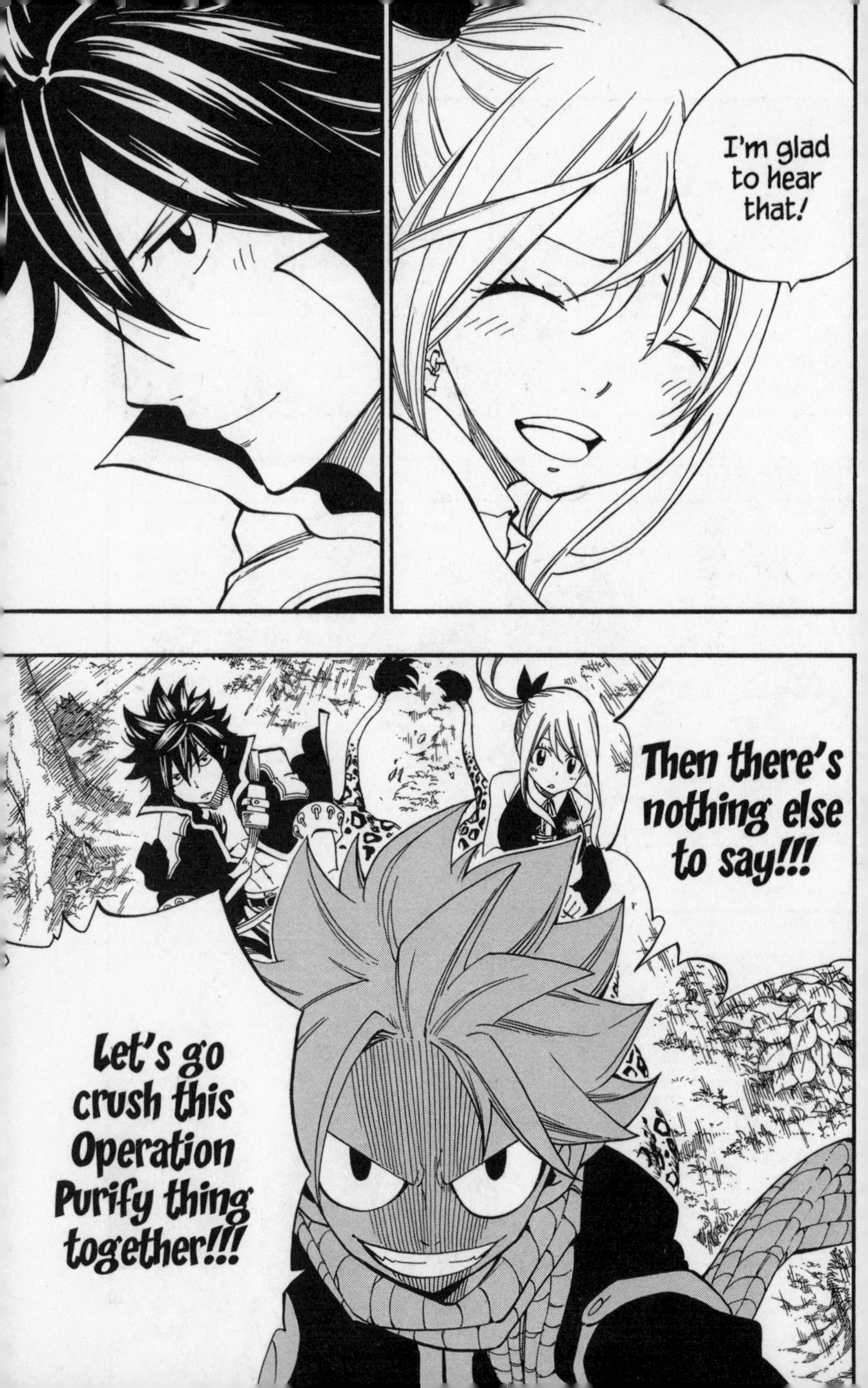
I'm glad to hear that!
Then there's nothing else to say!!!
Let's go crush this Operation Purify thing together!!!

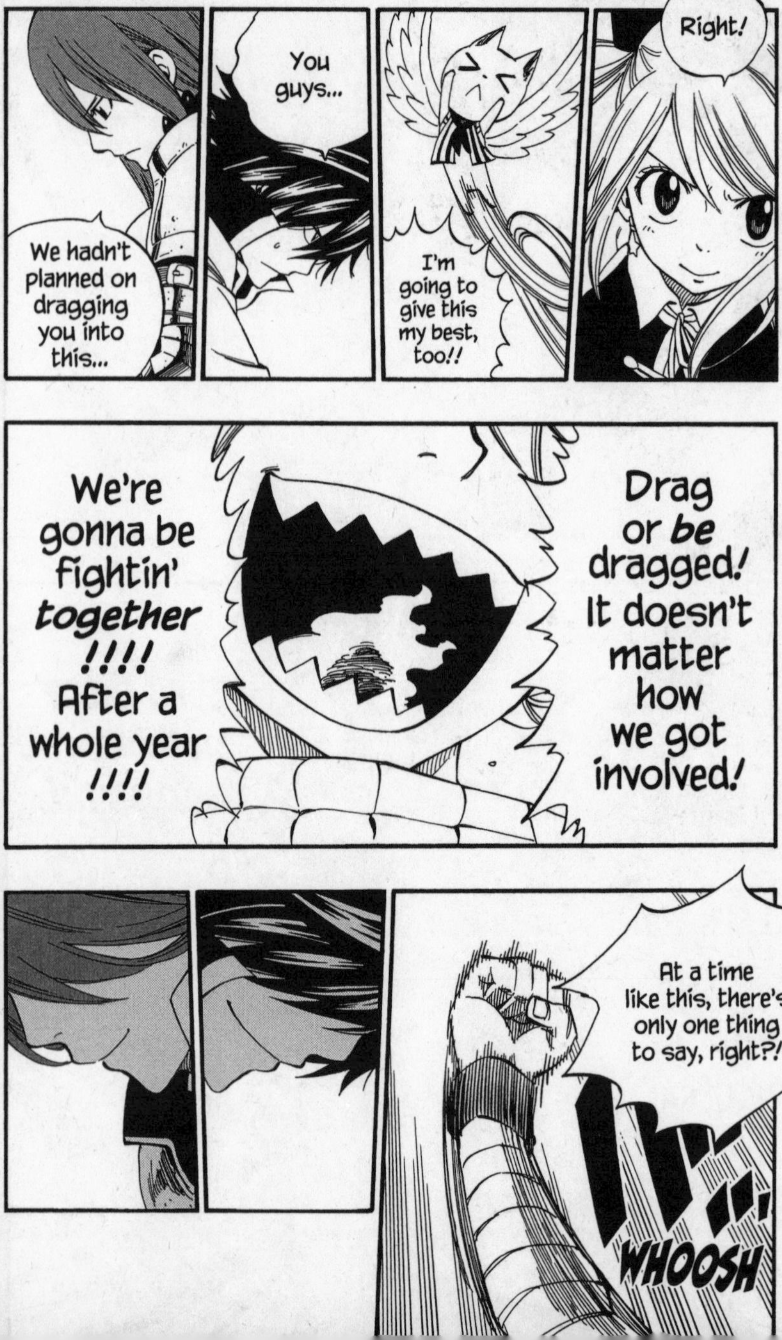
Right!
I'm going to give this my best, too!!
You guys...
We hadn't planned on dragging you into this...
Drag or *be* dragged! It doesn't matter how we got involved!
We're gonna be fightin' *together*!!!! After a whole year!!!!
At a time like this, there's only one thing to say, right?!
WHOOSH

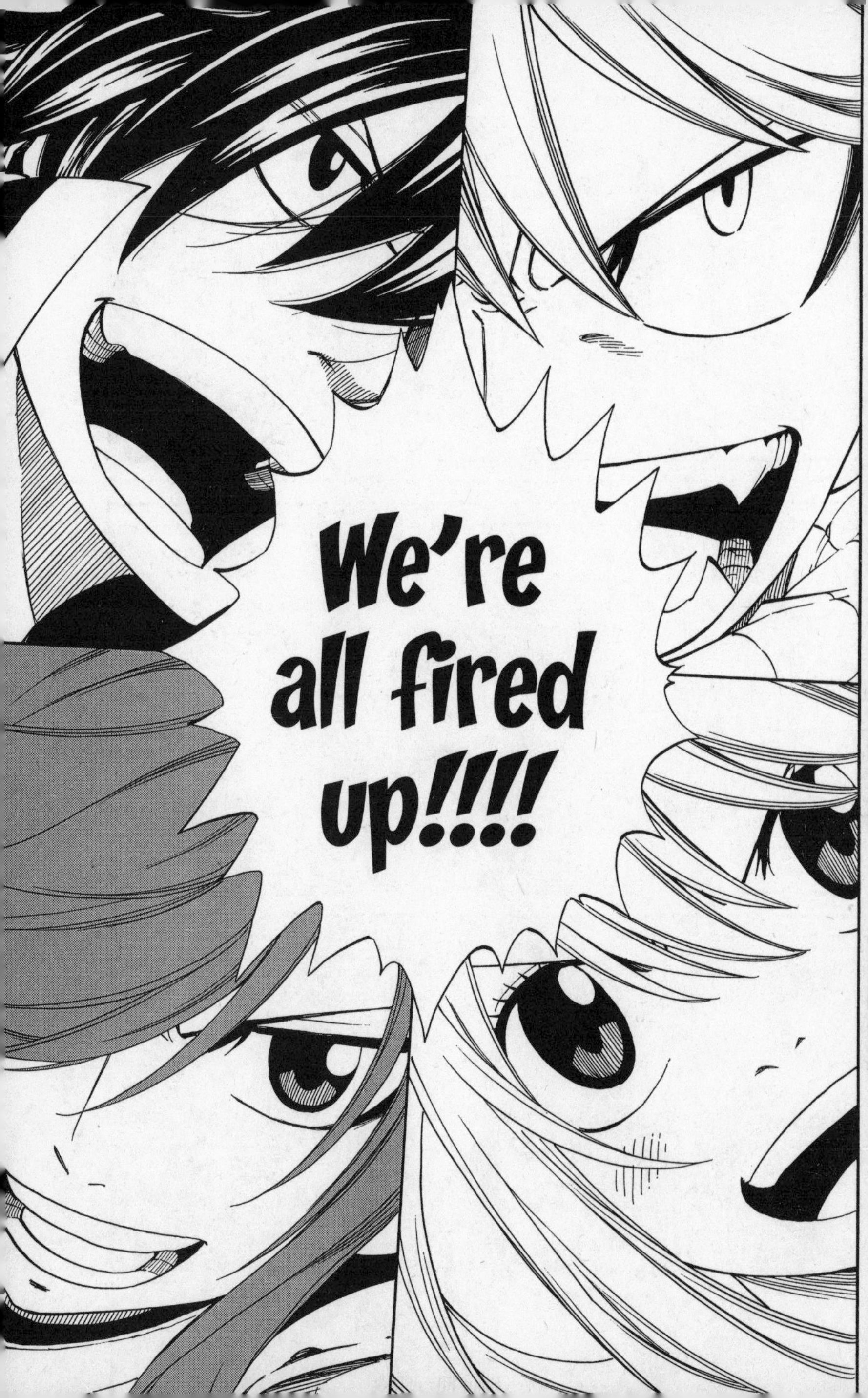
We're all fired up!!!!

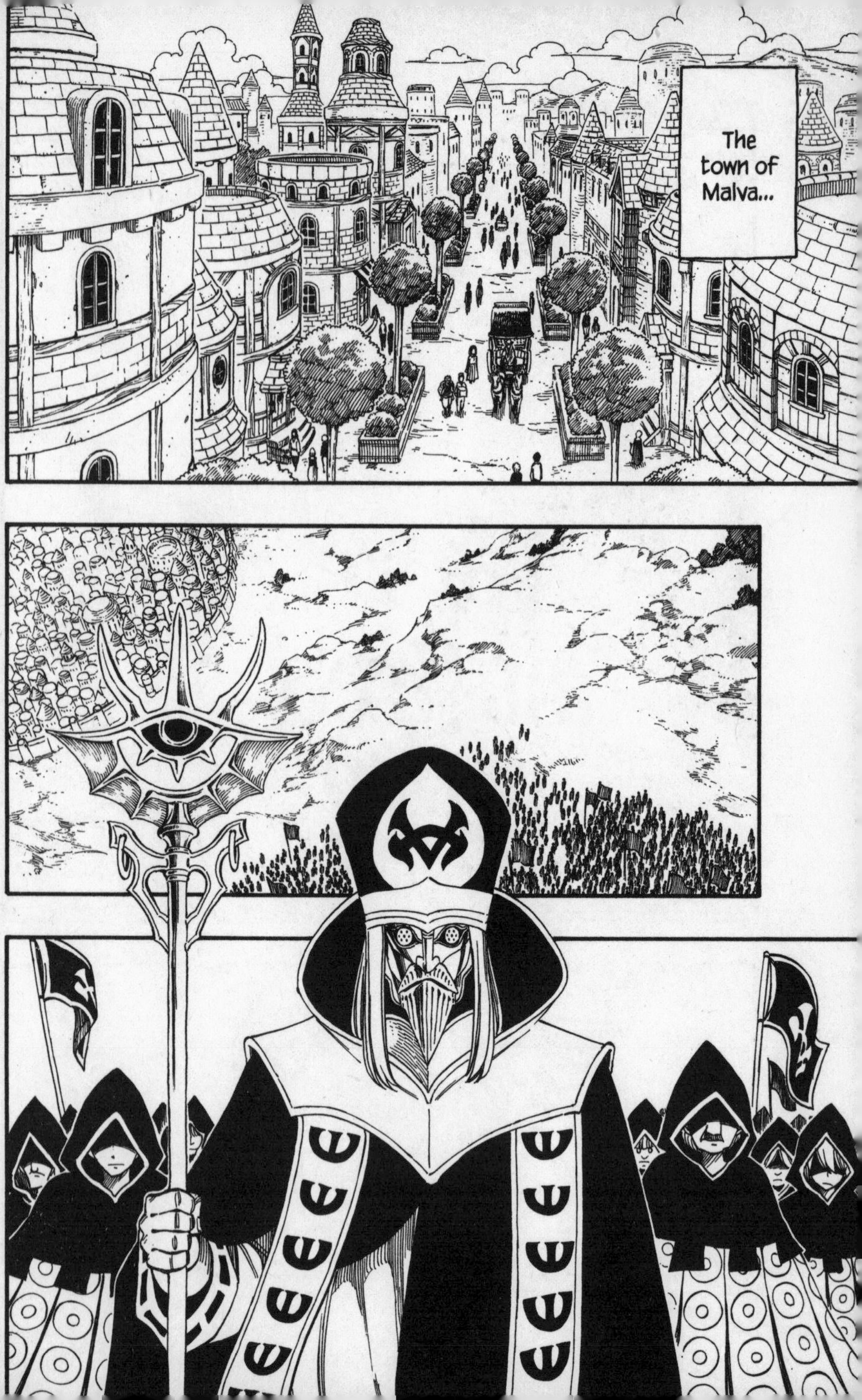
The town of Malva...

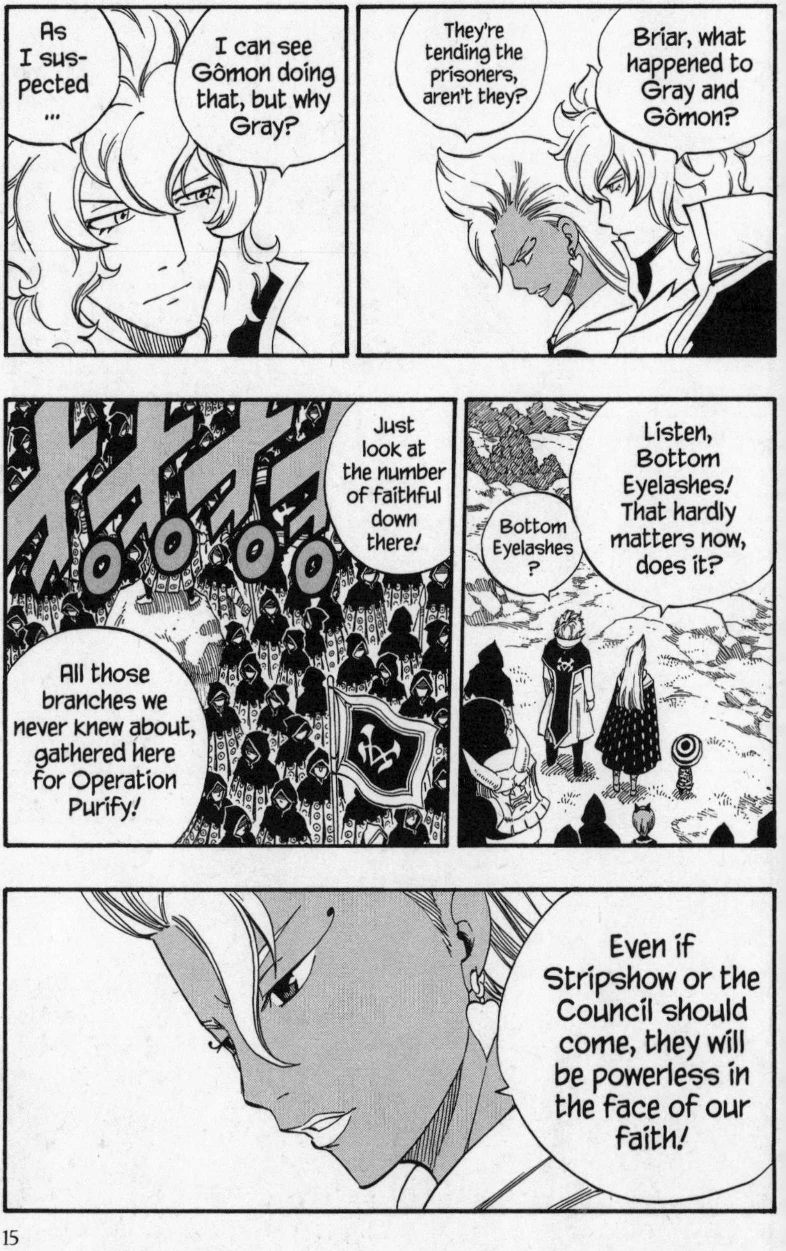

Briar, what happened to Gray and Gômon?
They're tending the prisoners, aren't they?
I can see Gômon doing that, but why Gray?
As I sus-pected ...
Listen, Bottom Eyelashes! That hardly matters now, does it?
Bottom Eyelashes?
Just look at the number of faithful down there!
All those branches we never knew about, gathered here for Operation Purify!
Even if Stripshow or the Council should come, they will be powerless in the face of our faith!

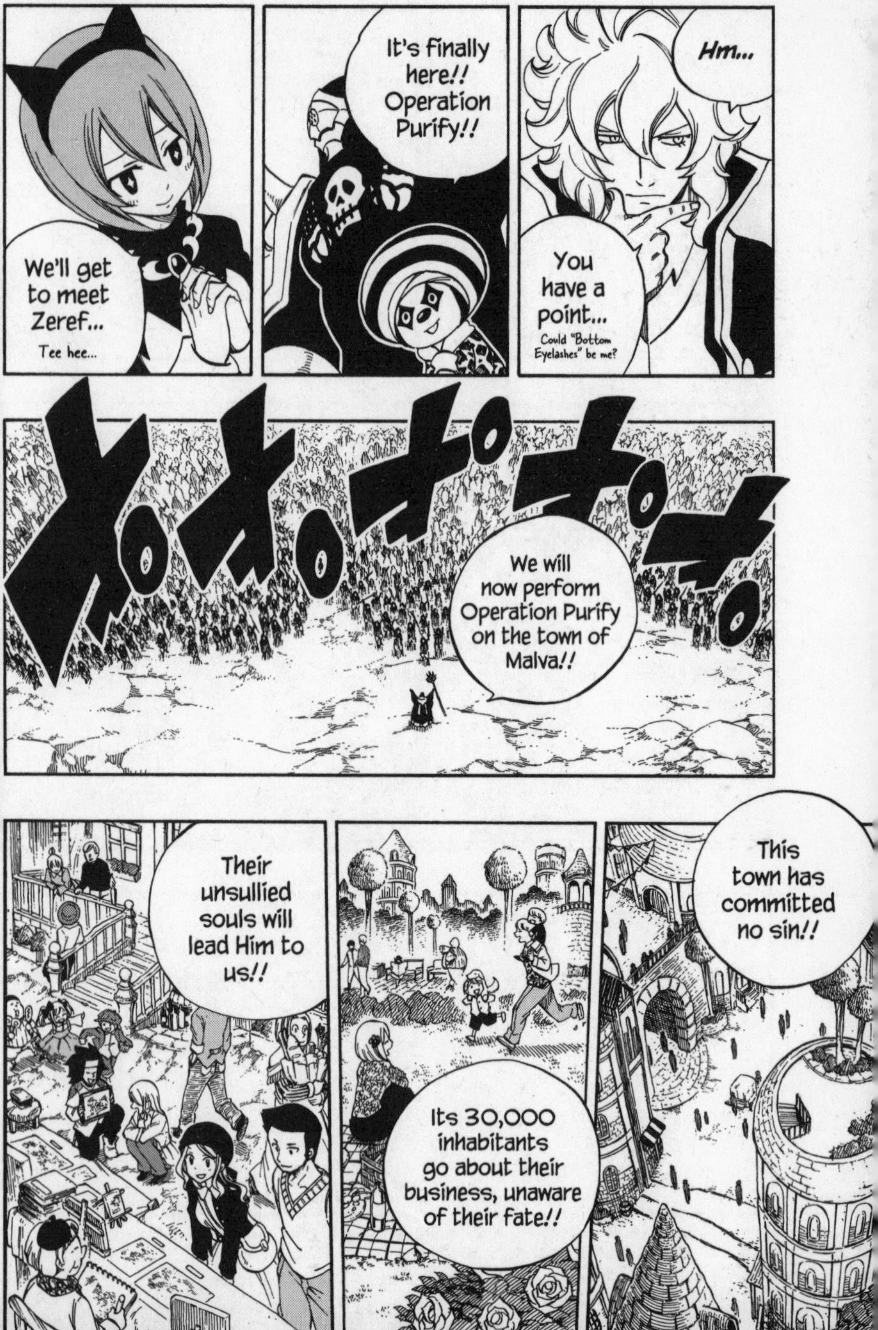
Hm...
You have a point...
Could "Bottom Eyelashes" be me?
It's finally here!! Operation Purify!!
We'll get to meet Zeref...
Tee hee...
We will now perform Operation Purify on the town of Malva!!
This town has committed no sin!!
Its 30,000 inhabitants go about their business, unaware of their fate!!
Their unsullied souls will lead Him to us!!

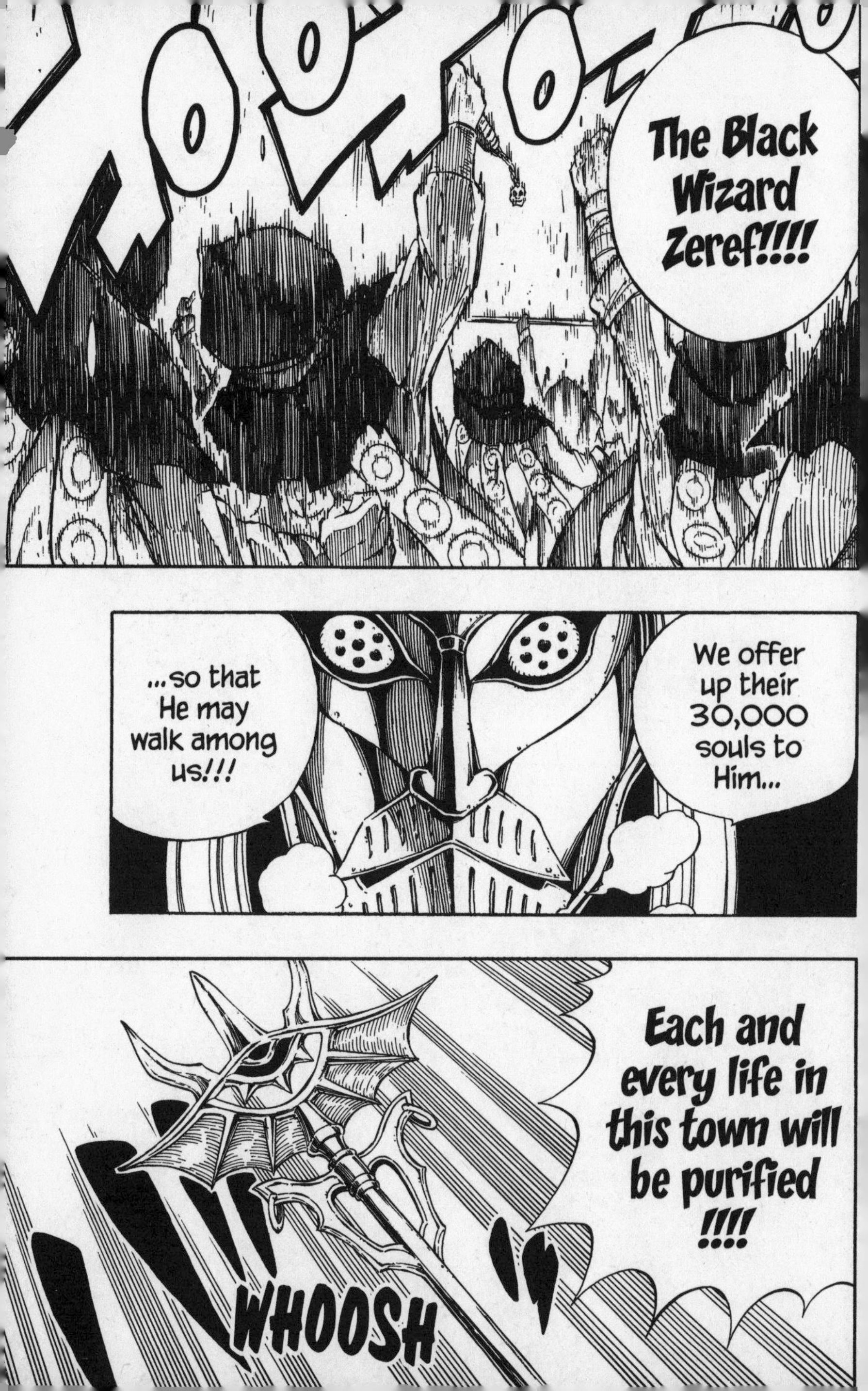
The Black Wizard Zeref!!!!
We offer up their 30,000 souls to Him...
...so that He may walk among us!!!
Each and every life in this town will be purified!!!!
WHOOSH

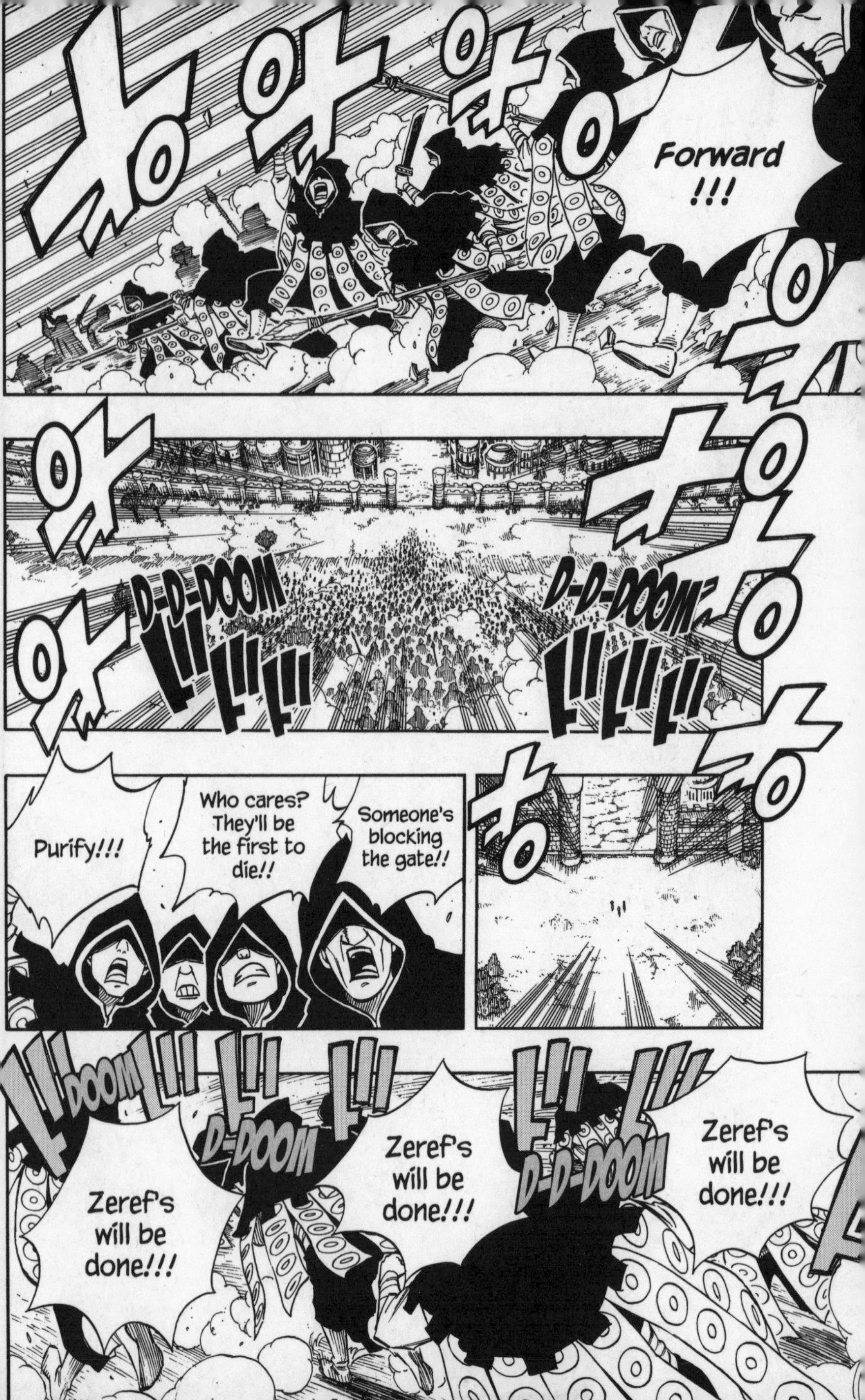
Forward !!!
D-D-DOOM
D-D-DOOM
Someone's blocking the gate!!
Who cares? They'll be the first to die!!
Purify!!!
Zeref's will be done!!!
D-D-DOOM
Zeref's will be done!!!
D-DOOM
Zeref's will be done!!!
DOOM

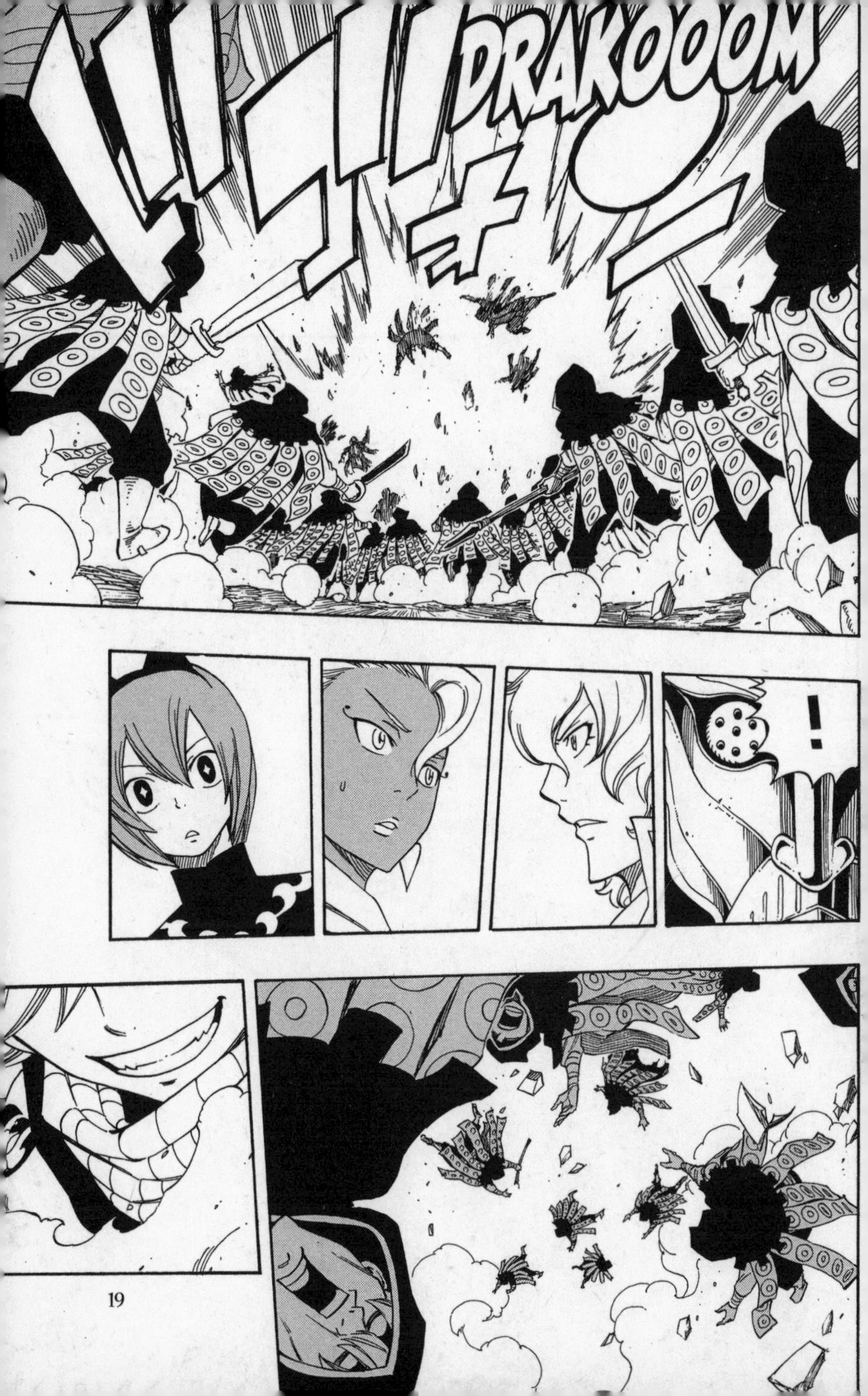
DRAKOOOM
!

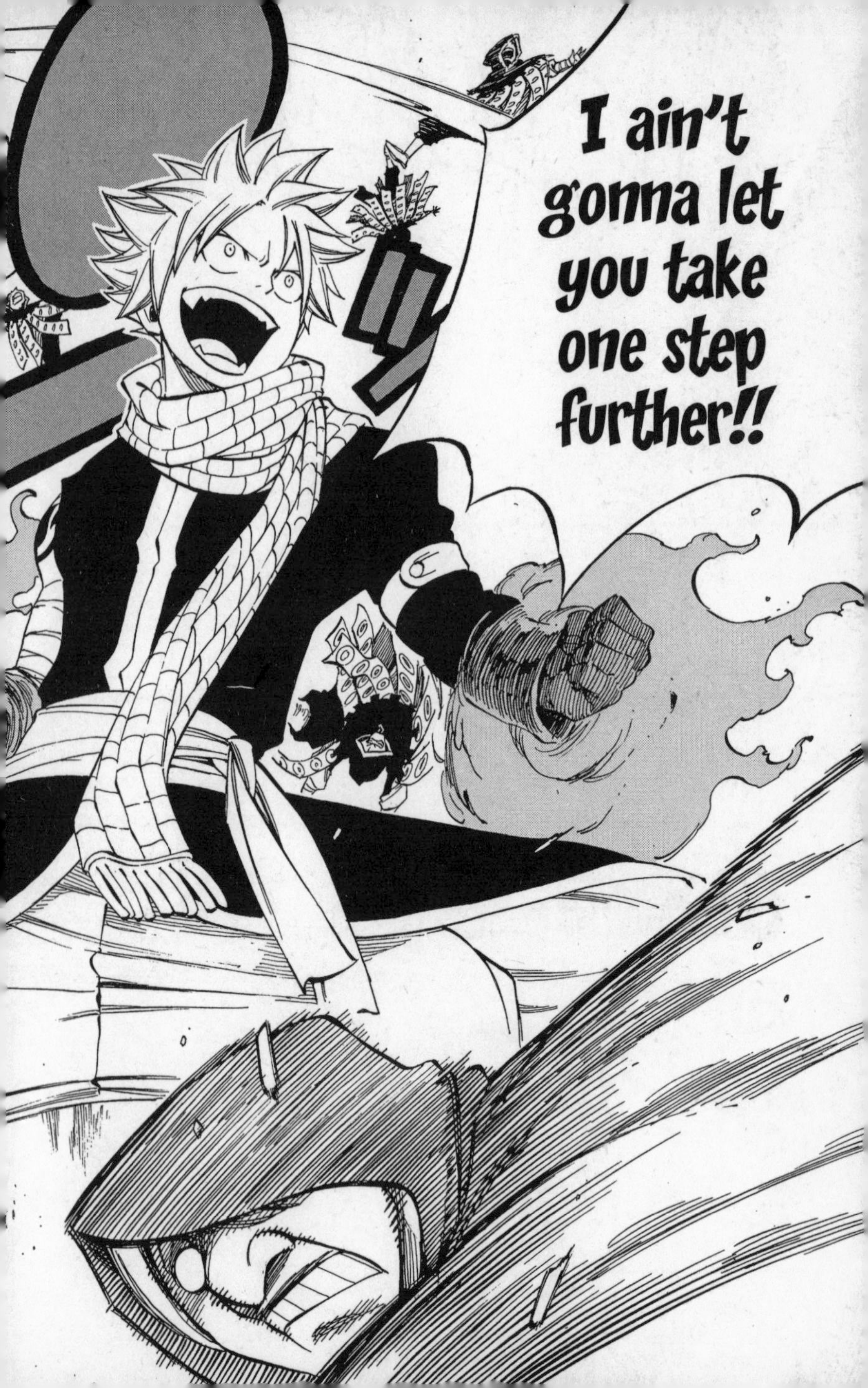
I ain't gonna let you take one step further!!

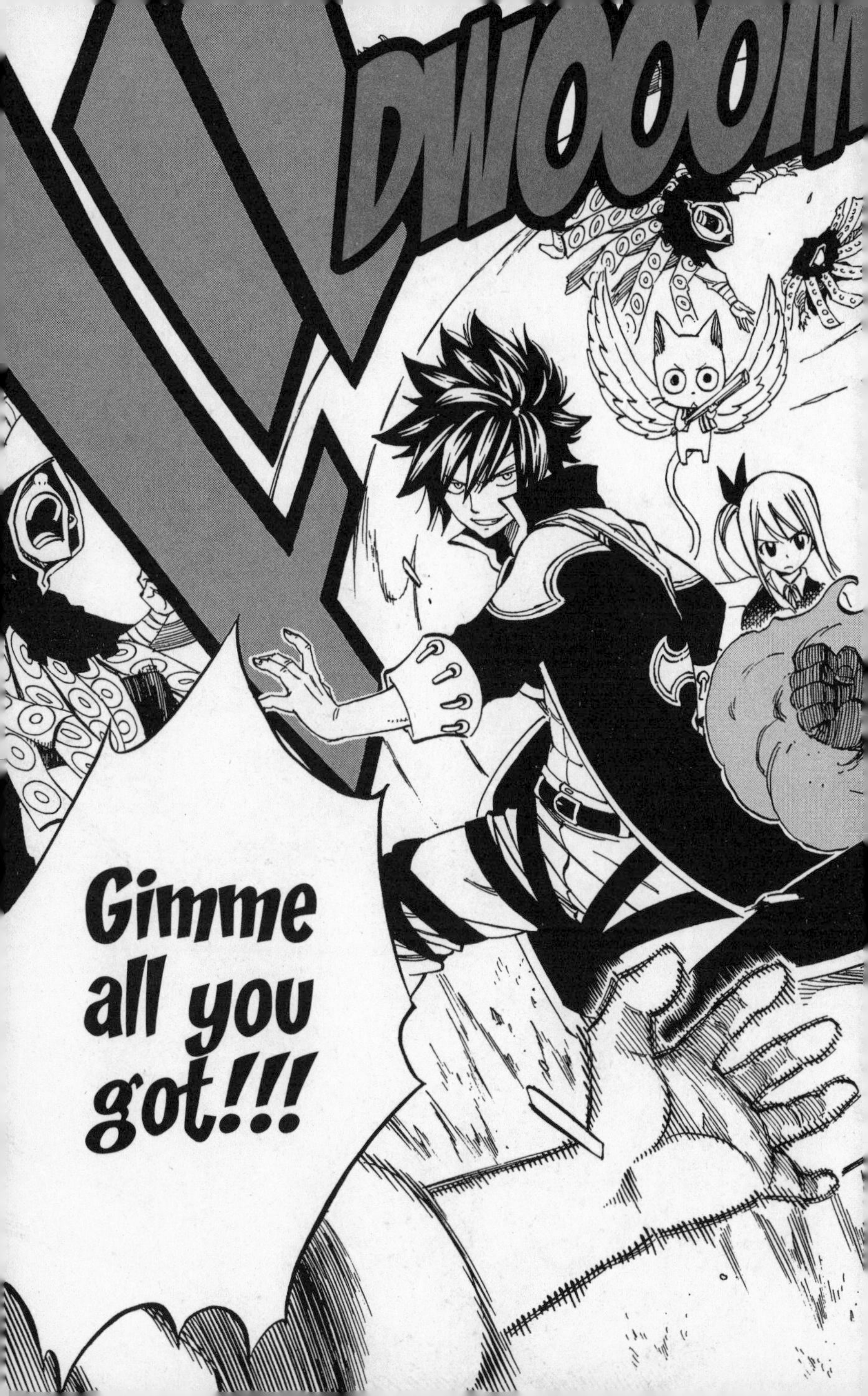
DWOOOM
Gimme all you got!!!

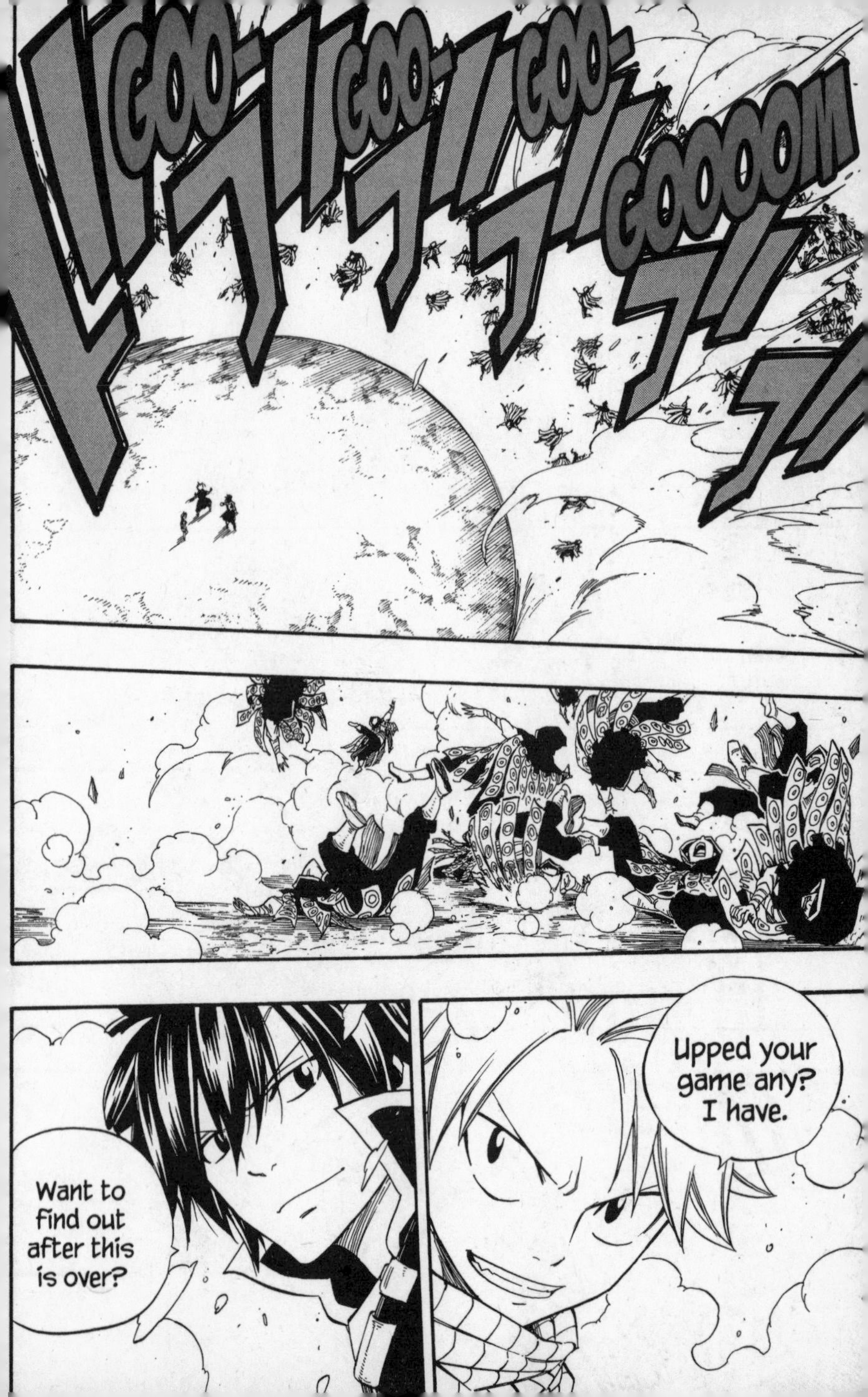
COO-
COO-
COO-
COOOOM
Upped your game any? I have.
Want to find out after this is over?

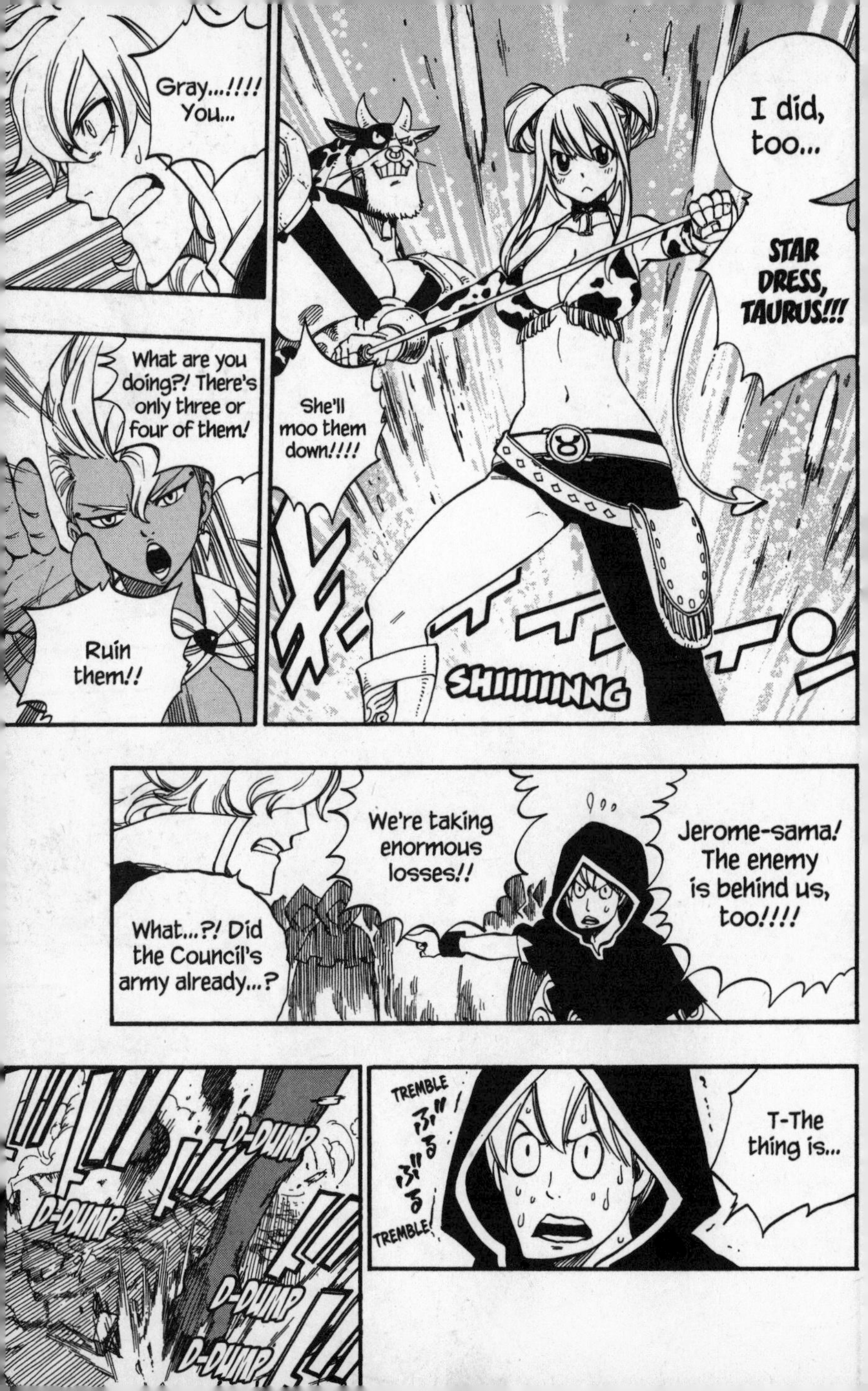
I did, too...
STAR DRESS, TAURUS!!!
She'll moo them down!!!!
SHIIIIIIINNG
Gray...!!!! You...
What are you doing?! There's only three or four of them!
Ruin them!!
Jerome-sama! The enemy is behind us, too!!!!
We're taking enormous losses!!
What...?! Did the Council's army already...?
TREMBLE
ぶるぶる
TREMBLE
T-The thing is...
D-DUMP
D-DUMP
D-DUMP
D-DUMP

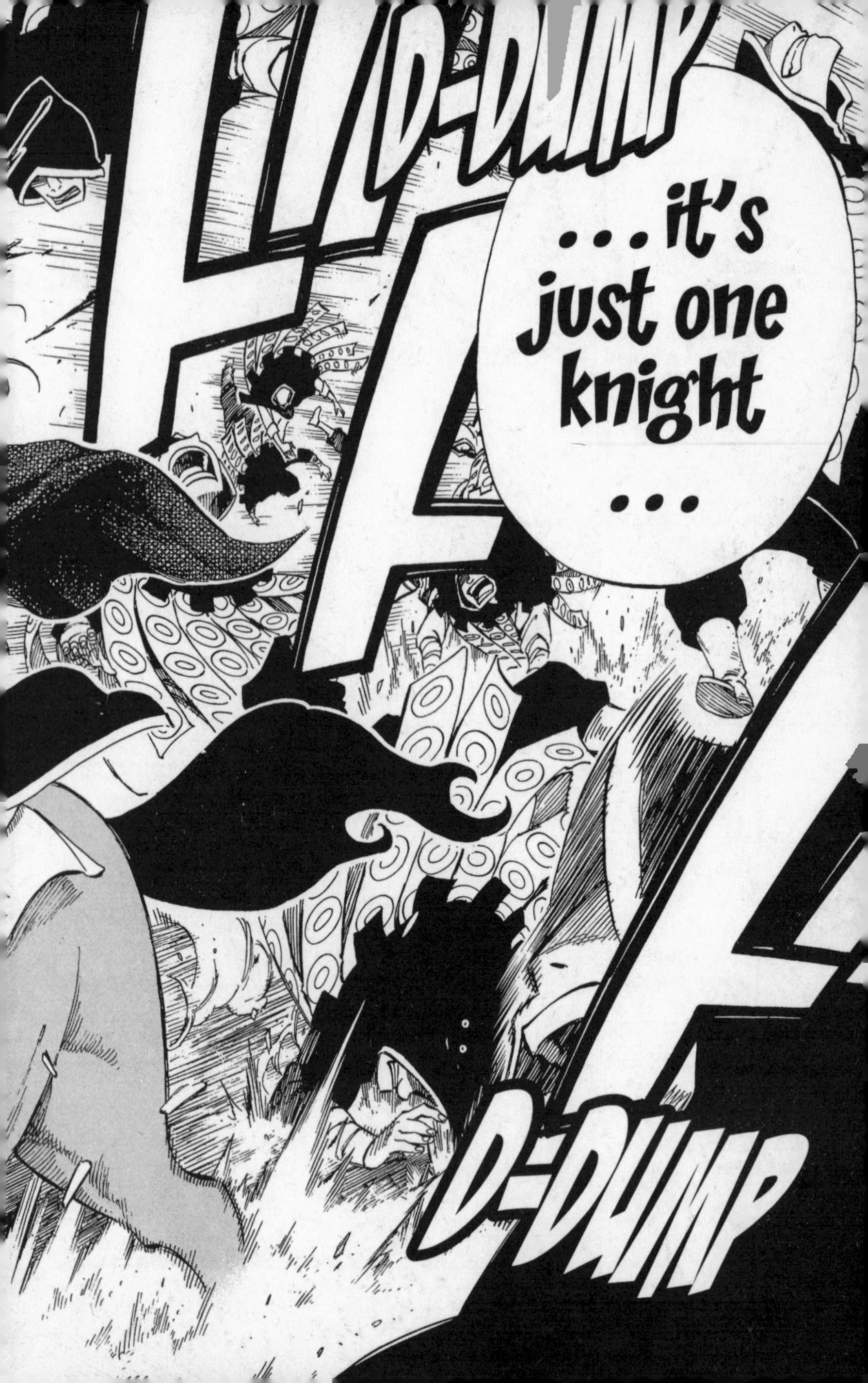
D-DUMP
...it's just one knight ...
D-DUMP

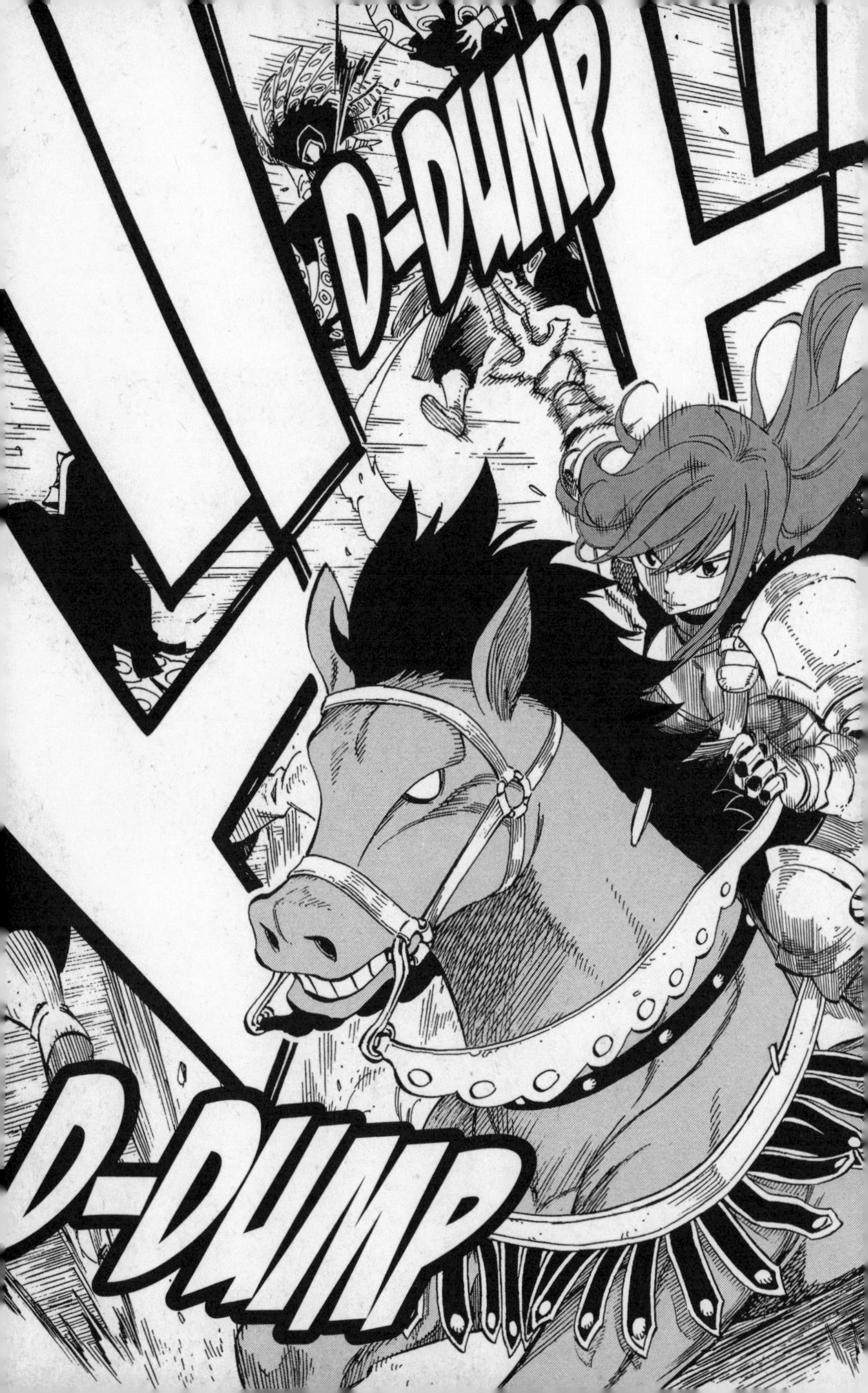
D-DUMP
D-DUMP

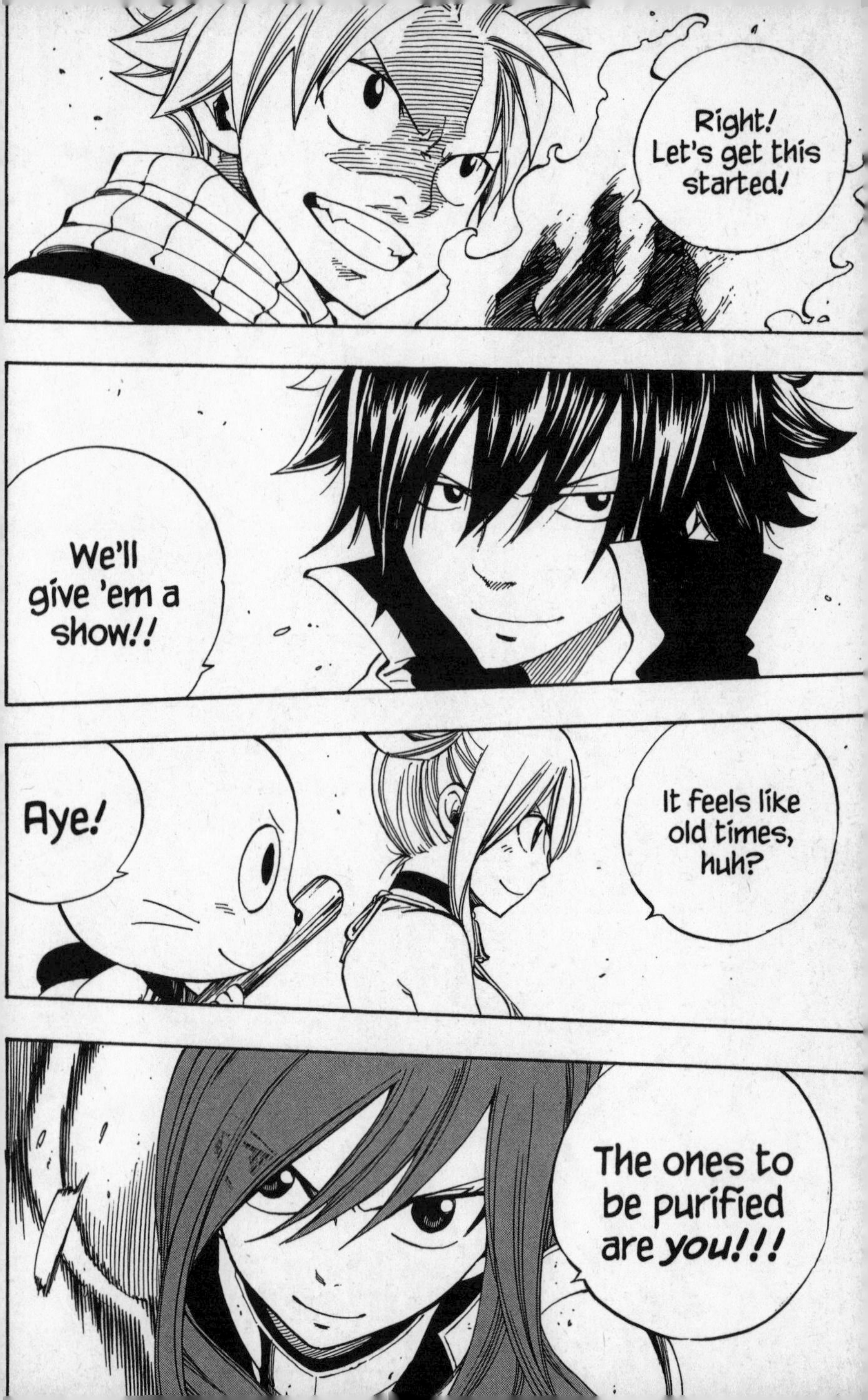
Right! Let's get this started!
We'll give 'em a show!!
It feels like old times, huh?
Aye!
The ones to be purified are *you*!!!

Chapter 431: My Sword

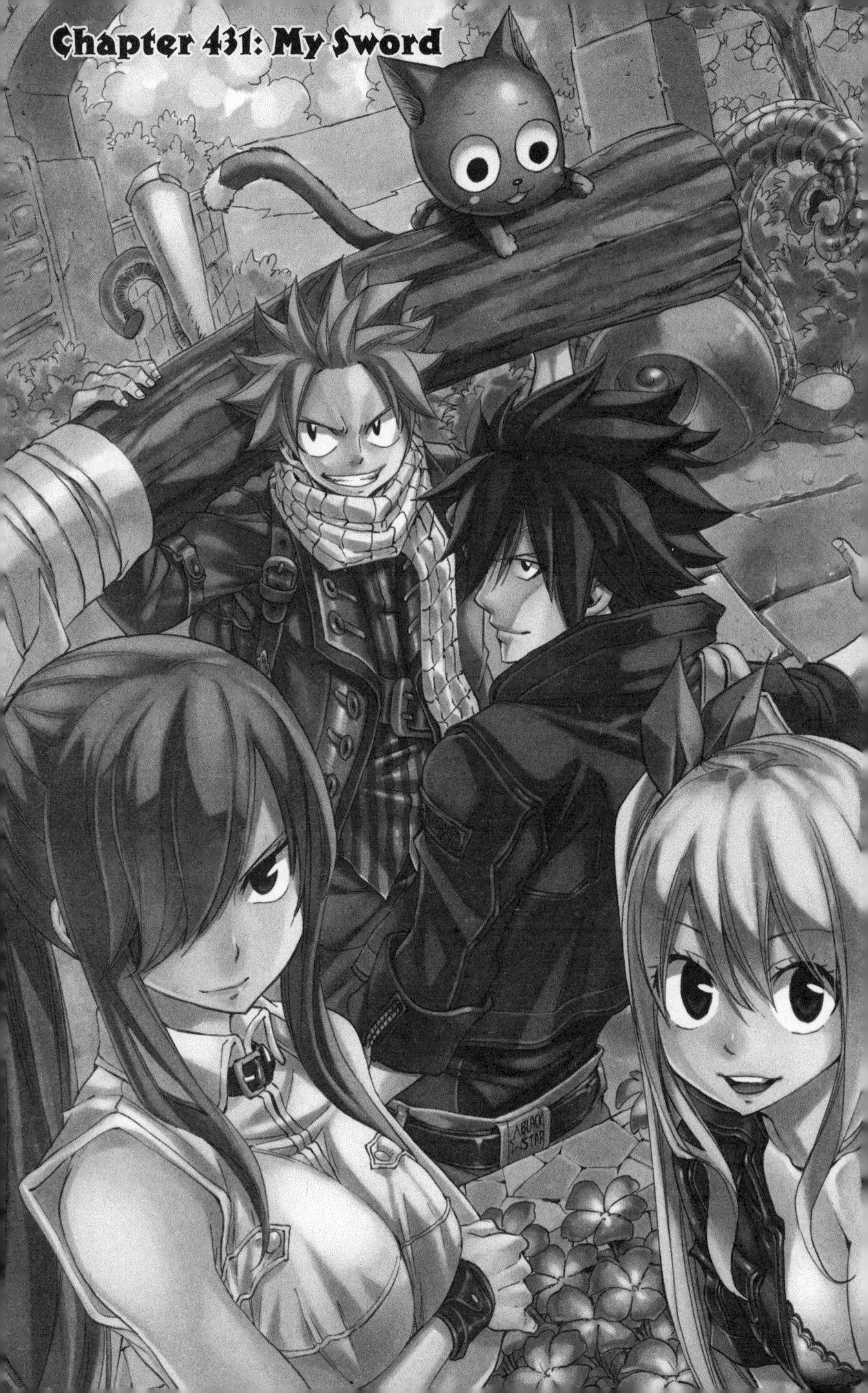
BLACK STAR

FAIRY TAIL
フェアリーテイル

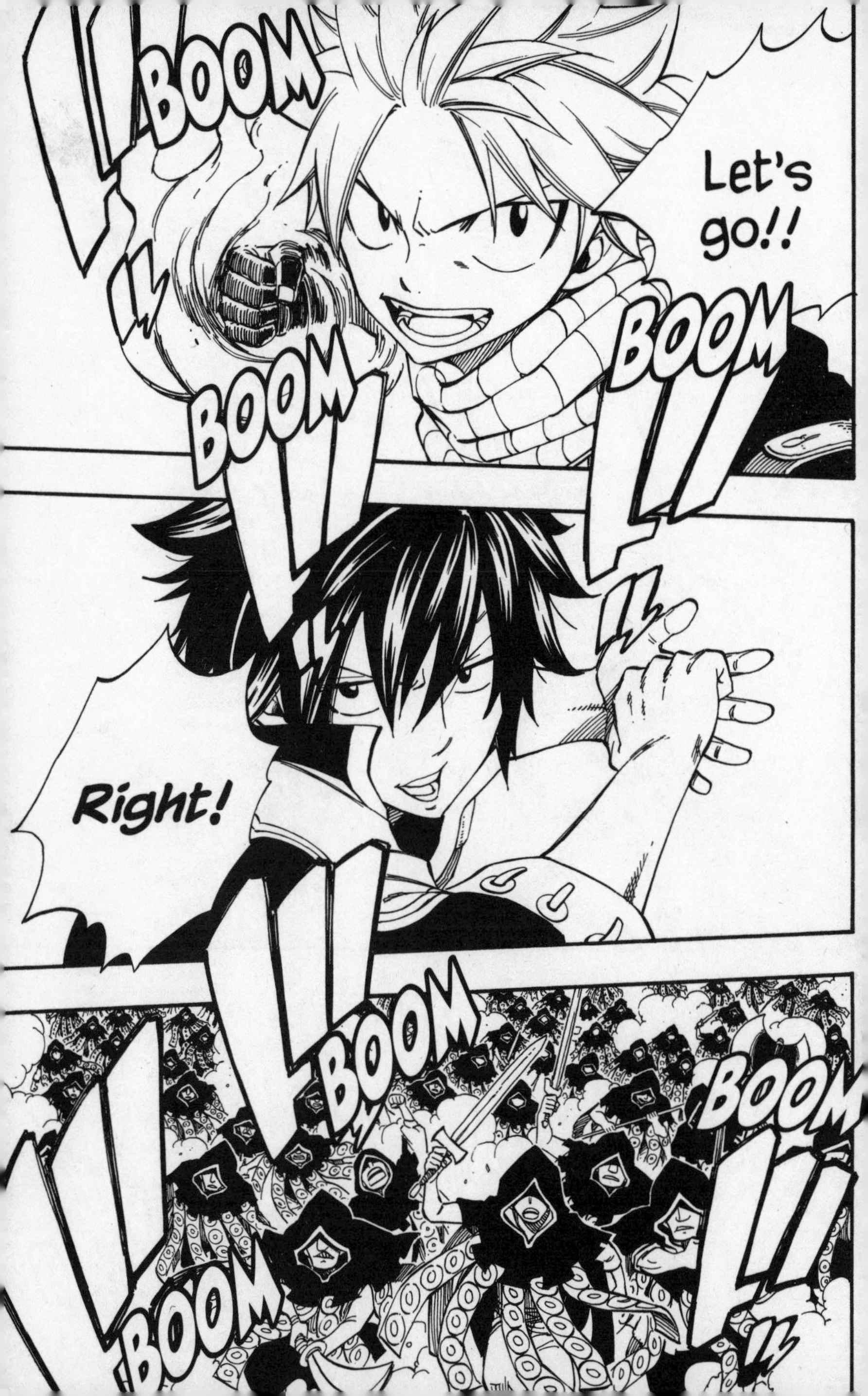

BOOM
Let's go!!
BOOM
BOOM
Right!
BOOM
BOOM
BOOM

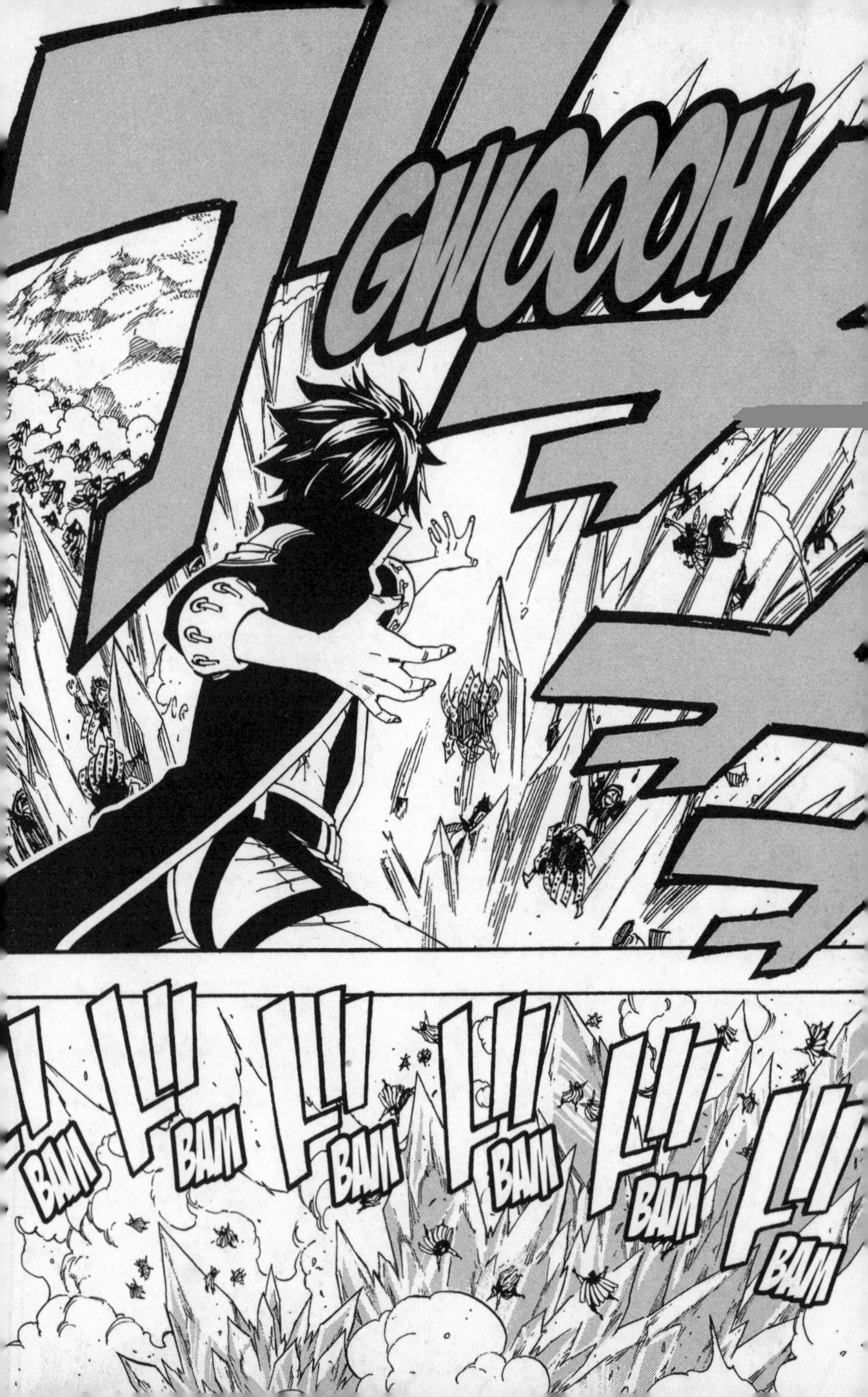
GWOOOH
BAM
BAM
BAM
BAM
BAM
BAM

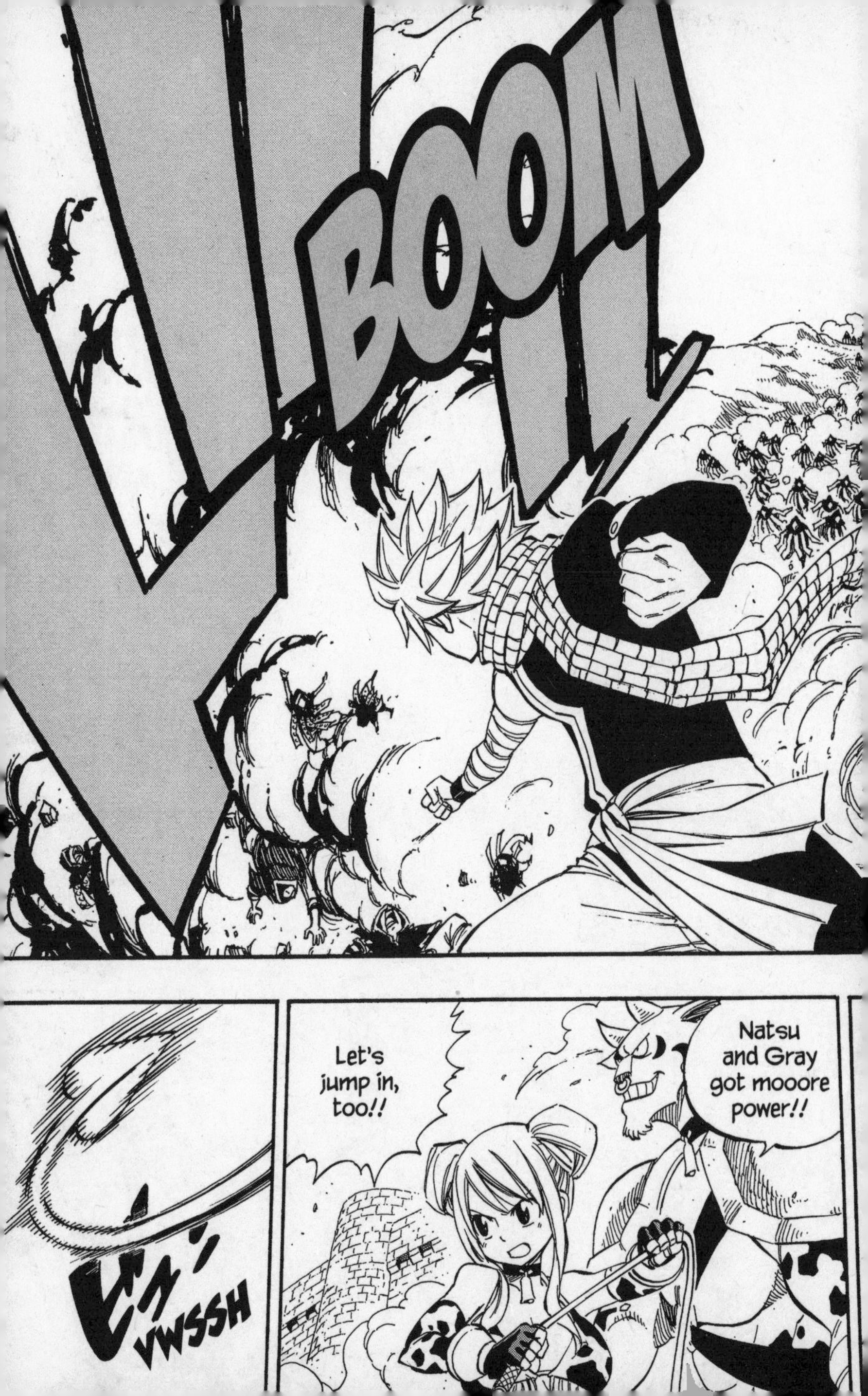
BOOM
Natsu and Gray got mooore power!!
Let's jump in, too!!
VWSSH

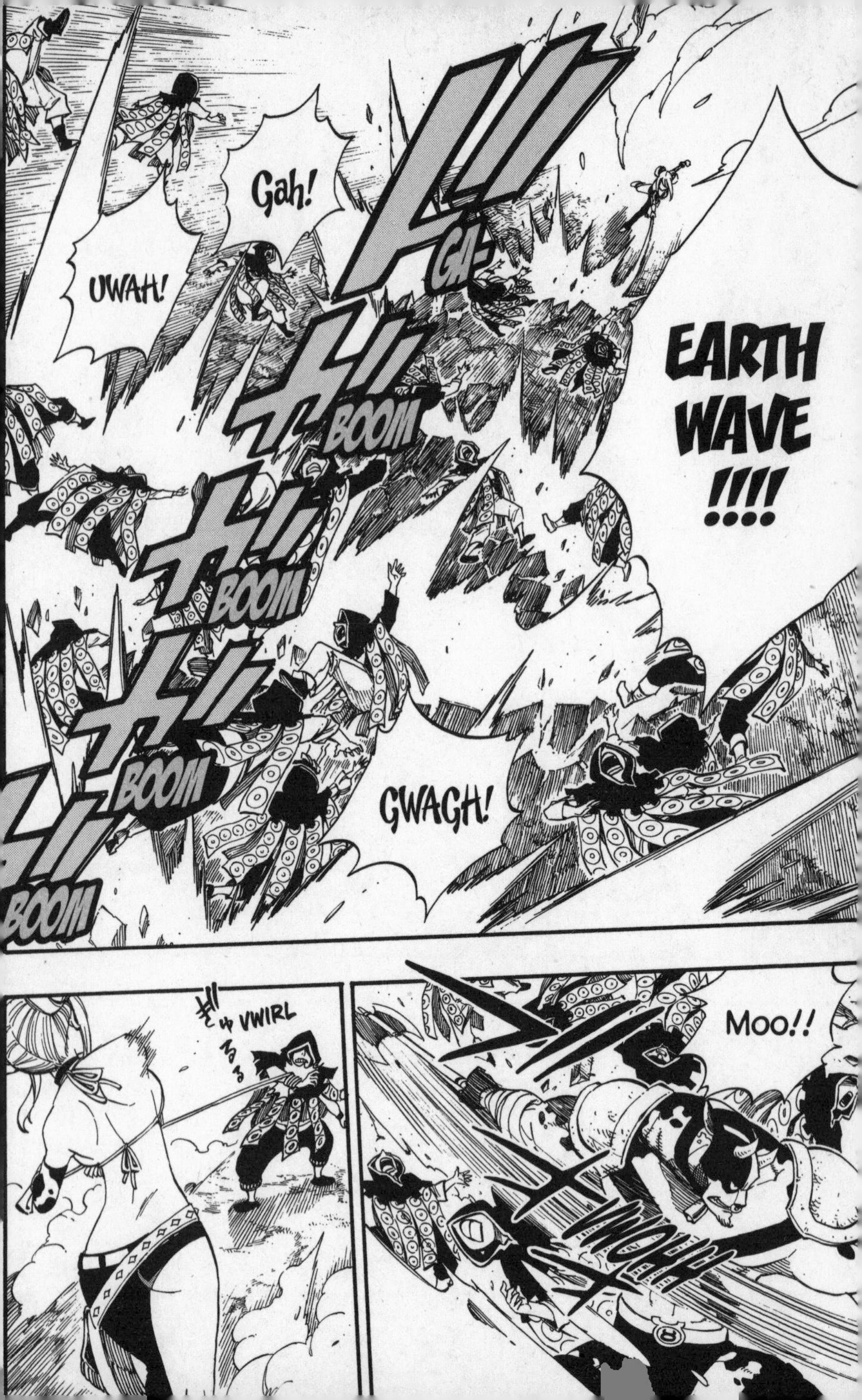
EARTH WAVE!!!!
GA-
Gah!
UWAH!
BOOM
BOOM
BOOM
GWAGH!
BOOM
Moo!!
VWIRL

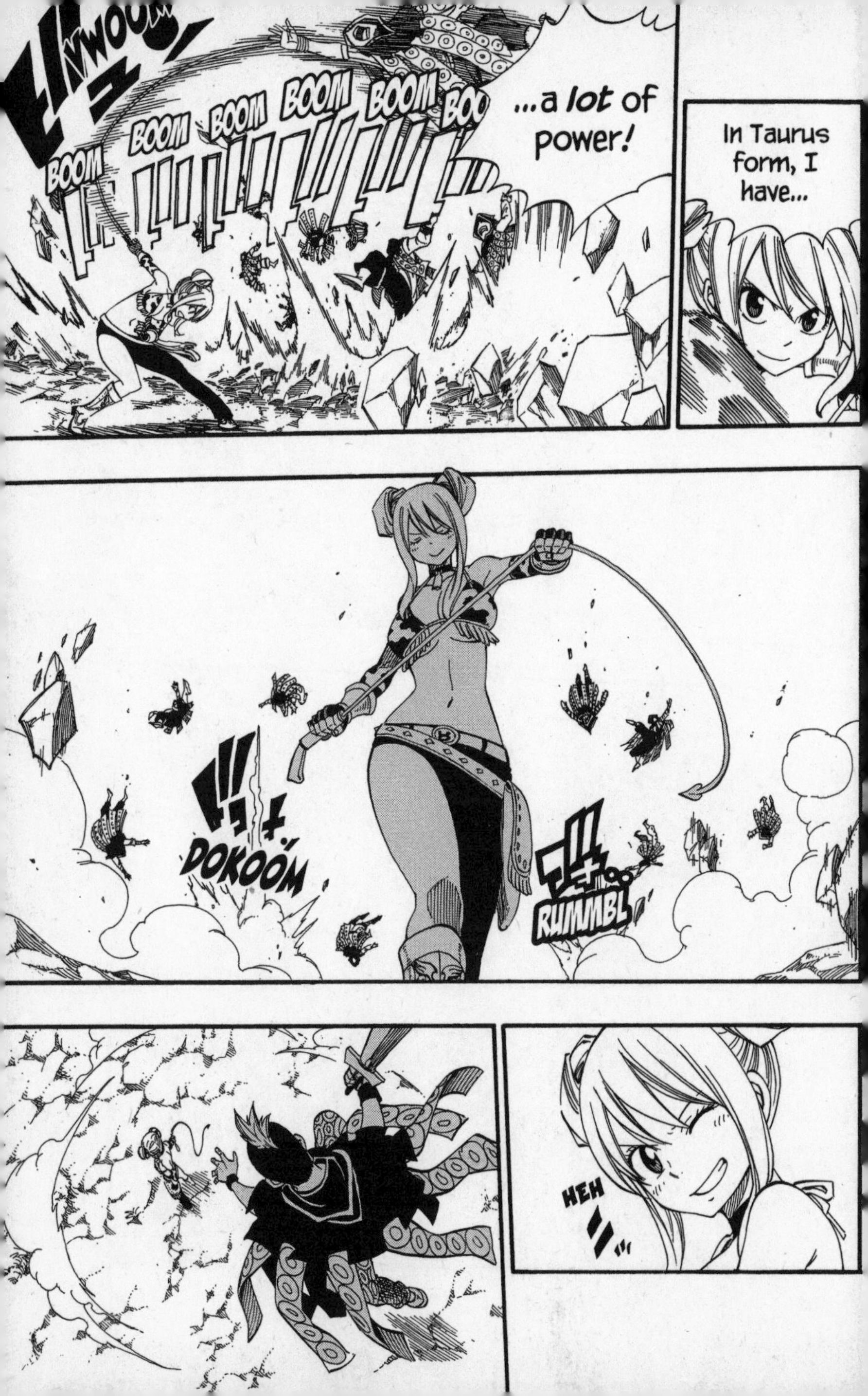
In Taurus form, I have...
...a lot of power!
WOOM
BOOM BOOM BOOM BOOM BOOM BOO
RUMMBL
DOKOOM
HEH

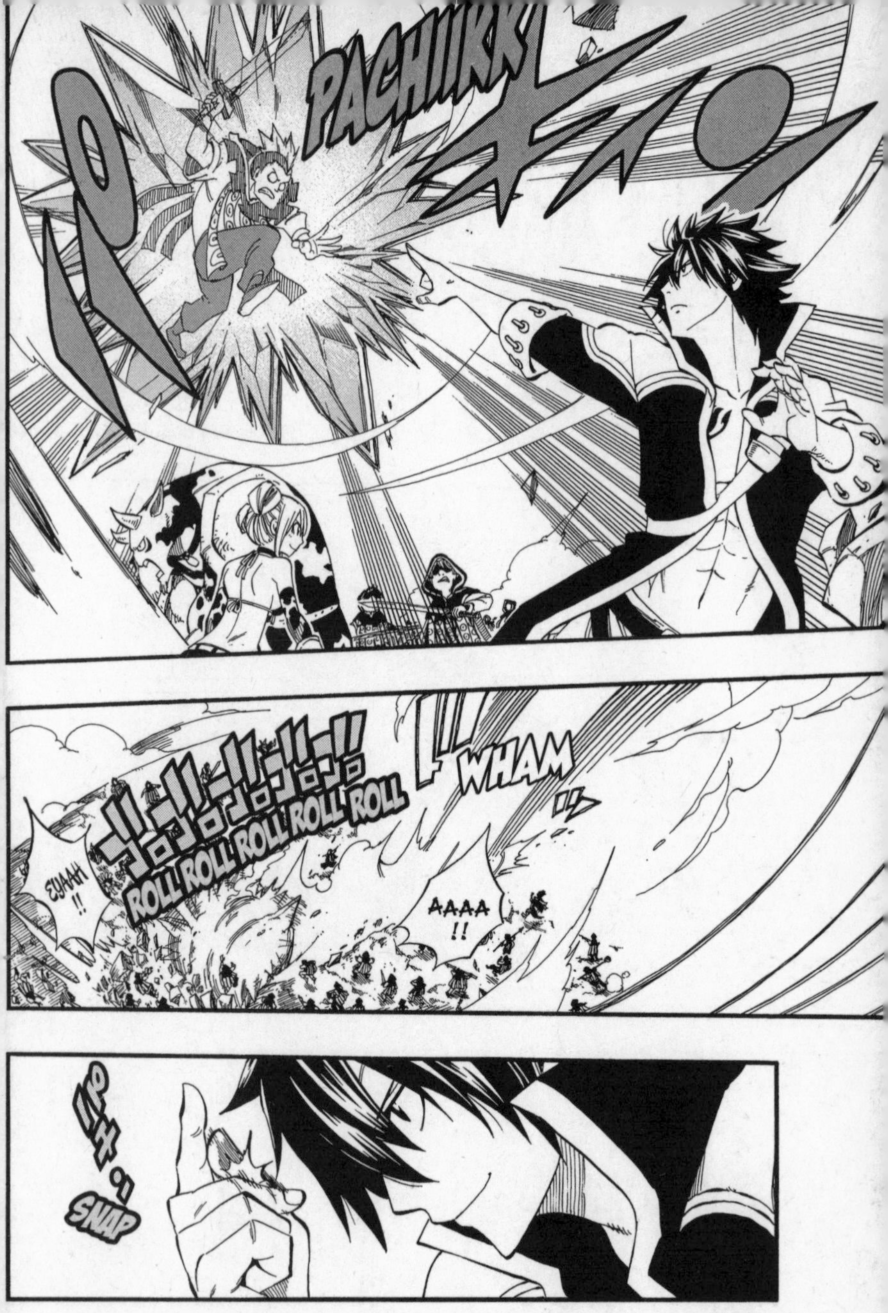
PACHIIKK
WHAM
ROLL ROLL ROLL ROLL ROLL
AAAA !!
EYAAH !!
SNAP

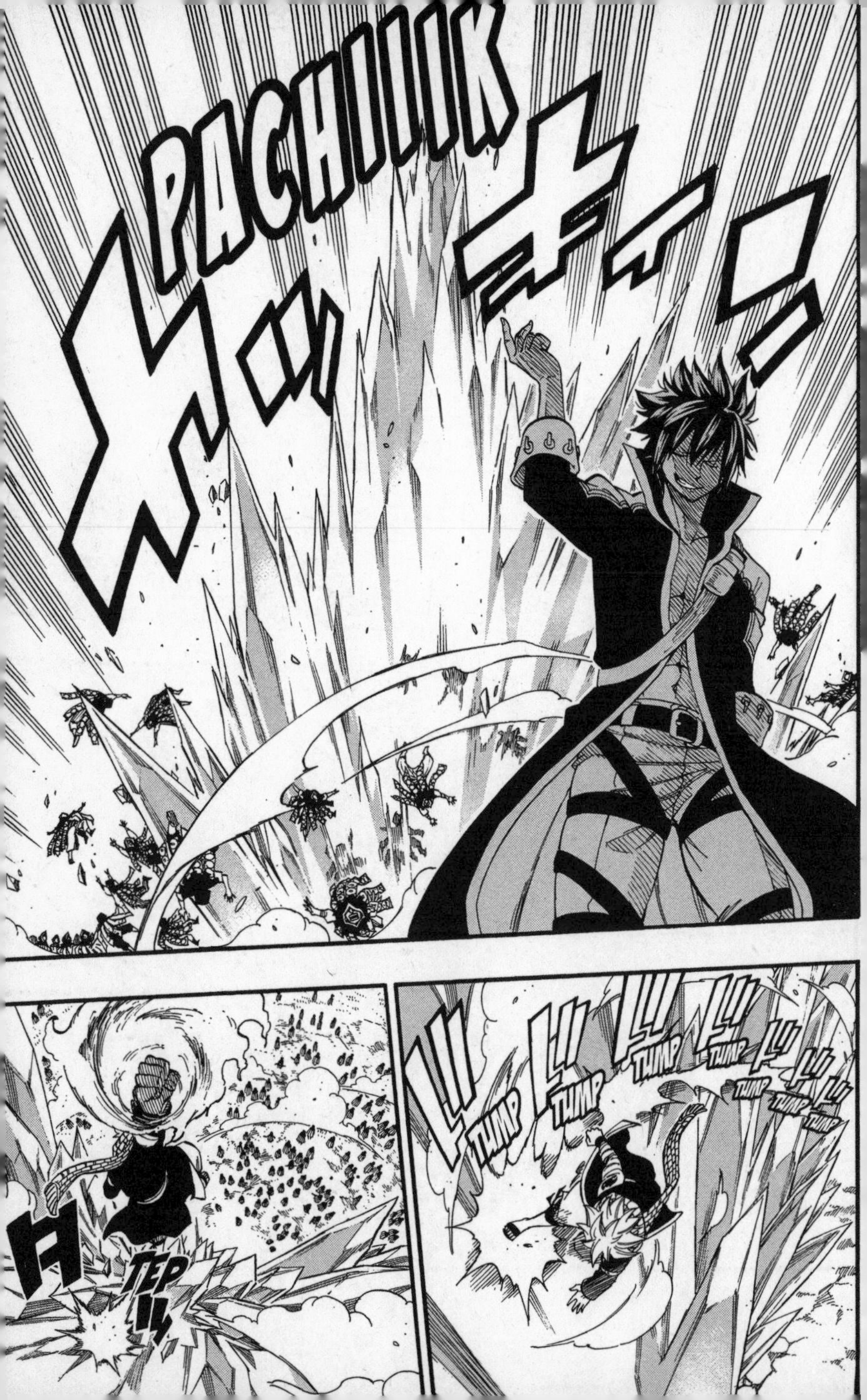
PACHIIIK
THUMP
THUMP
THUMP
THUMP
THUMP
THUMP
THUMP
TEP

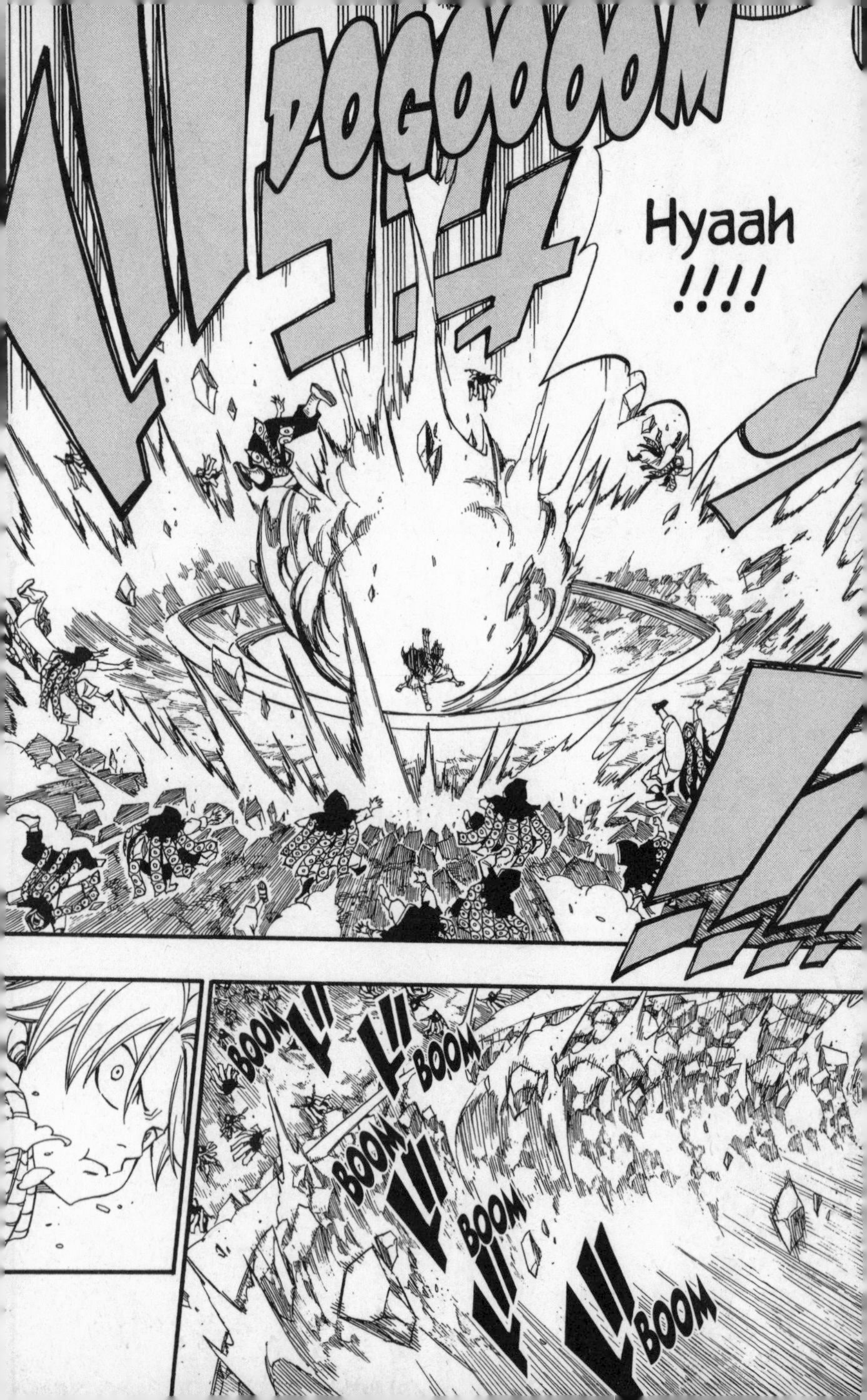
Hyaah !!!!
DOGOOOOM
BOOM!!
BOOM!!
BOOM!!
BOOM!!
BOOM!!

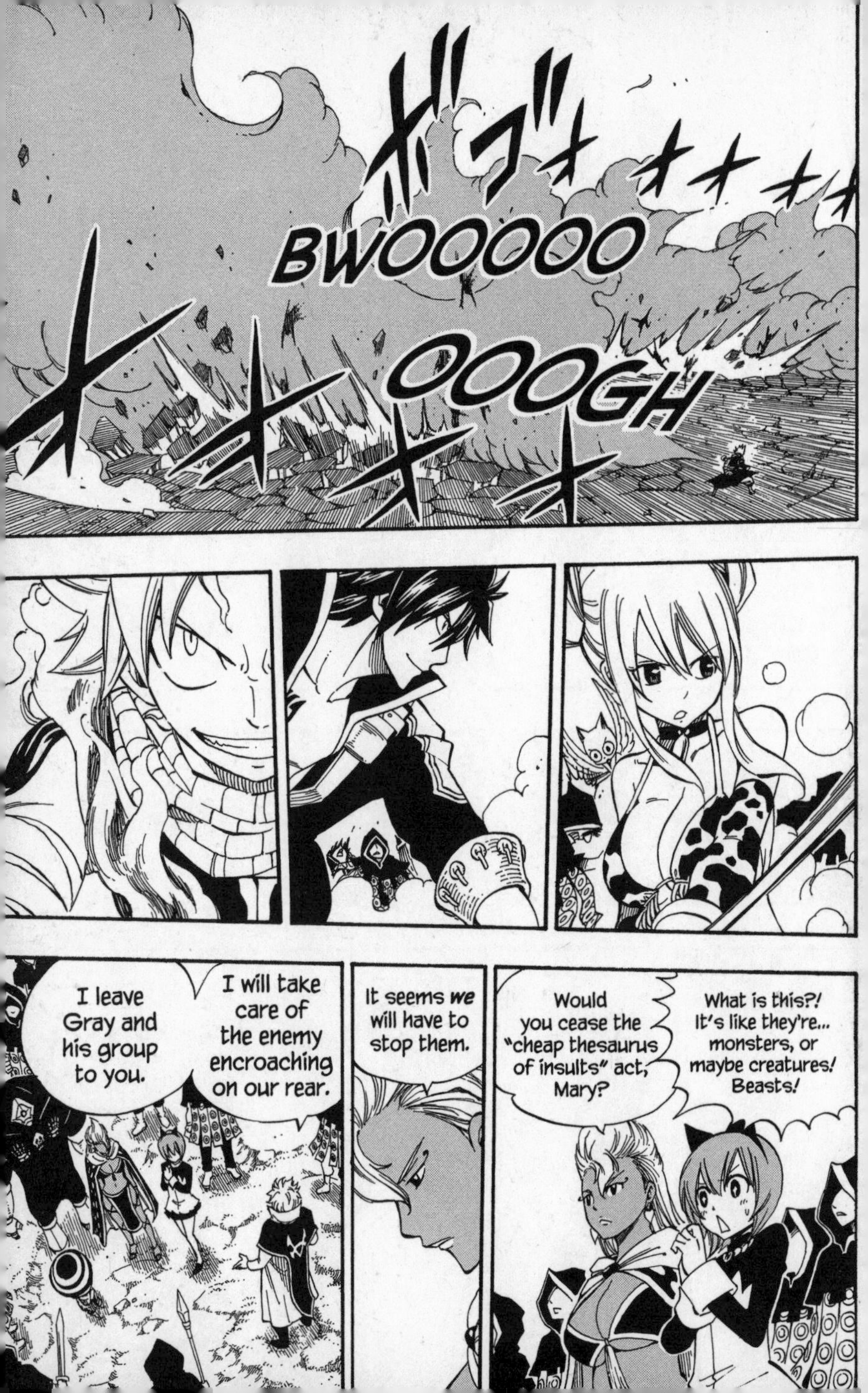
BWOOOOO
OOOGH
What is this?! It's like they're... monsters, or maybe creatures! Beasts!
Would you cease the "cheap thesaurus of insults" act, Mary?
It seems *we* will have to stop them.
I will take care of the enemy encroaching on our rear.
I leave Gray and his group to you.

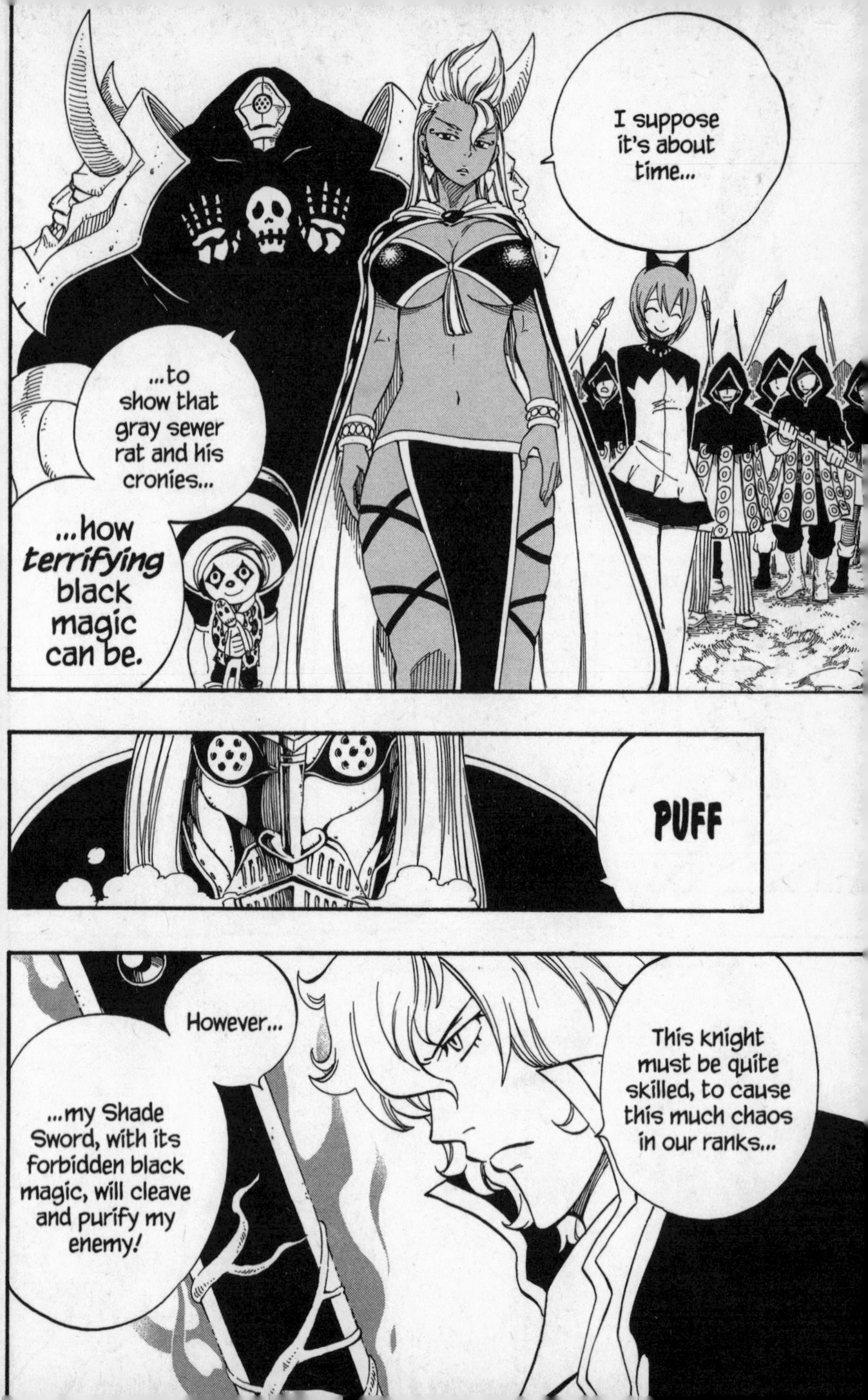
I suppose it's about time...
...to show that gray sewer rat and his cronies...
...how *terrifying* black magic can be.
PUFF
This knight must be quite skilled, to cause this much chaos in our ranks...
However...
...my Shade Sword, with its forbidden black magic, will cleave and purify my enemy!

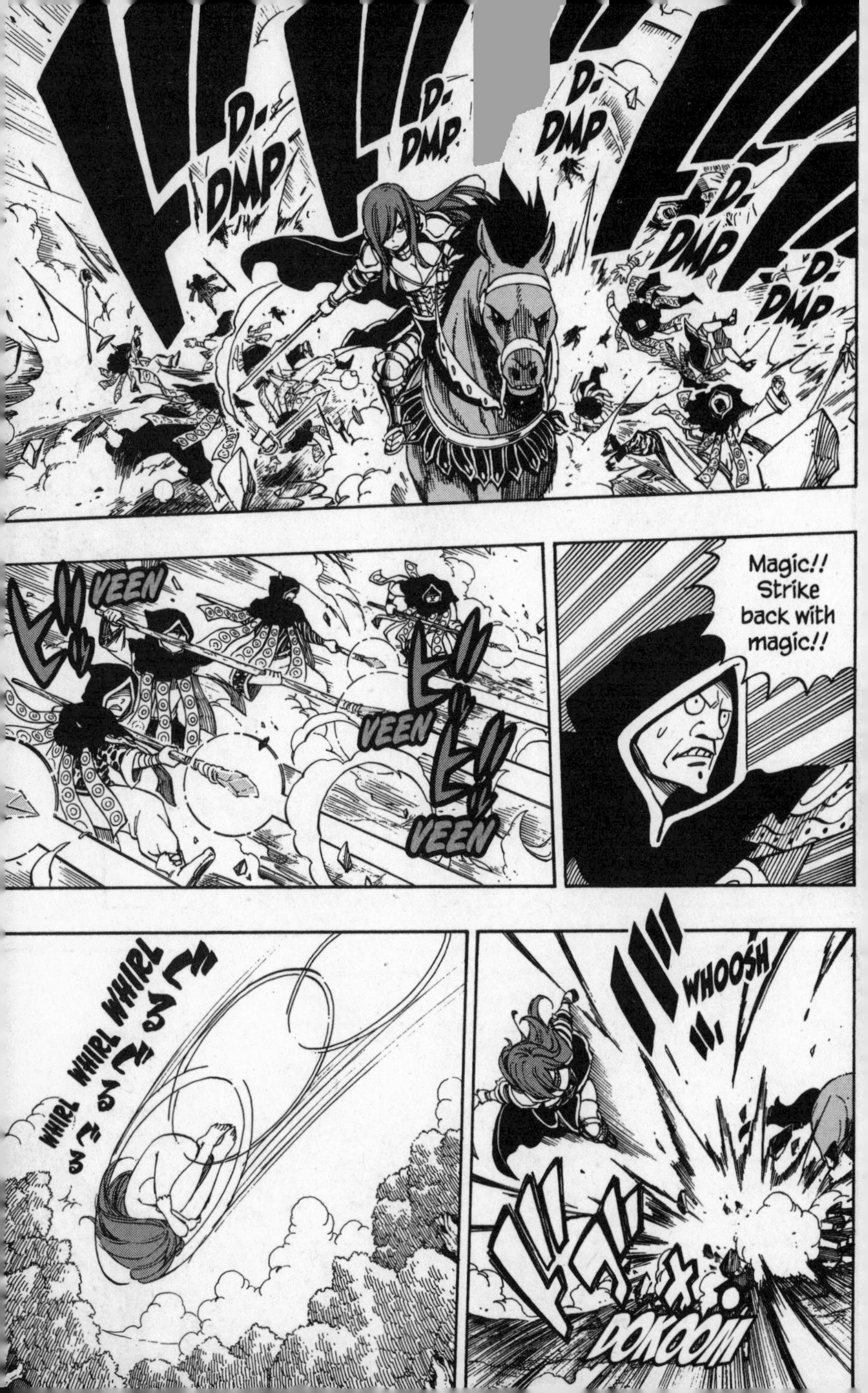
D-DMP
D-DMP
D-DMP
D-DMP
D-DMP
D-DMP
Magic!! Strike back with magic!!
VEEN
VEEN
VEEN
WHOOSH
DOKOOM
WHIRL WHIRL WHIRL

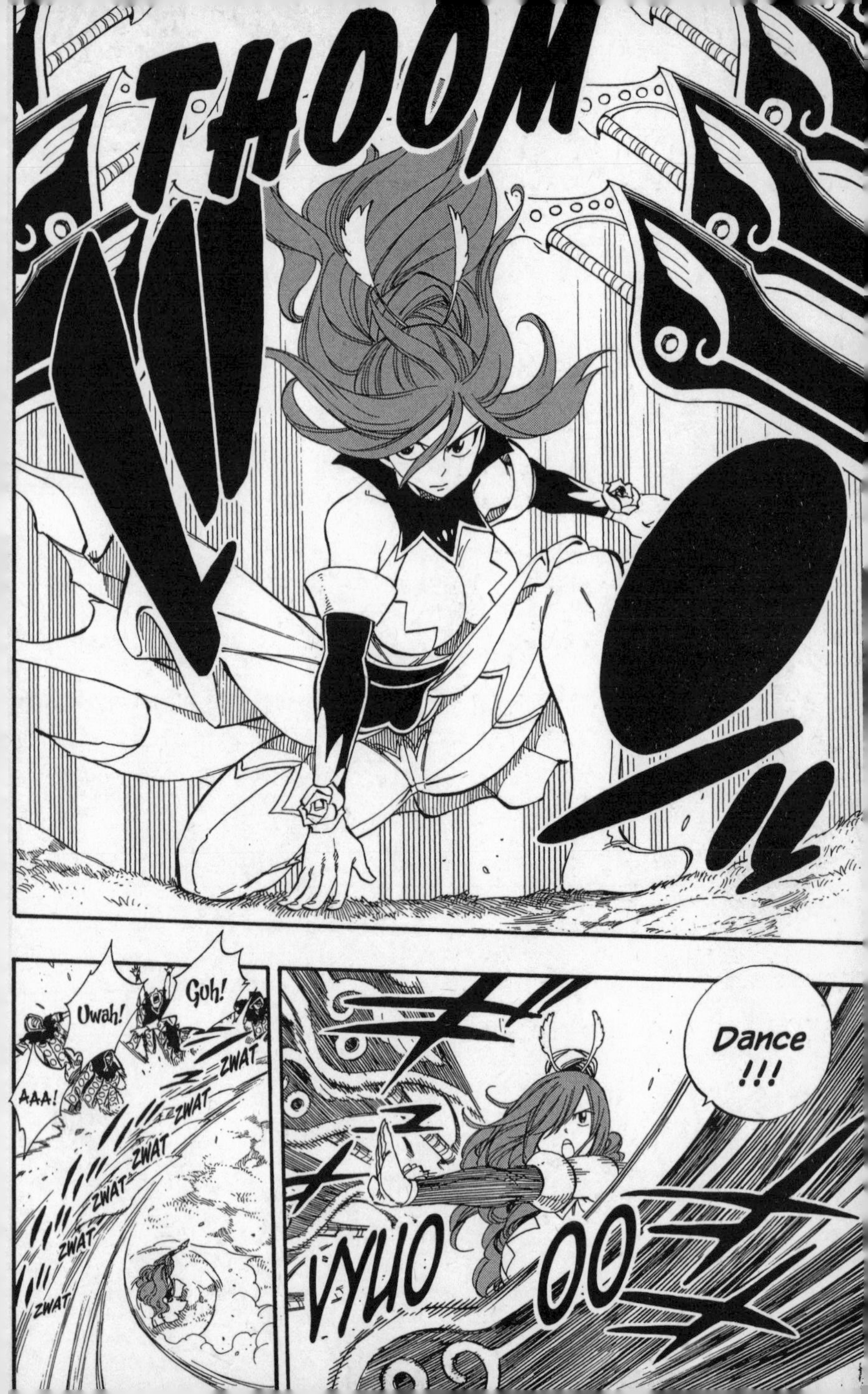
THOOM
Dance !!!
VYUO OO
Guh!
Uwah!
ZWAT
ZWAT
AAA!
ZWAT
ZWAT
ZWAT
ZWAT

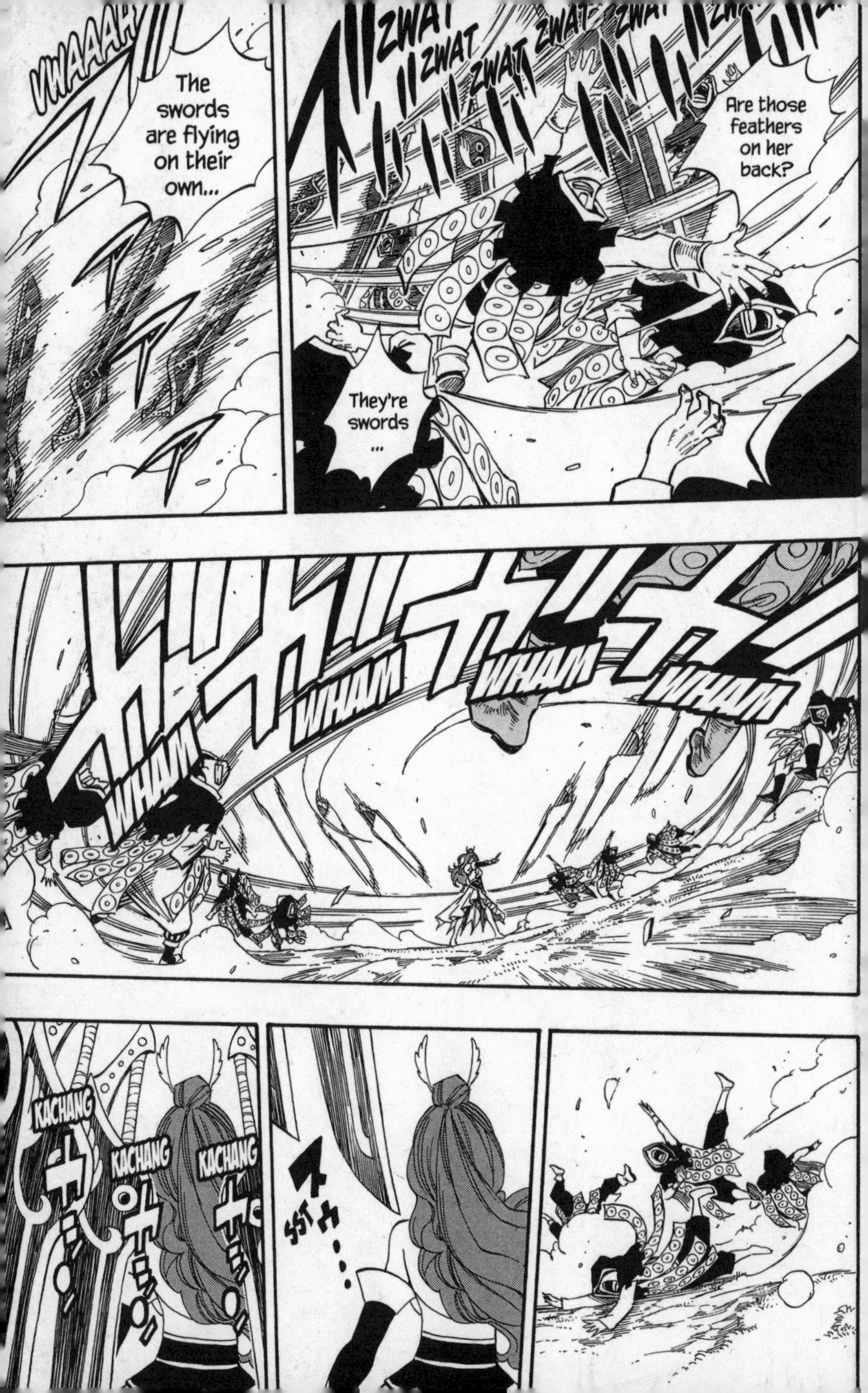
ZWAT ZWAT ZWAT ZWAT ZWAT
Are those feathers on her back?
They're swords ...
VWAAAH
The swords are flying on their own...
WHAM WHAM WHAM WHAM WHAM
SST
KACHANG KACHANG KACHANG

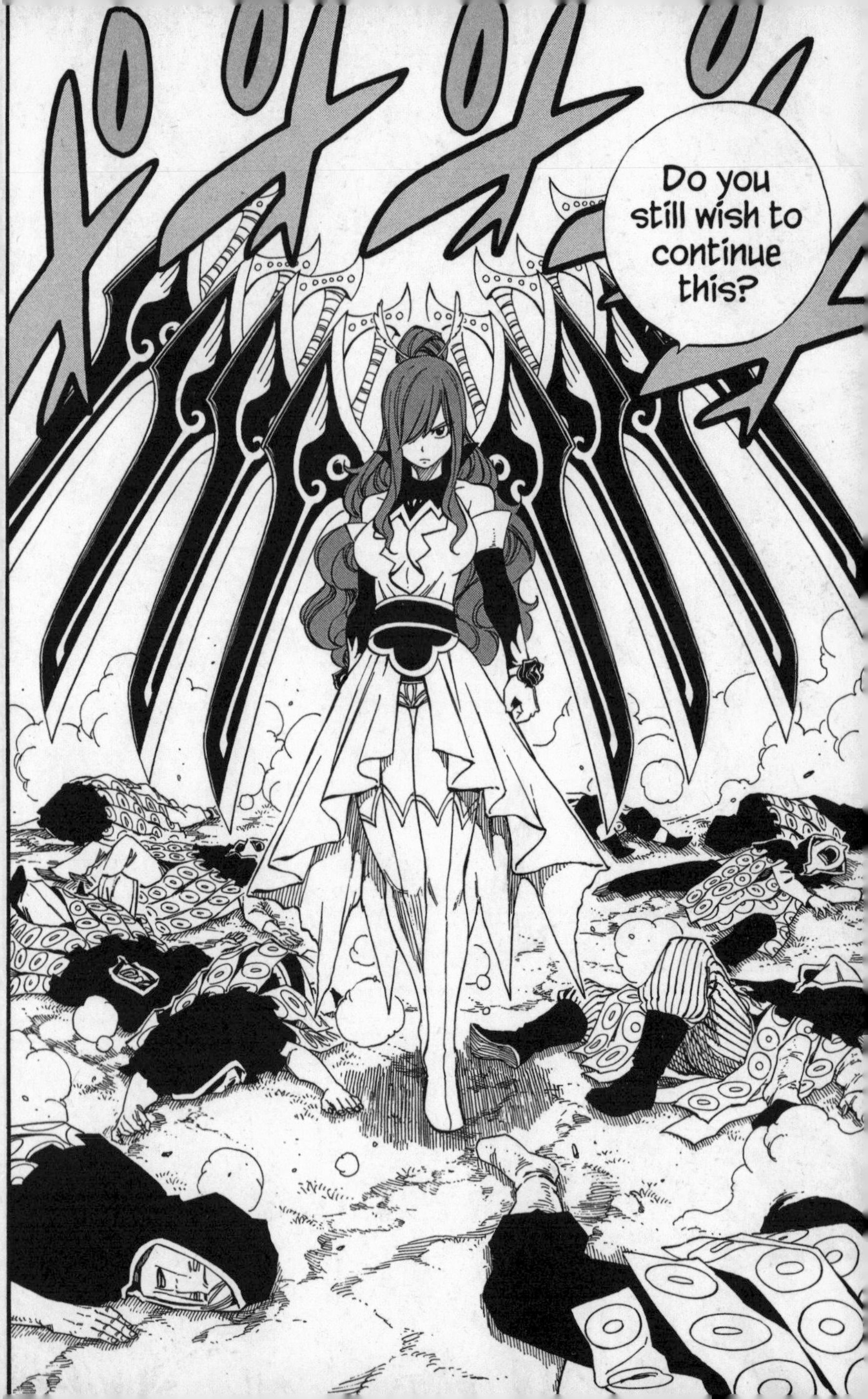
Do you still wish to continue this?

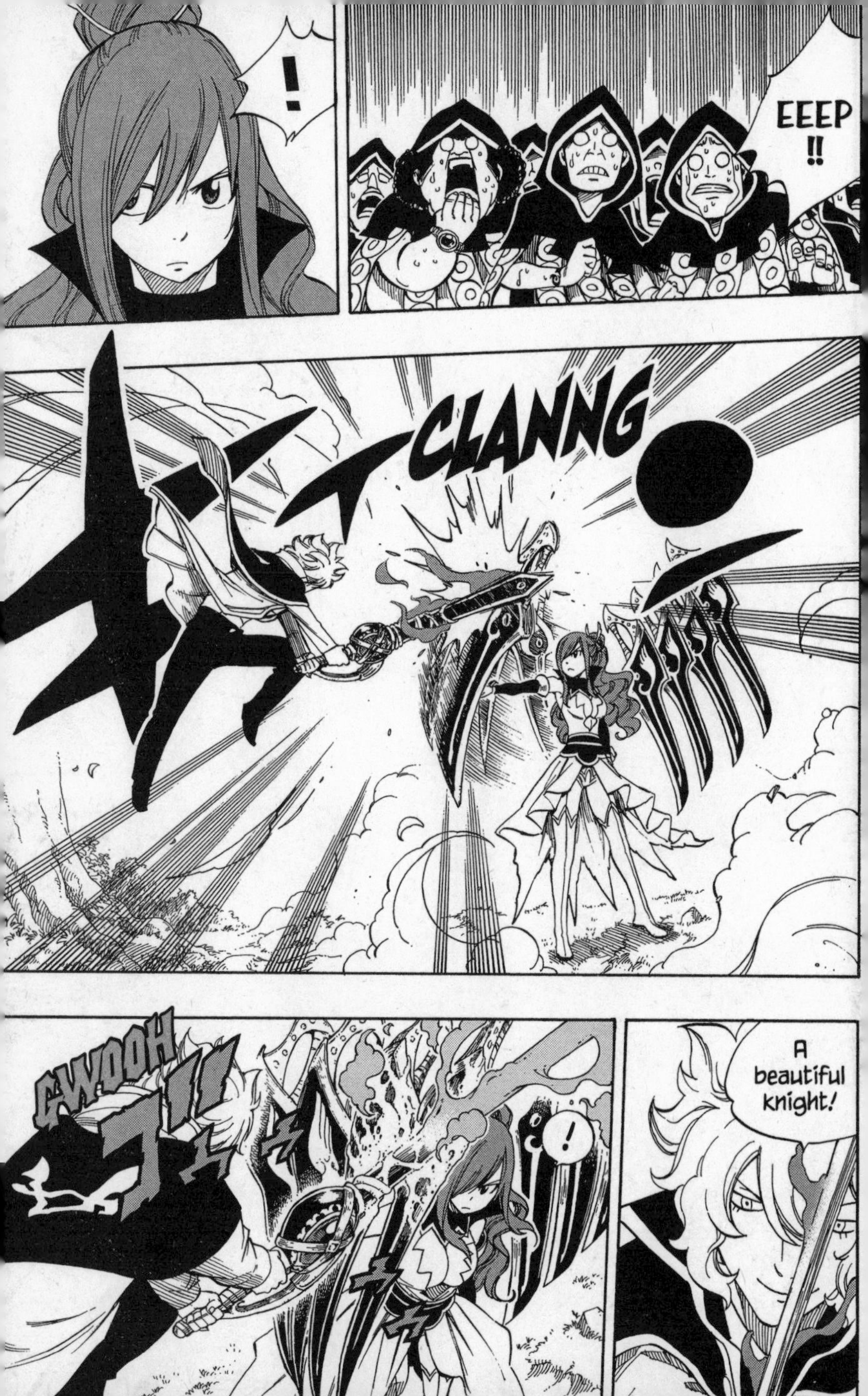
EEEP !!
!
CLANNG
A beautiful knight!
GWOOH
!

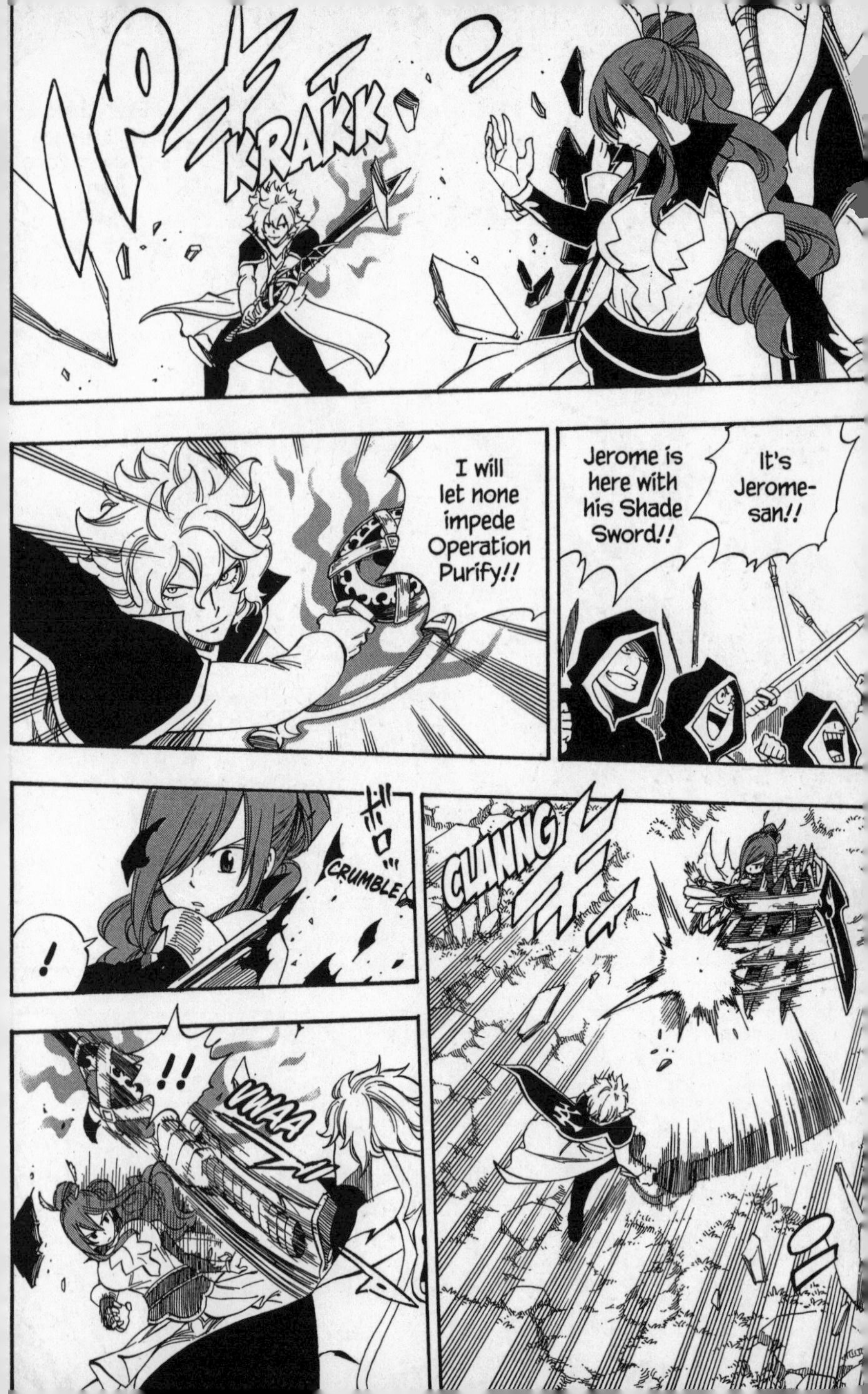
KRAKK
It's Jerome-san!!
Jerome is here with his Shade Sword!!
I will let none impede Operation Purify!!
CLANNG
CRUMBLE
!
!!
UWAA

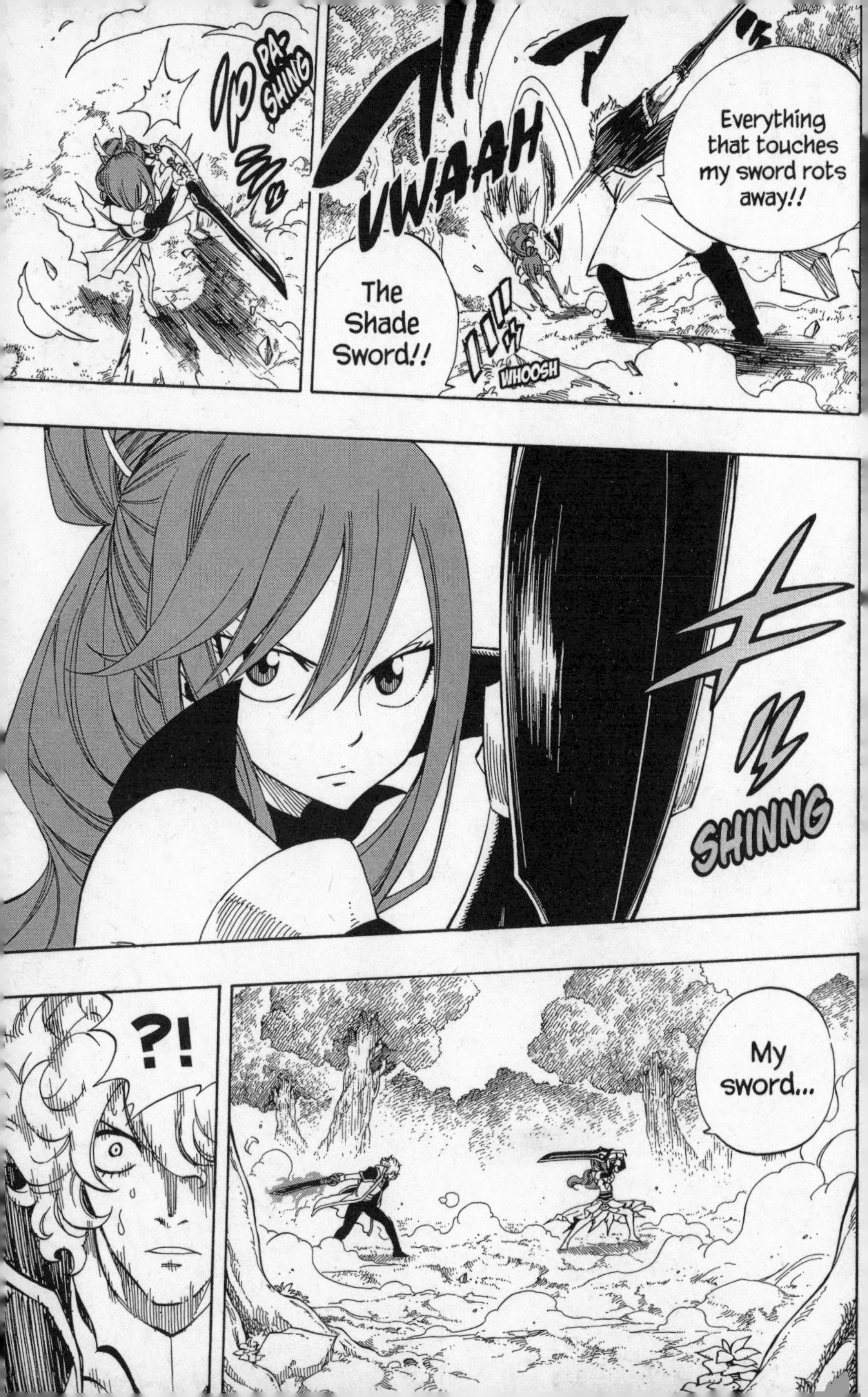
UWAAH
Everything that touches my sword rots away!!
The Shade Sword!!
WHOOSH
PA-SHING
SHINNG
My sword...
?!

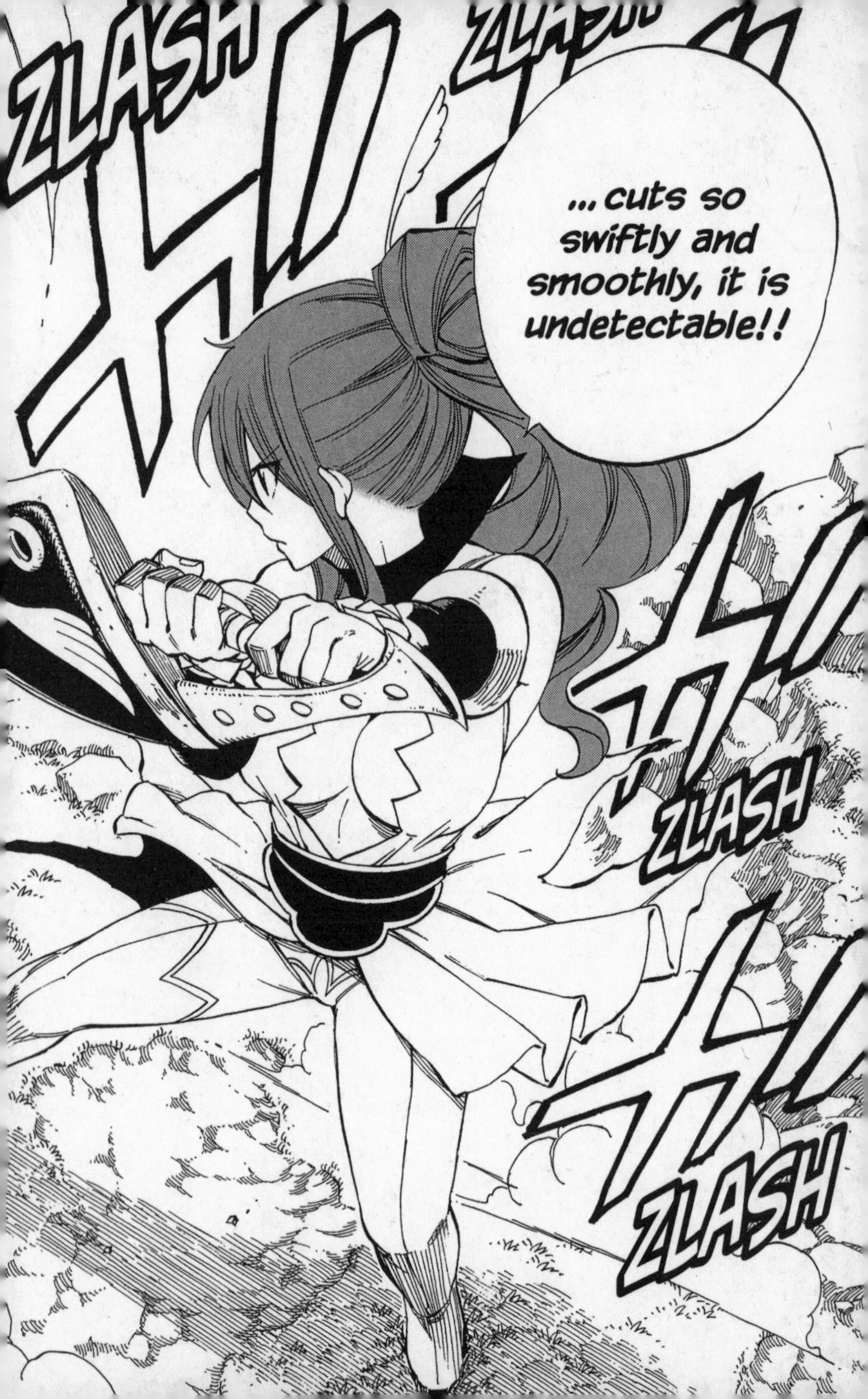
...cuts so swiftly and smoothly, it is undetectable!!
ZLASH
ZLASH
ZLASH

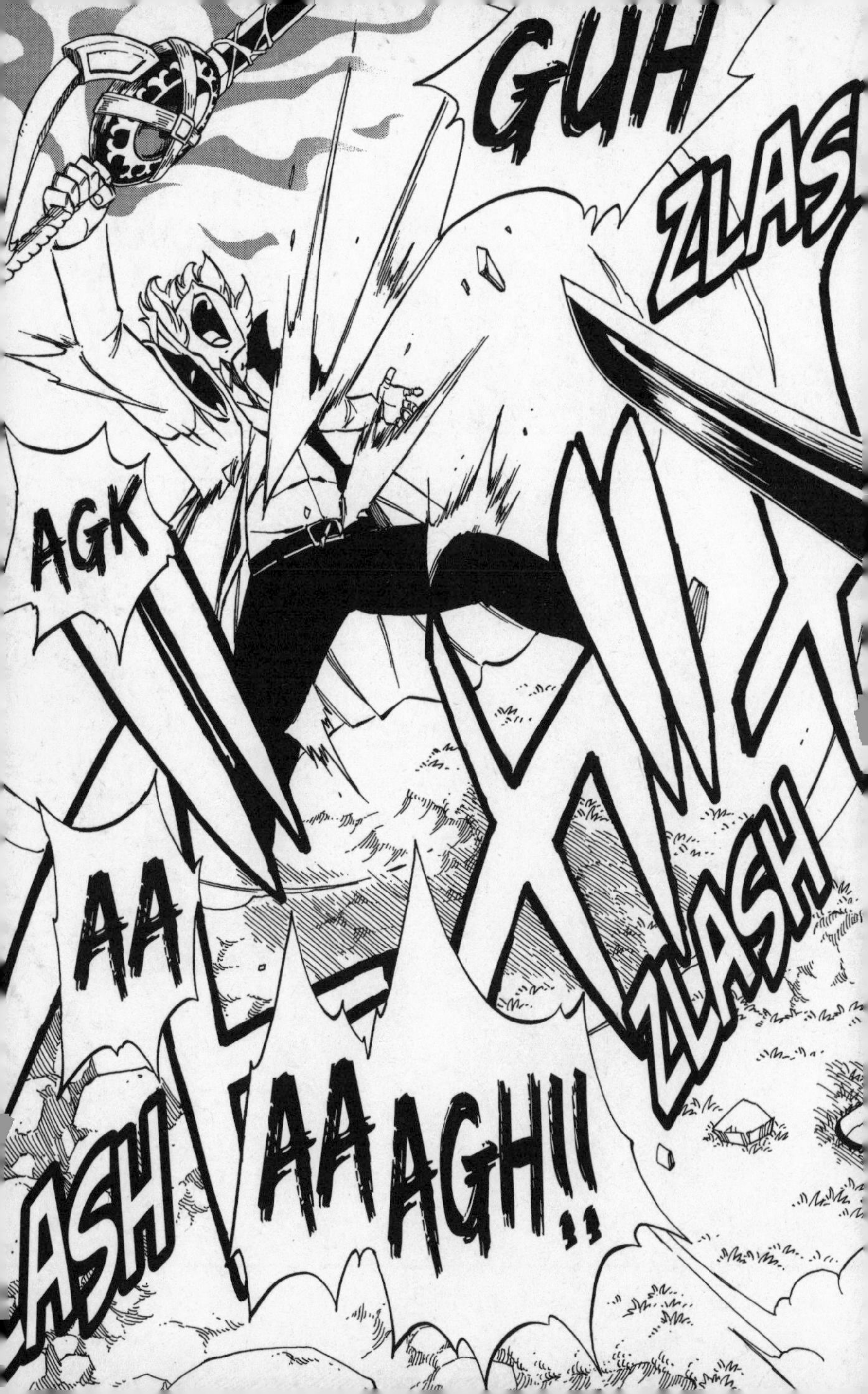

GUH
ZLAS
AGK
ZLASH
AA
AAAGH!!
ASH

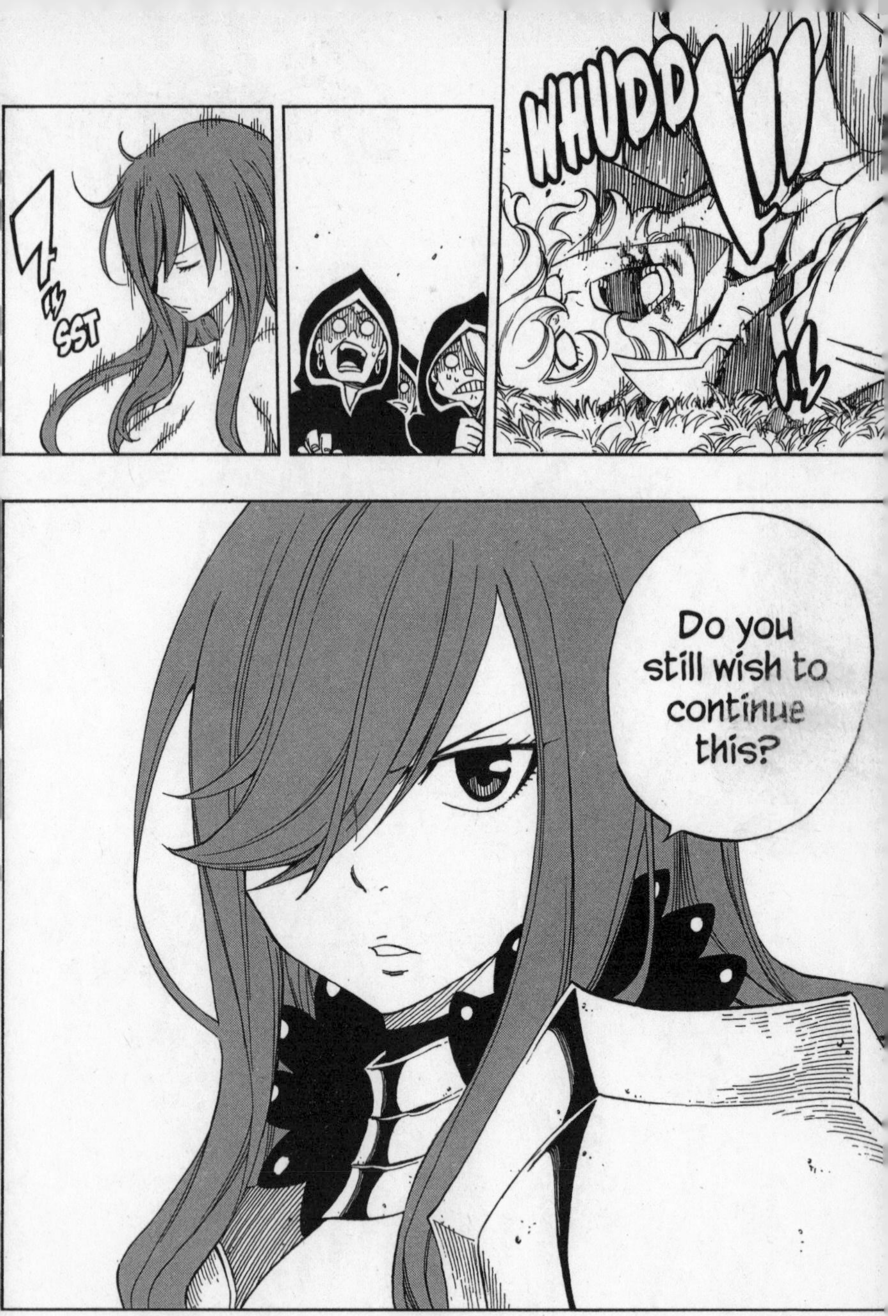
WHUDD
SST
Do you still wish to continue this?

FAIRY TAIL

フェアリーテイル

Chapter 432: Briar in Love

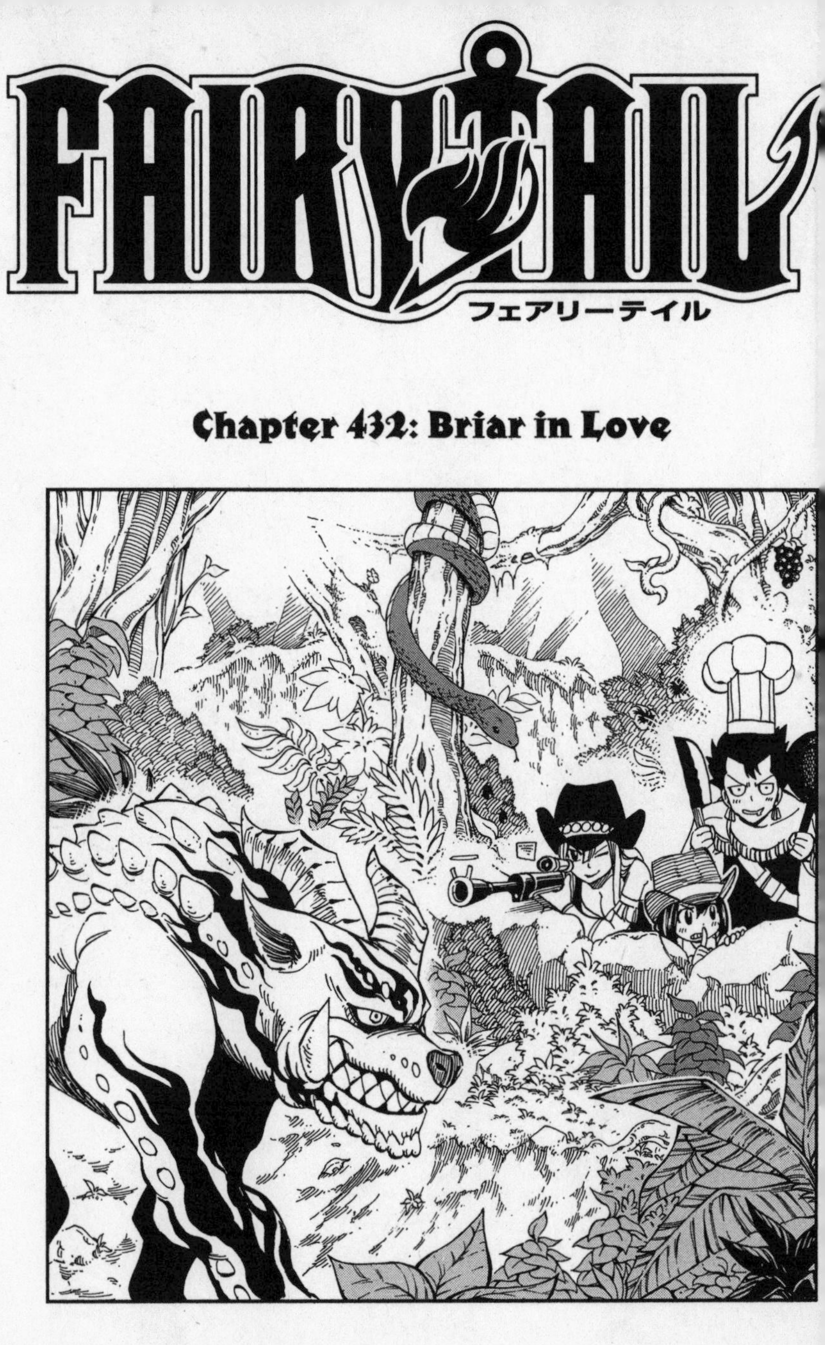

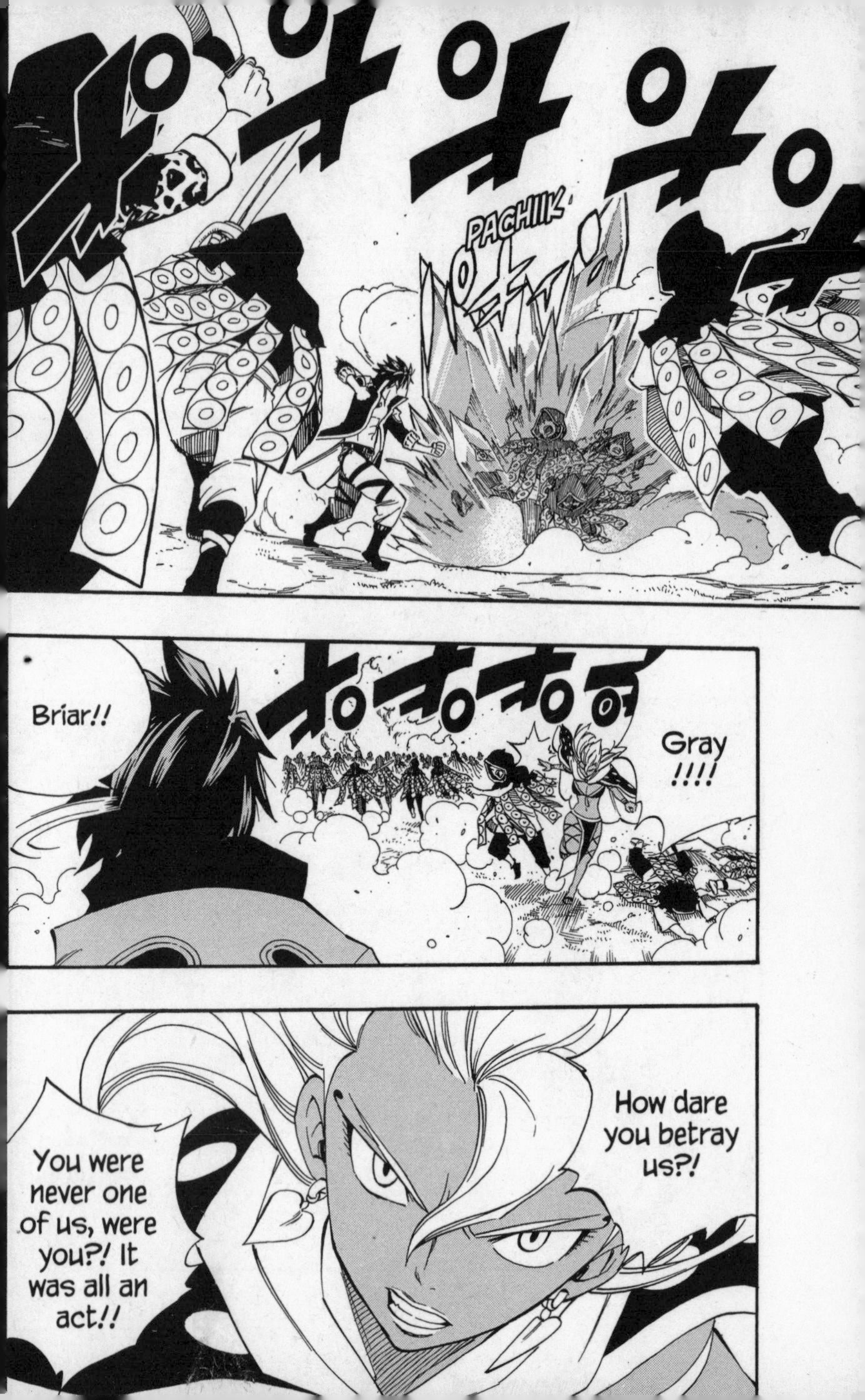
PACHIIK
Gray!!!!
Briar!!
How dare you betray us?!
You were never one of us, were you?! It was all an act!!

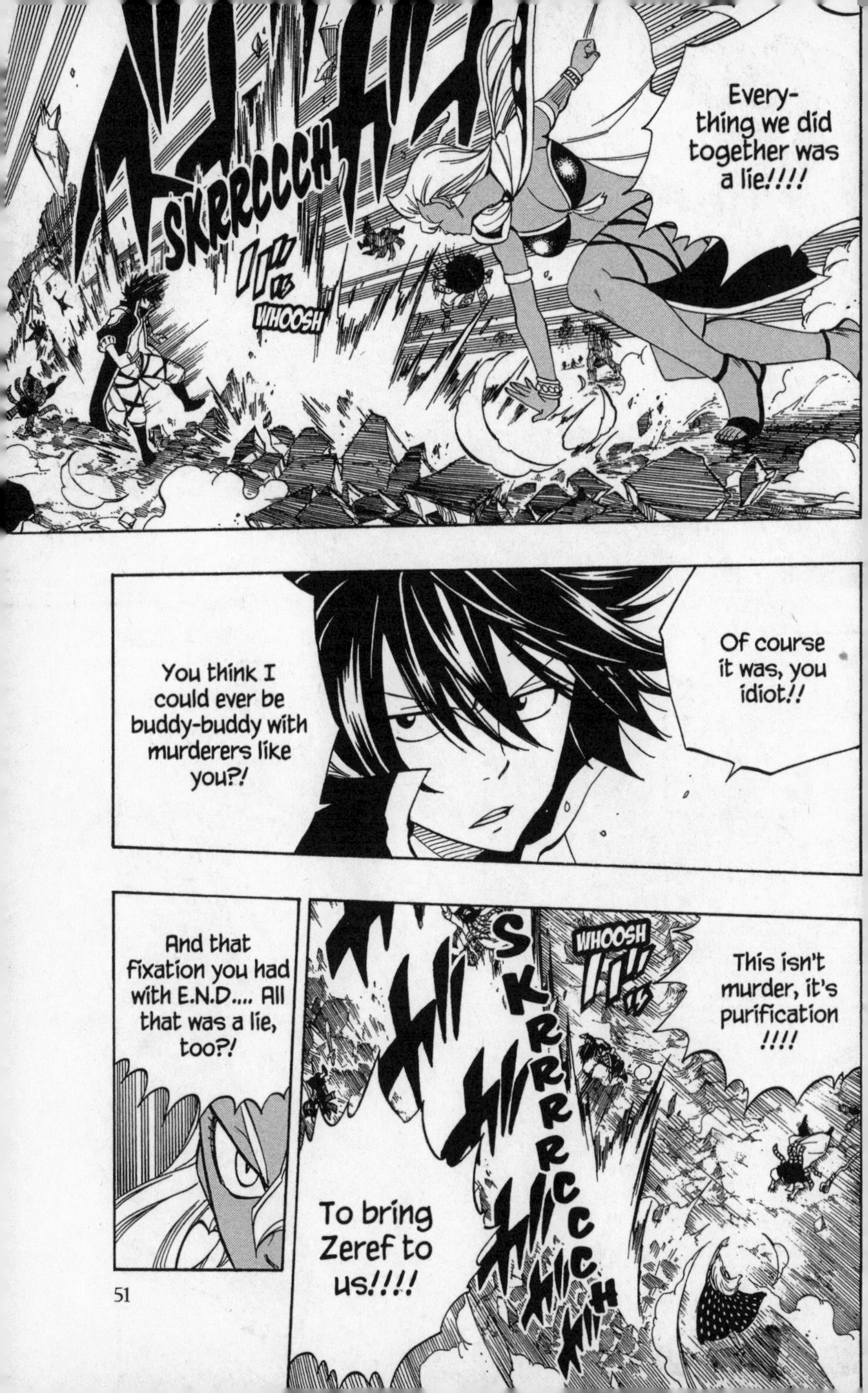
Every-thing we did together was a lie!!!!
SKRRCCCH
WHOOSH
Of course it was, you idiot!!
You think I could ever be buddy-buddy with murderers like you?!
This isn't murder, it's purification!!!!
WHOOSH
SKRRRRCCCH
To bring Zeref to us!!!!
And that fixation you had with E.N.D.... All that was a lie, too?!

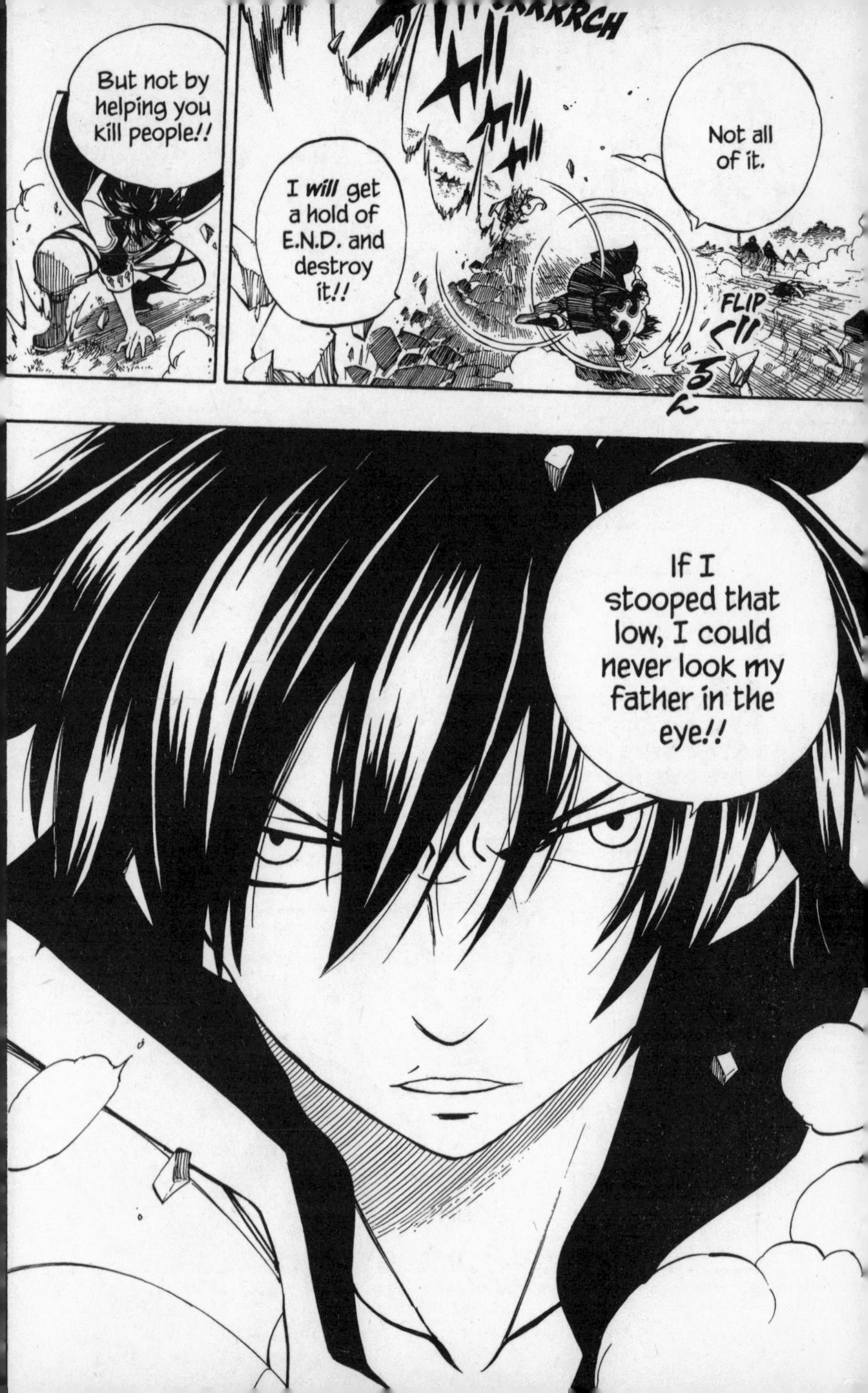

Not all of it.
I *will* get a hold of E.N.D. and destroy it!!
FLIP
ぐるん
But not by helping you kill people!!
If I stooped that low, I could never look my father in the eye!!

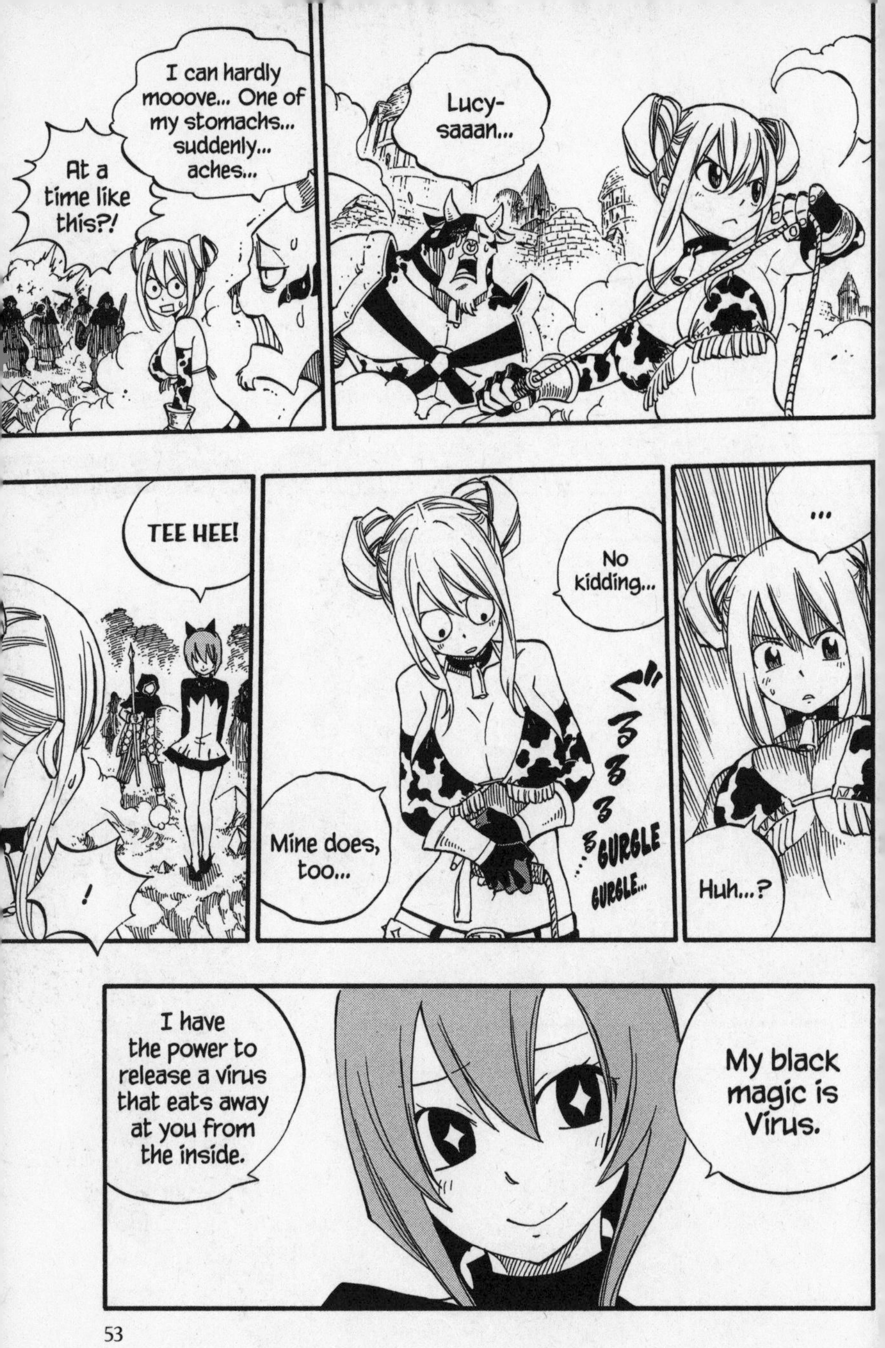
Lucy-saaan...
I can hardly mooove... One of my stomachs... suddenly... aches...
At a time like this?!
...
Huh...?
No kidding...
ぐるるるる...
GURGLE
GURGLE...
Mine does, too...
TEE HEE!
!
My black magic is Virus.
I have the power to release a virus that eats away at you from the inside.

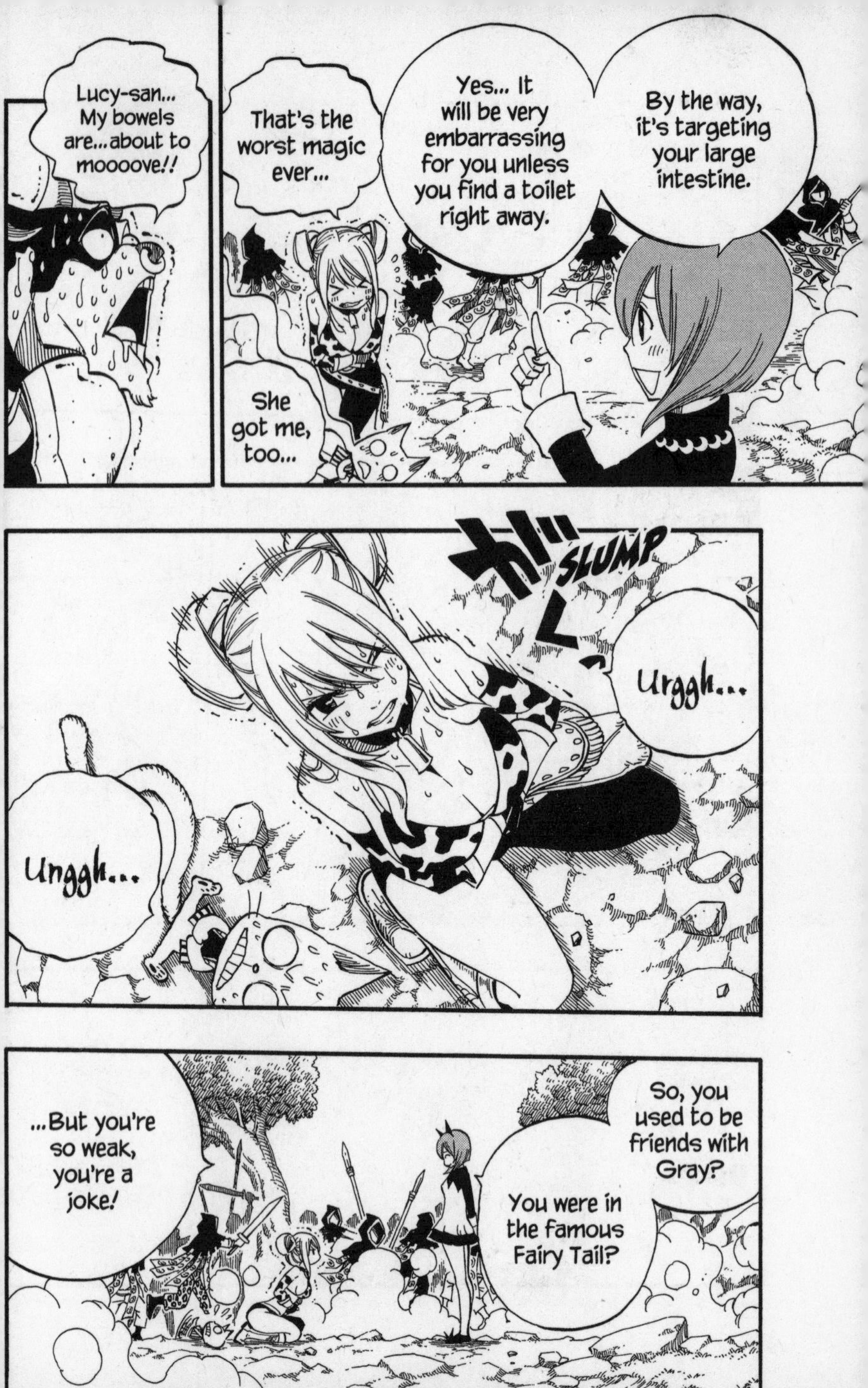
By the way, it's targeting your large intestine.
Yes... It will be very embarrassing for you unless you find a toilet right away.
That's the worst magic ever...
She got me, too...
Lucy-san... My bowels are...about to moooove!!
SLUMP
Urggh...
Unggh...
So, you used to be friends with Gray?
You were in the famous Fairy Tail?
...But you're so weak, you're a joke!

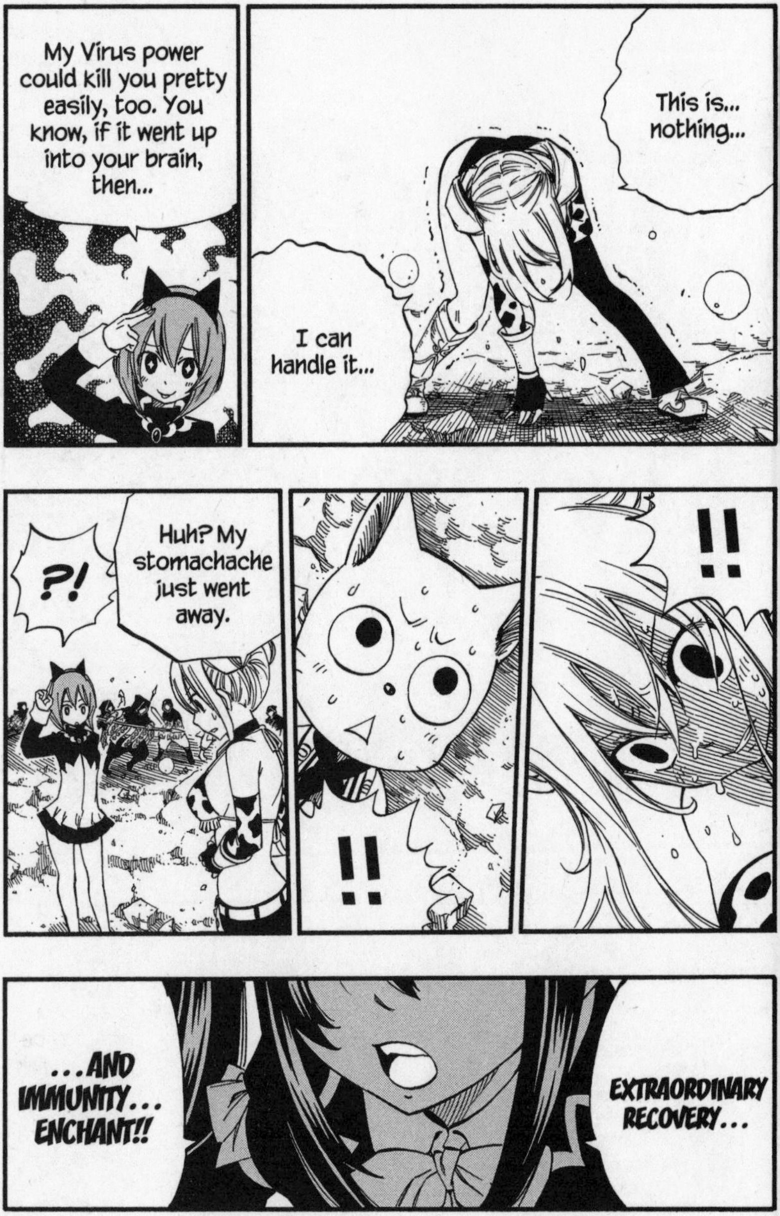
This is... nothing...
I can handle it...
My Virus power could kill you pretty easily, too. You know, if it went up into your brain, then...
!!
!!
Huh? My stomachache just went away.
?!
EXTRAORDINARY RECOVERY...
...AND IMMUNITY... ENCHANT!!

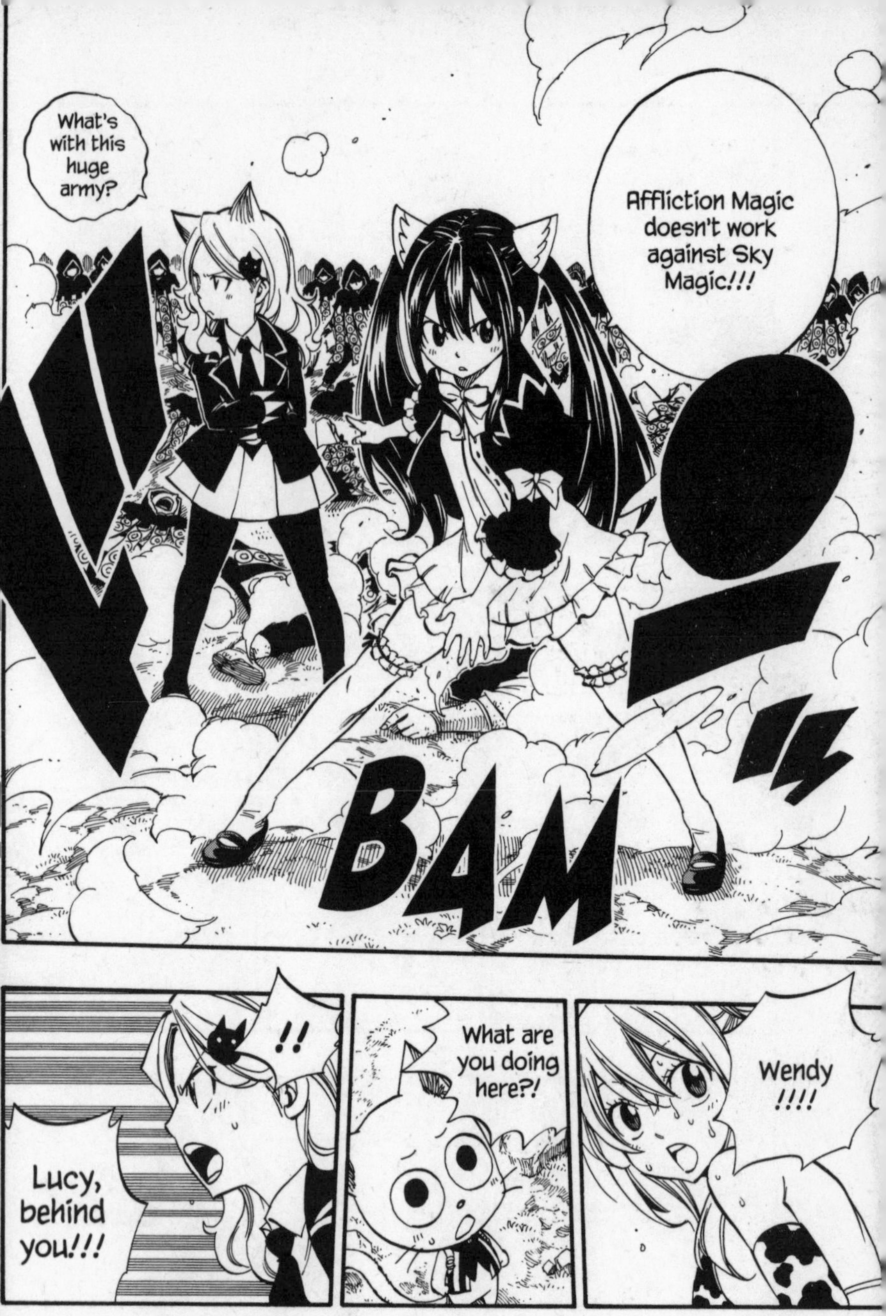
Affliction Magic doesn't work against Sky Magic!!!
What's with this huge army?
BAM
Wendy!!!!
What are you doing here?!
!!
Lucy, behind you!!!

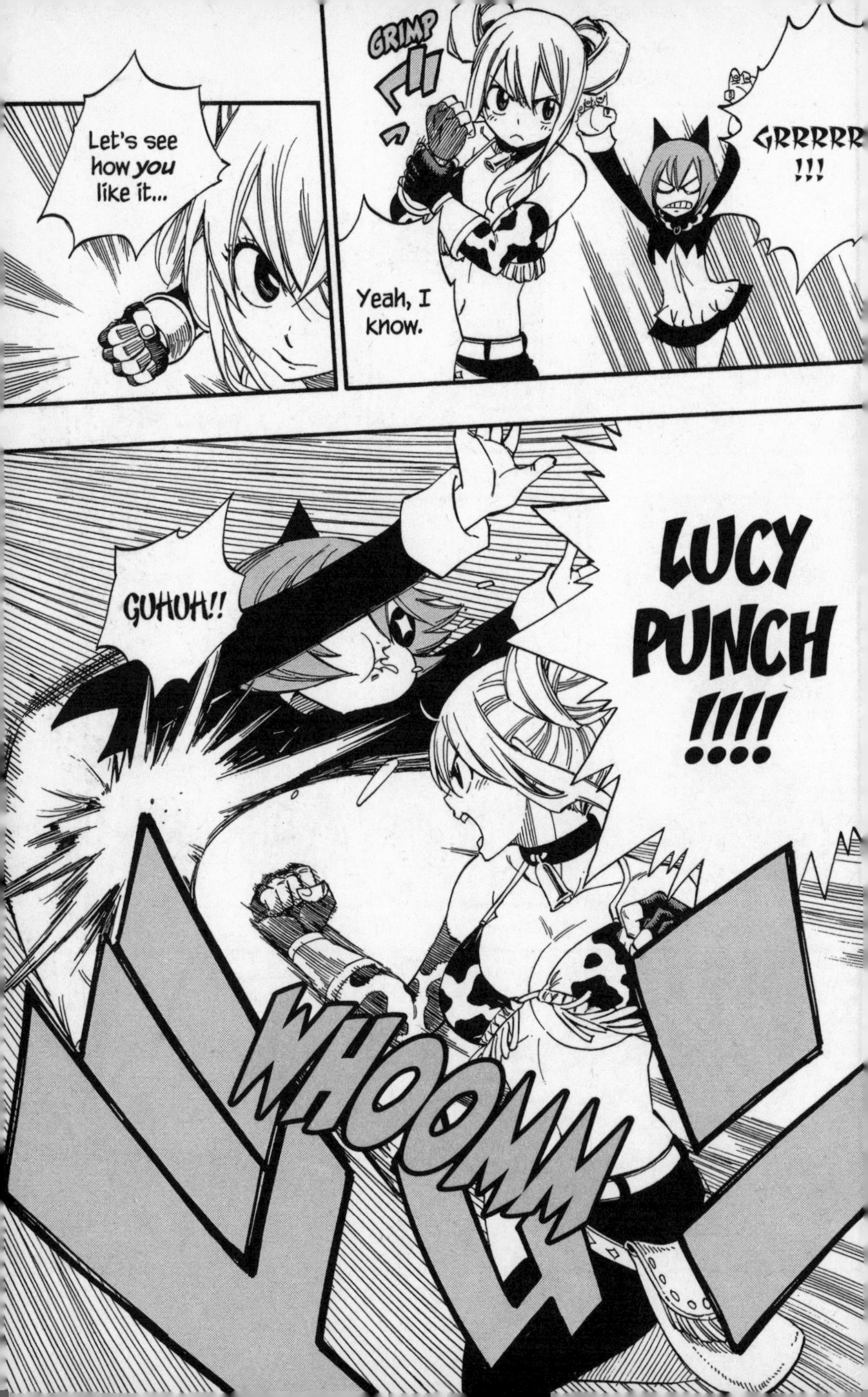
GRRRRR !!!
GRIMP
Yeah, I know.
Let's see how *you* like it...
LUCY PUNCH !!!!
GUHUH!!
WHOOMM

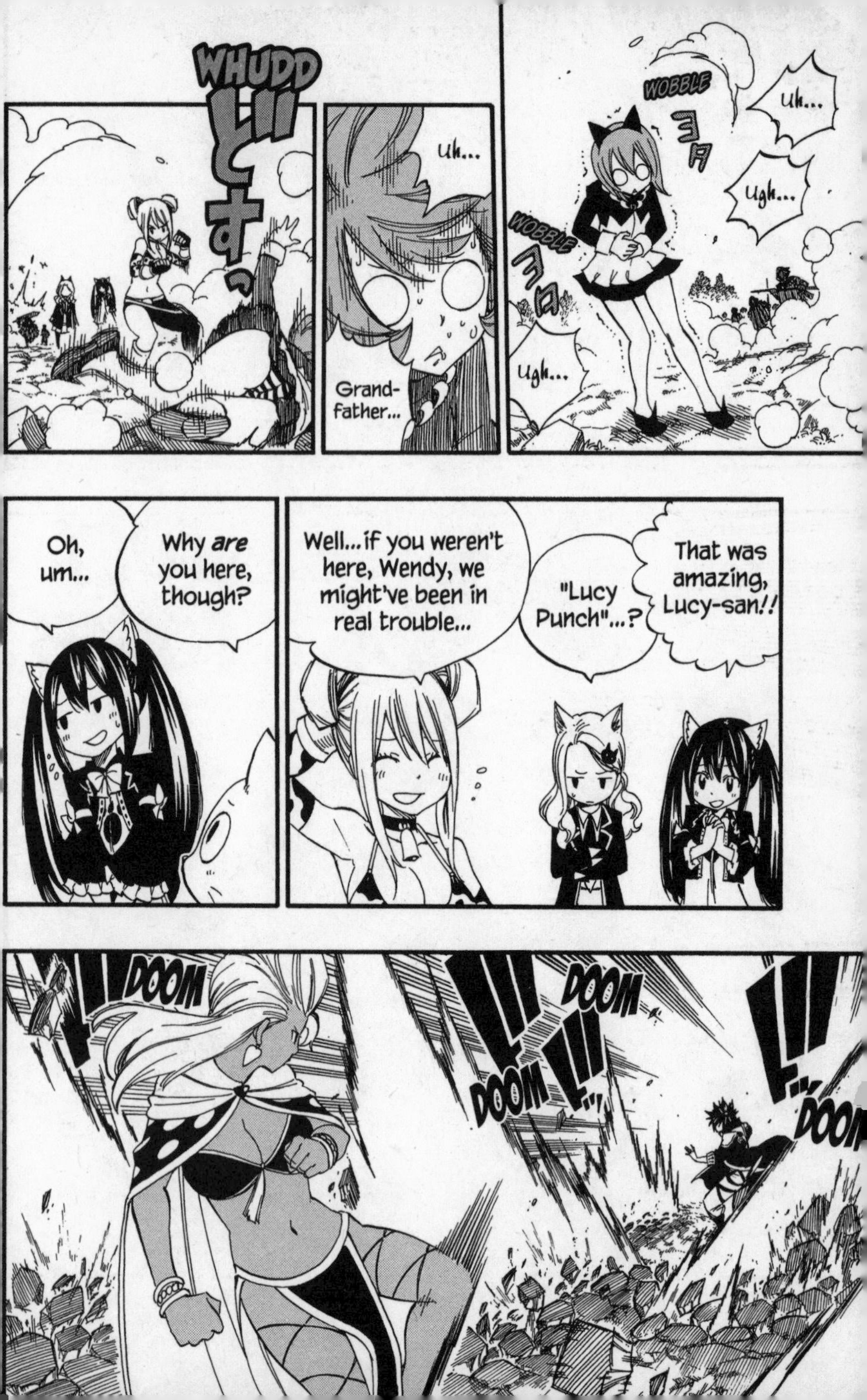

Uh...
WOBBLE
ヨタ
Ugh...
WOBBLE
ヨロ
Ugh...
Uh...
Grand-father...
WHUDD
どすっ
That was amazing, Lucy-san!!
"Lucy Punch"...?
Well...if you weren't here, Wendy, we might've been in real trouble...
Why *are* you here, though?
Oh, um...
DOOM
DOOM
DOOM
DOOM

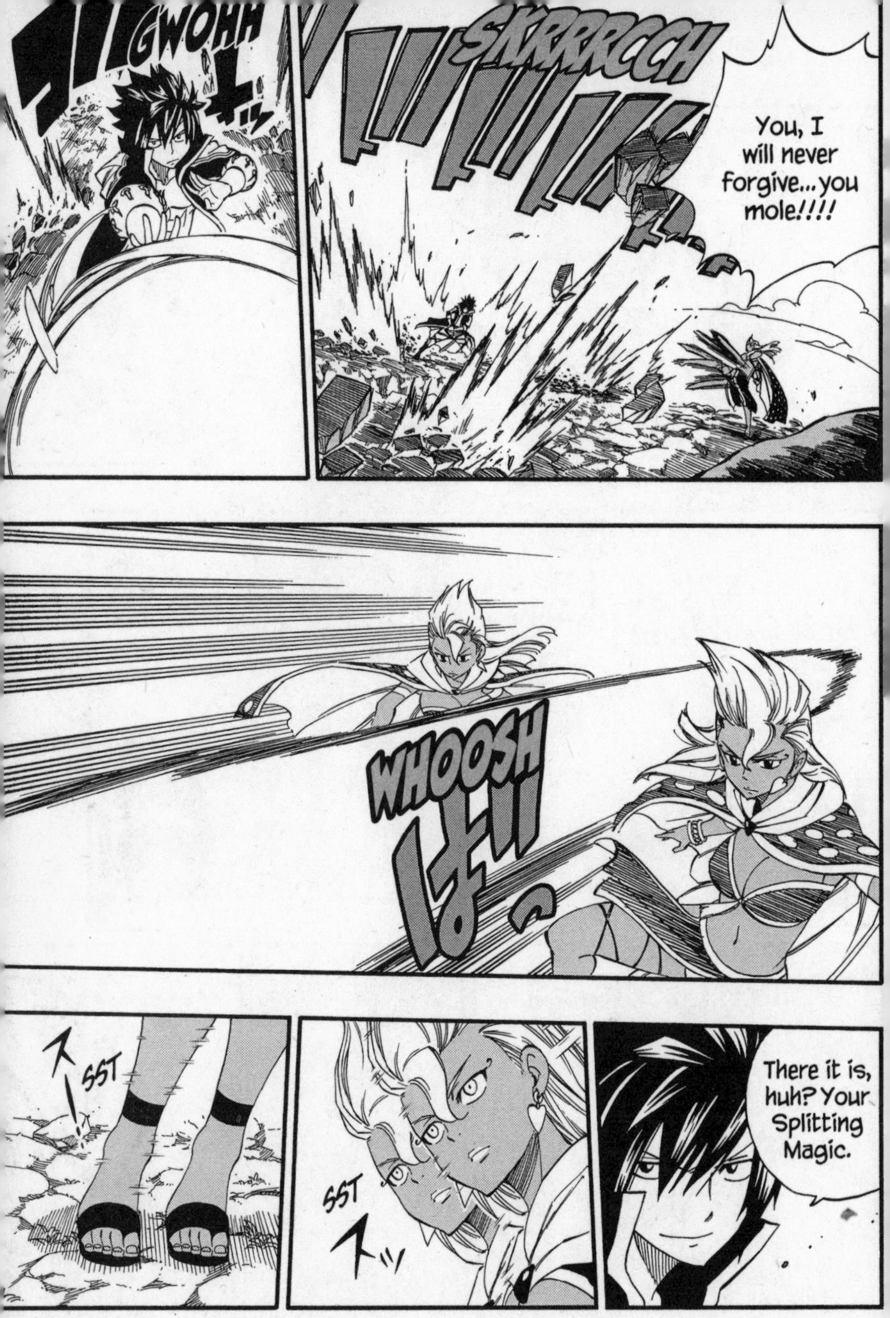
SKRRRCCH
You, I will never forgive...you mole!!!!
GWOHH
WHOOSH
There it is, huh? Your Splitting Magic.
SST
SST

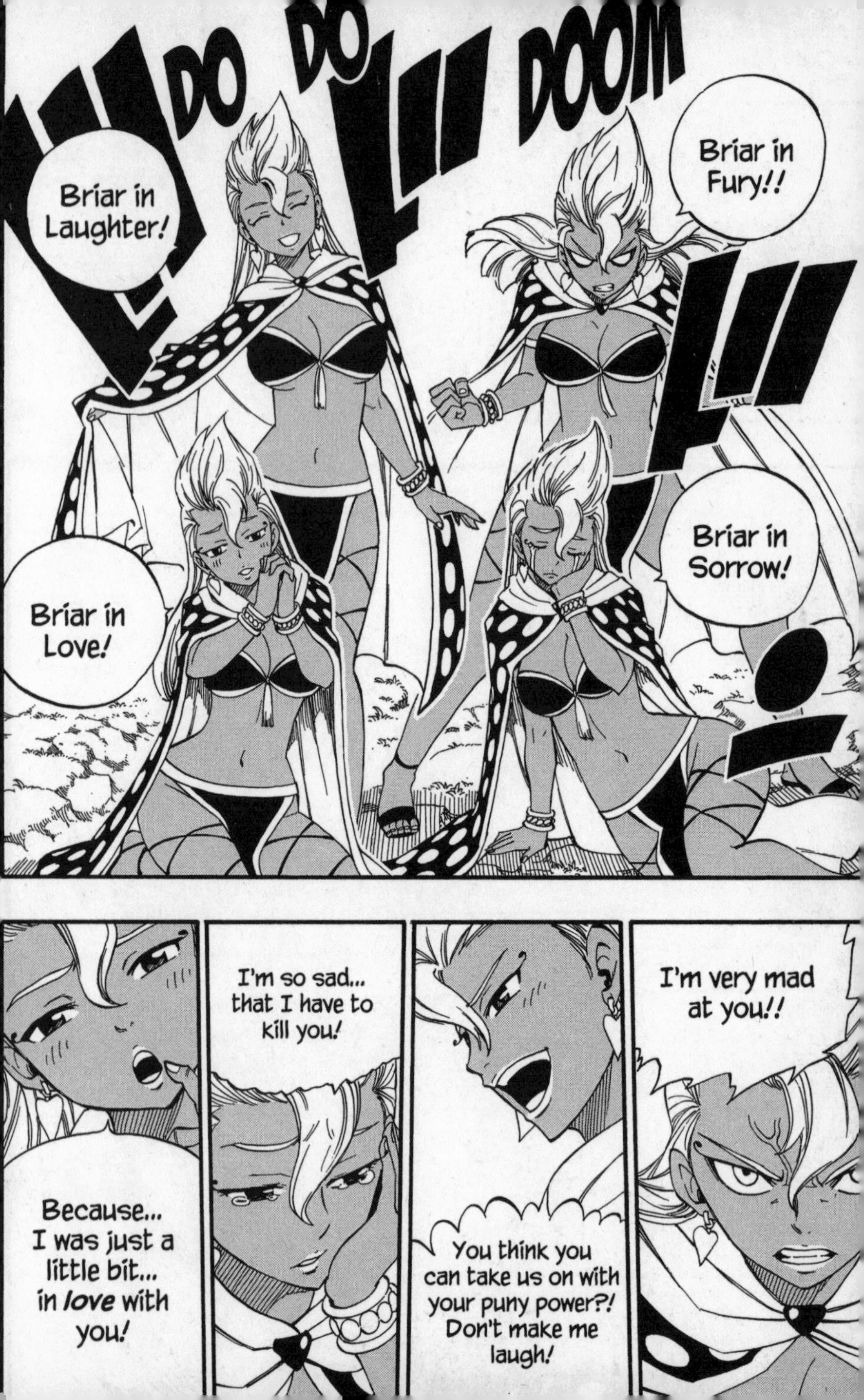
DO DO DOOM
Briar in Fury!!
Briar in Laughter!
Briar in Sorrow!
Briar in Love!
I'm very mad at you!!
You think you can take us on with your puny power?! Don't make me laugh!
I'm so sad... that I have to kill you!
Because... I was just a little bit... in *love* with you!

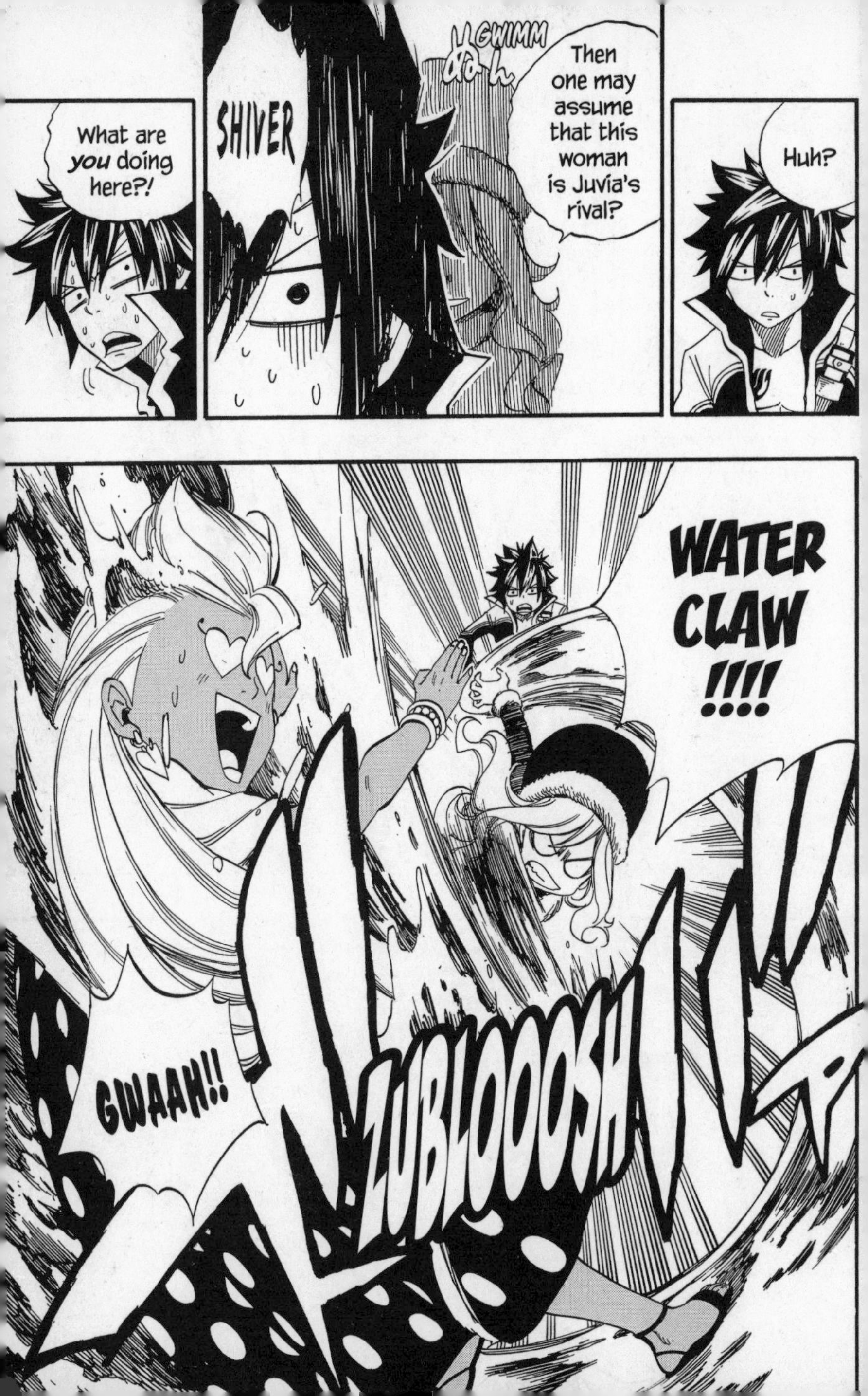
Huh?
GWIMM
Then one may assume that this woman is Juvia's rival?
SHIVER
What are *you* doing here?!
WATER CLAW !!!!
ZUBLOOOSH
GWAAH!!

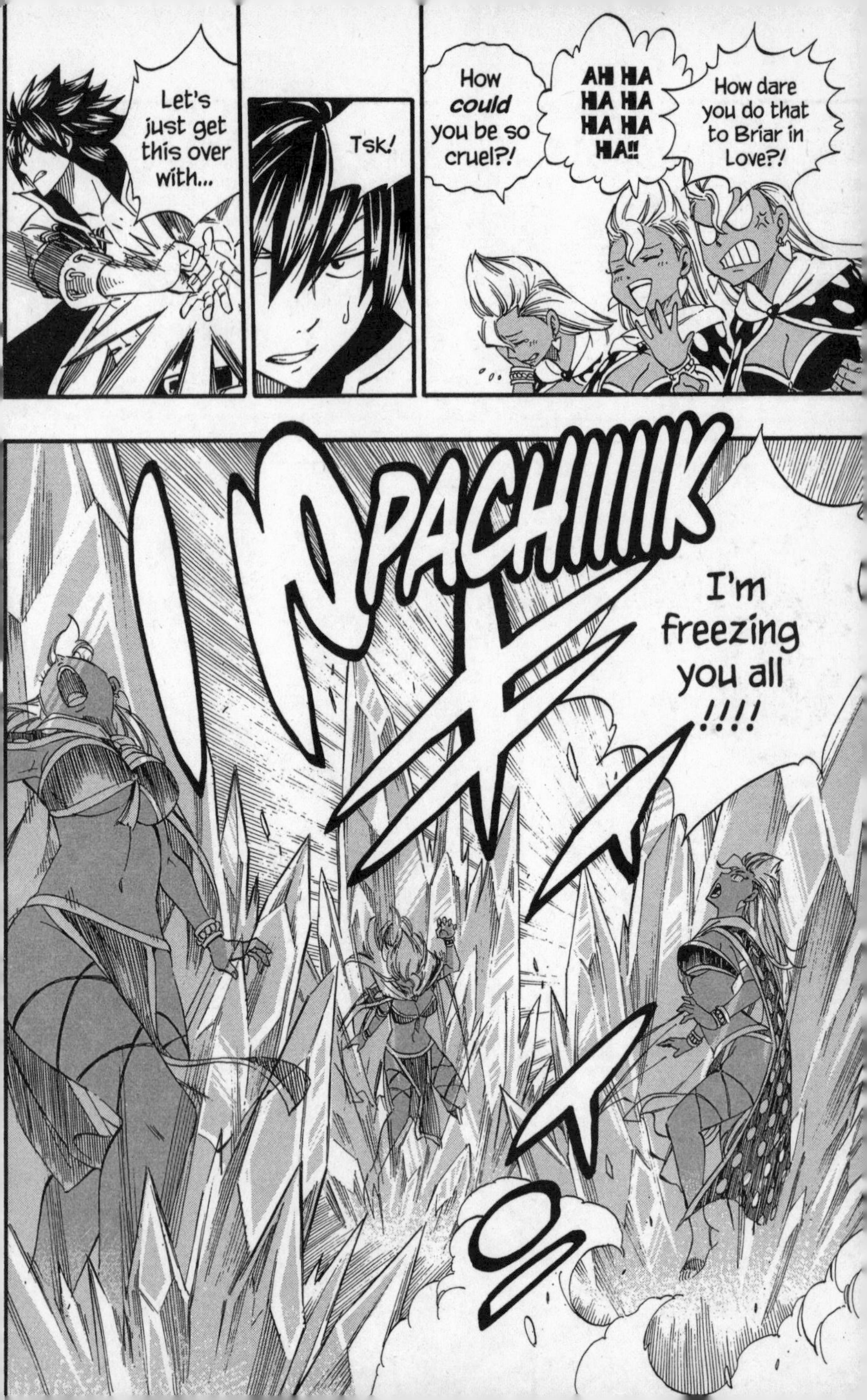
How dare you do that to Briar in Love?!
AH HA HA HA HA HA HA!!
How *could* you be so cruel?!
Tsk!
Let's just get this over with...
I'm freezing you all !!!!
PACHIIIIK

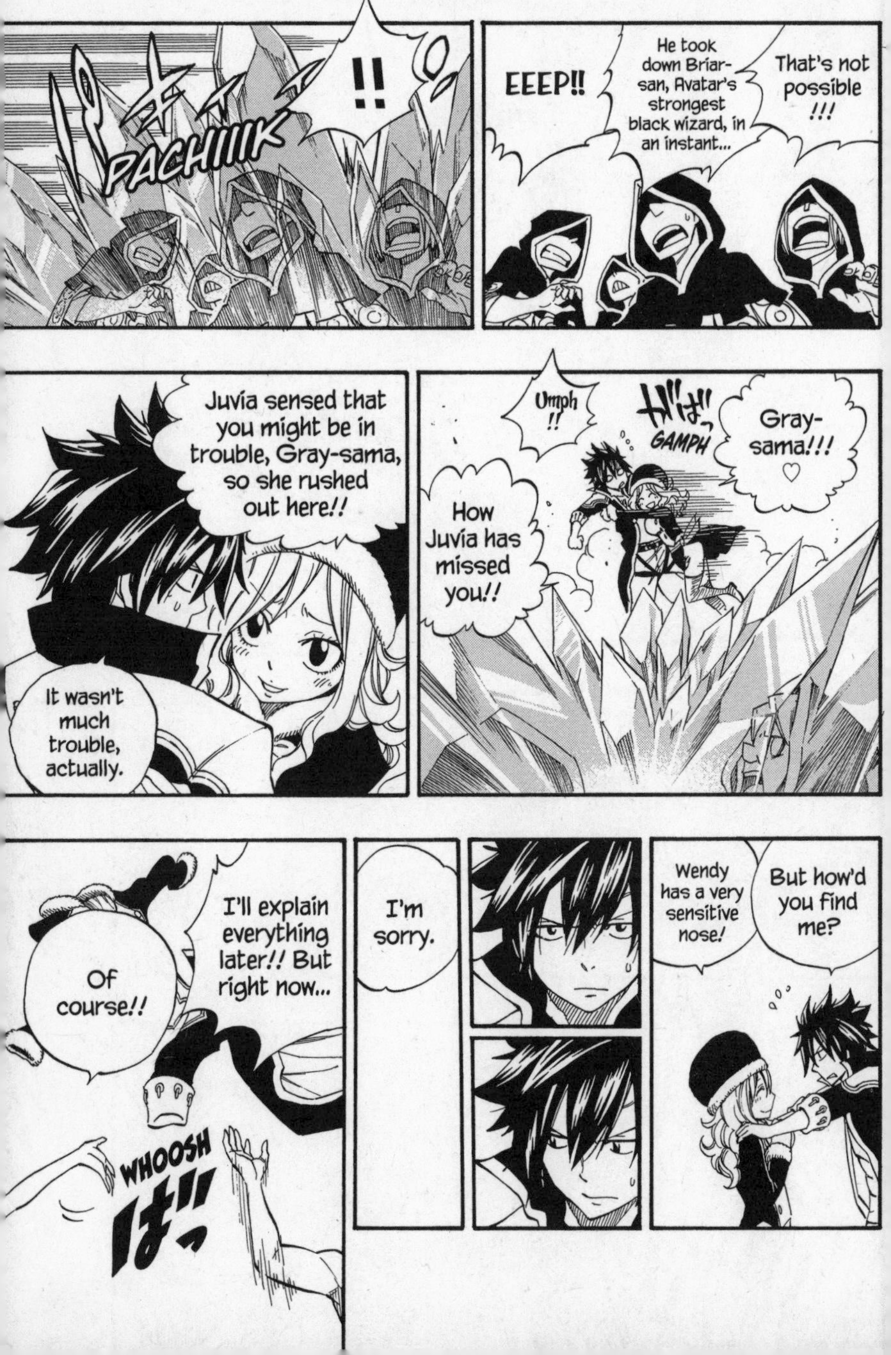
That's not possible!!!
He took down Briar-san, Avatar's strongest black wizard, in an instant...
EEEP!!
!!
PACHIIIIK
Gray-sama!!! ♡
GAMPH
Umph!!
How Juvia has missed you!!
Juvia sensed that you might be in trouble, Gray-sama, so she rushed out here!!
It wasn't much trouble, actually.
But how'd you find me?
Wendy has a very sensitive nose!
I'm sorry.
I'll explain everything later!! But right now...
Of course!!
WHOOSH

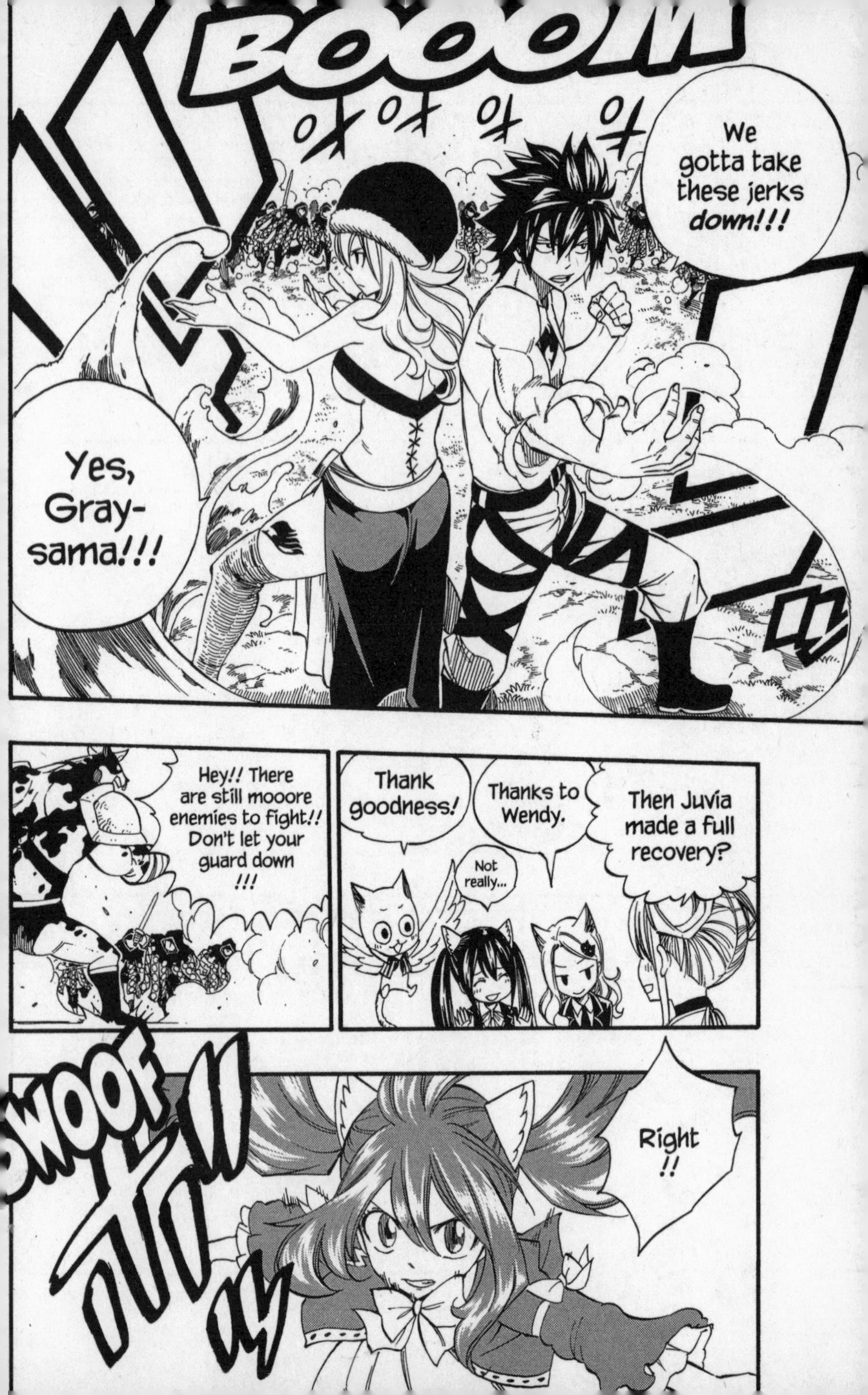
BOOOM
We gotta take these jerks down!!!
Yes, Gray-sama!!!
Then Juvia made a full recovery?
Thanks to Wendy.
Thank goodness!
Not really...
Hey!! There are still mooore enemies to fight!! Don't let your guard down !!!
Right !!
SWOOF

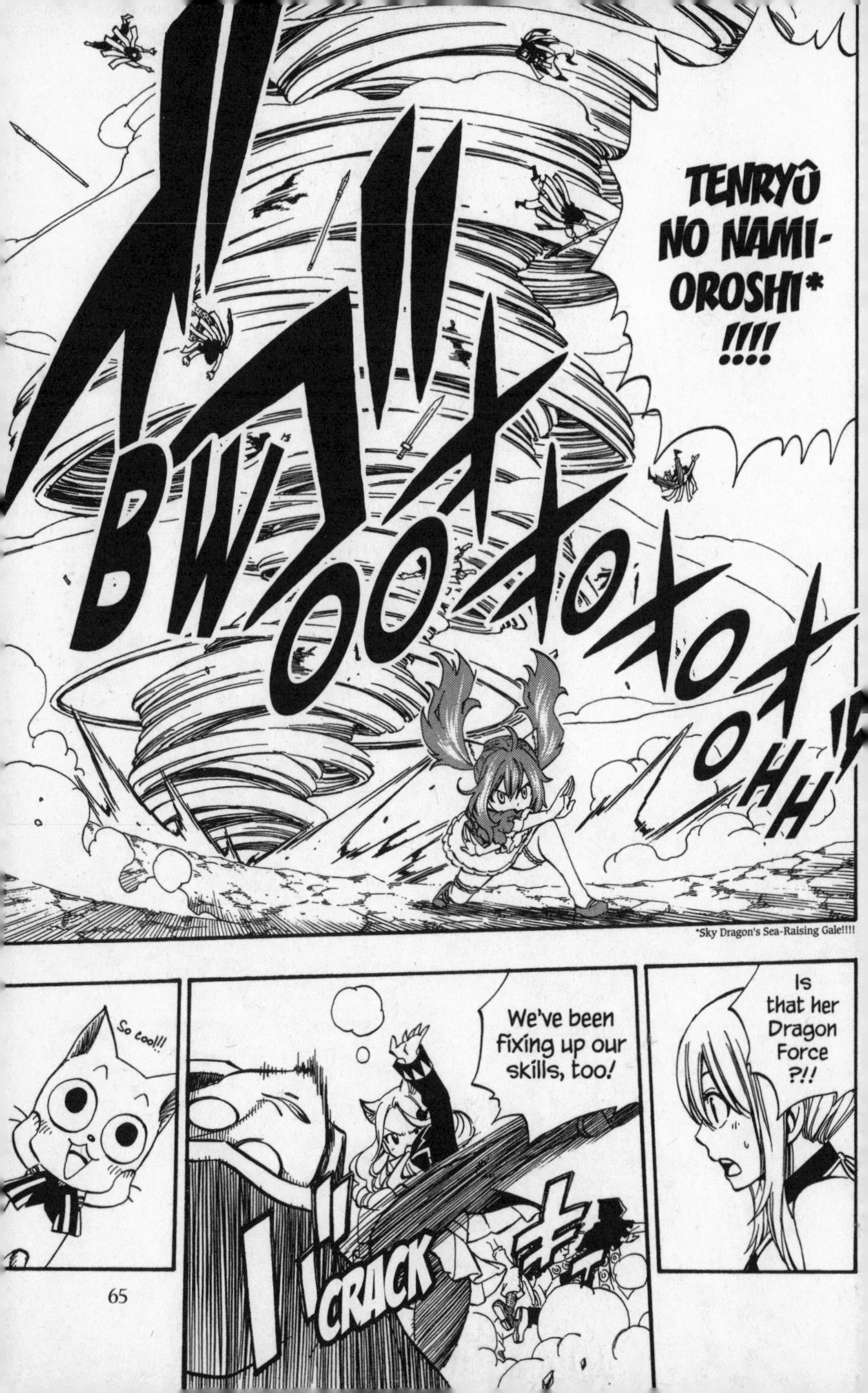
TENRYÛ NO NAMI-OROSHI* !!!!
BWOOOOOOHH
Is that her Dragon Force ?!!
We've been fixing up our skills, too!
CRACK
So cool!!
*Sky Dragon's Sea-Raising Gale!!!!

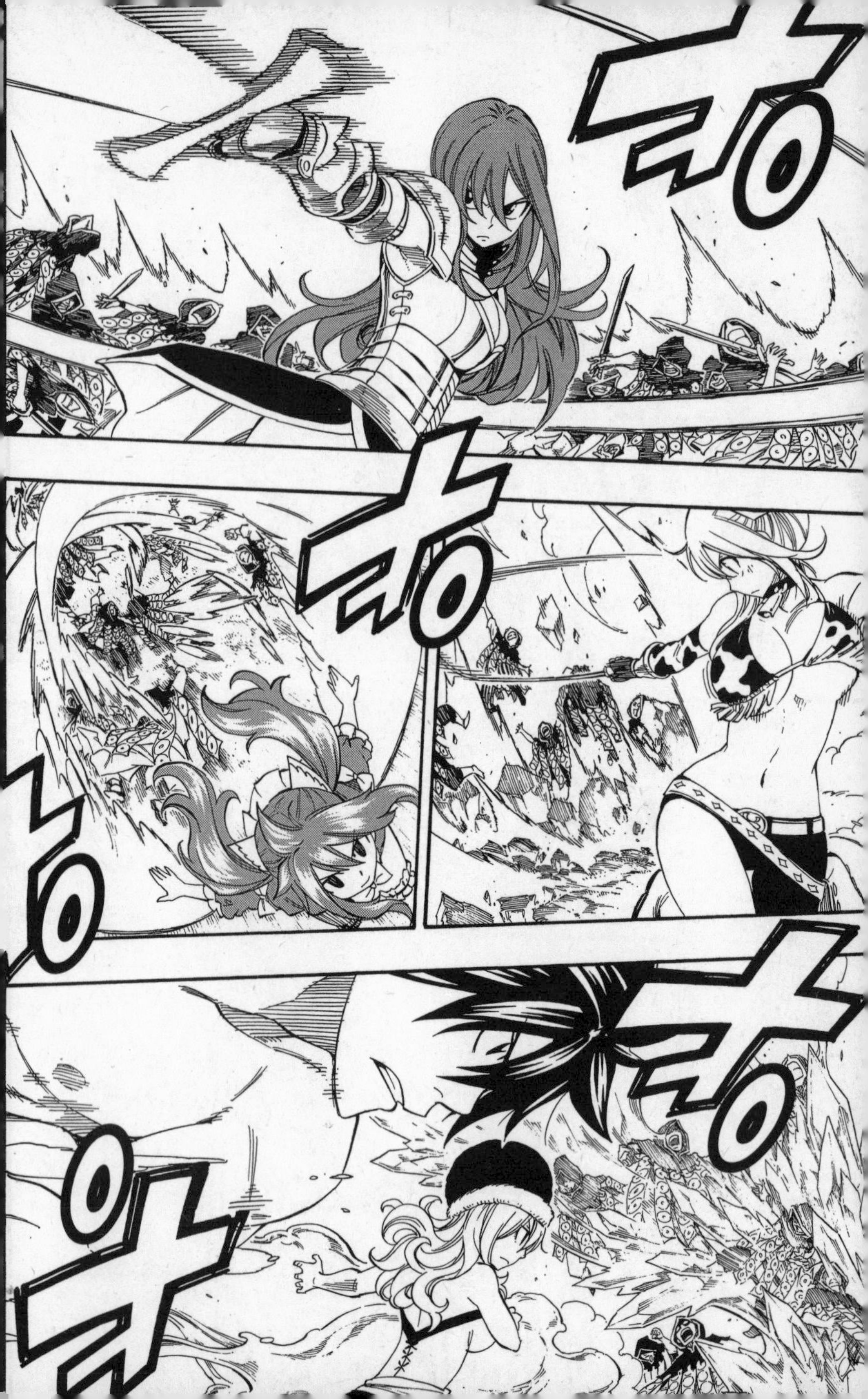

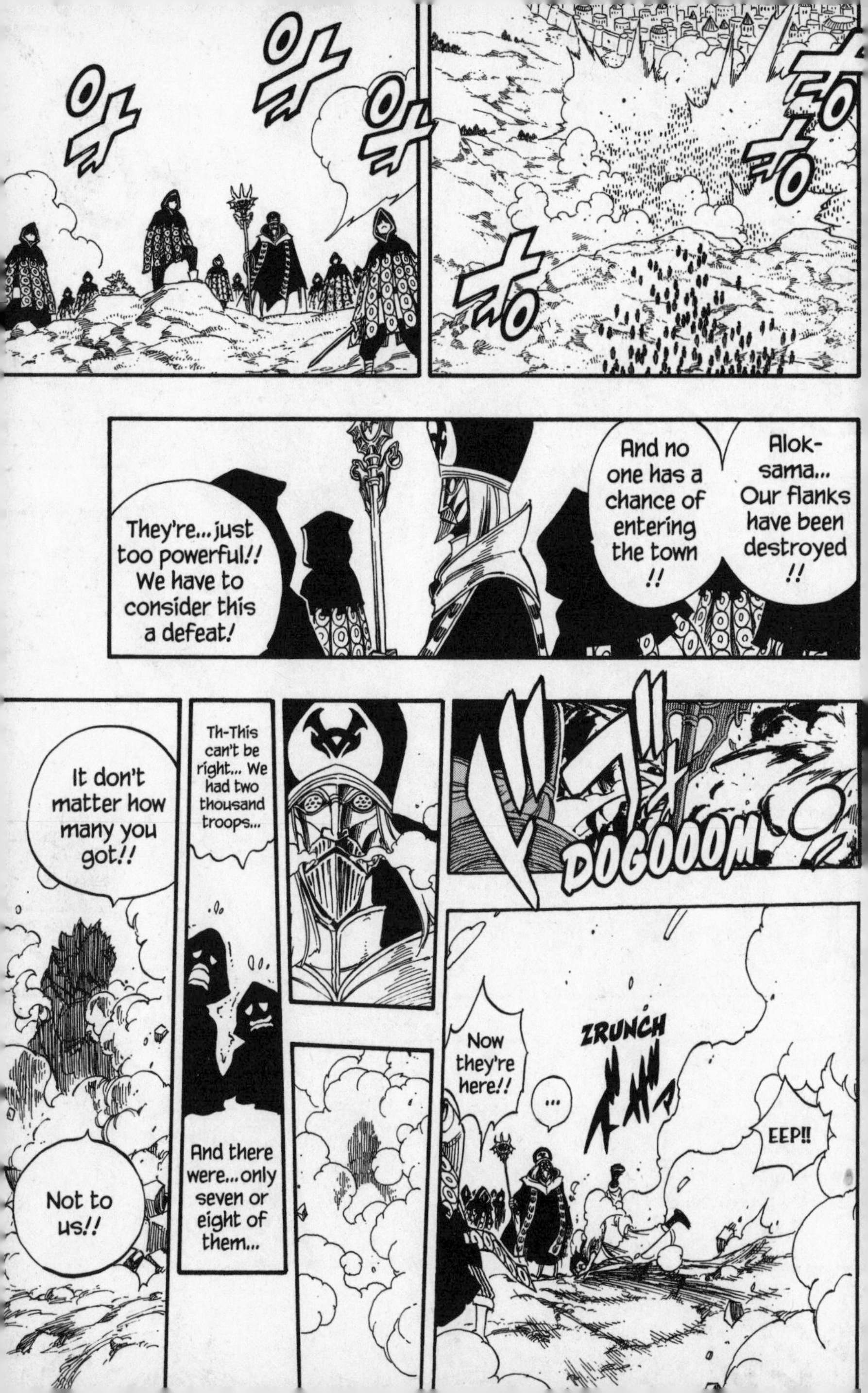
Alok-sama... Our flanks have been destroyed!!
And no one has a chance of entering the town!!
They're...just too powerful!! We have to consider this a defeat!
DOGOOOM
Now they're here!!
...
ZRUNCH
EEP!!
Th-This can't be right... We had two thousand troops...
And there were...only seven or eight of them...
It don't matter how many you got!!
Not to us!!

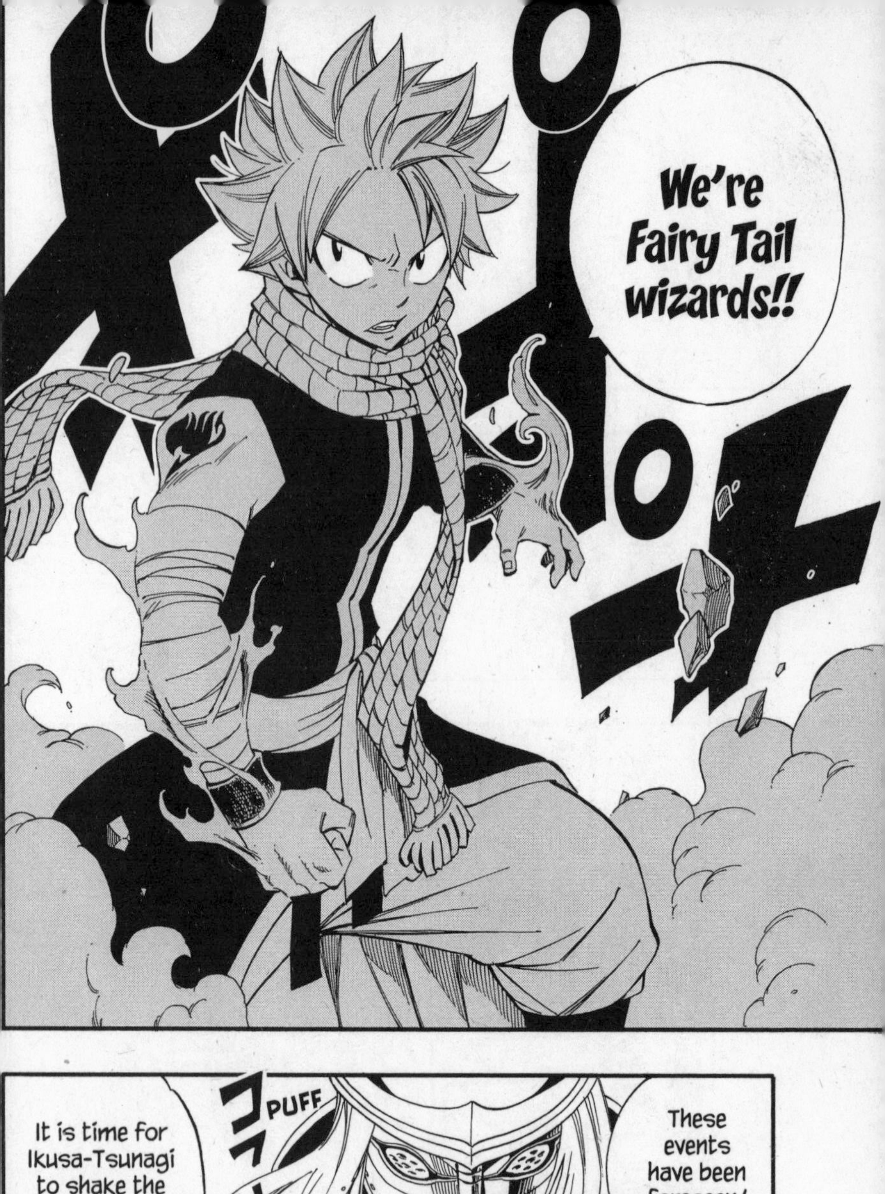
We're Fairy Tail wizards!!
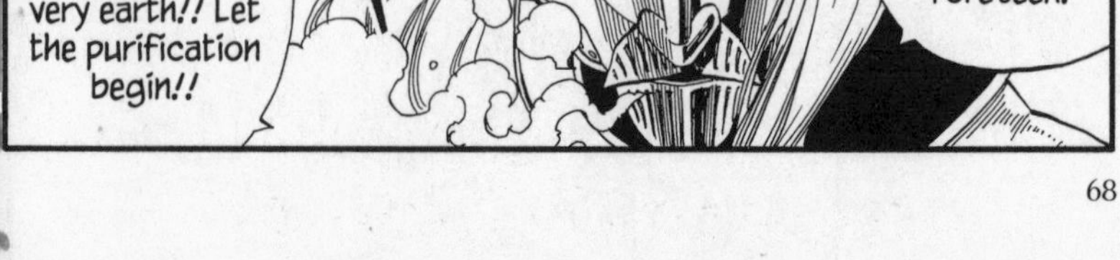
These events have been foreseen!
PUFF
It is time for Ikusa-Tsunagi to shake the very earth!! Let the purification begin!!

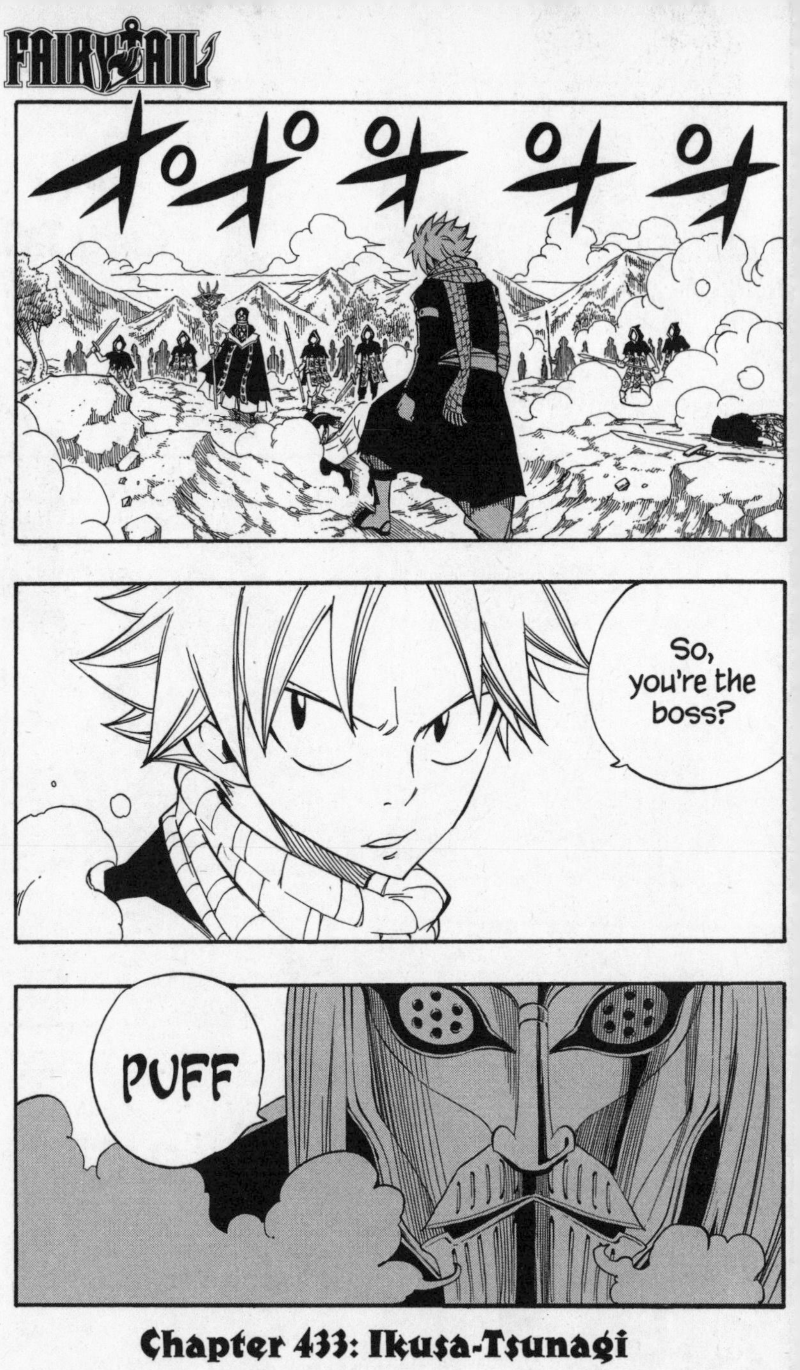

So, you're the boss?
PUFF

Chapter 433: Ikusa-Tsunagi

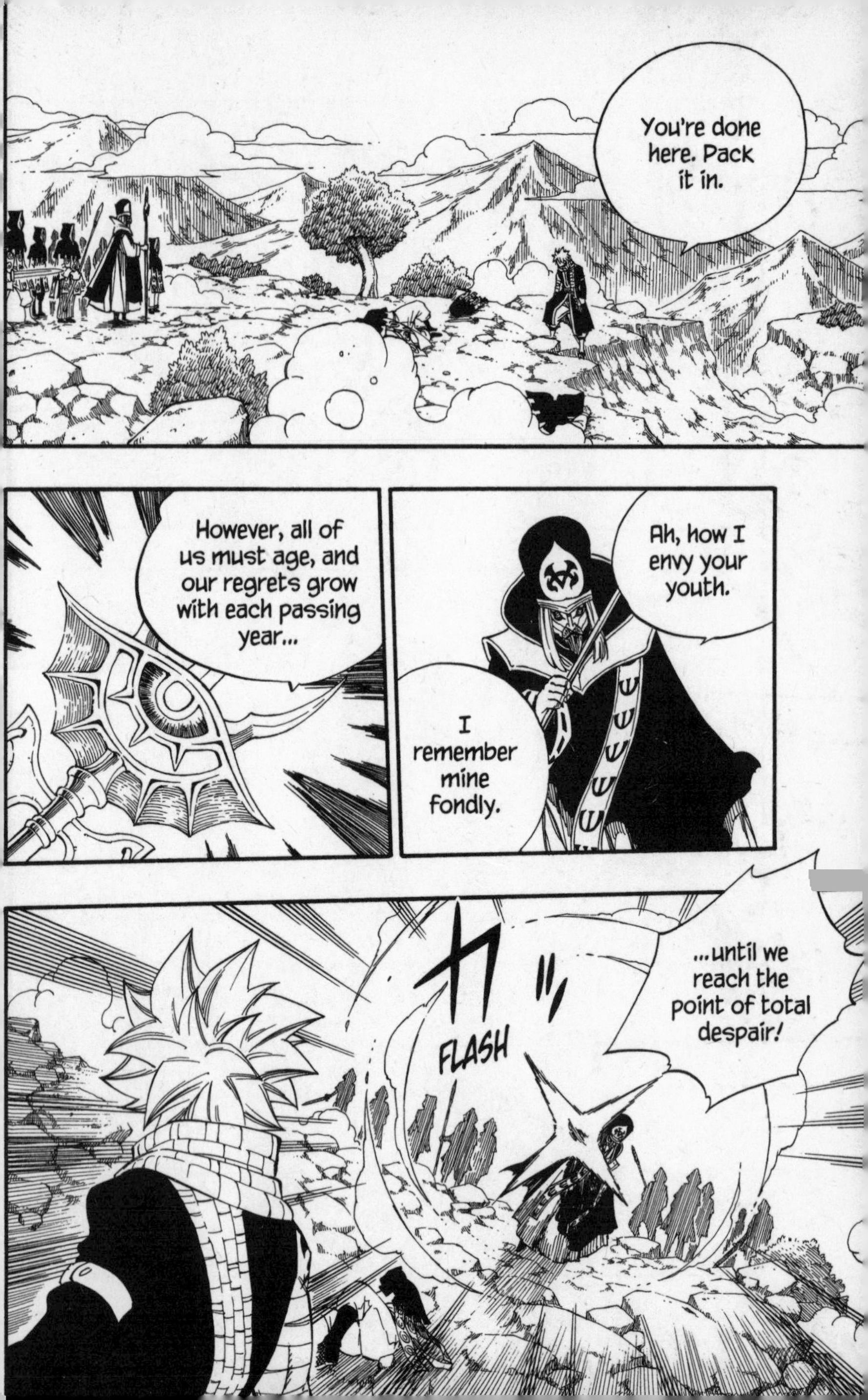
You're done here. Pack it in.
Ah, how I envy your youth.
I remember mine fondly.
However, all of us must age, and our regrets grow with each passing year...
...until we reach the point of total despair!
FLASH

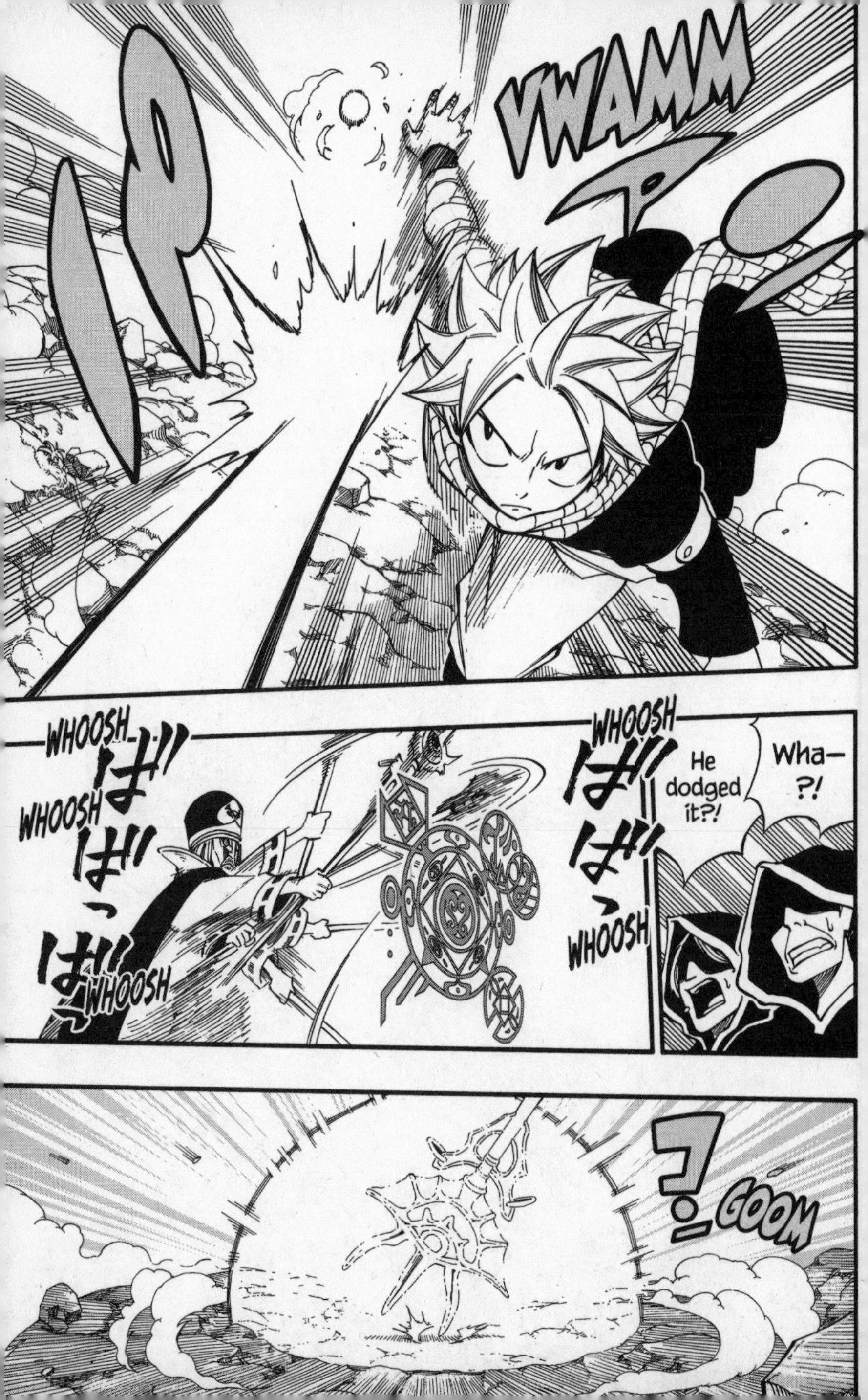
VWAMM
Wha-?!
He dodged it?!
WHOOSH
WHOOSH
WHOOSH
WHOOSH
WHOOSH
GOOM

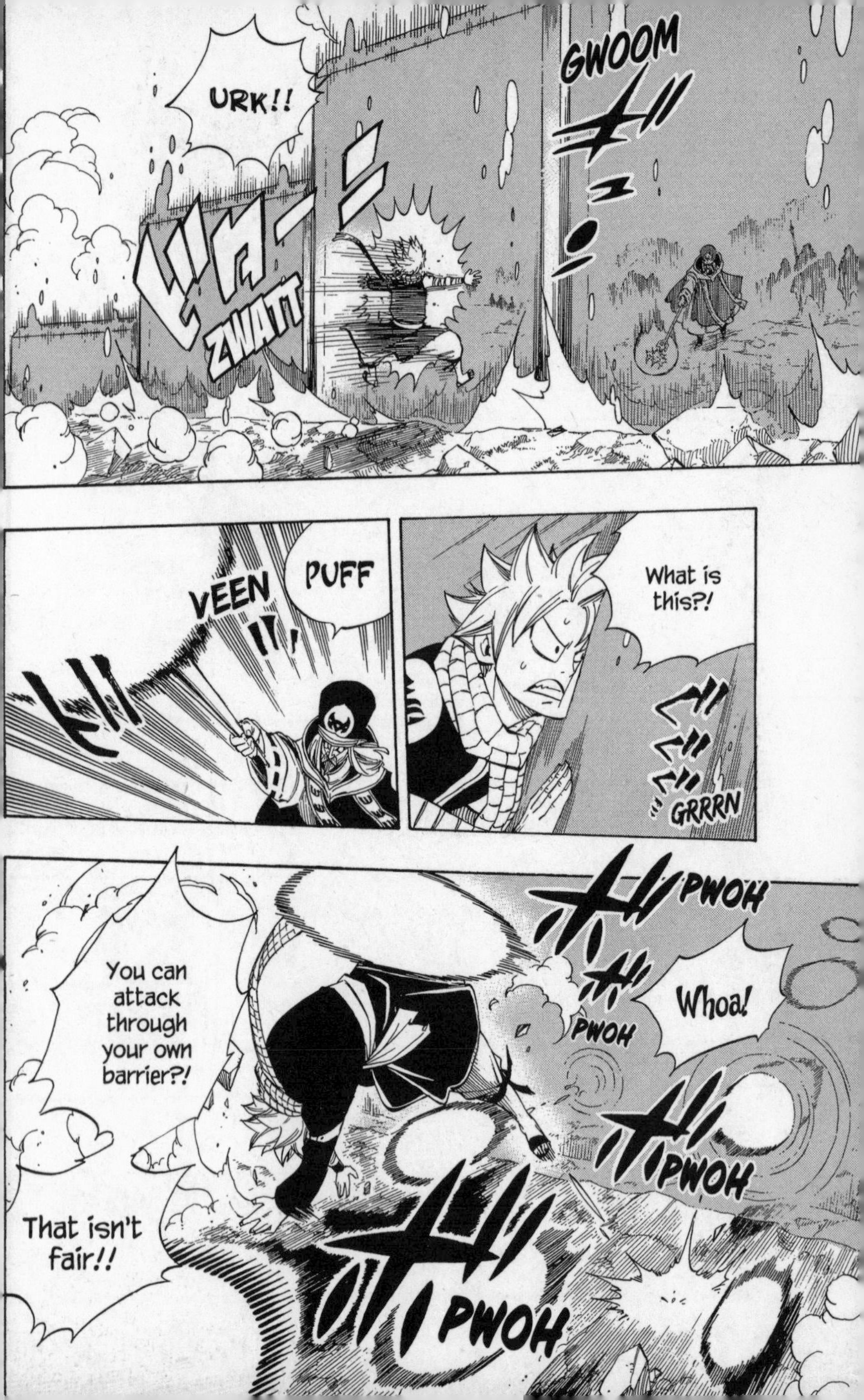
GWOOM
URK!!
ZWATT
What is this?!
GRRRN
PUFF
VEEN
PWOH
Whoa!
PWOH
PWOH
You can attack through your own barrier?!
That isn't fair!!
PWOH

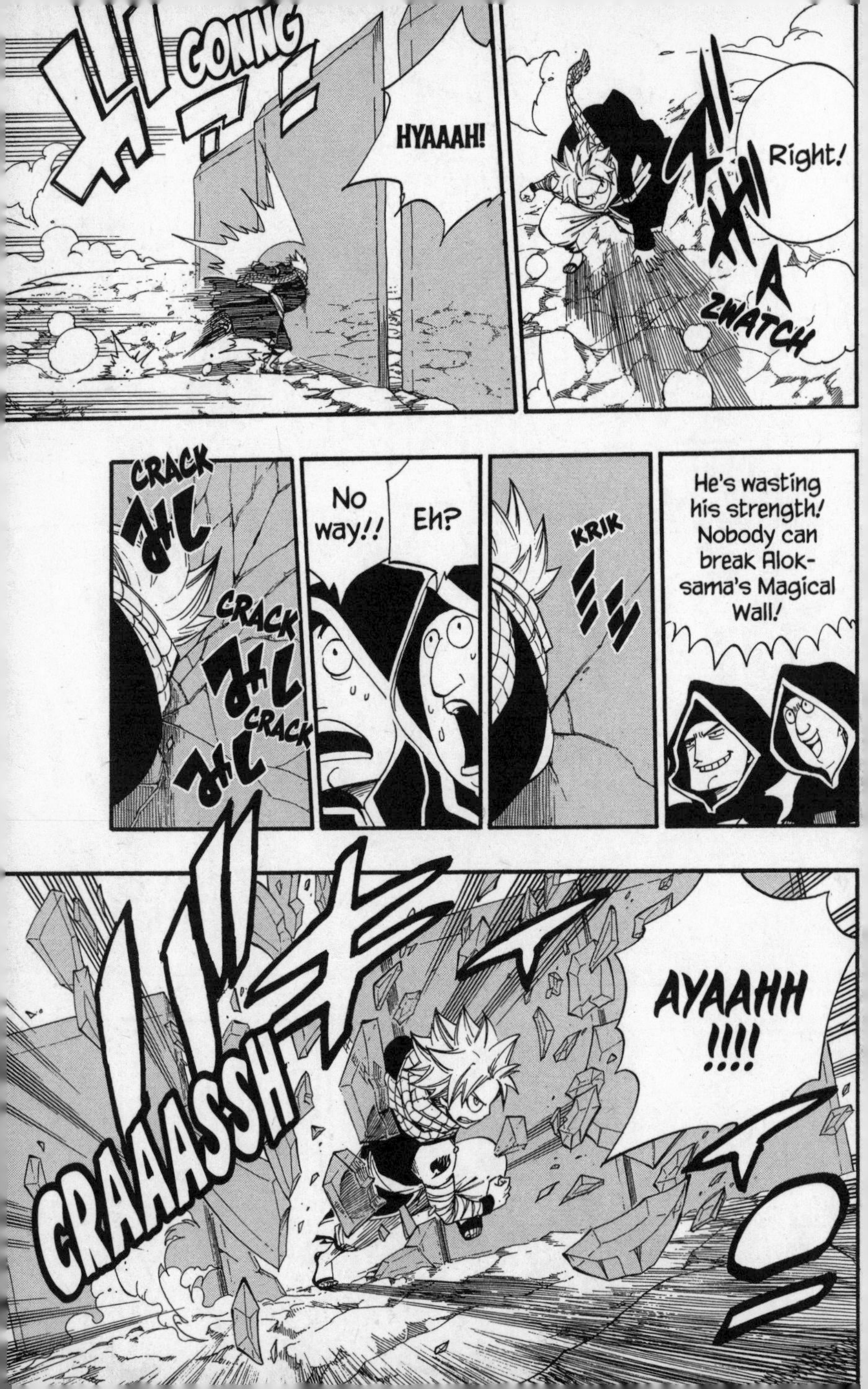
Right!
ZWATCH
HYAAAH!
GONNG
He's wasting his strength! Nobody can break Alok-sama's Magical Wall!
KRIK
Eh?
No way!!
CRACK
CRACK
CRACK
AYAAHH!!!!
CRAAASSH

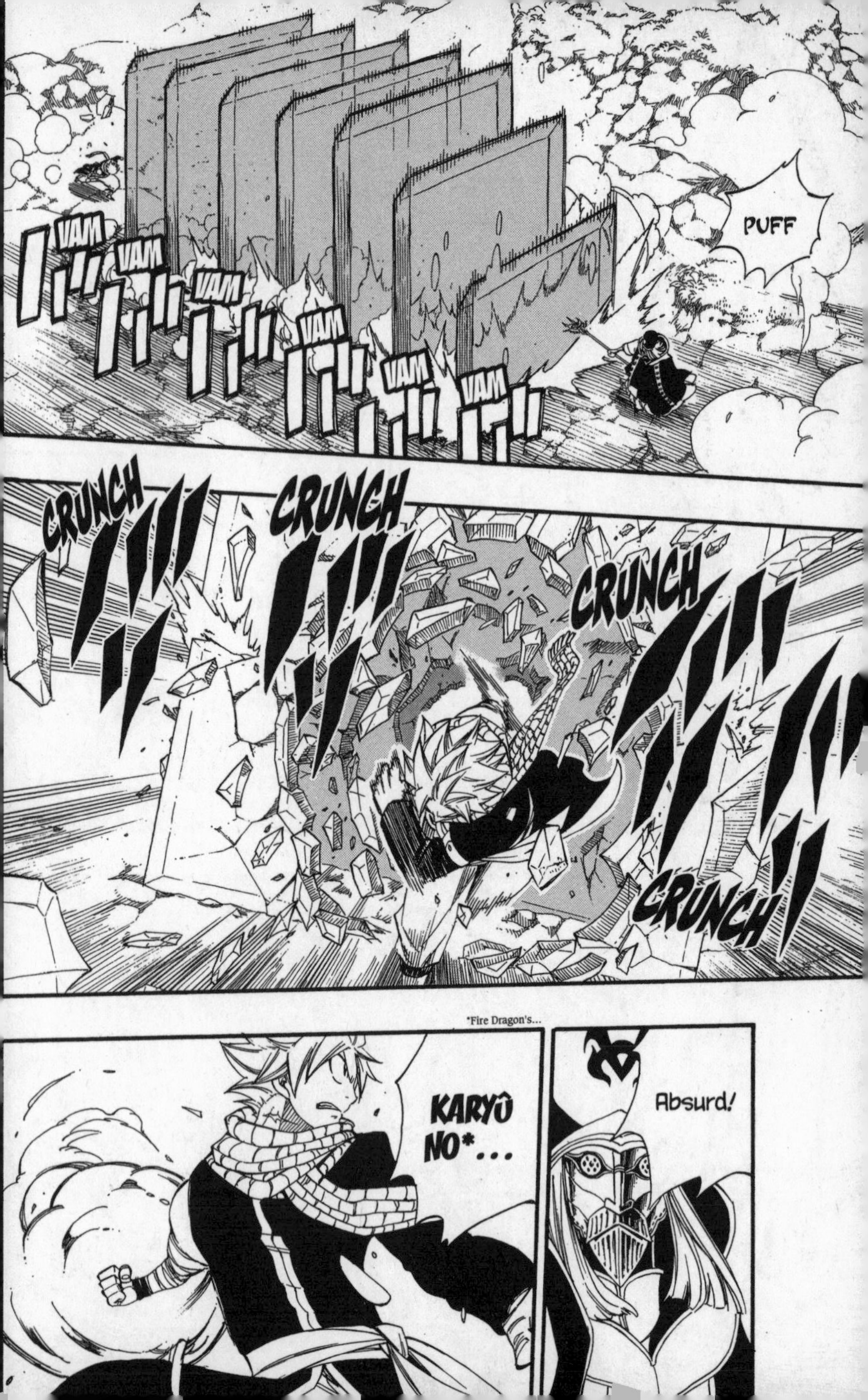
PUFF
VAM
VAM
VAM
VAM
VAM
VAM
CRUNCH
CRUNCH
CRUNCH
CRUNCH
Absurd!
KARYÛ NO*...
*Fire Dragon's...

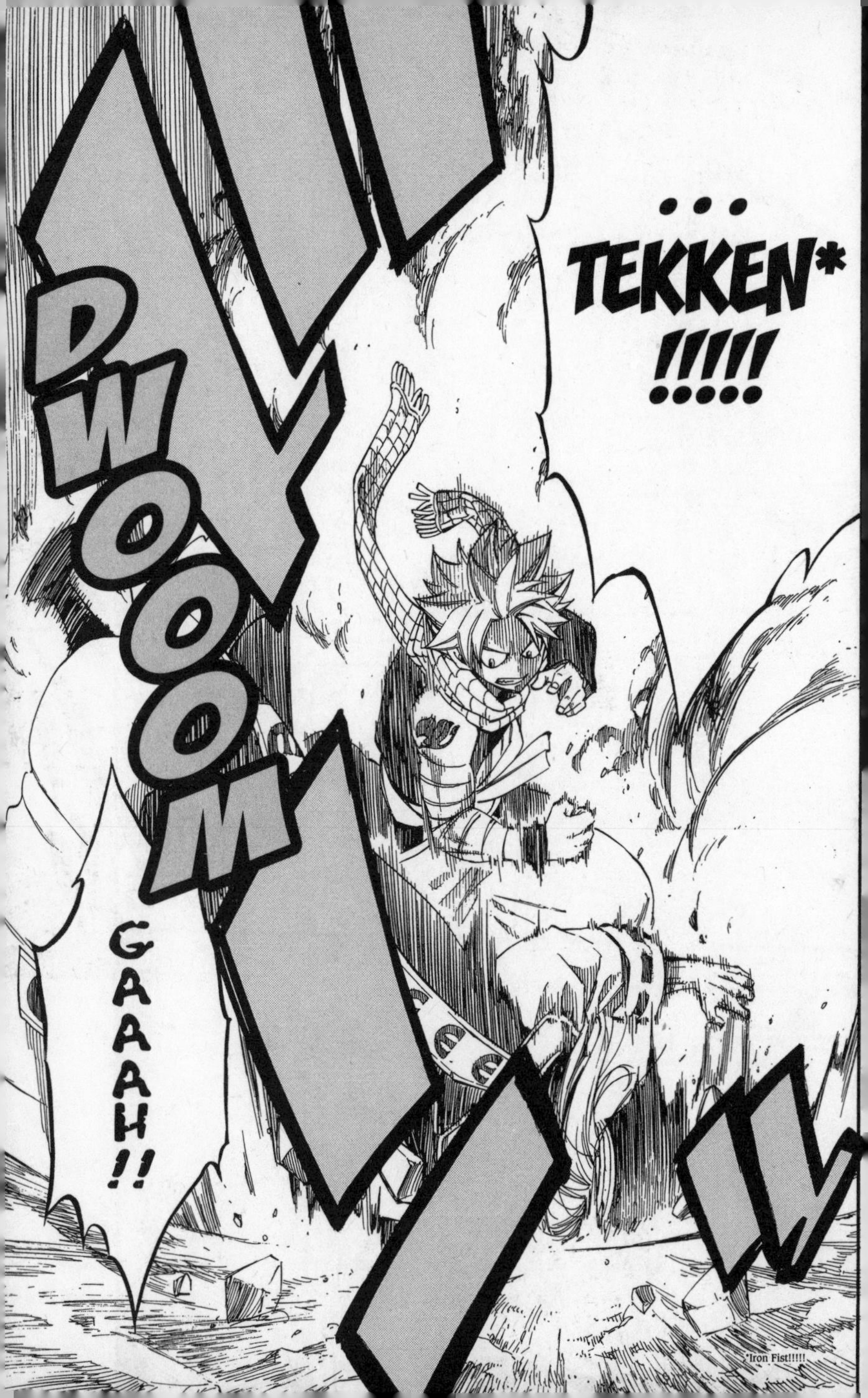
...TEKKEN* !!!!!
DWOOOM
GAAAH!!
*Iron Fist!!!!!

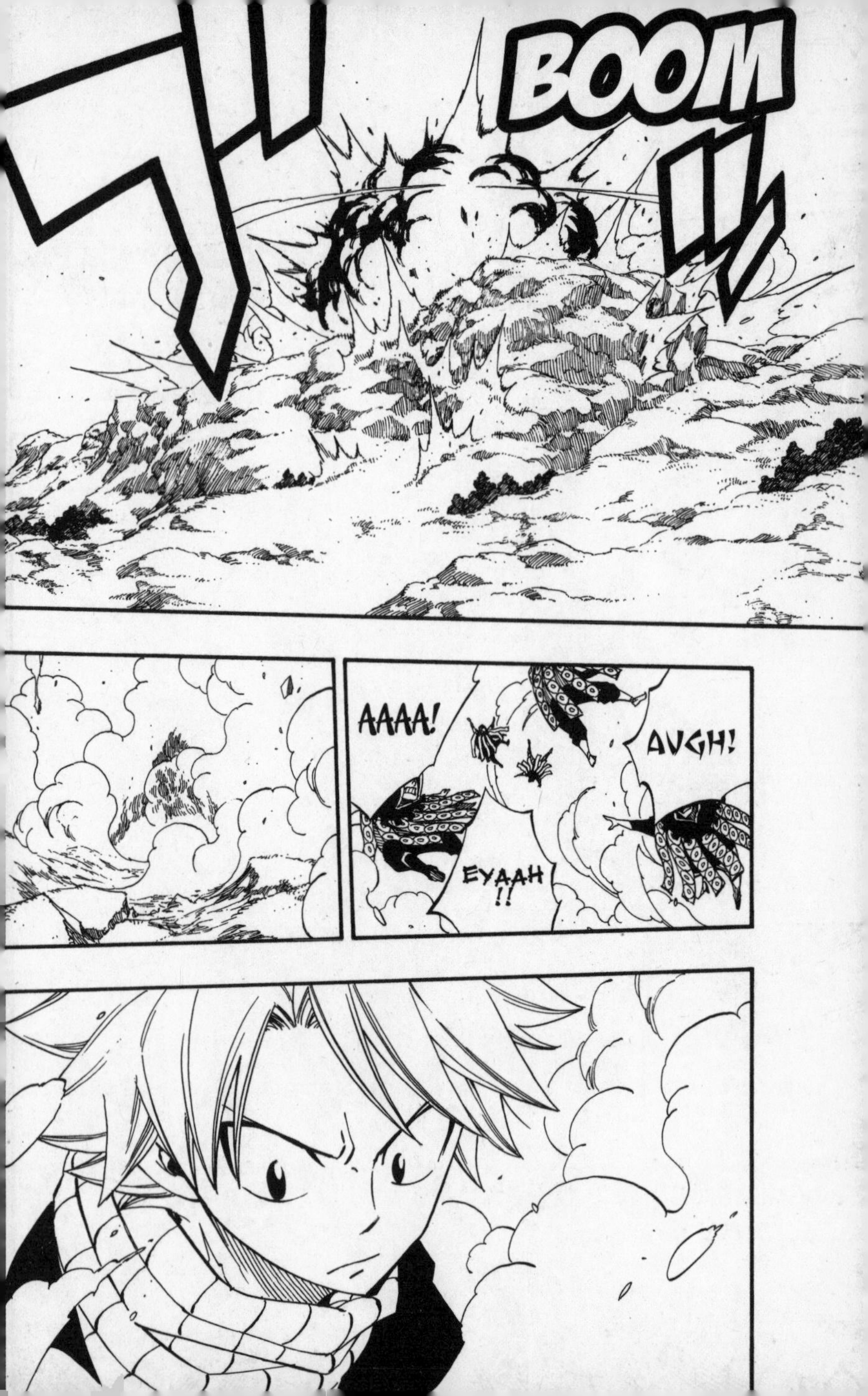
BOOM!!
AUGH!
AAAA!
EYAAH!!

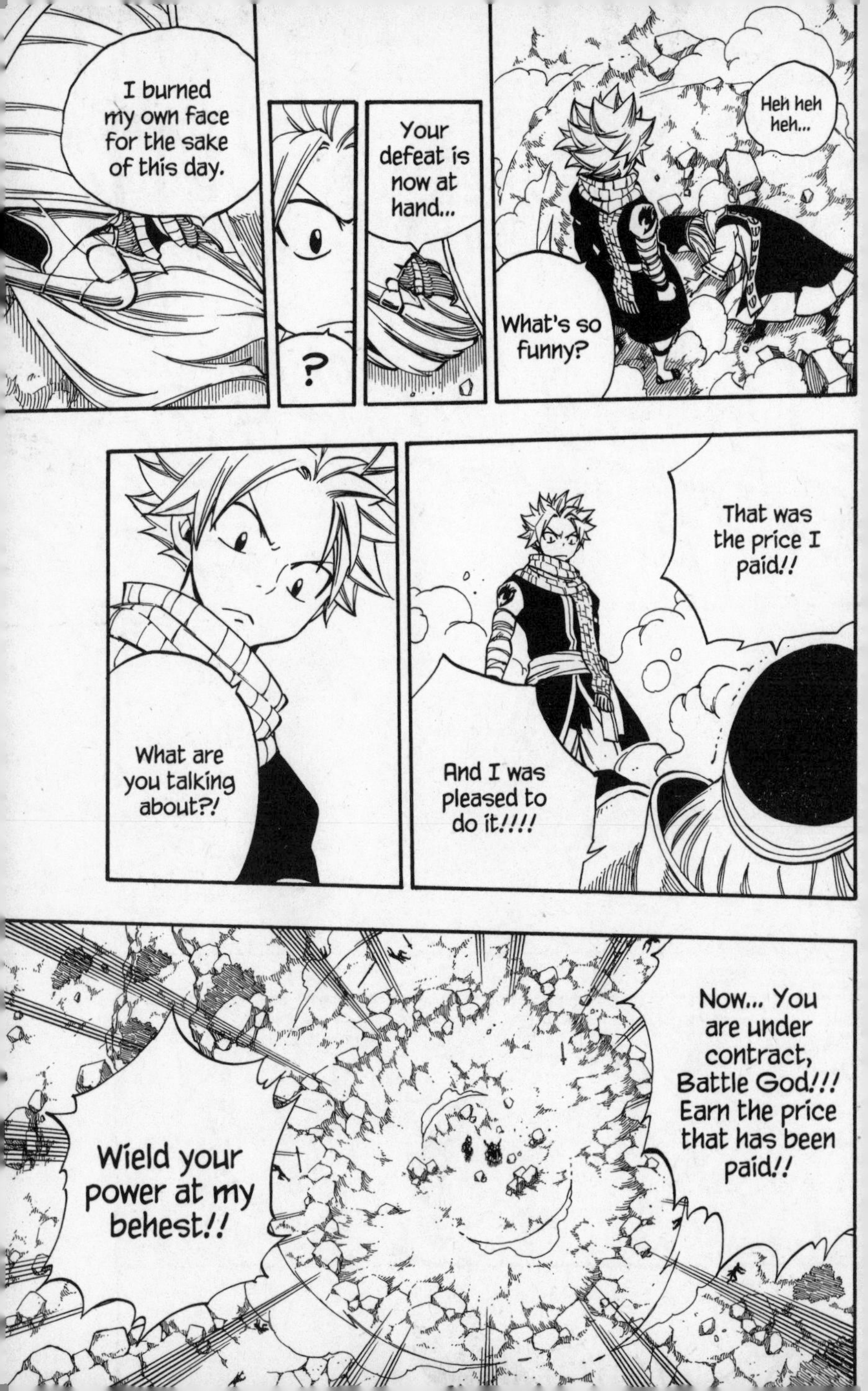
Heh heh heh...
What's so funny?
Your defeat is now at hand...
?
I burned my own face for the sake of this day.
That was the price I paid!!
And I was pleased to do it!!!!
What are you talking about?!
Now... You are under contract, Battle God!!! Earn the price that has been paid!!
Wield your power at my behest!!

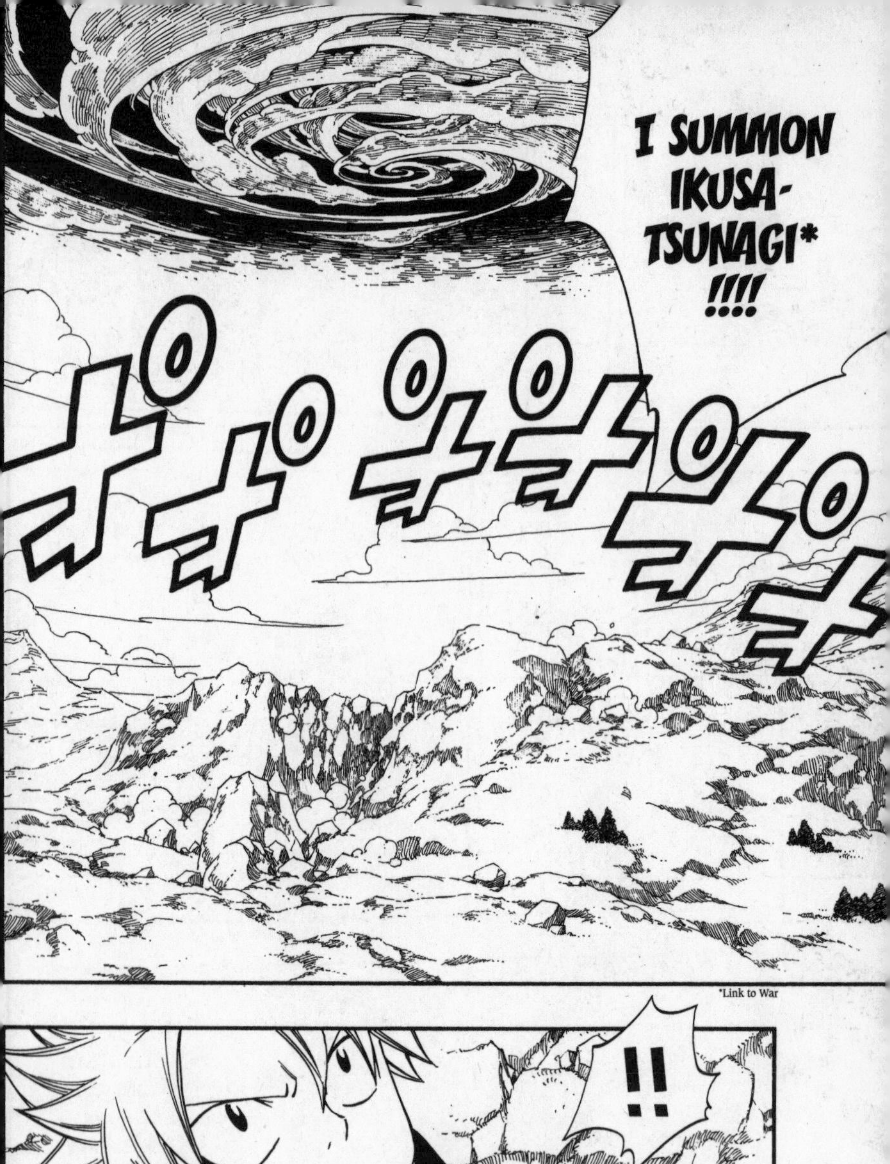
I SUMMON IKUSA-TSUNAGI* !!!!
ポポポポポポ

*Link to War

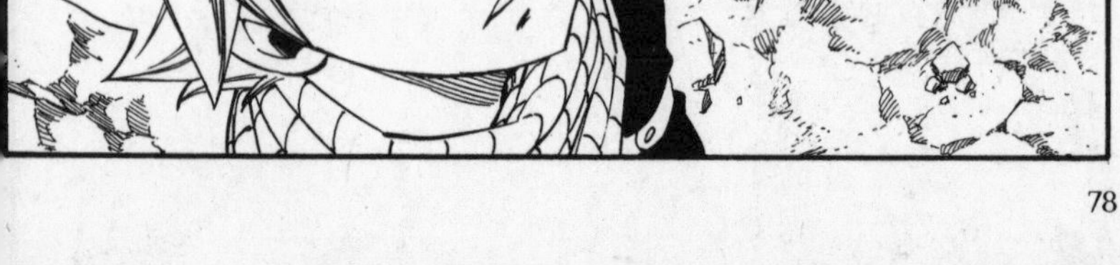
!!

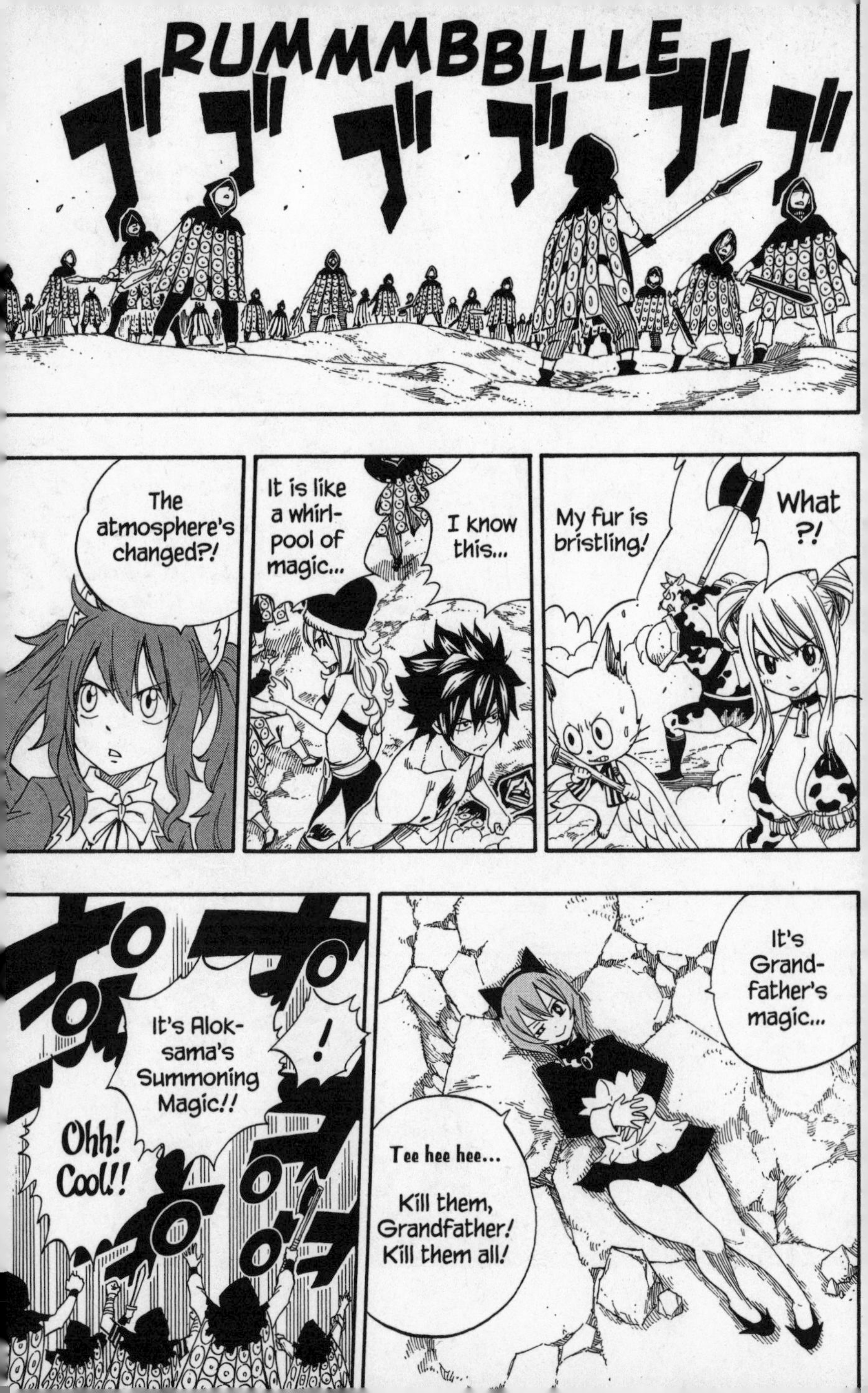
RUMMMBBLLLE
ゴゴゴゴゴゴ
What ?!
My fur is bristling!
I know this...
It is like a whirl-pool of magic...
The atmosphere's changed?!
It's Grand-father's magic...
Tee hee hee...
Kill them, Grandfather! Kill them all!
!
It's Alok-sama's Summoning Magic!!
Ohh! Cool!!

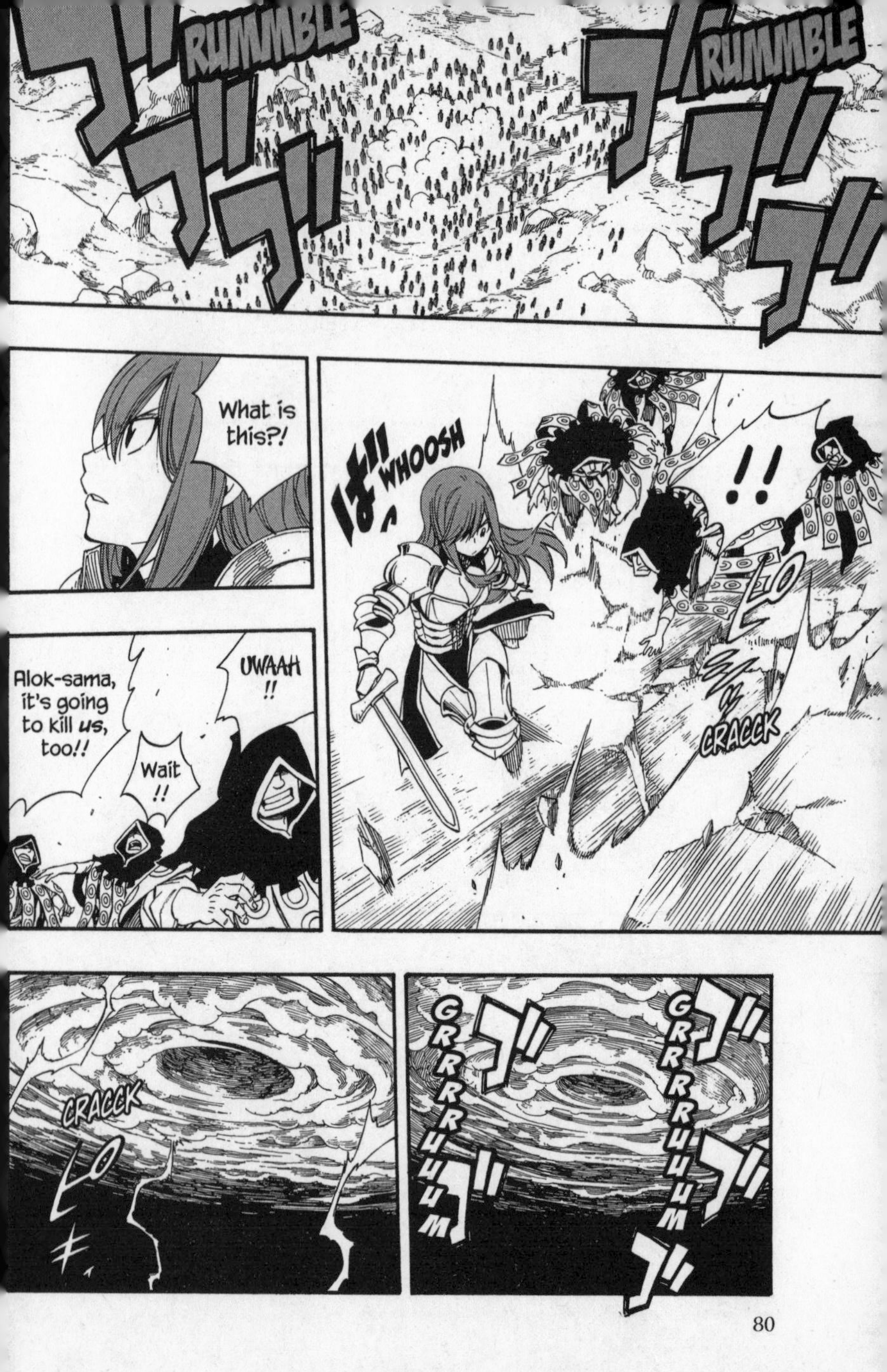
RUMMBLE
RUMMBLE
What is this?!
WHOOSH
!!
CRACCK
UWAAH !!
Alok-sama, it's going to kill us, too!!
Wait !!
GRRRRUUUM
GRRRRUUUM
CRACCK

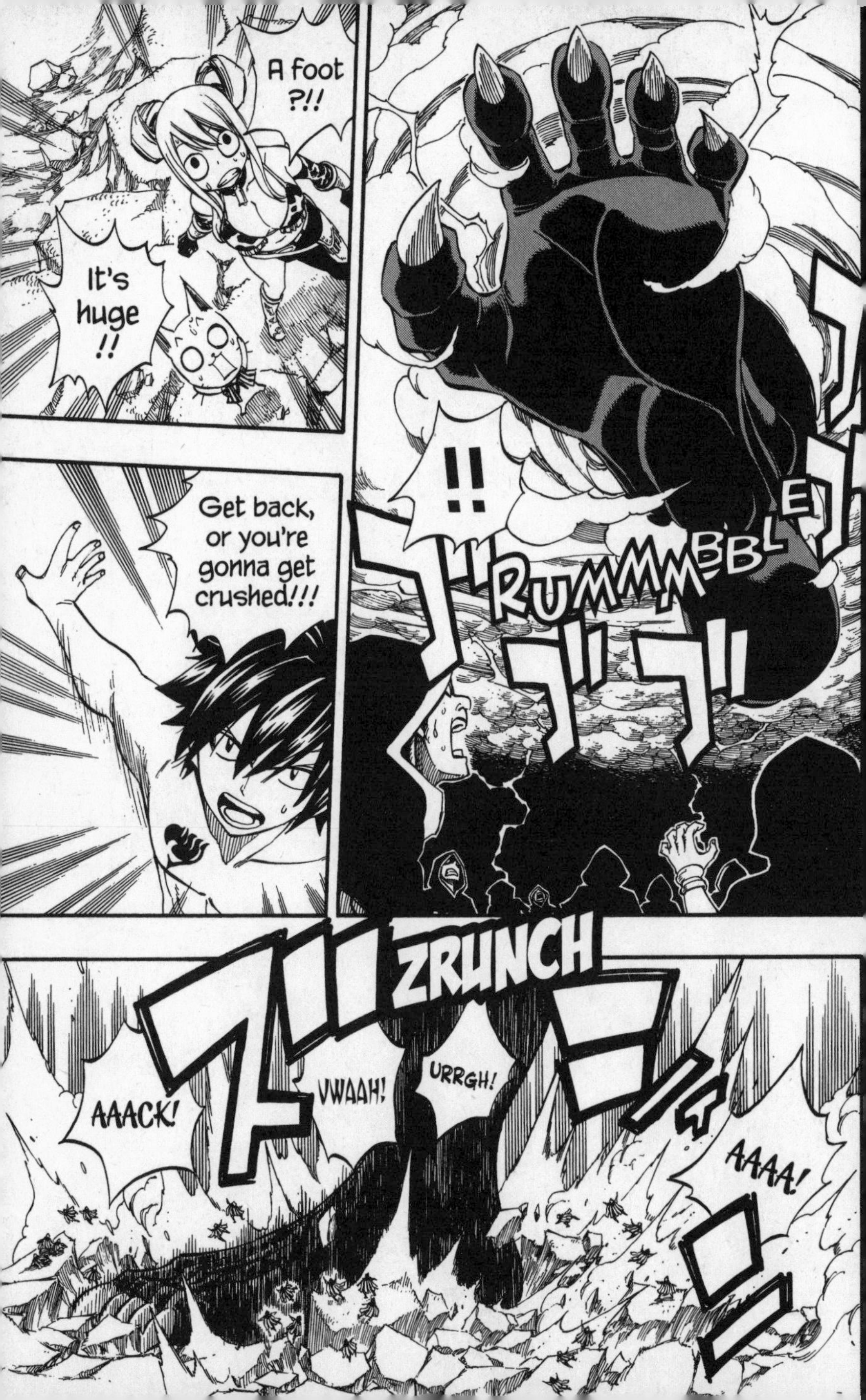
!!
RUMMMBBLE
A foot ?!!
It's huge !!
Get back, or you're gonna get crushed!!!
ZRUNCH
AAAA!
URRGH!
VWAAH!
AAACK!

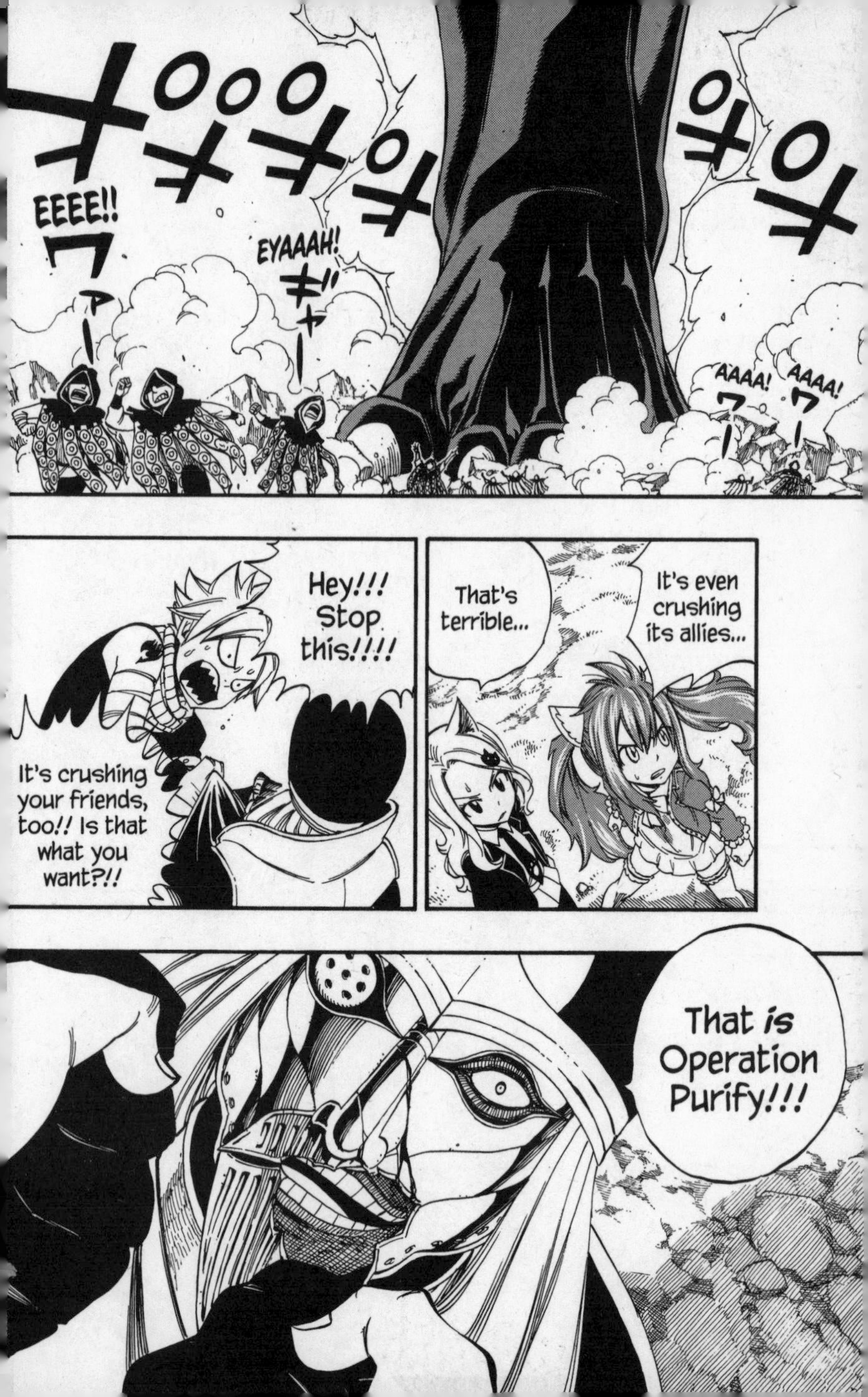
AAAA!
AAAA!
EYAAAH!
EEEE!!
It's even crushing its allies...
That's terrible...
Hey!!! Stop this!!!!
It's crushing your friends, too!! Is that what you want?!!
That *is* Operation Purify!!!

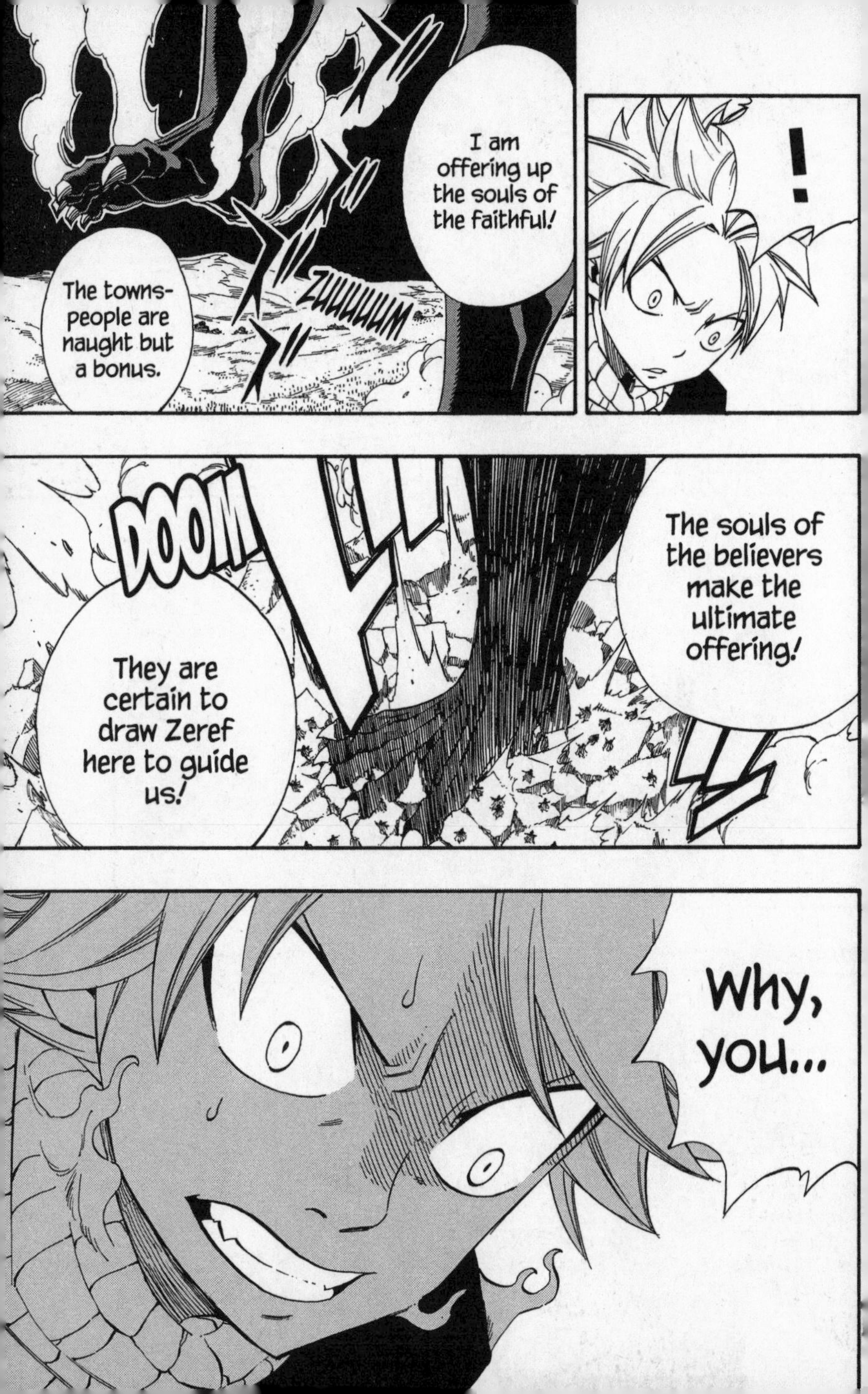
!
I am offering up the souls of the faithful!
ZUUUUUM
The towns-people are naught but a bonus.
The souls of the believers make the ultimate offering!
DOOM
They are certain to draw Zeref here to guide us!
Why, you...

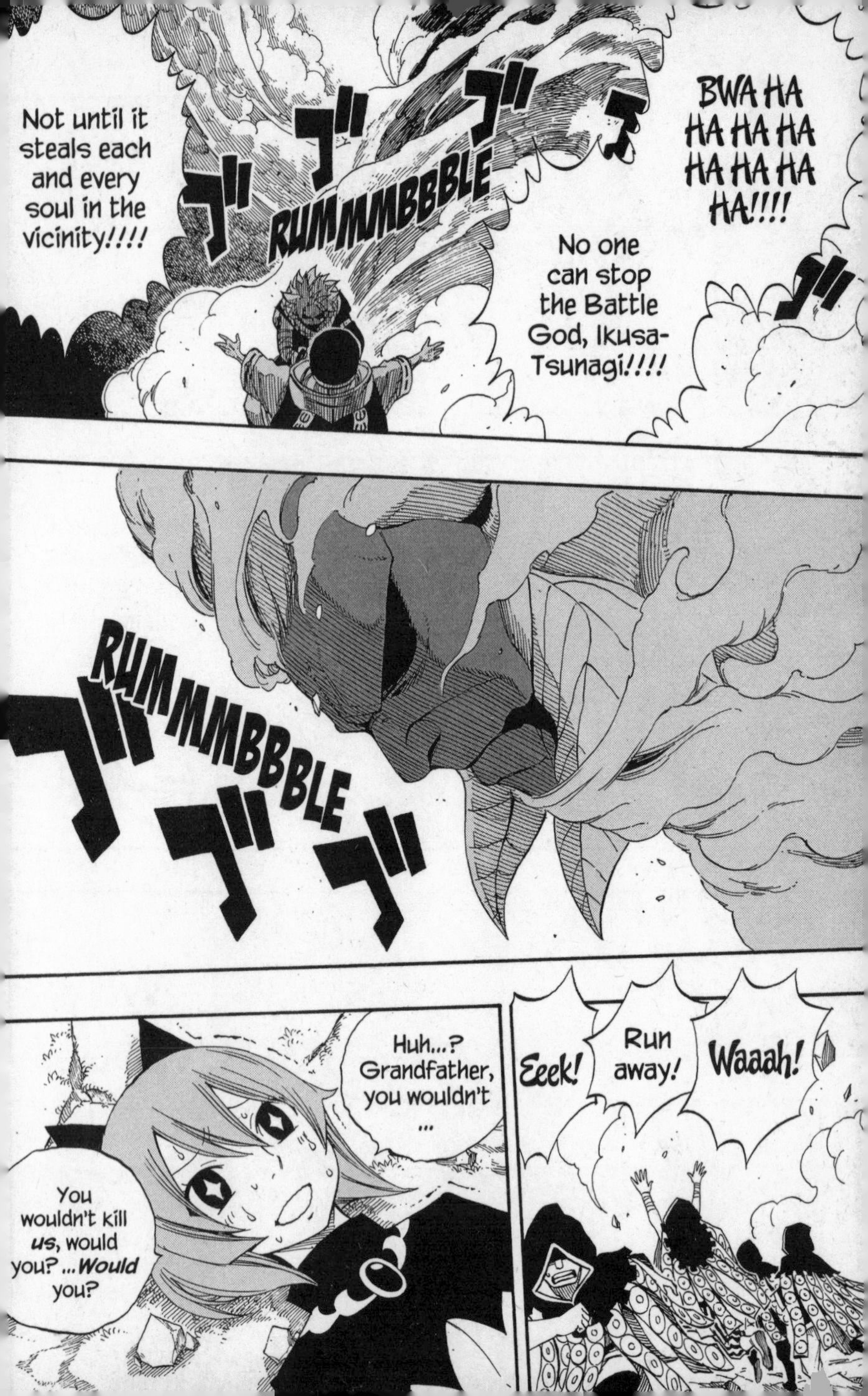
BWA HA HA HA HA HA HA HA HA!!!!
No one can stop the Battle God, Ikusa-Tsunagi!!!!
RUMMMBBBLE
Not until it steals each and every soul in the vicinity!!!!
RUMMMBBBLE
Waaah!
Run away!
Eeek!
Huh...? Grandfather, you wouldn't ...
You wouldn't kill *us*, would you? ...*Would* you?

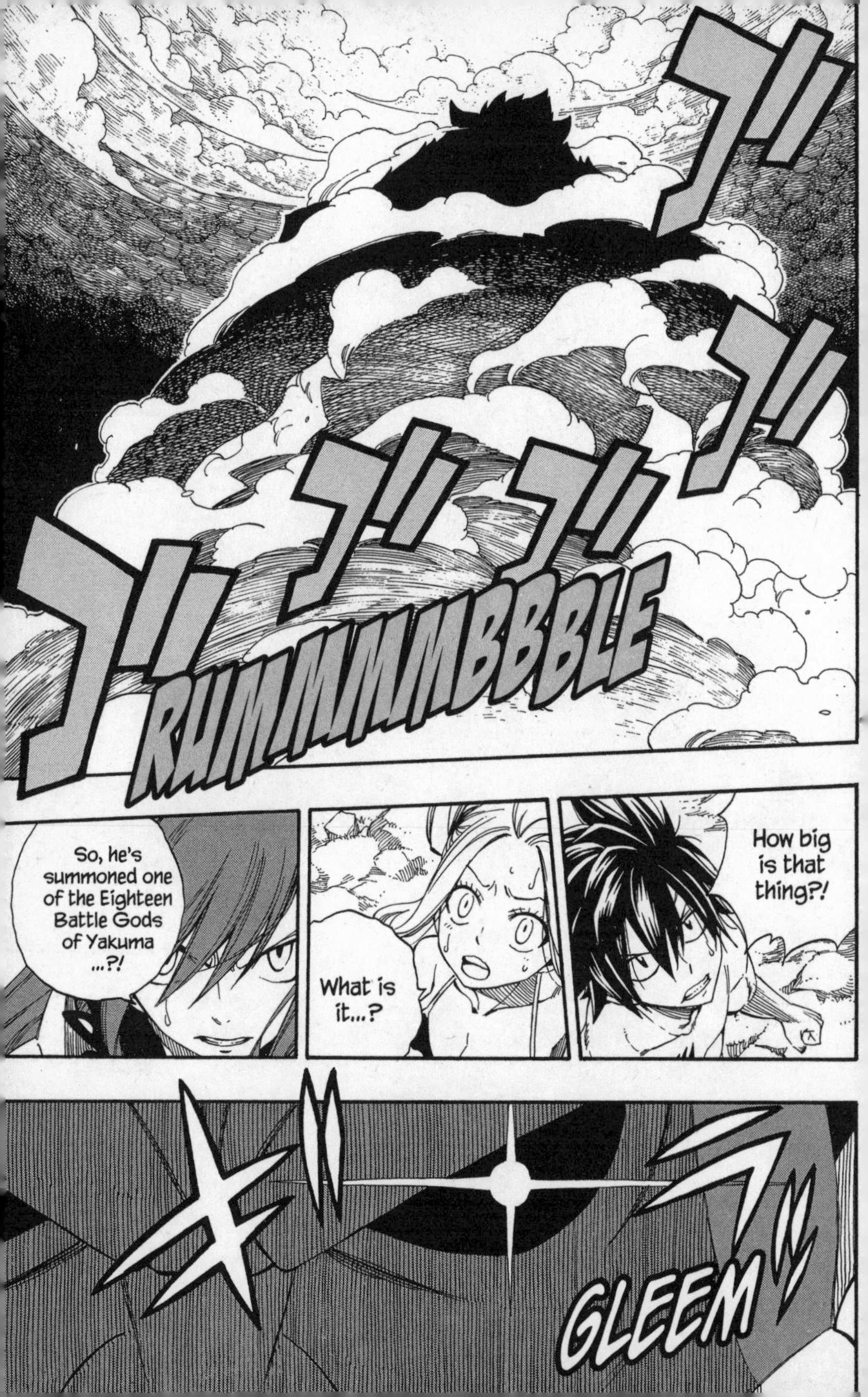
RUMMMMMBBBLE
How big is that thing?!
What is it...?
So, he's summoned one of the Eighteen Battle Gods of Yakuma ...?!
GLEEM

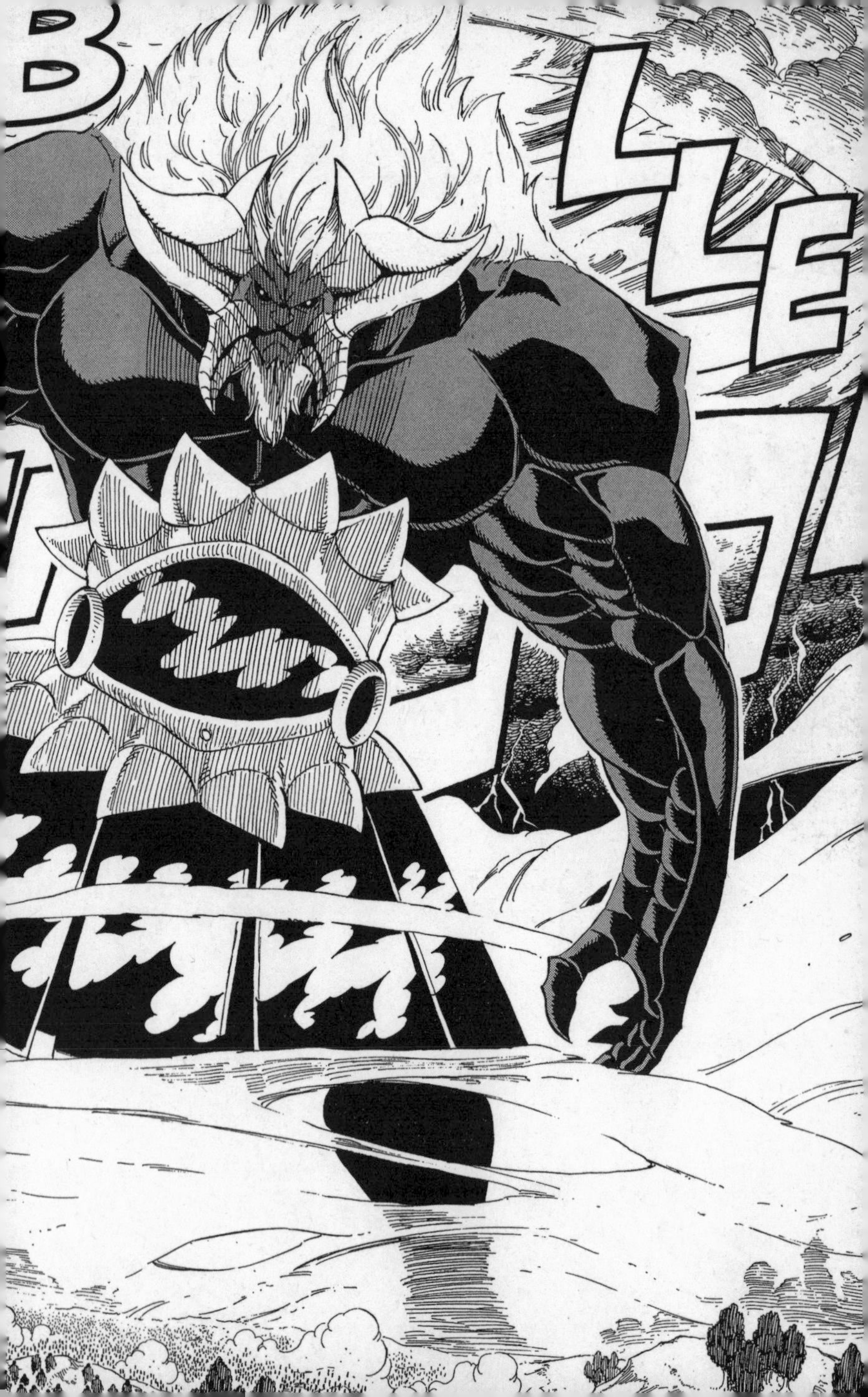
B
LLE

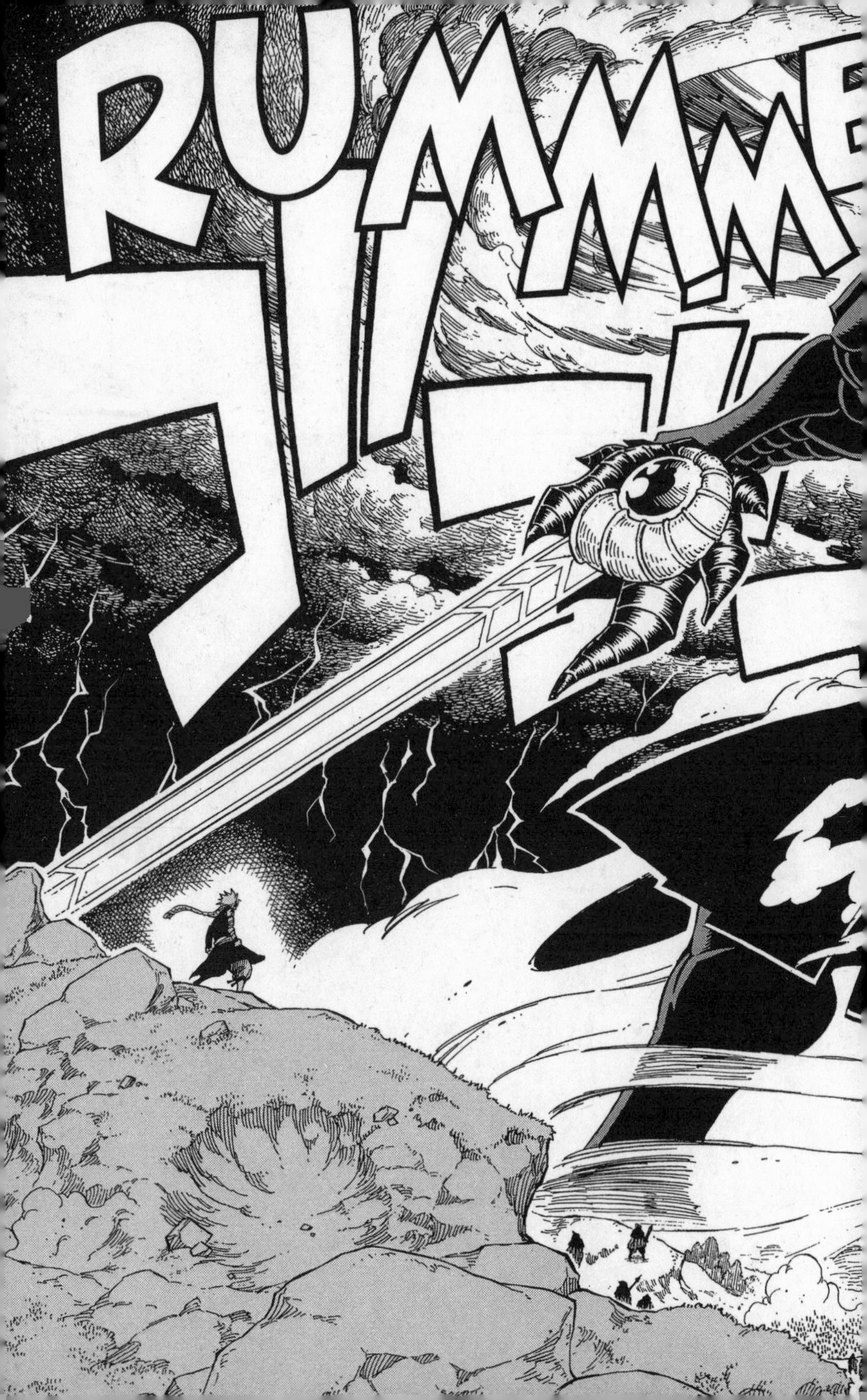

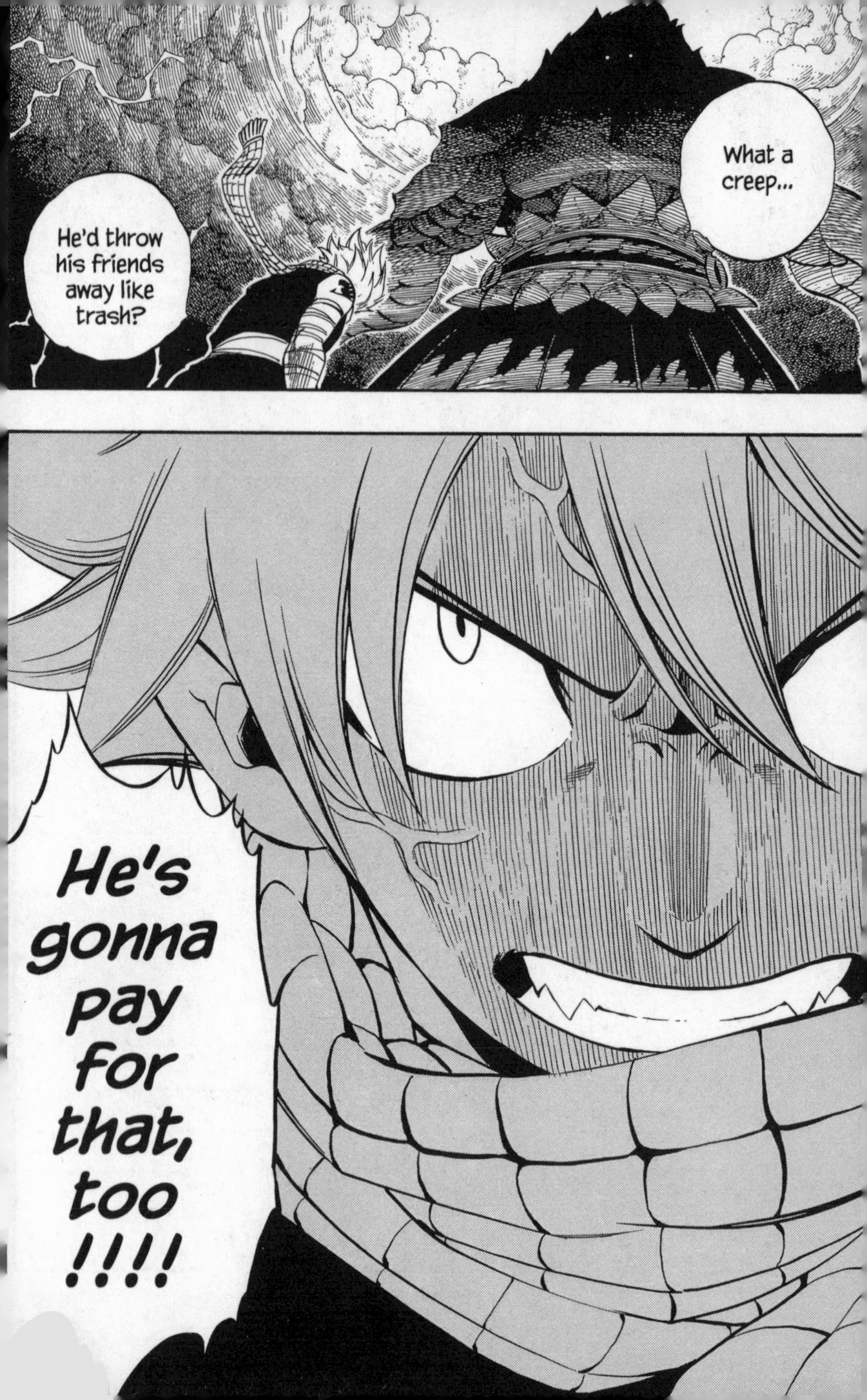
What a creep...
He'd throw his friends away like trash?
He's gonna pay for that, too!!!!

FAIRY TAIL
フェアリーテイル

Chapter 434: Hôken

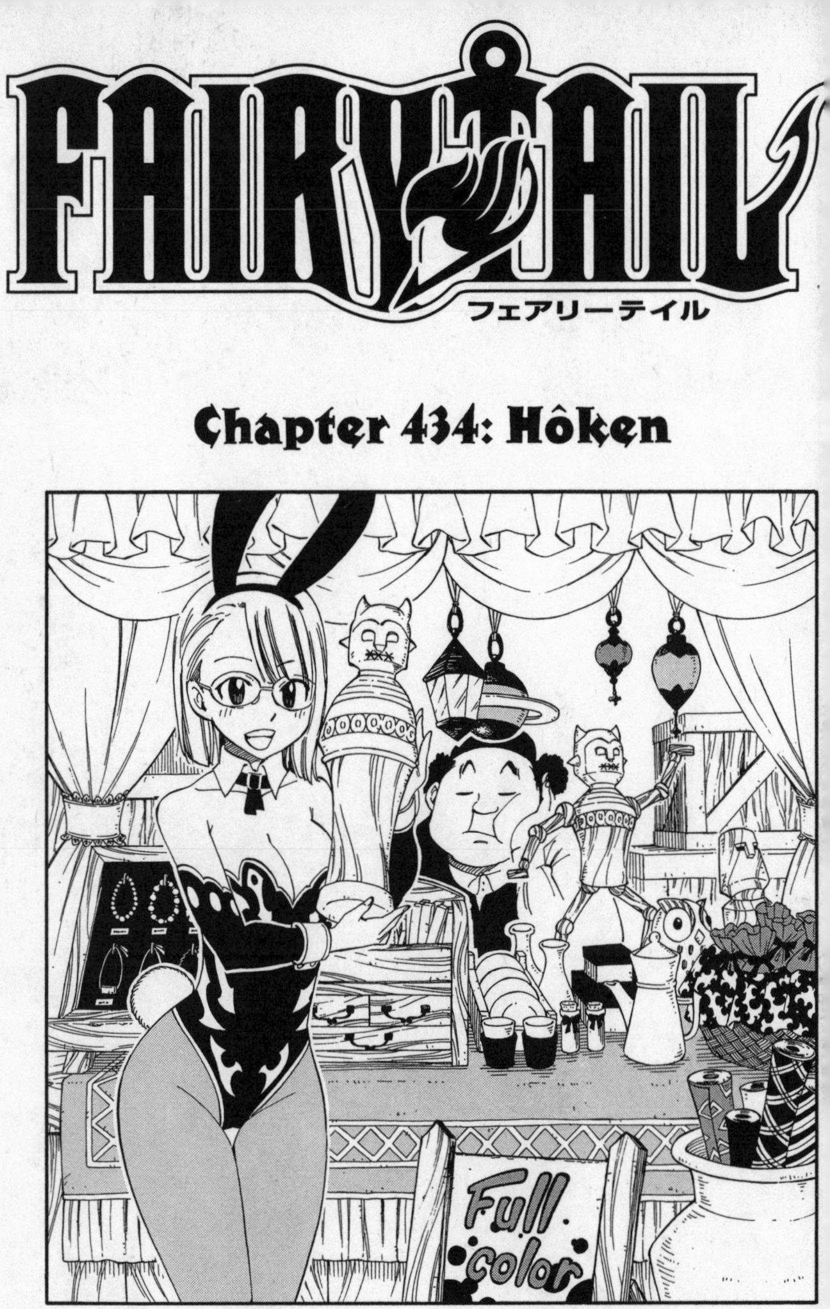
Full color

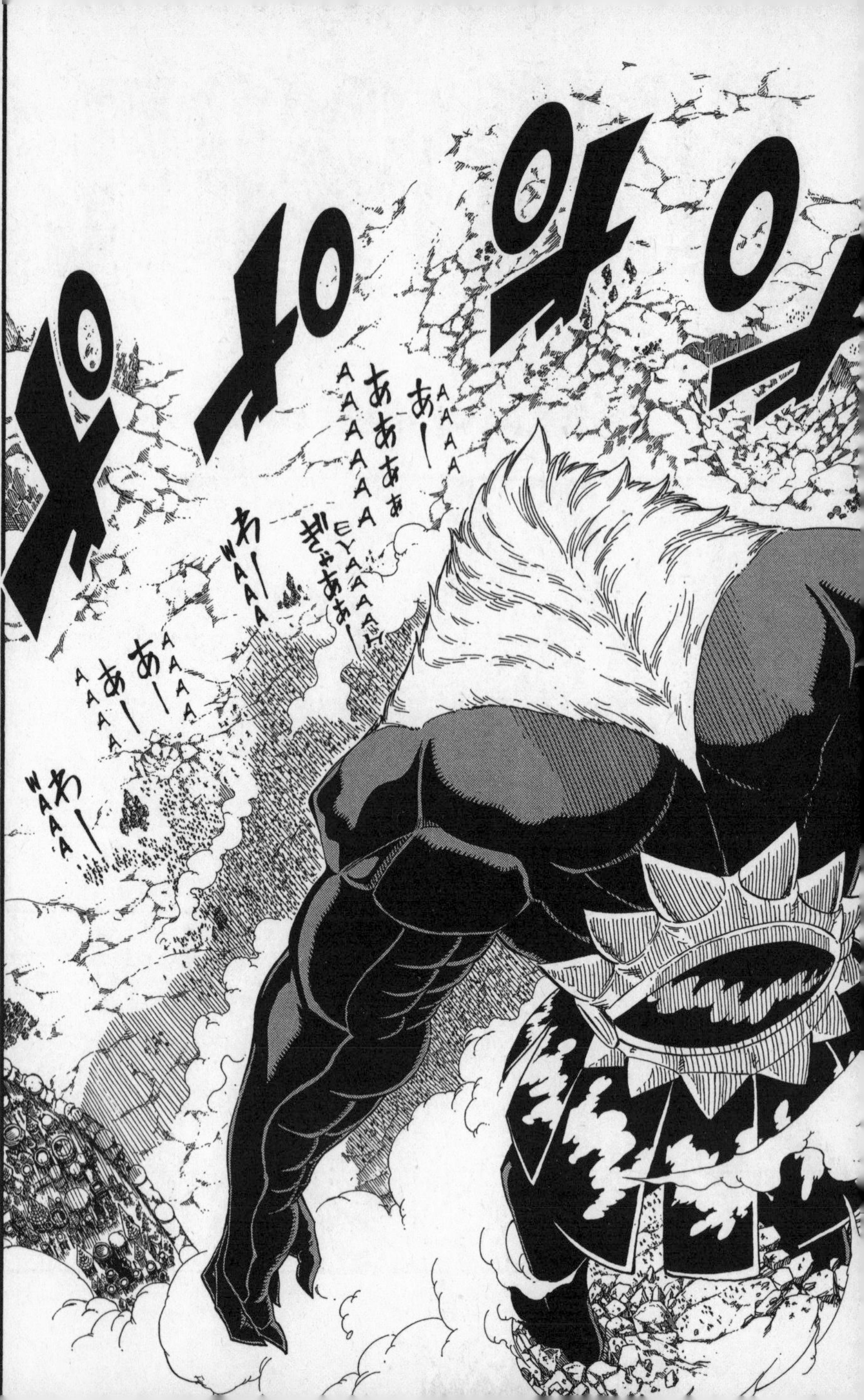
あー AAAA
あああぁ AAAAAAAA
ぎゃあああー EYAAAAAH
わー WAAAA
あー AAAA
あー AAAA
わー WAAAA

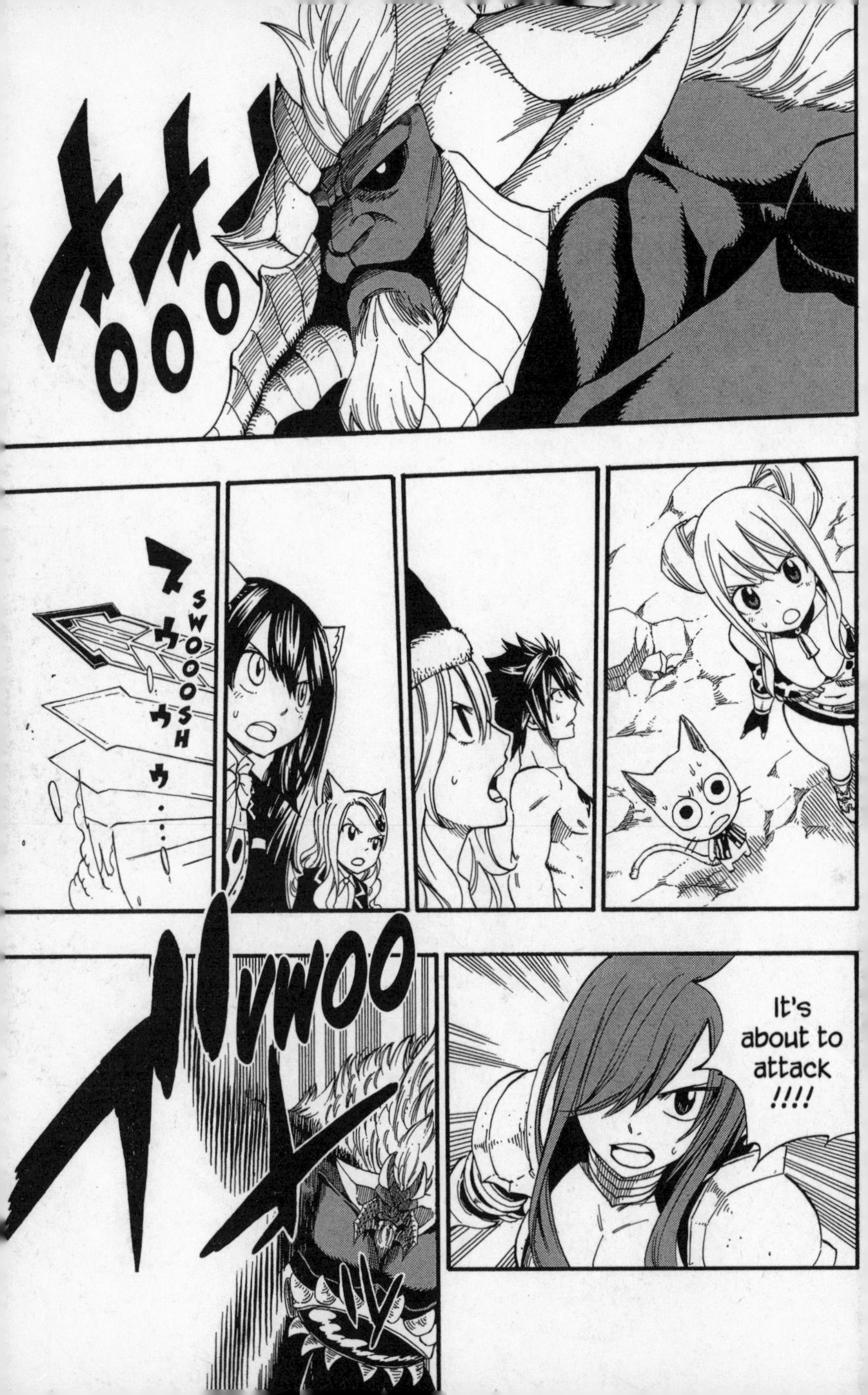
OOO
SWOOOOSH
It's about to attack !!!!
WOO

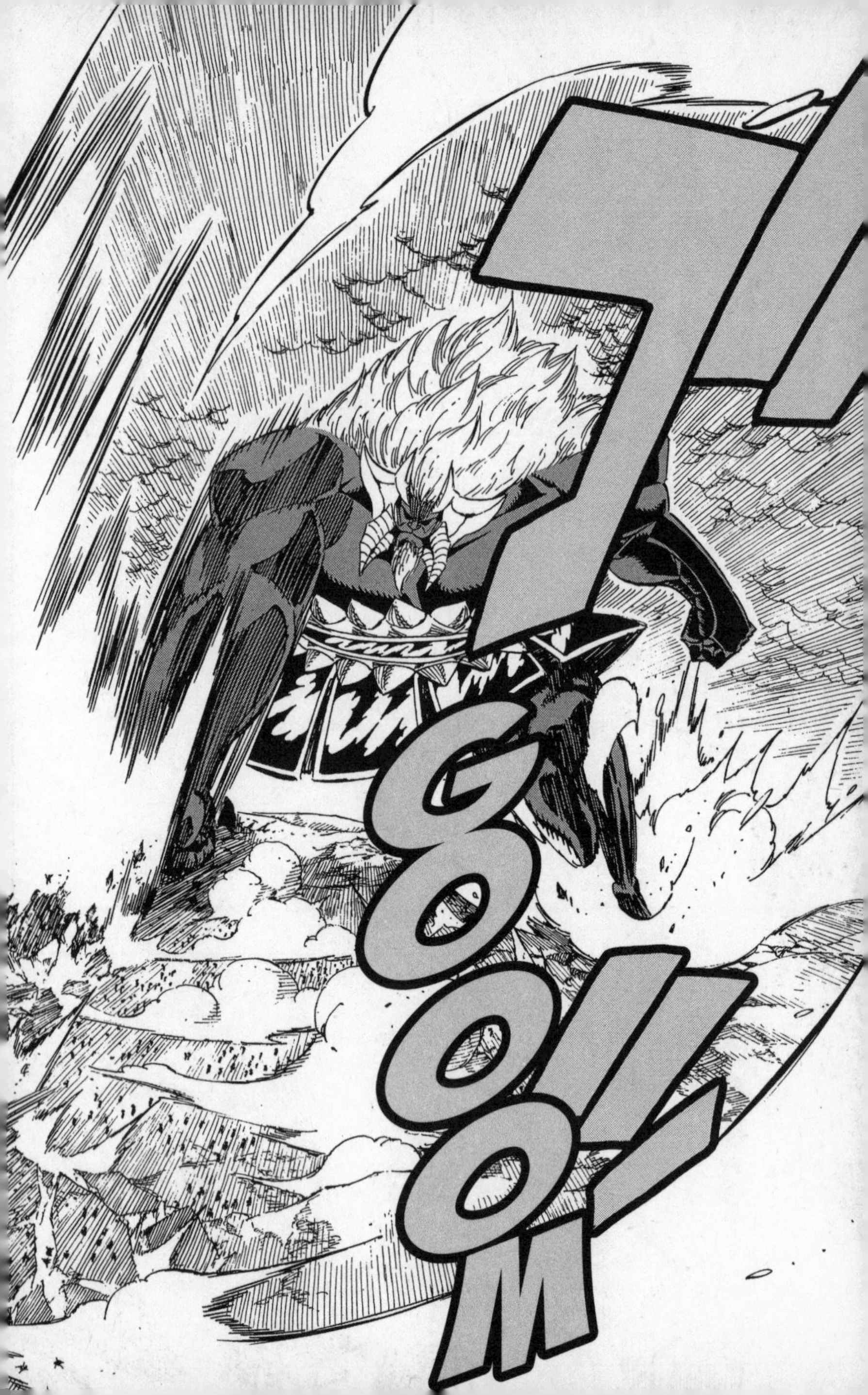
GOOOM

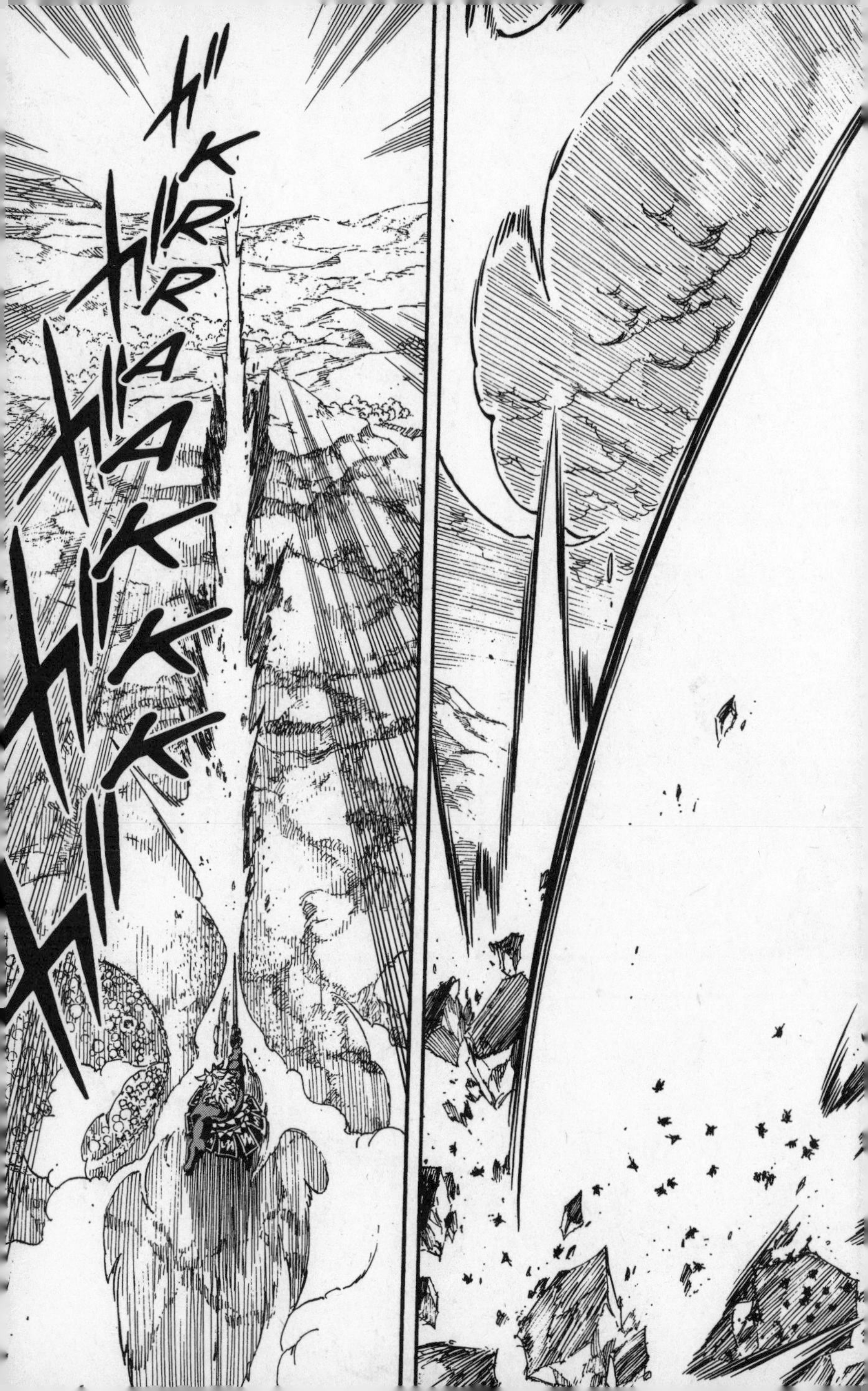
KRRAAKKKK

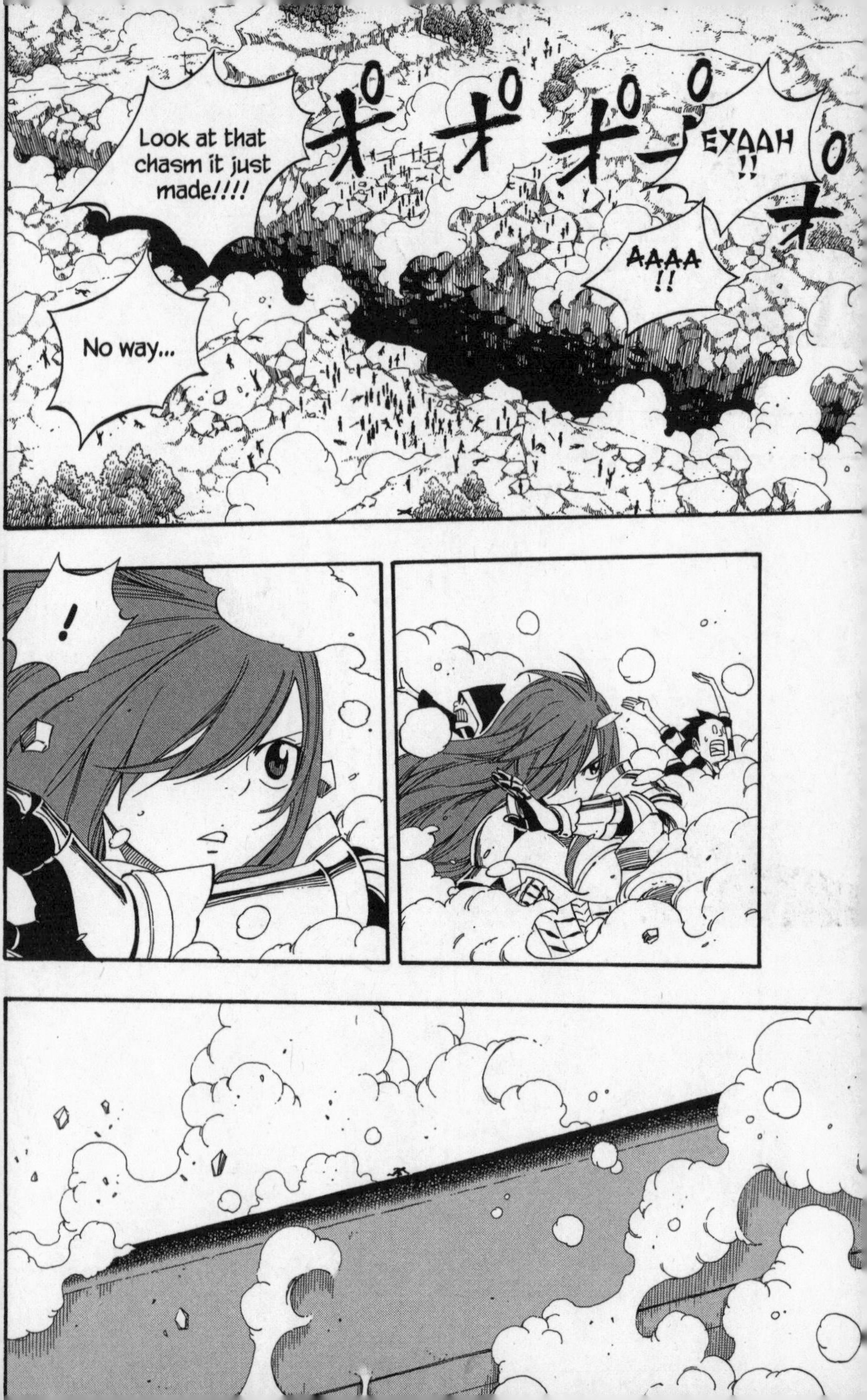
EYAAH!!
AAAA!!
Look at that chasm it just made!!!!
No way...
!

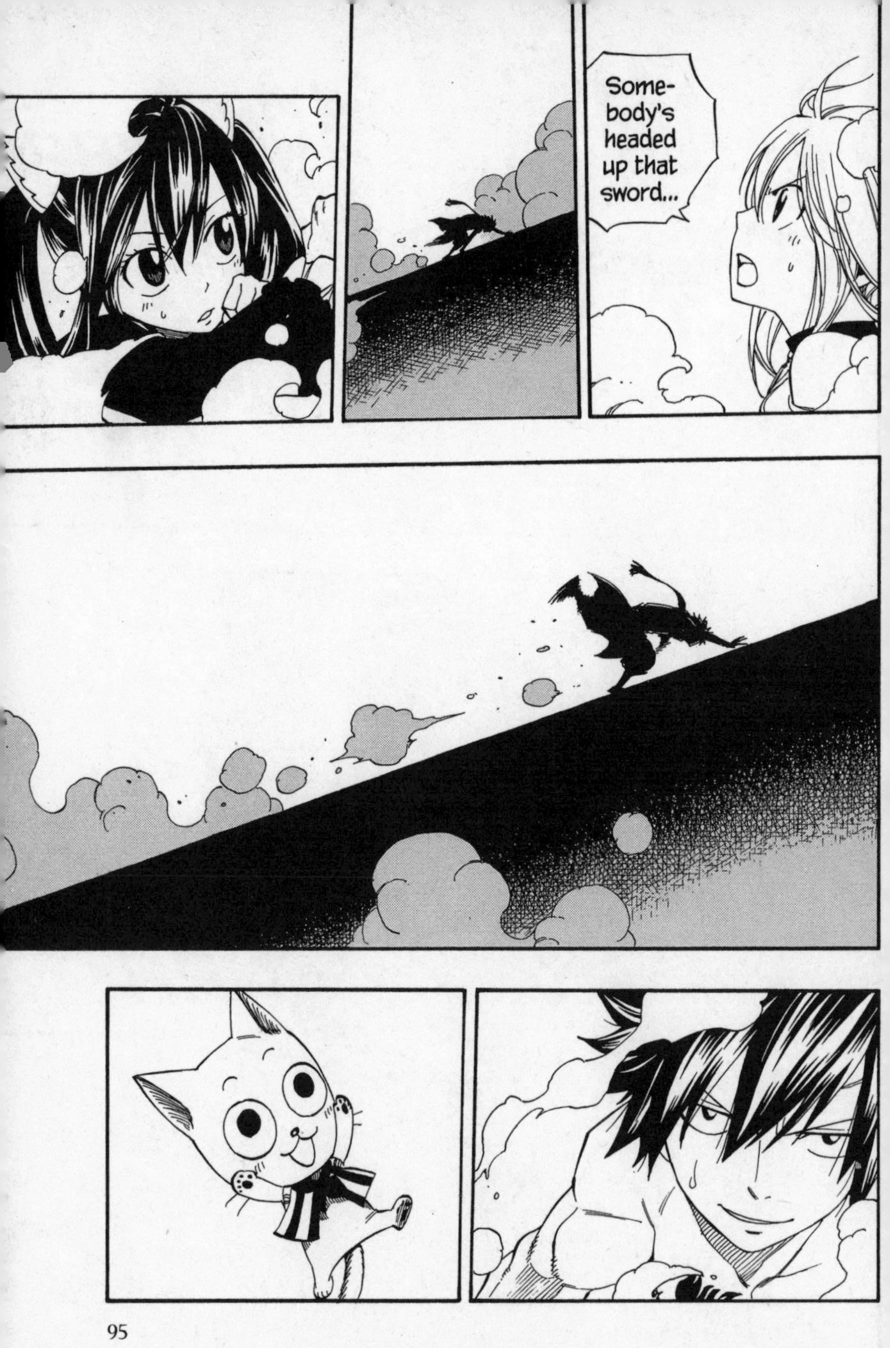
Some-body's headed up that sword...

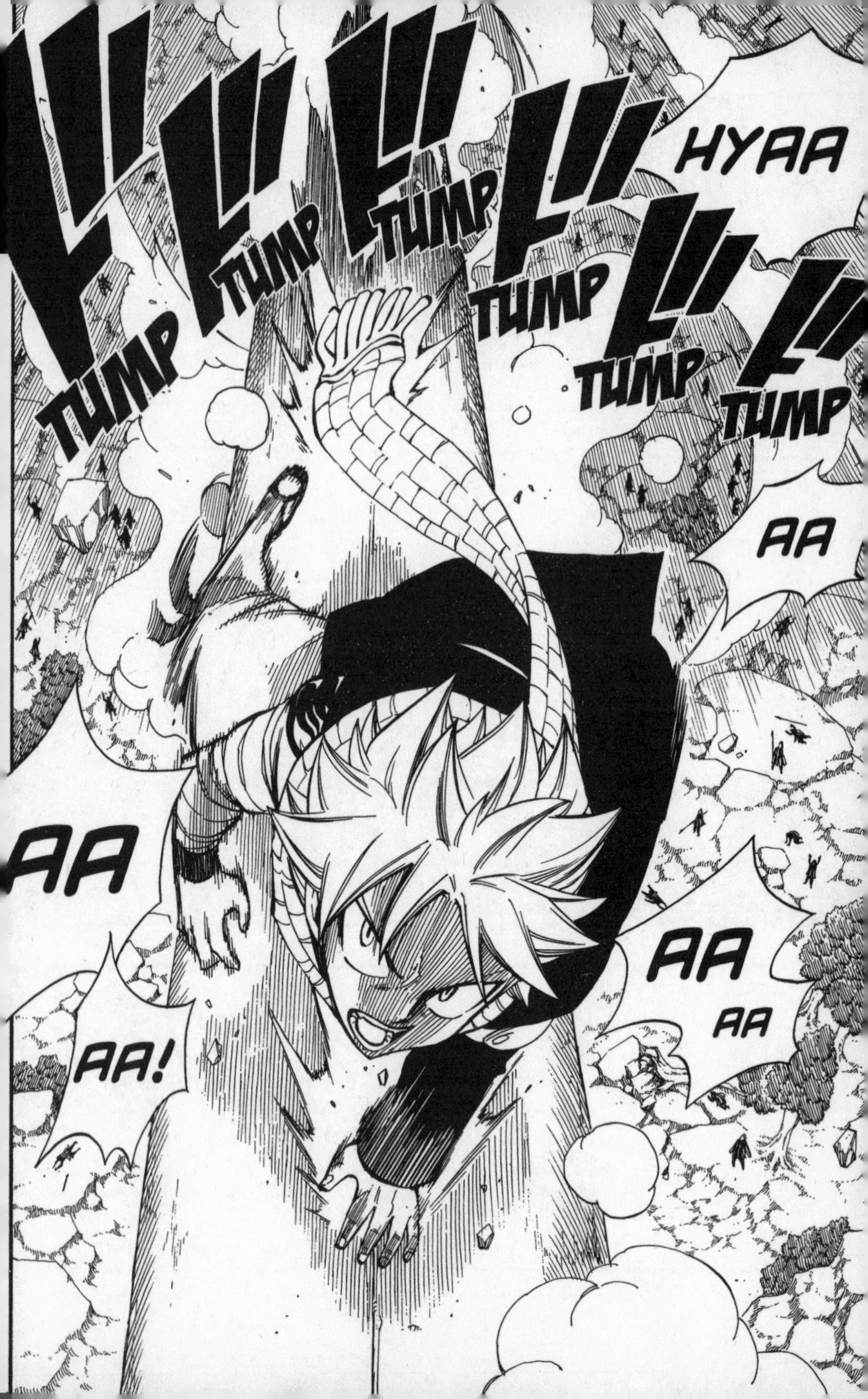

TUMP
TUMP
TUMP
TUMP
TUMP
TUMP
HYAA
AA
AA
AA
AA
AA!

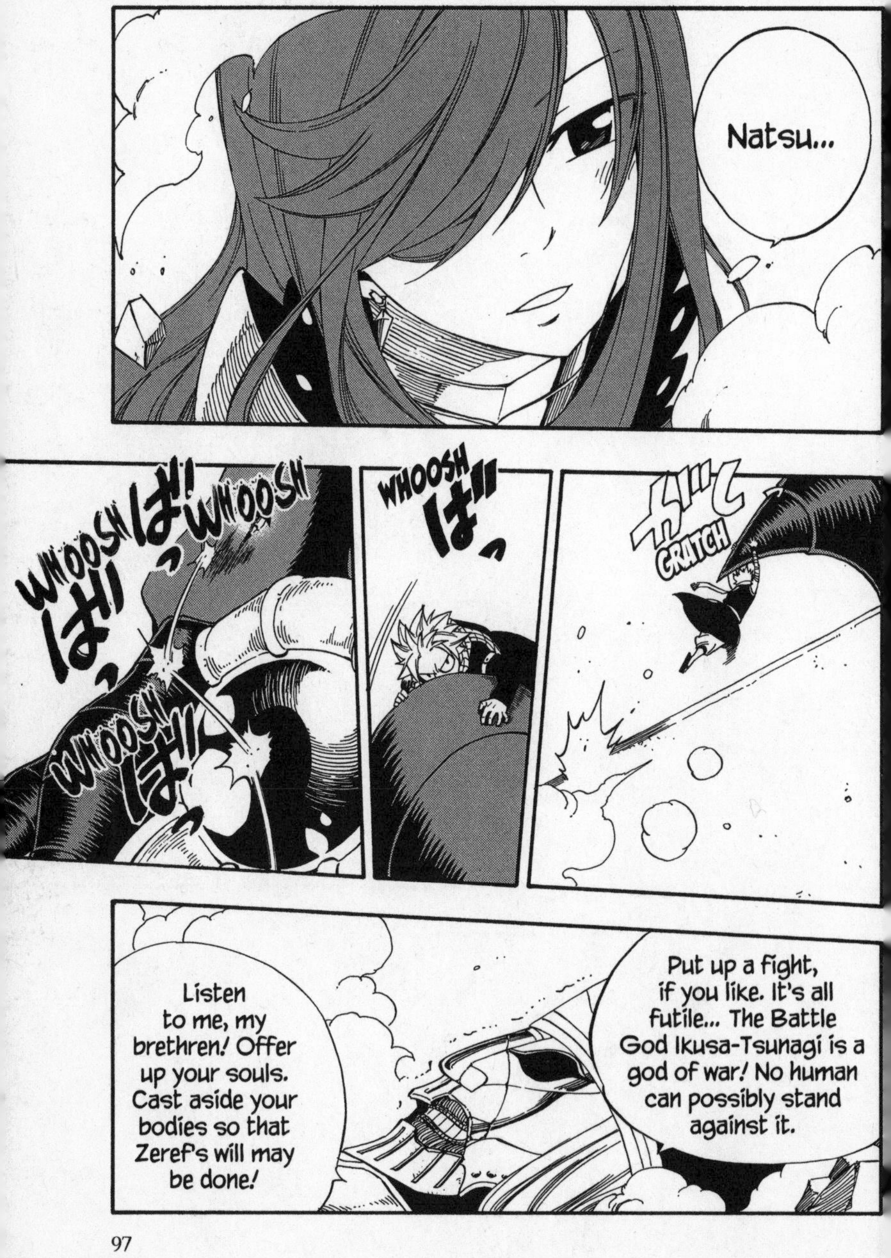
Natsu...
ちぎっ
GRATCH
ばっ
WHOOSH
ばっ
WHOOSH
ばっ
WHOOSH
ばっ
WHOOSH
ばっ
WHOOSH
Put up a fight, if you like. It's all futile... The Battle God Ikusa-Tsunagi is a god of war! No human can possibly stand against it.
Listen to me, my brethren! Offer up your souls. Cast aside your bodies so that Zeref's will may be done!

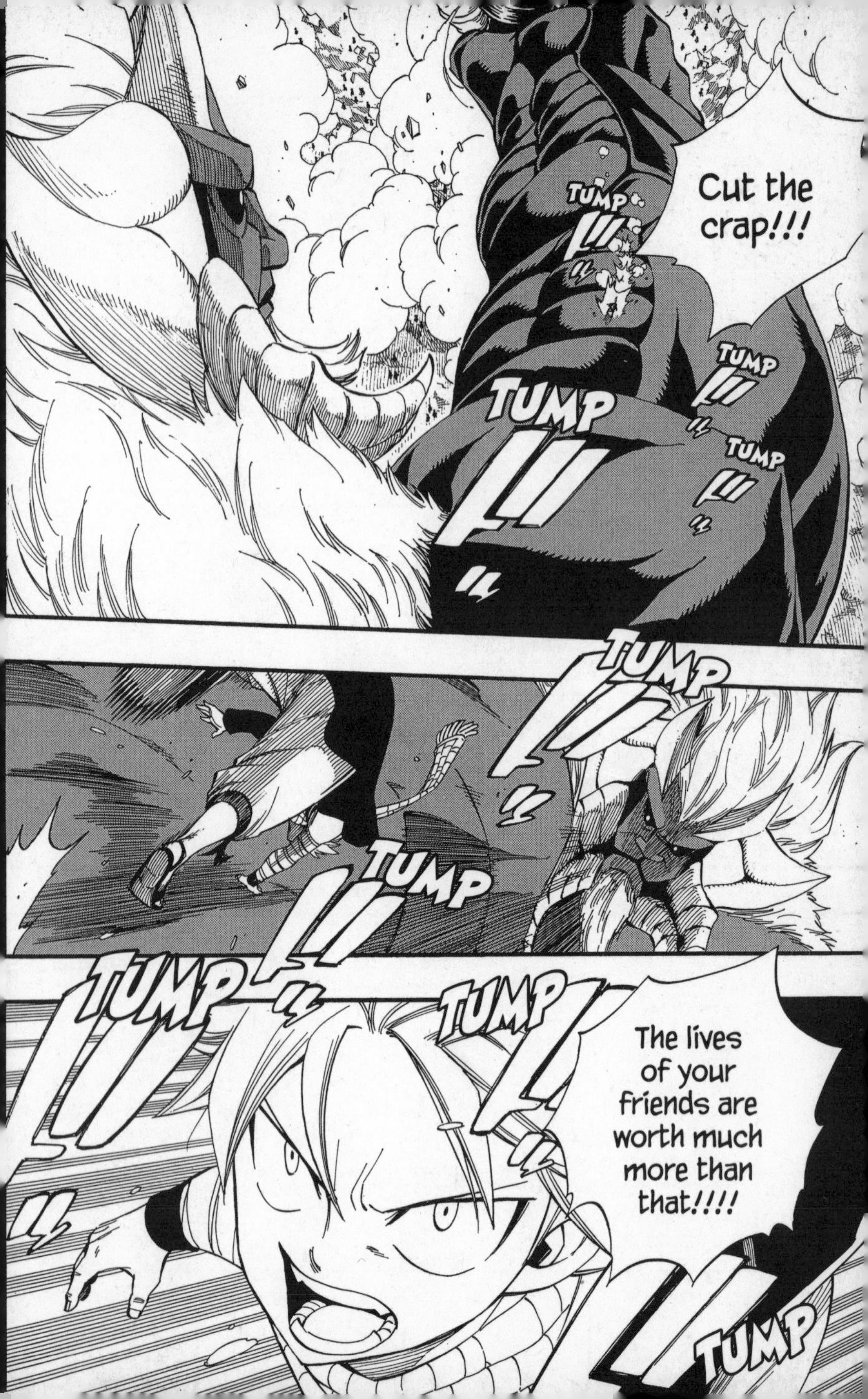
Cut the crap!!!
TUMP
TUMP
TUMP
TUMP
TUMP
TUMP
TUMP
TUMP
The lives of your friends are worth much more than that!!!!
TUMP

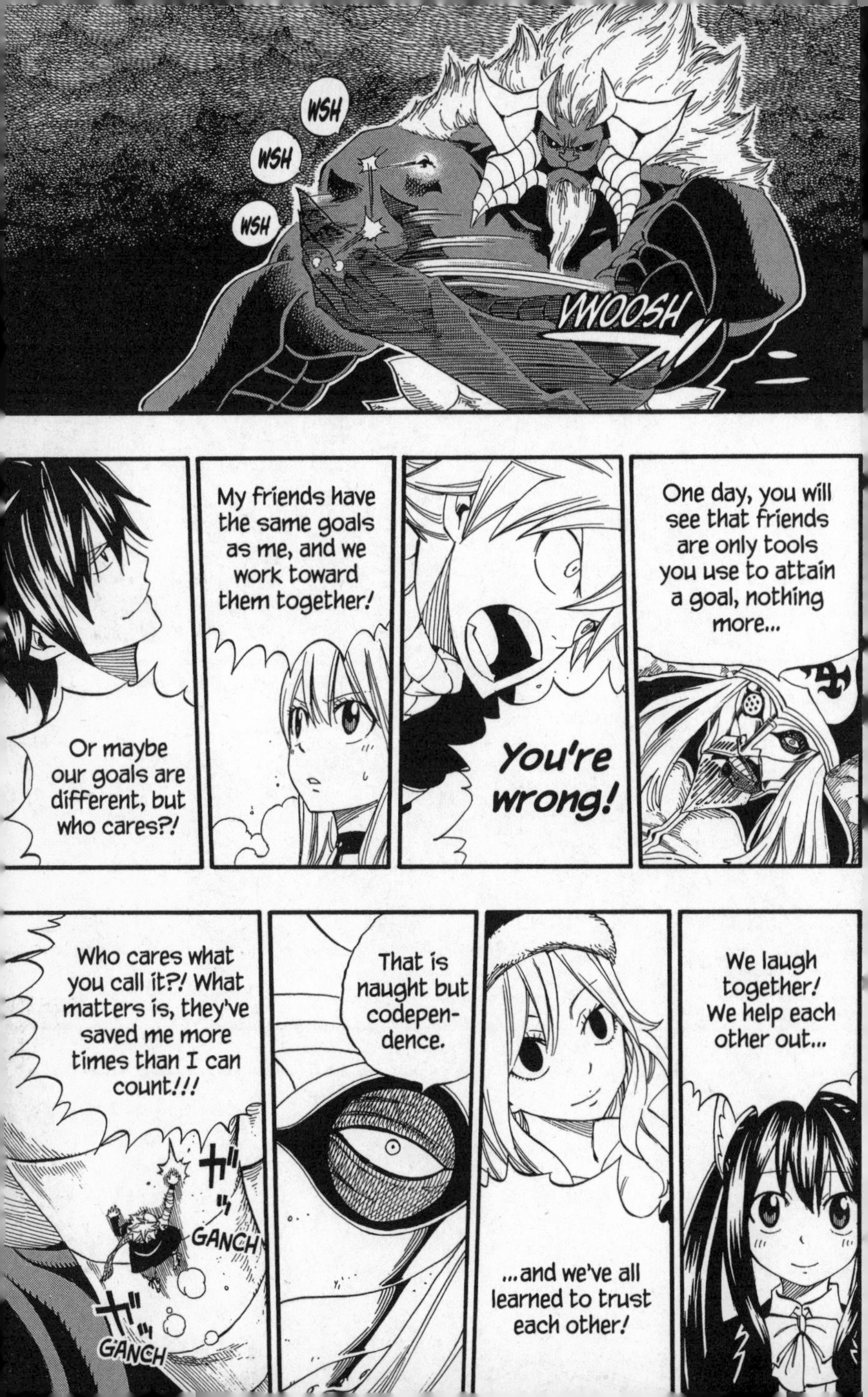
WSH
WSH
WSH
VWOOSH
One day, you will see that friends are only tools you use to attain a goal, nothing more...
You're wrong!
My friends have the same goals as me, and we work toward them together!
Or maybe our goals are different, but who cares?!
We laugh together! We help each other out...
...and we've all learned to trust each other!
That is naught but codepen- dence.
Who cares what you call it?! What matters is, they've saved me more times than I can count!!!
GANCH
GANCH

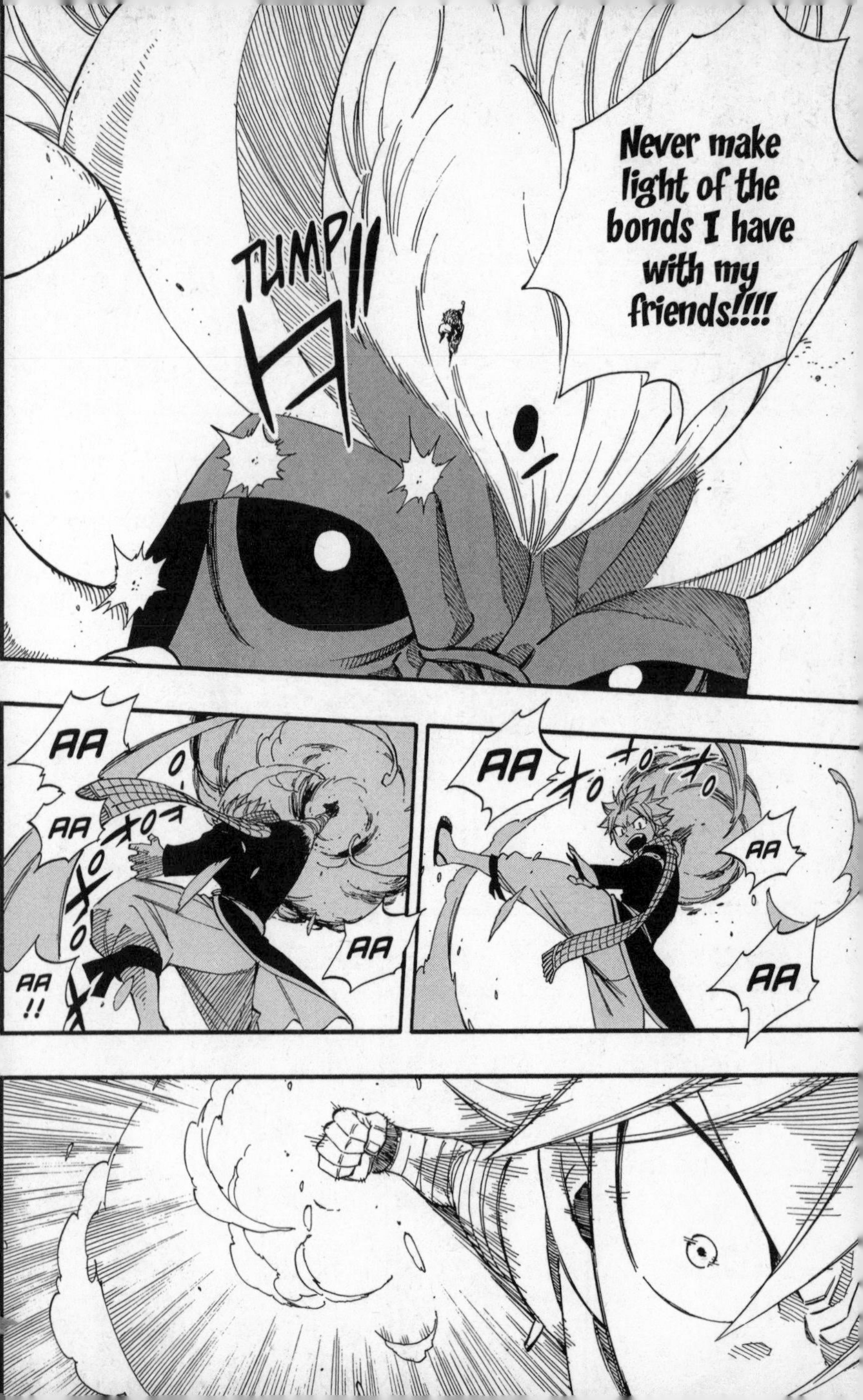
Never make light of the bonds I have with my friends!!!!
TUMP!!
AA
AA
AA
AA
AA
AA
AA !!

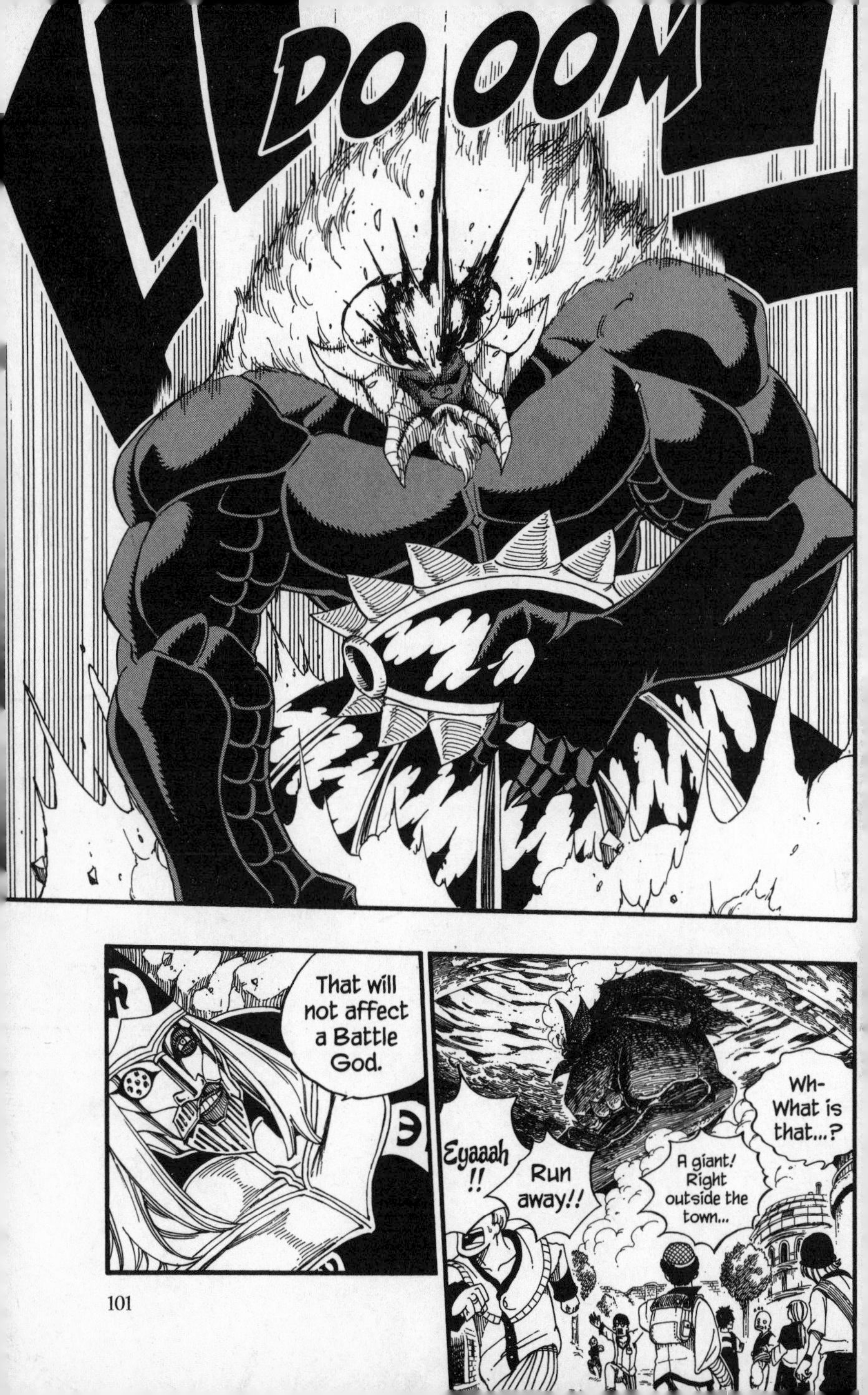
DO OOM
Wh- What is that...?
A giant! Right outside the town...
Run away!!
Eyaaah!!
That will not affect a Battle God.

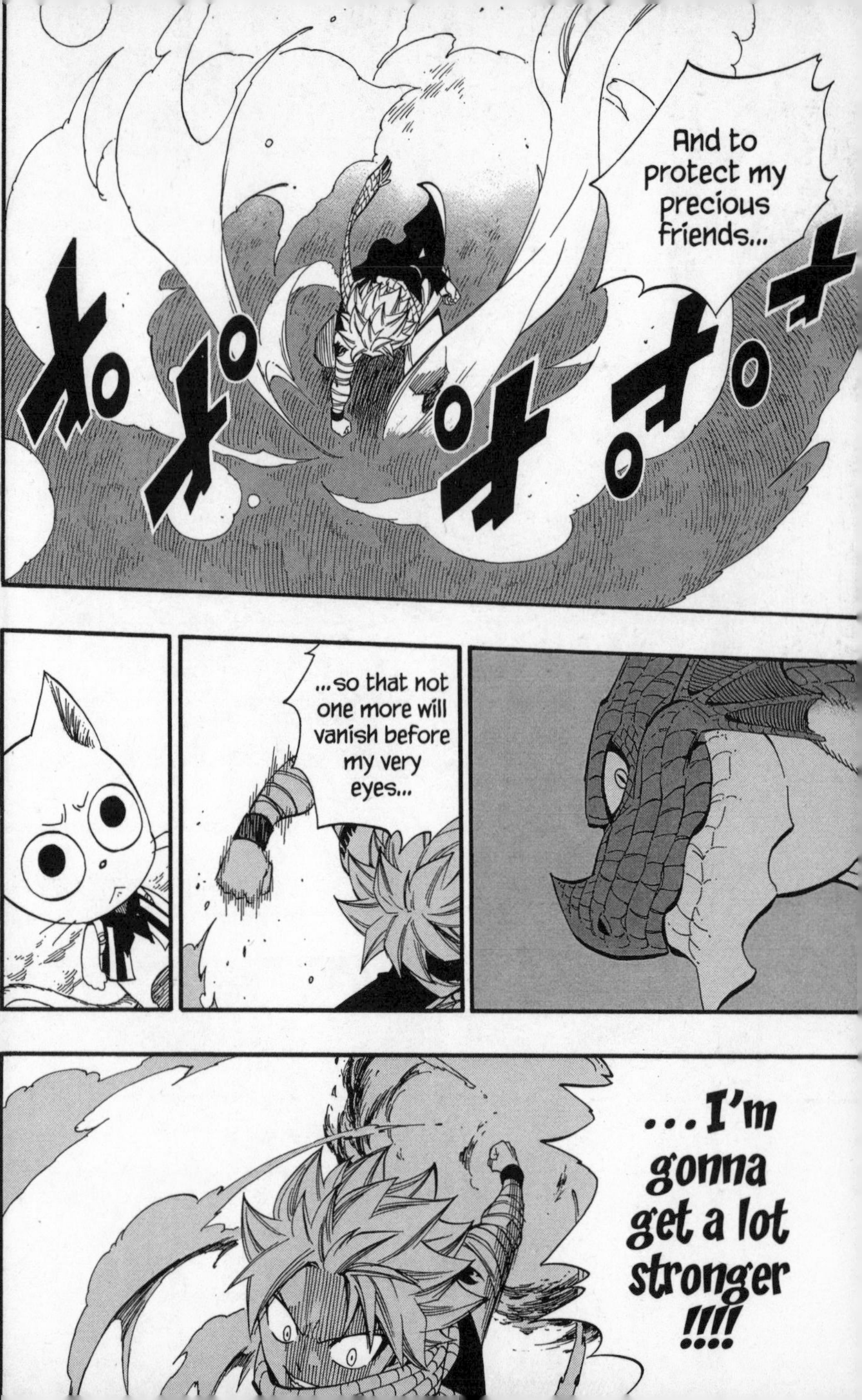
And to protect my precious friends...
...so that not one more will vanish before my very eyes...
...I'm gonna get a lot stronger!!!!

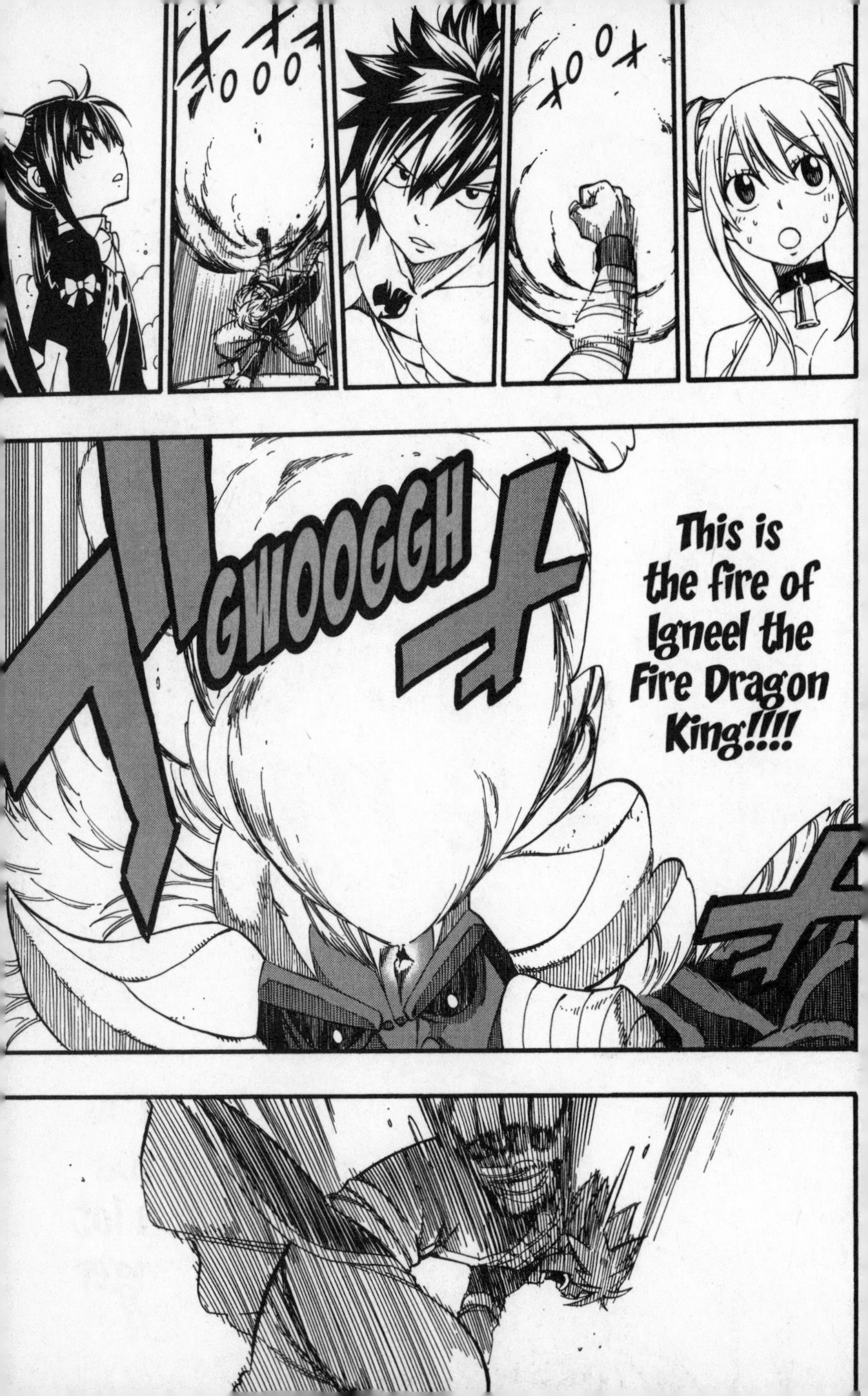
This is the fire of Igneel the Fire Dragon King!!!!
GWOOGGH

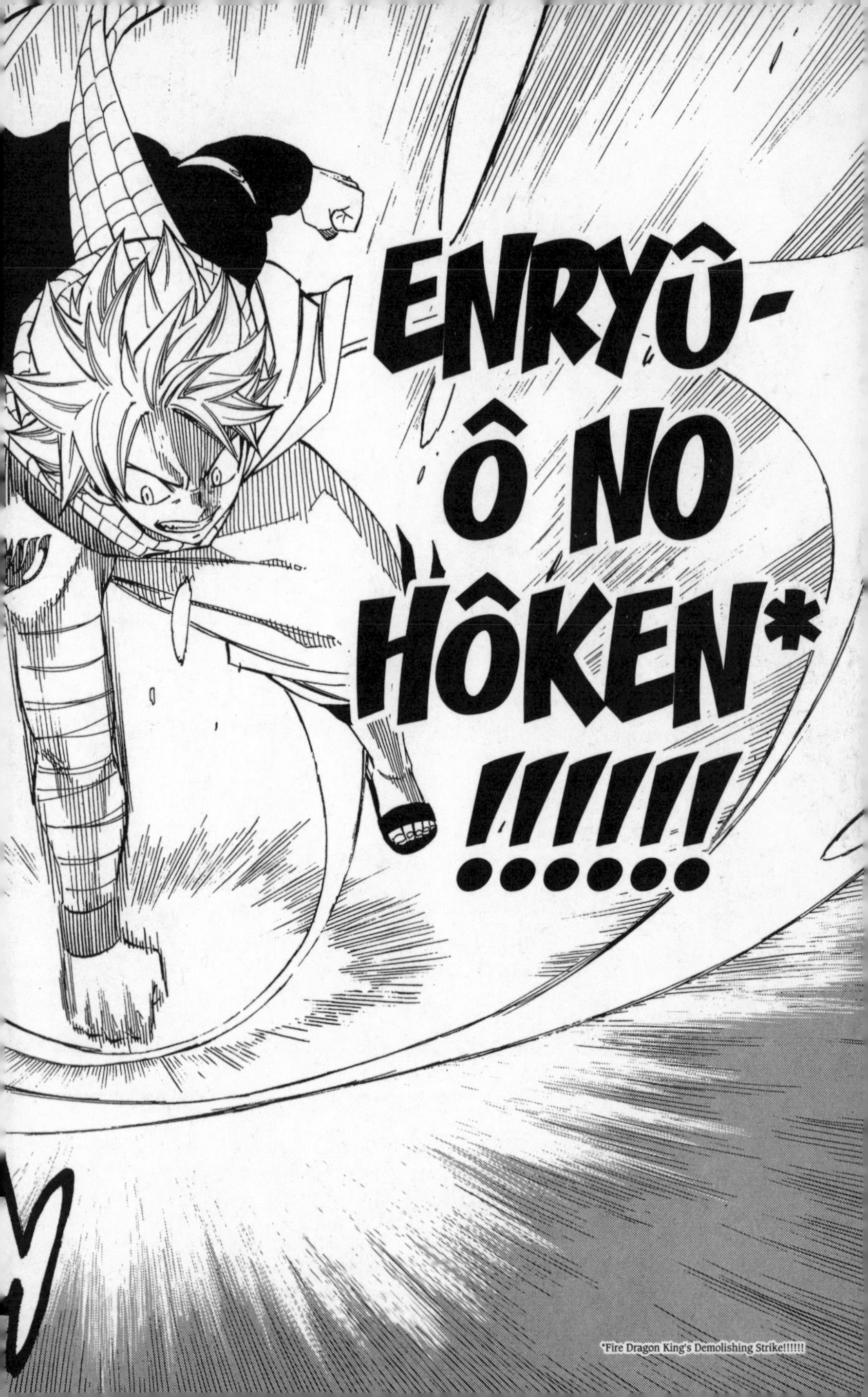
ENRYÔ-
Ô NO
HÔKEN*
!!!!!!
*Fire Dragon King's Demolishing Strike!!!!!!

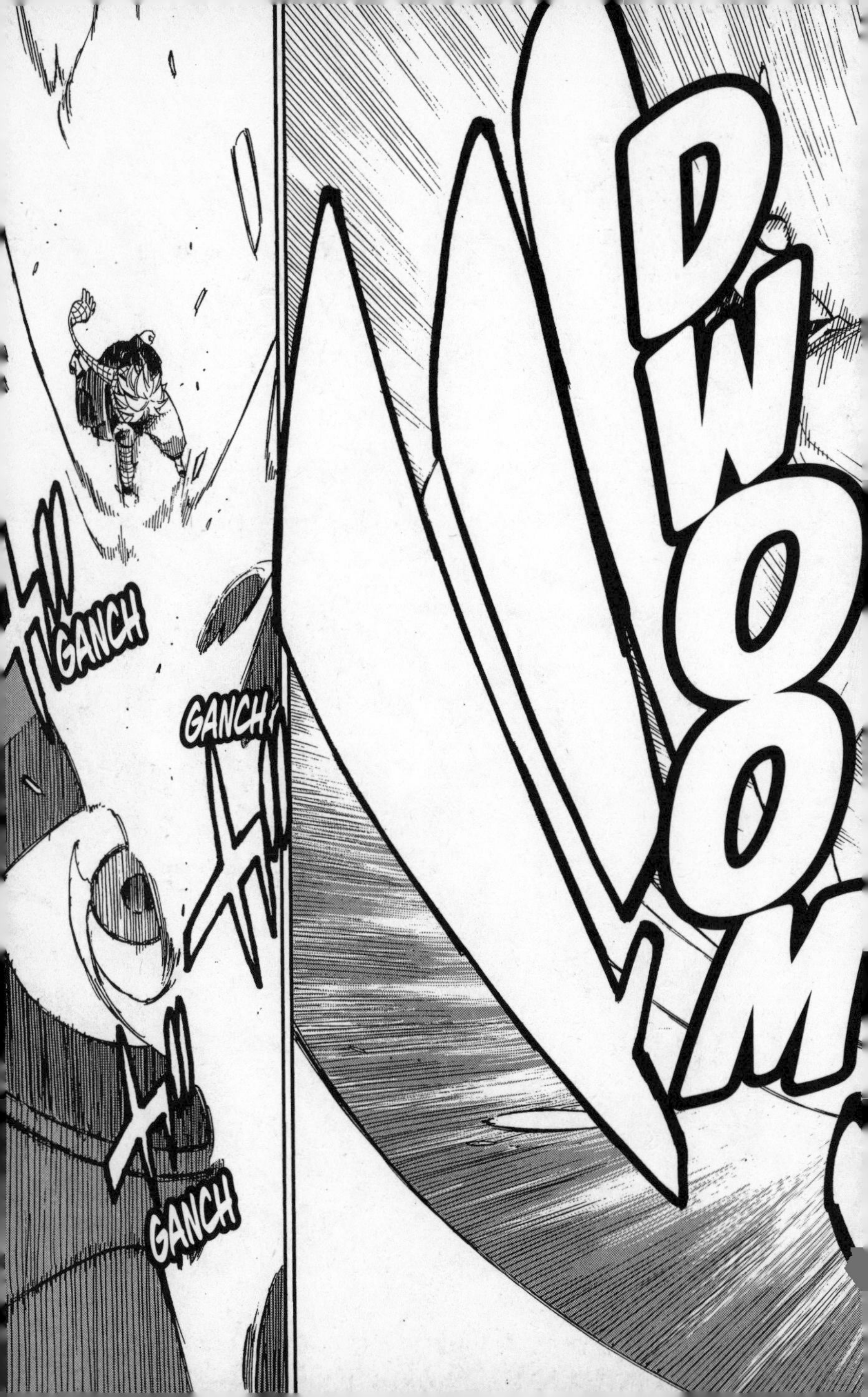
DWOOM
GANCH
GANCH
GANCH

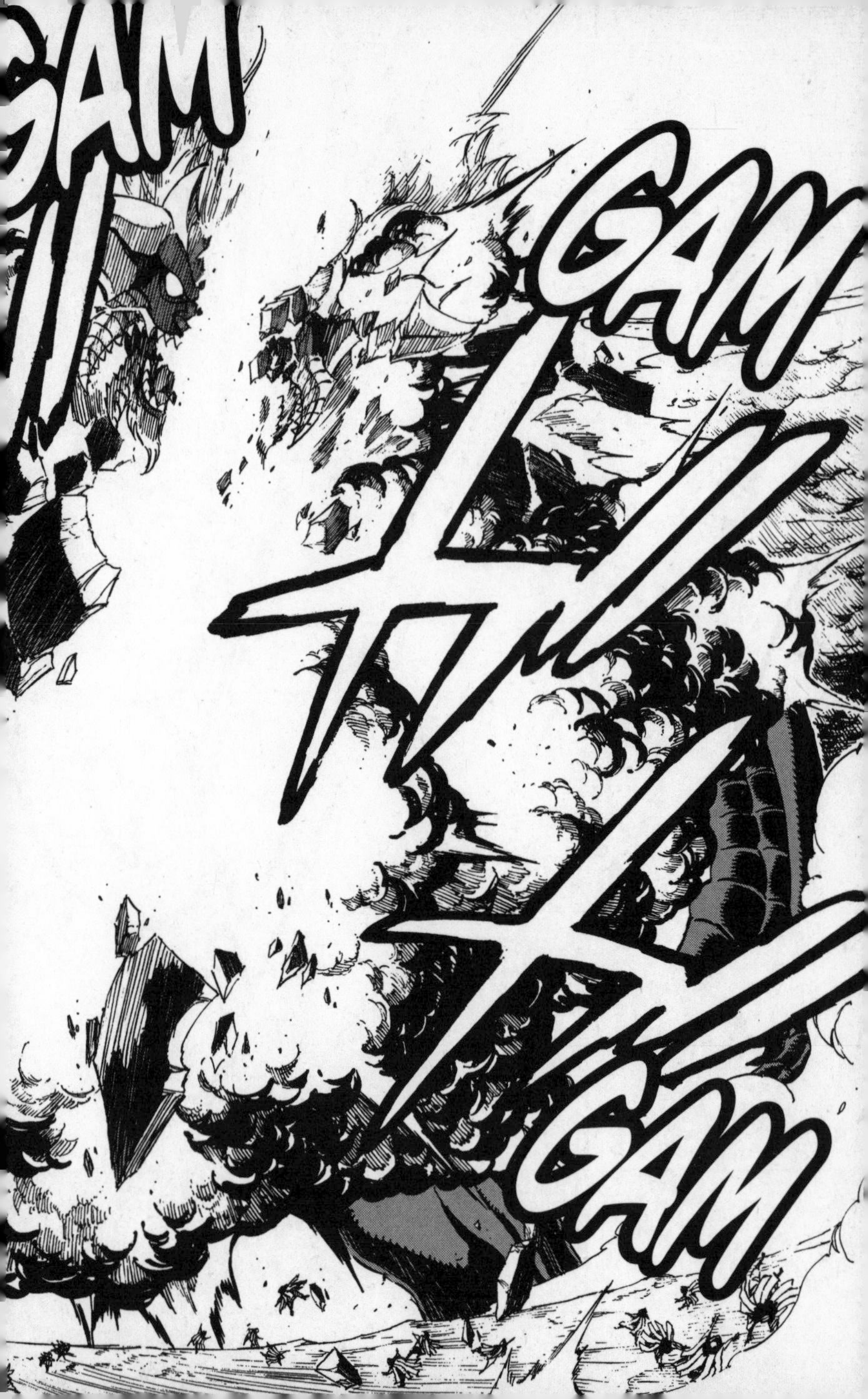
GAM
GAM
GAM

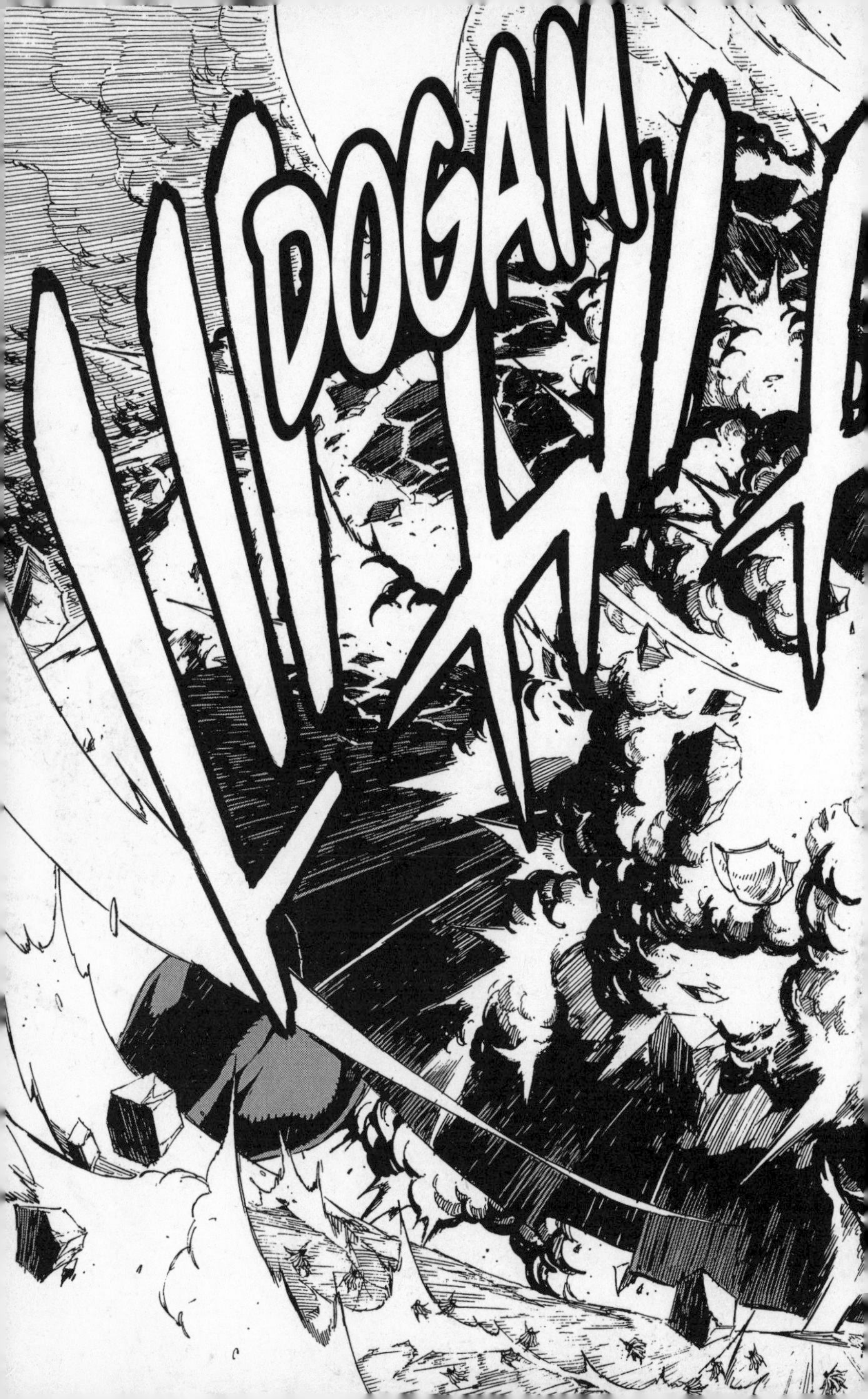

DOGAM

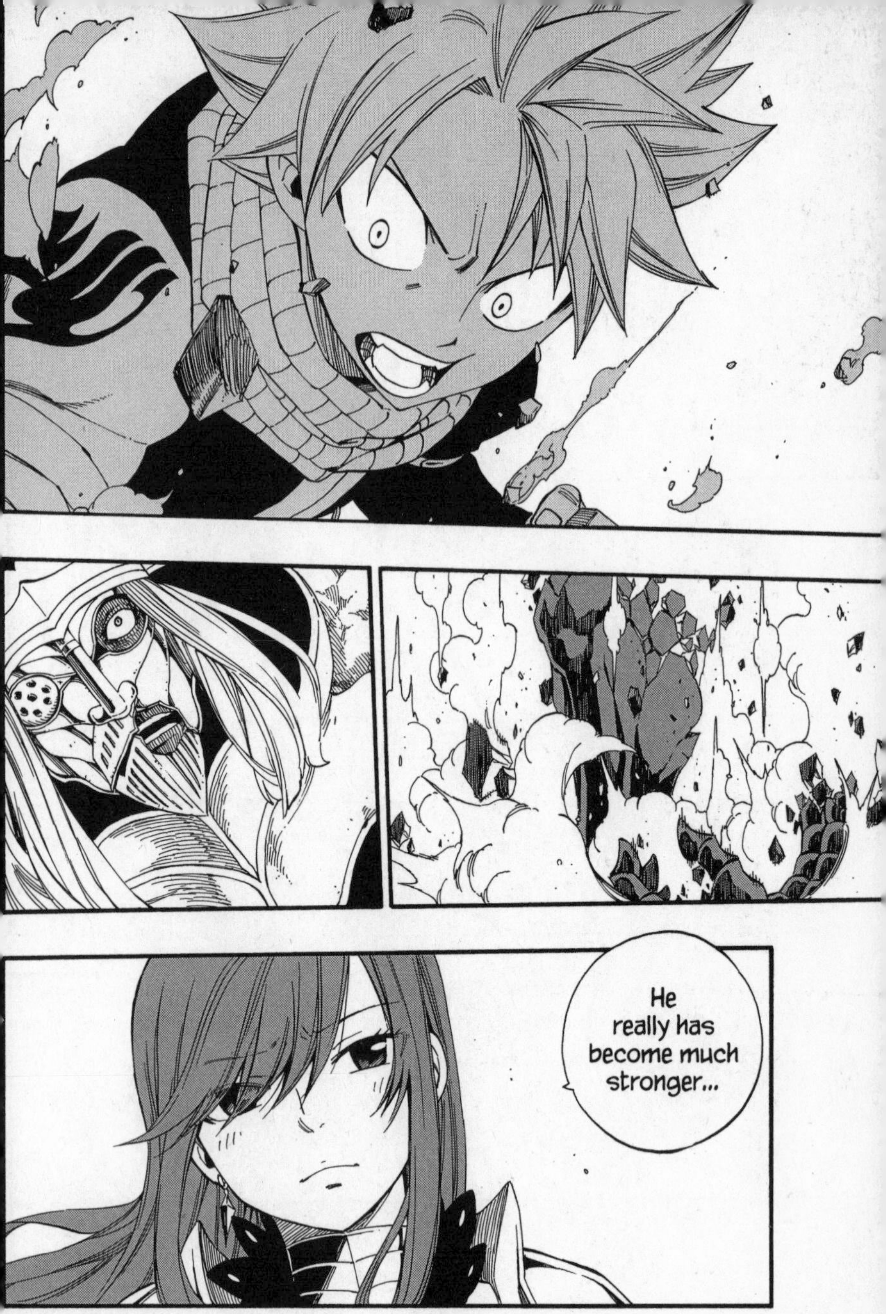
He really has become much stronger...

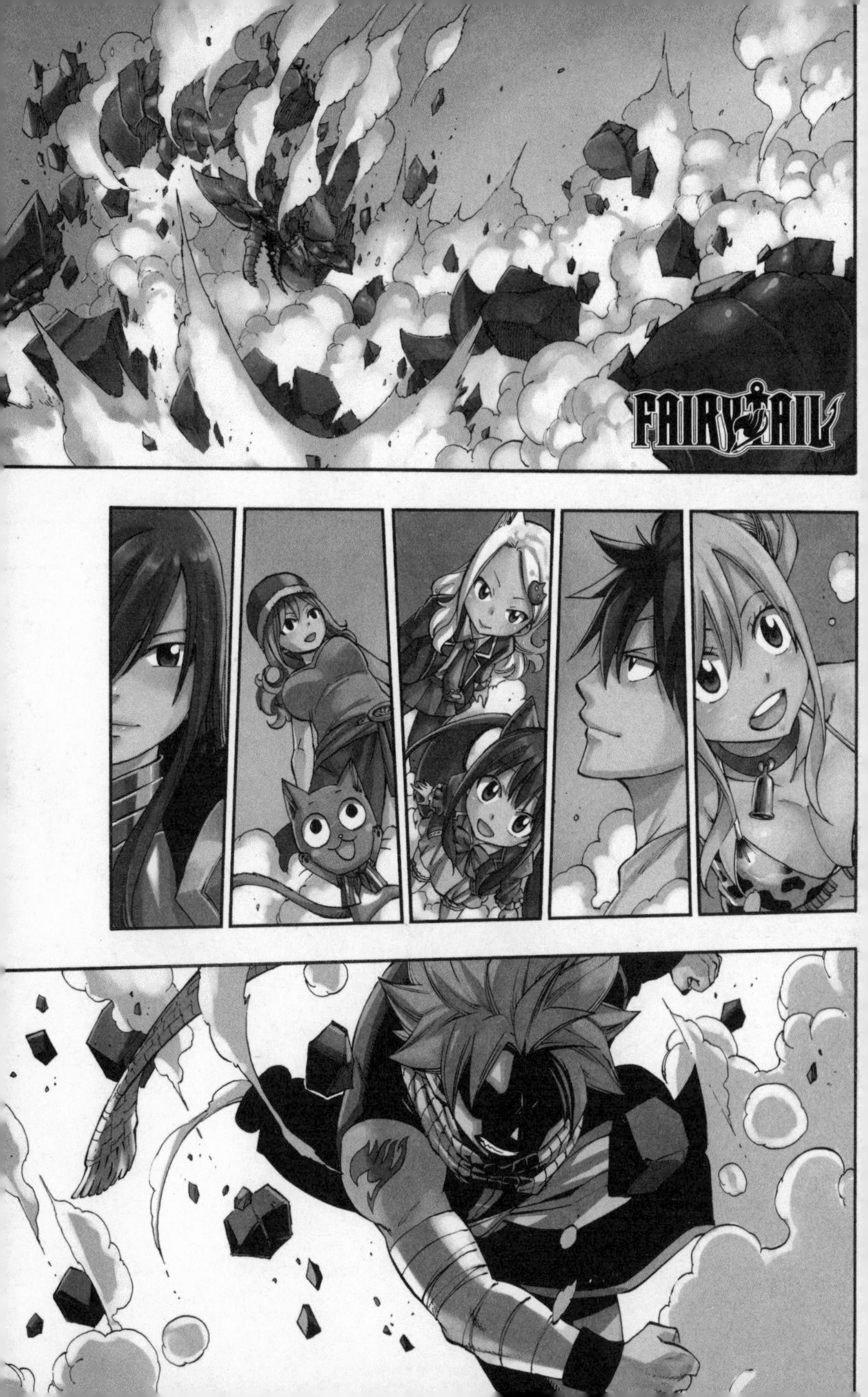

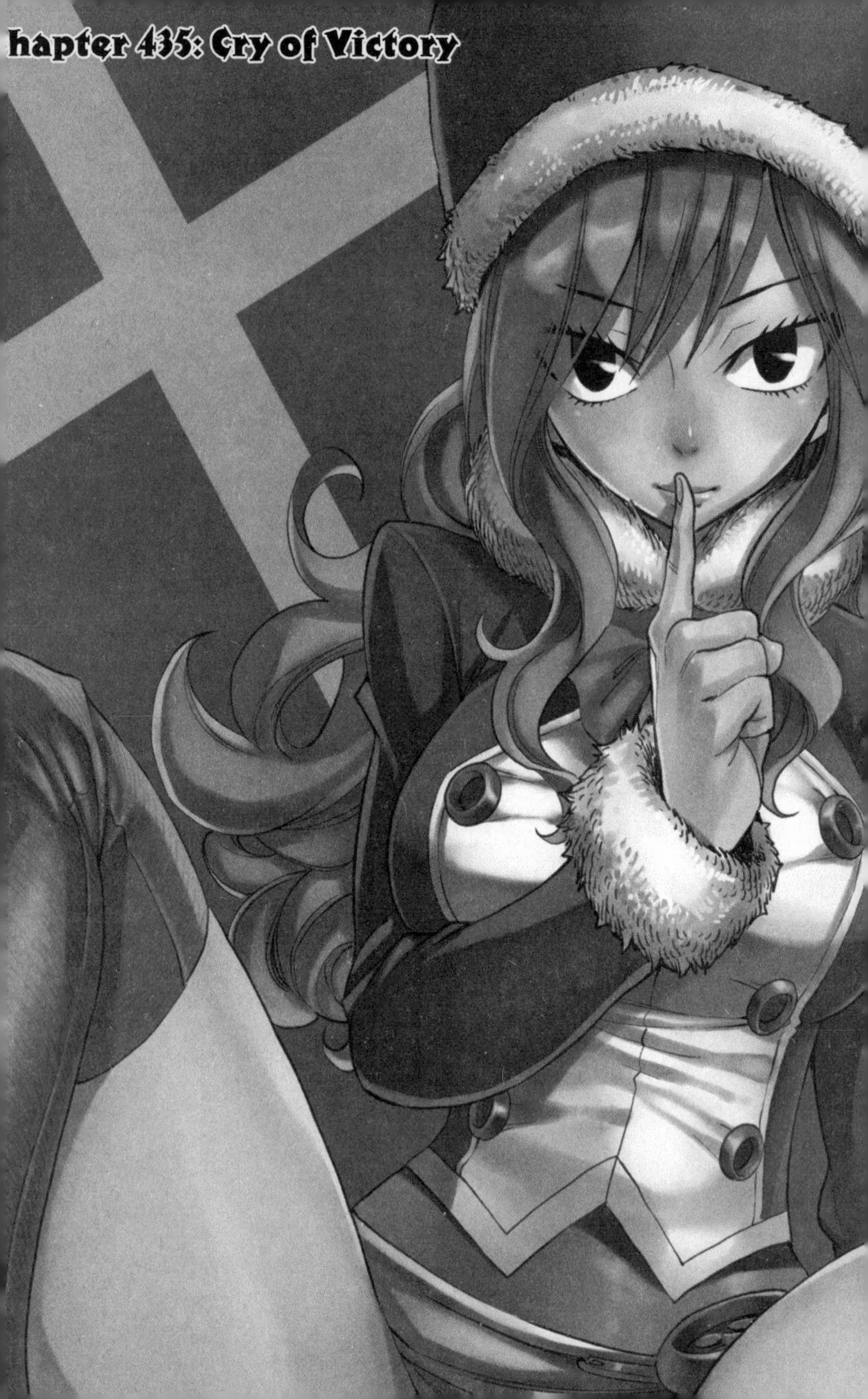
hapter 435: Cry of Victory

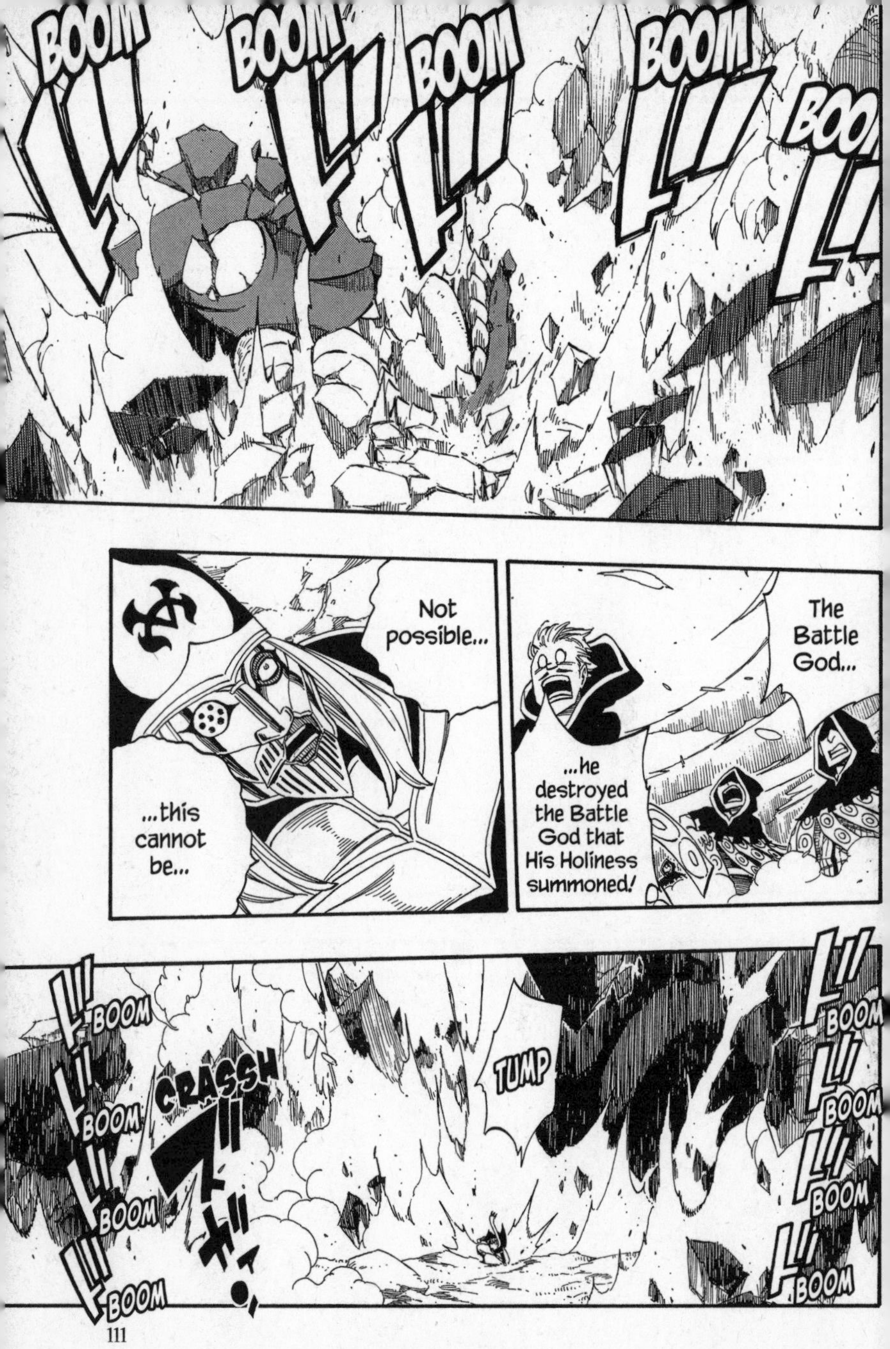
BOOM
BOOM
BOOM
BOOM
BOOM
The Battle God...
...he destroyed the Battle God that His Holiness summoned!
Not possible...
...this cannot be...
BOOM
BOOM
BOOM
BOOM
TUMP
CRASSH
BOOM
BOOM
BOOM
BOOM

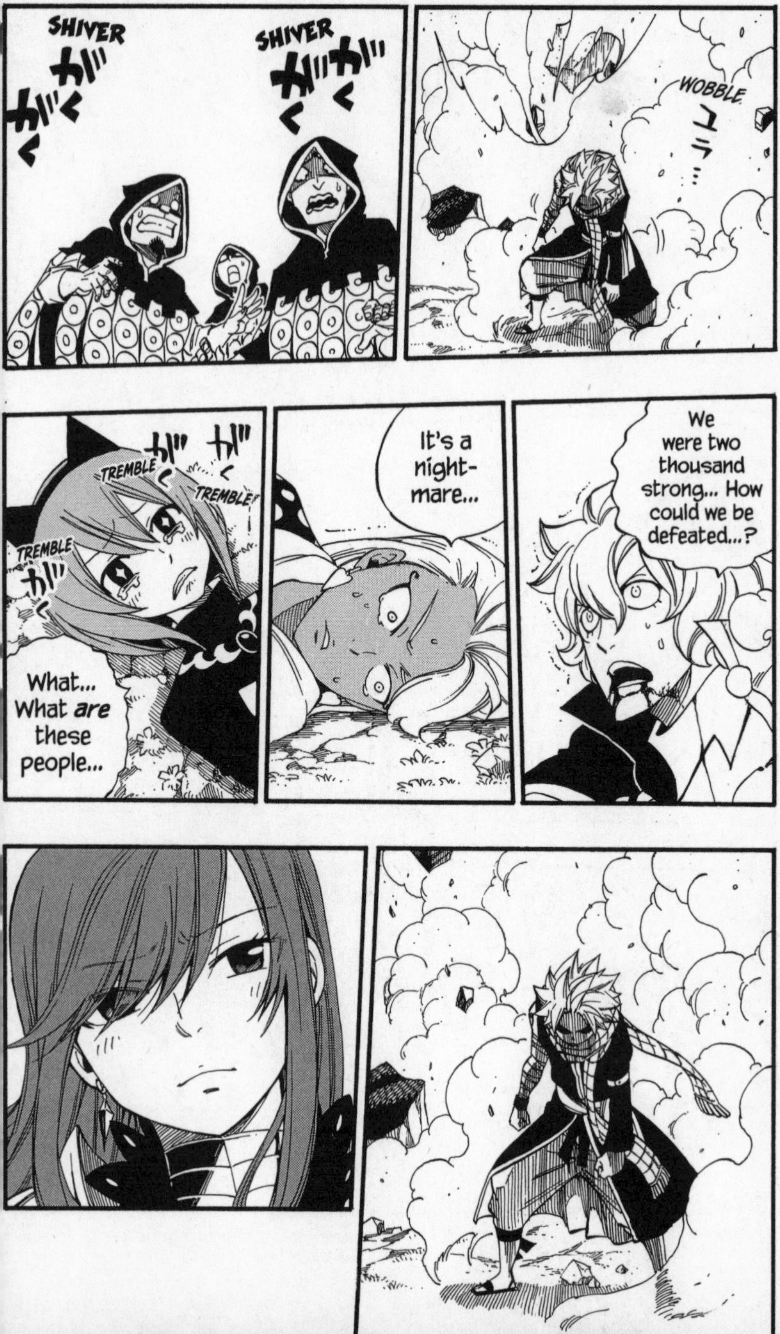
WOBBLE
ユラ…
SHIVER
がくがく
SHIVER
がくがく
We were two thousand strong... How could we be defeated...?
It's a nightmare...
TREMBLE
がく
TREMBLE
がく
TREMBLE
がく
What... What are these people...

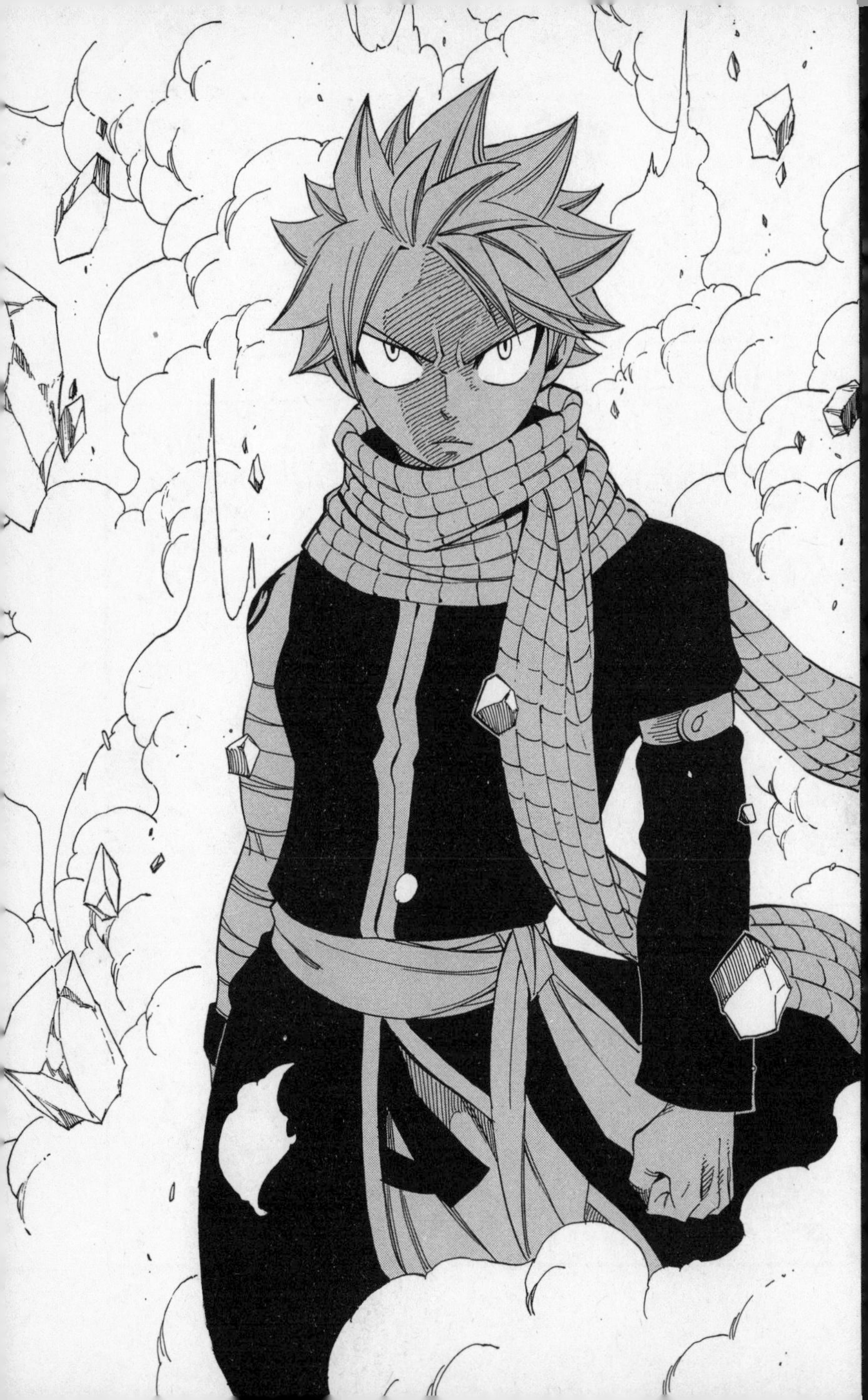

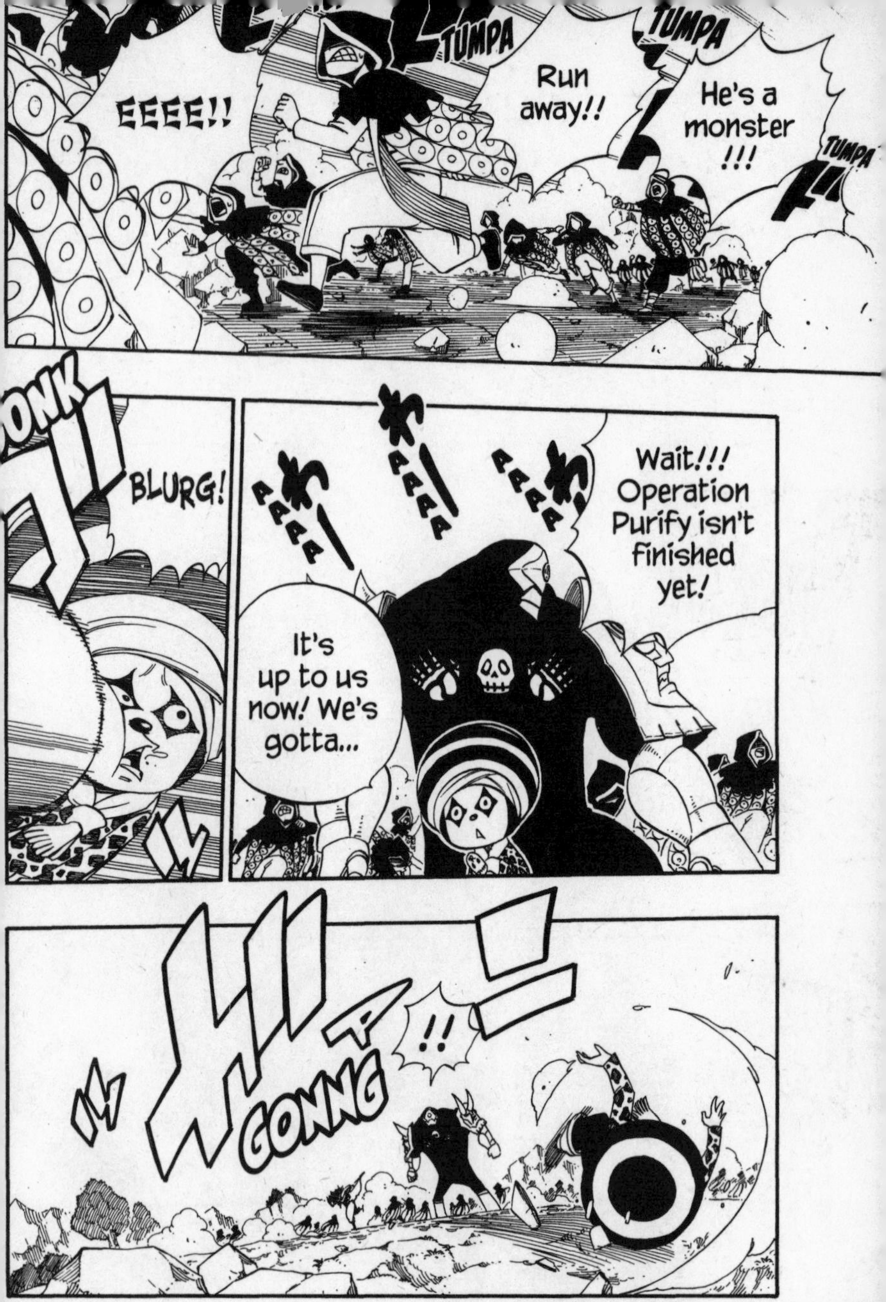
TUMPA
He's a monster!!!
TUMPA
Run away!!
TUMPA
EEEE!!
Wait!!! Operation Purify isn't finished yet!
AAAA
AAAA
AAAA
It's up to us now! We's gotta...
BLURG!
!!
GONNG

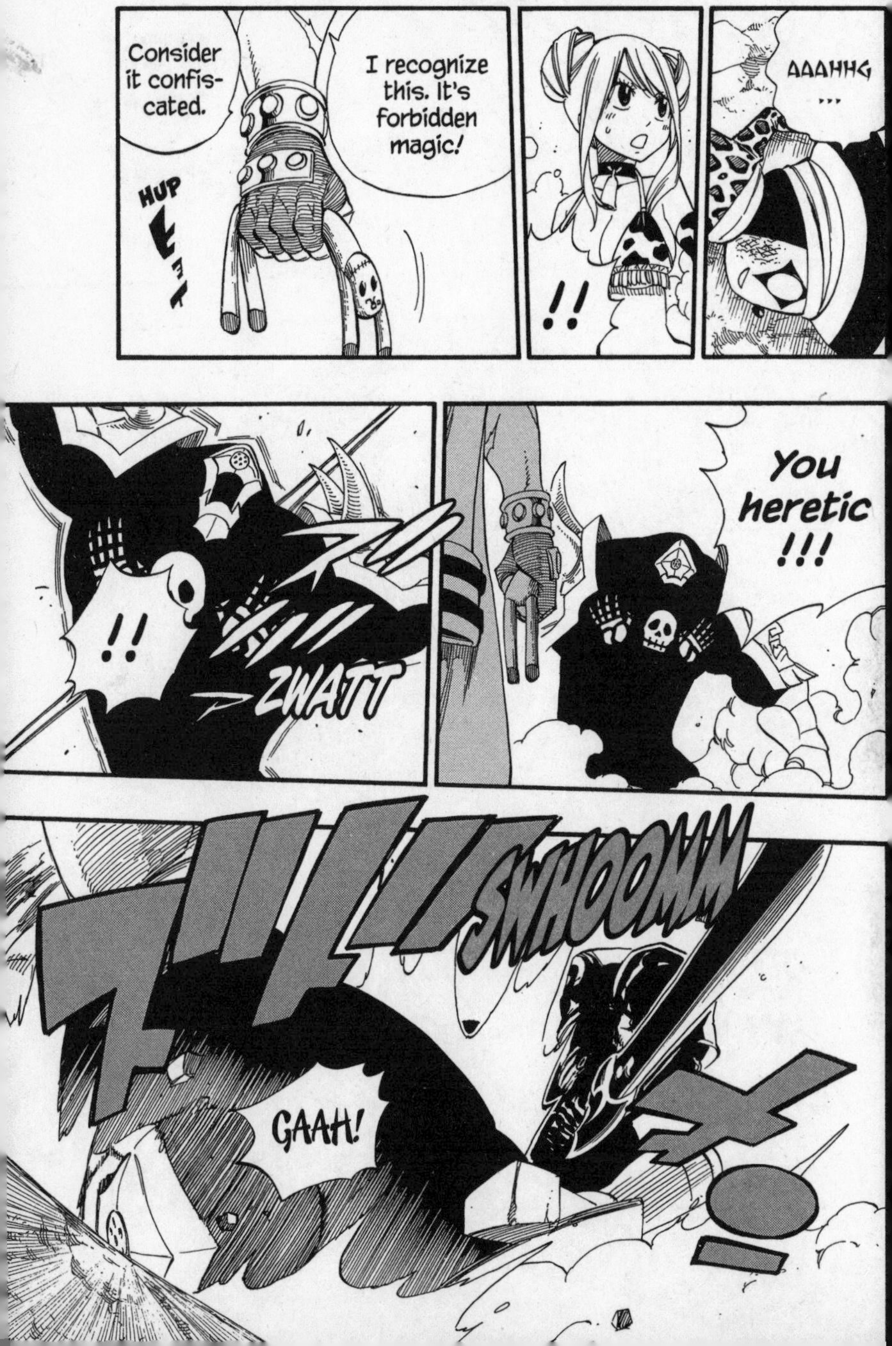
AAAHHG ...
!!
I recognize this. It's forbidden magic!
Consider it confiscated.
HUP
You heretic !!!
!!
ZWATT
SWHOOMM
GAAH!

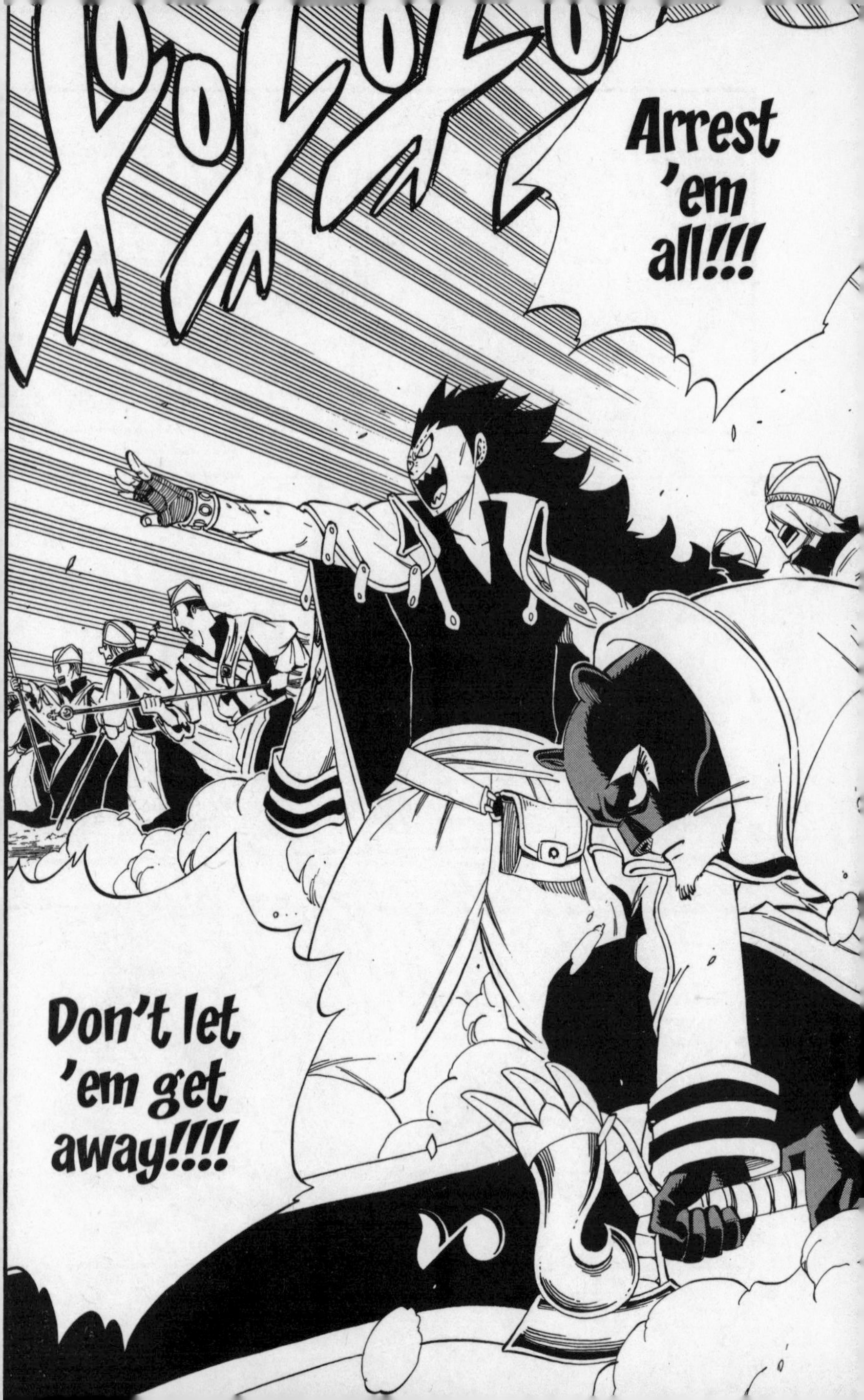
Arrest 'em all!!!
Don't let 'em get away!!!!

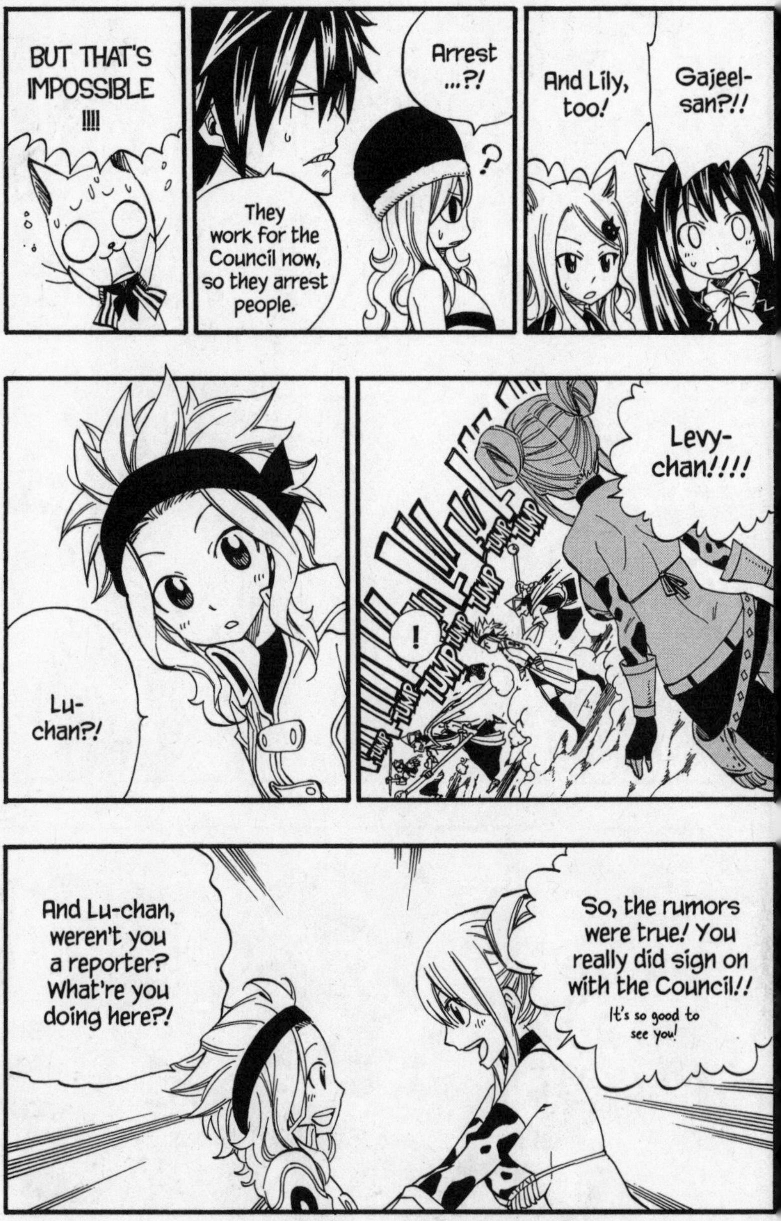
Gajeel-san?!!
And Lily, too!
Arrest ...?!
They work for the Council now, so they arrest people.
BUT THAT'S IMPOSSIBLE !!!!!
Levy-chan!!!!
TUMP TUMP TUMP TUMP TUMP TUMP TUMP
!
Lu-chan?!
So, the rumors were true! You really did sign on with the Council!!
It's so good to see you!
And Lu-chan, weren't you a reporter? What're you doing here?!

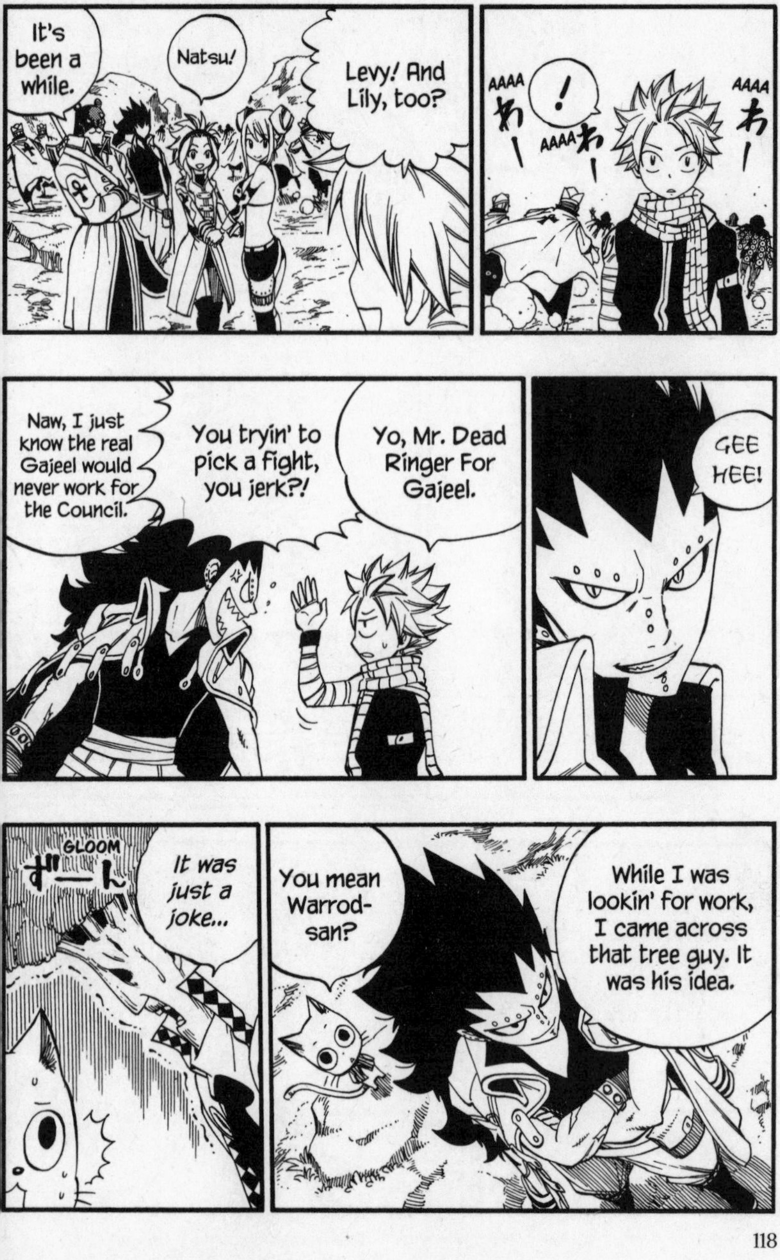
AAAA
わー
!
AAAA
わー
AAAA
わー
Levy! And Lily, too?
Natsu!
It's been a while.
GEE HEE!
Yo, Mr. Dead Ringer For Gajeel.
You tryin' to pick a fight, you jerk?!
Naw, I just know the real Gajeel would never work for the Council.
While I was lookin' for work, I came across that tree guy. It was his idea.
You mean Warrod-san?
It was just a joke...
GLOOM
ずーん

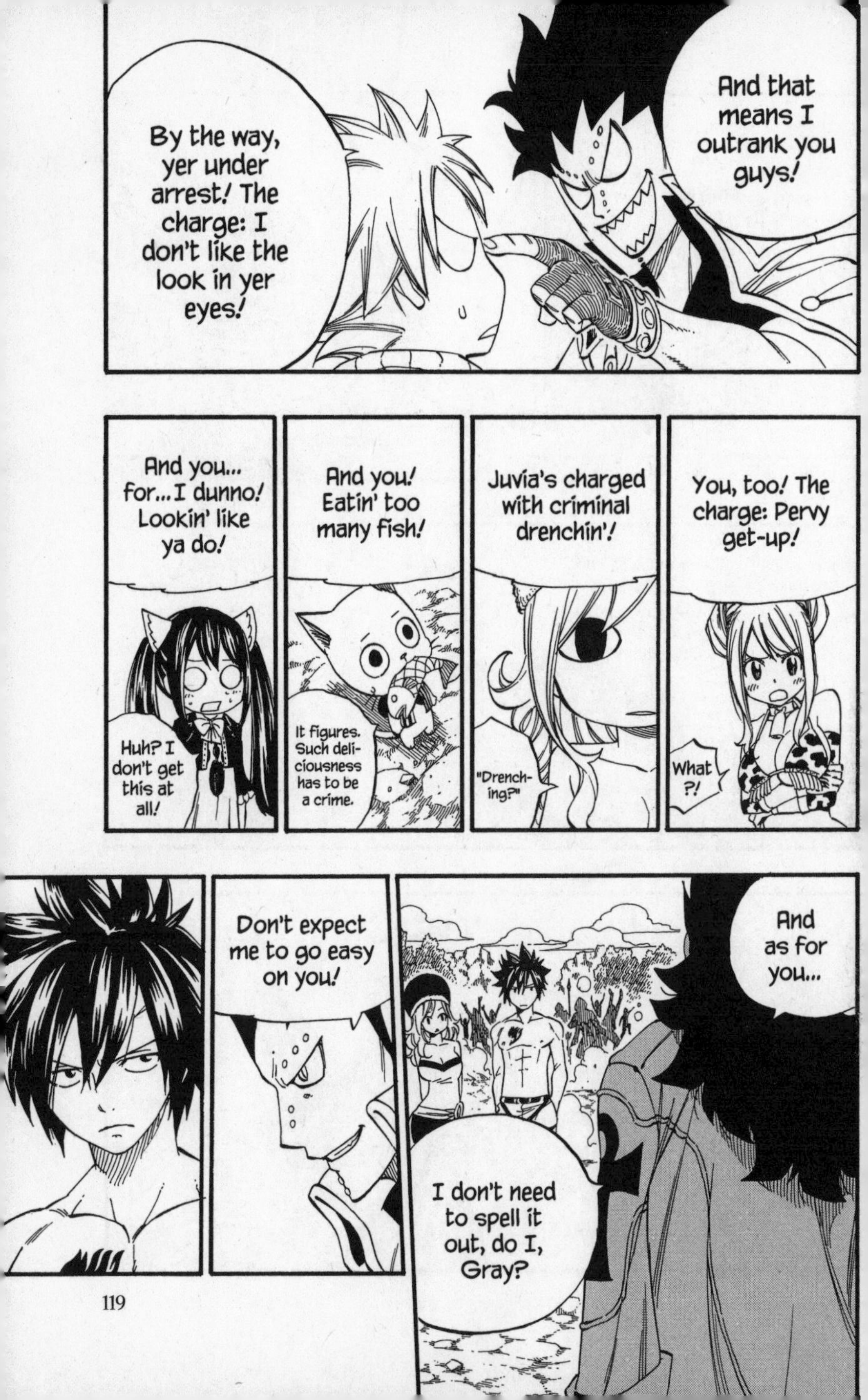
And that means I outrank you guys!
By the way, yer under arrest! The charge: I don't like the look in yer eyes!
You, too! The charge: Pervy get-up!
What?!
Juvia's charged with criminal drenchin'!
"Drenching?"
And you! Eatin' too many fish!
It figures. Such deliciousness has to be a crime.
And you... for...I dunno! Lookin' like ya do!
Huh? I don't get this at all!
And as for you...
I don't need to spell it out, do I, Gray?
Don't expect me to go easy on you!

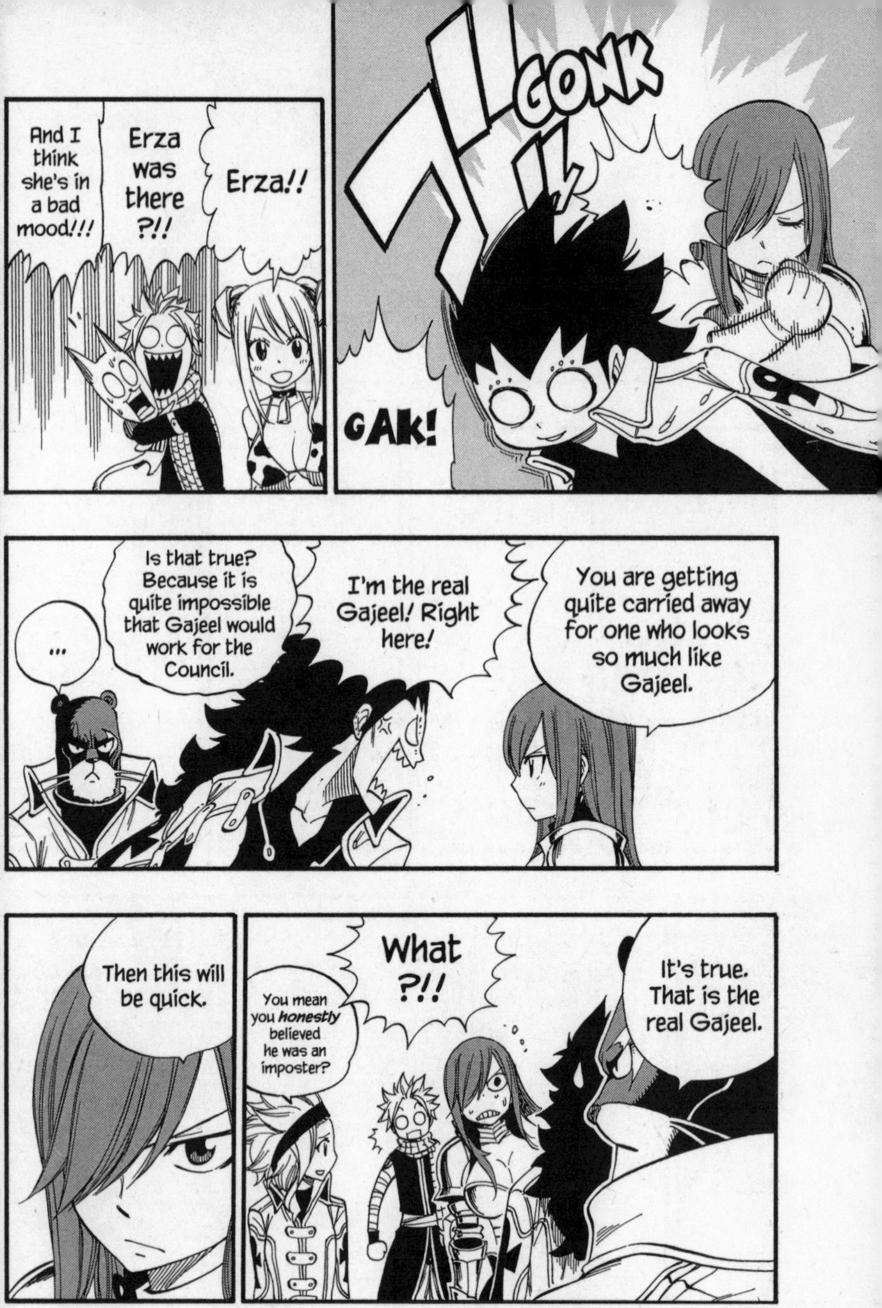
GONK
GAK!
Erza!!
Erza was there?!!
And I think she's in a bad mood!!!
You are getting quite carried away for one who looks so much like Gajeel.
I'm the real Gajeel! Right here!
Is that true? Because it is quite impossible that Gajeel would work for the Council.
...
It's true. That is the real Gajeel.
What?!!
You mean you *honestly* believed he was an imposter?
Then this will be quick.

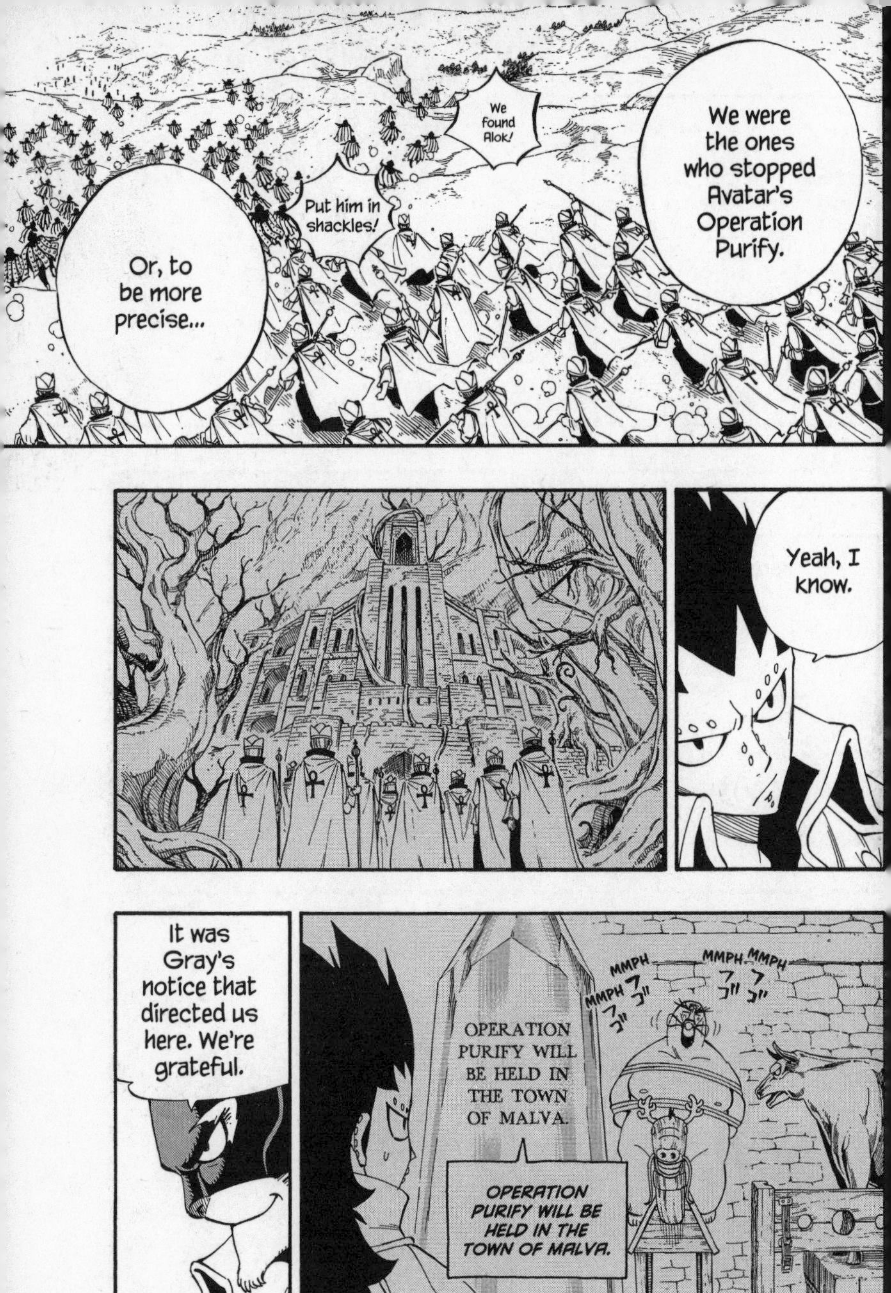
We were the ones who stopped Avatar's Operation Purify.
We found Alok!
Put him in shackles!
Or, to be more precise...
Yeah, I know.
MMPH MMPH
MMPH
MMPH
OPERATION PURIFY WILL BE HELD IN THE TOWN OF MALVA.
OPERATION PURIFY WILL BE HELD IN THE TOWN OF MALVA.
It was Gray's notice that directed us here. We're grateful.

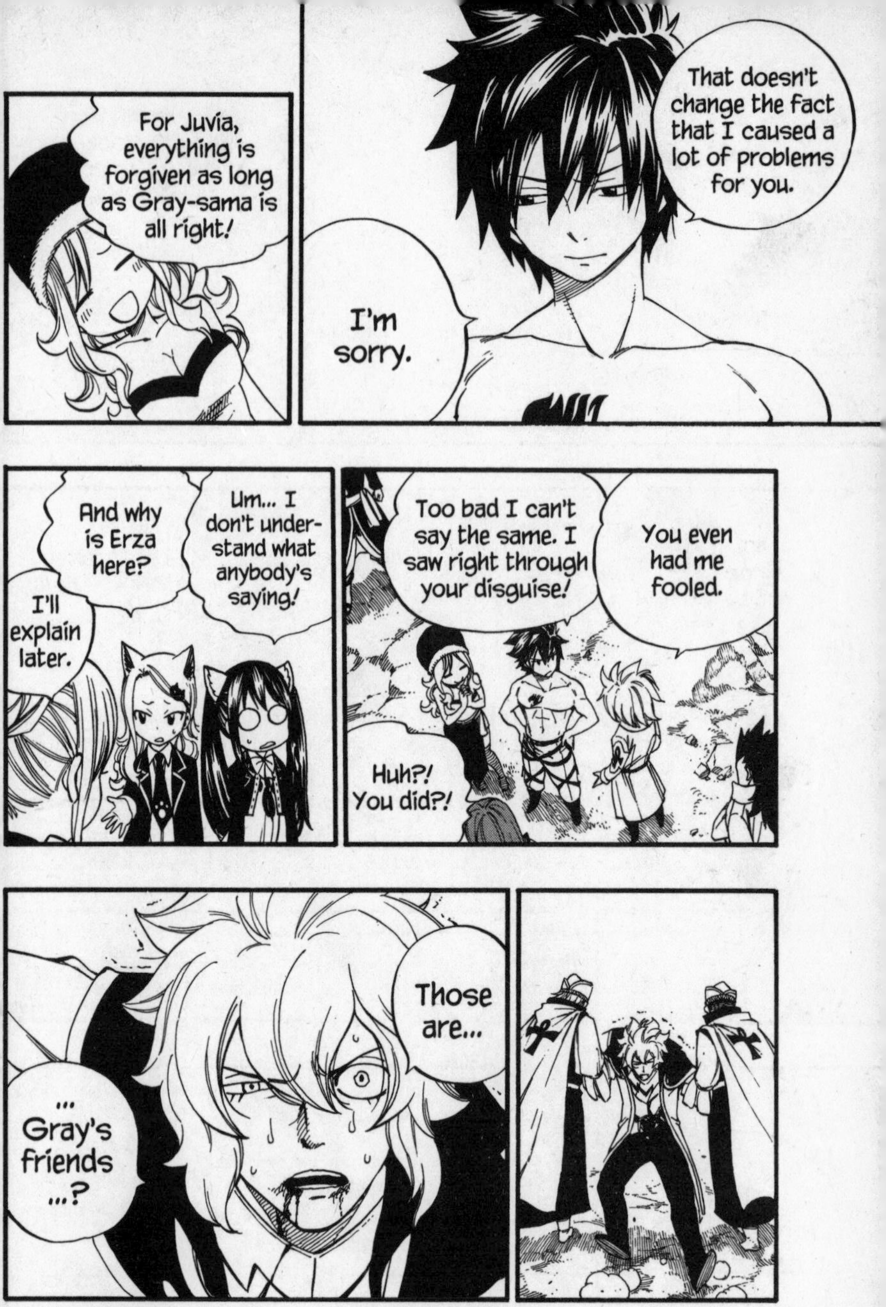
That doesn't change the fact that I caused a lot of problems for you.
I'm sorry.
For Juvia, everything is forgiven as long as Gray-sama is all right!
You even had me fooled.
Too bad I can't say the same. I saw right through your disguise!
Huh?! You did?!
Um... I don't under-stand what anybody's saying!
And why is Erza here?
I'll explain later.
Those are...
... Gray's friends ...?

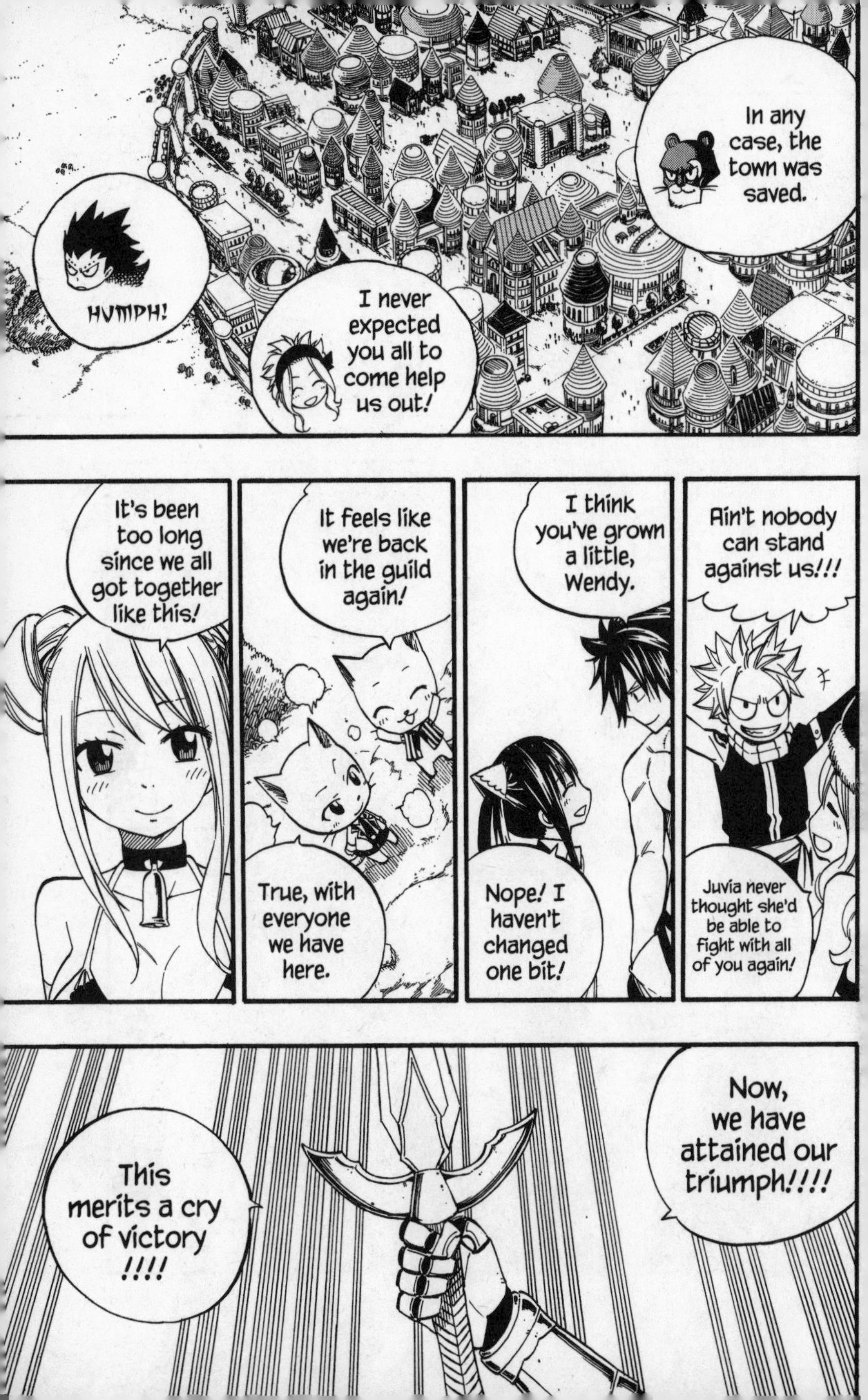
In any case, the town was saved.
I never expected you all to come help us out!
HUMPH!
Ain't nobody can stand against us!!!
Juvia never thought she'd be able to fight with all of you again!
I think you've grown a little, Wendy.
Nope! I haven't changed one bit!
It feels like we're back in the guild again!
True, with everyone we have here.
It's been too long since we all got together like this!
Now, we have attained our triumph!!!!
This merits a cry of victory !!!!

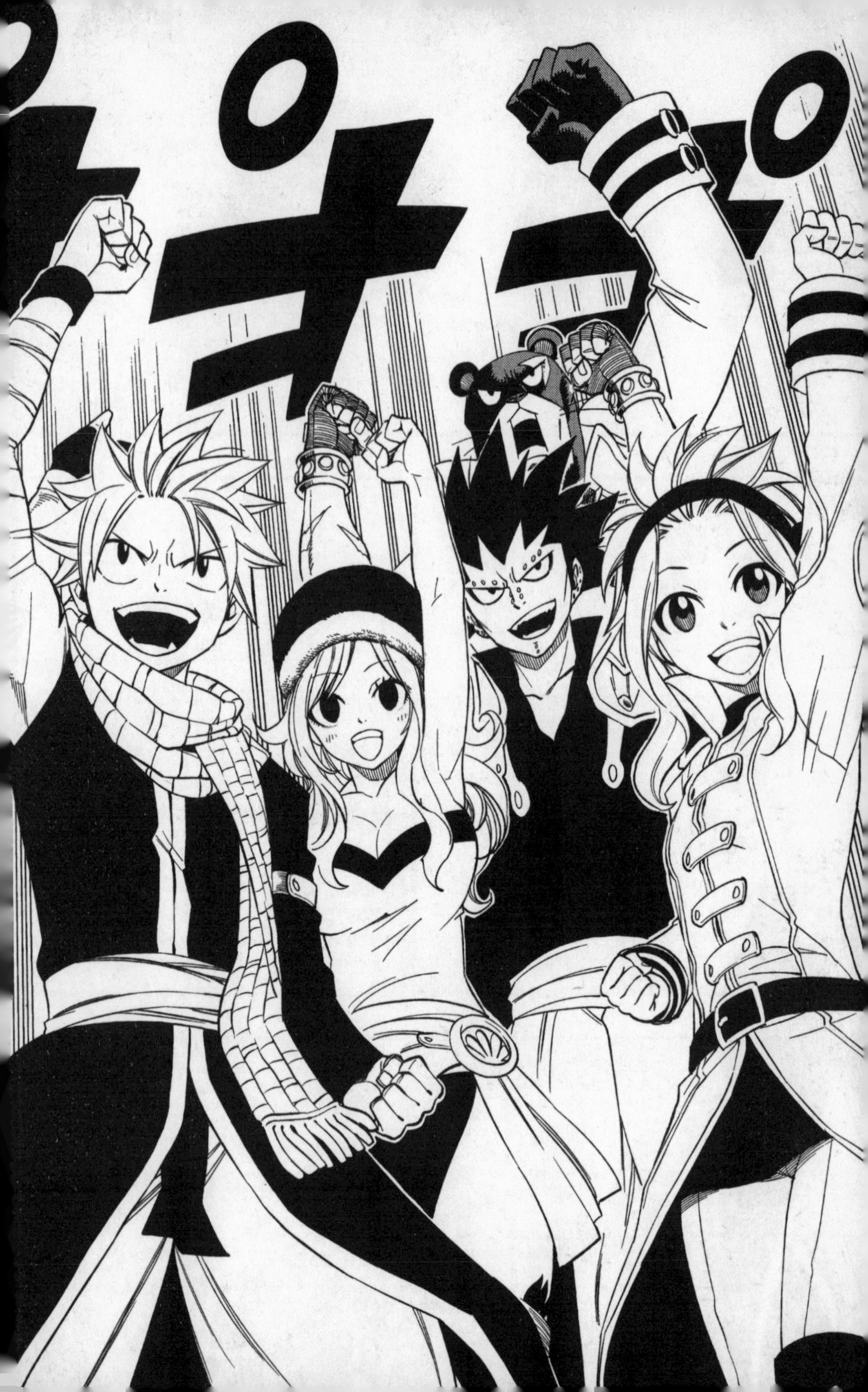

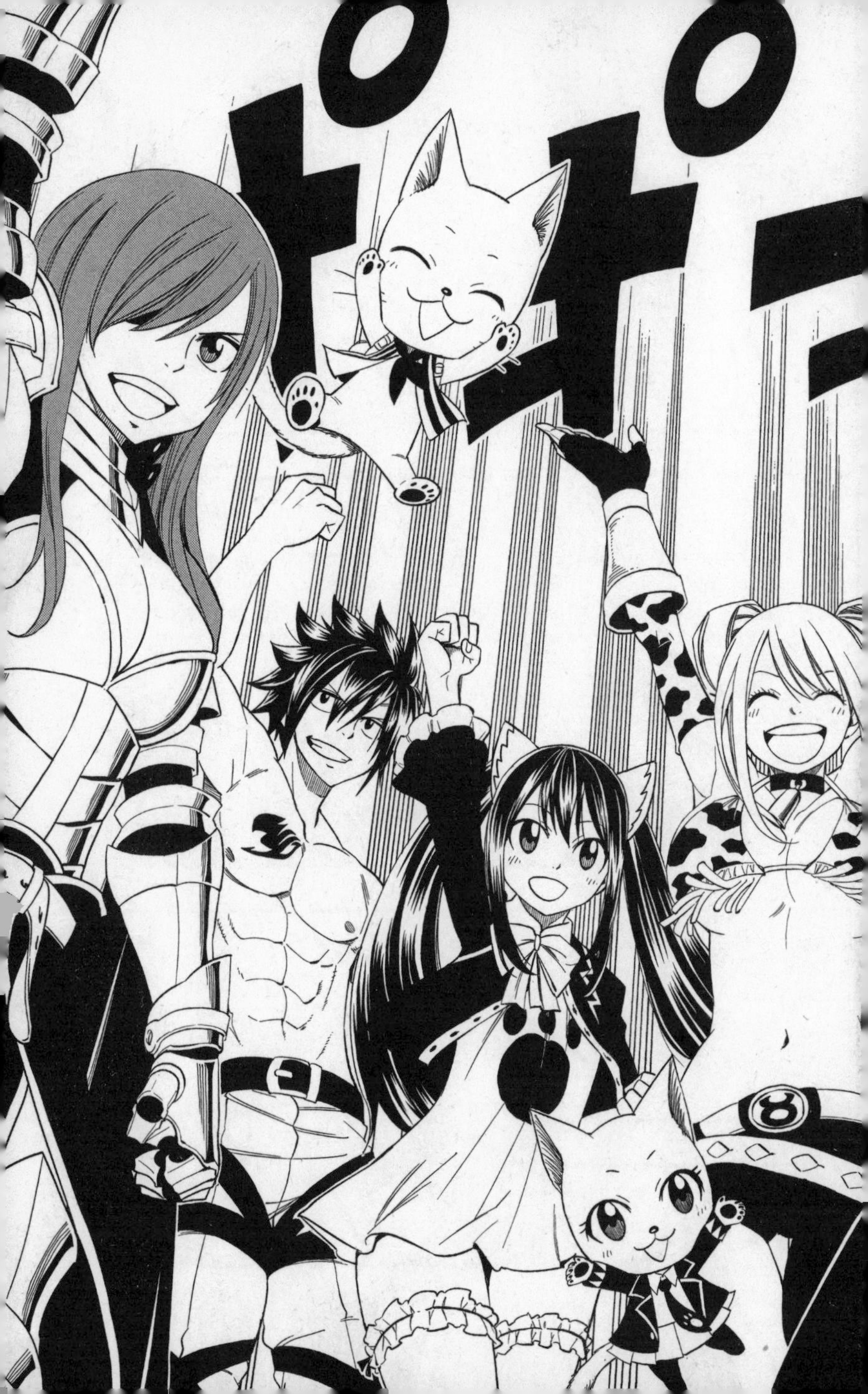

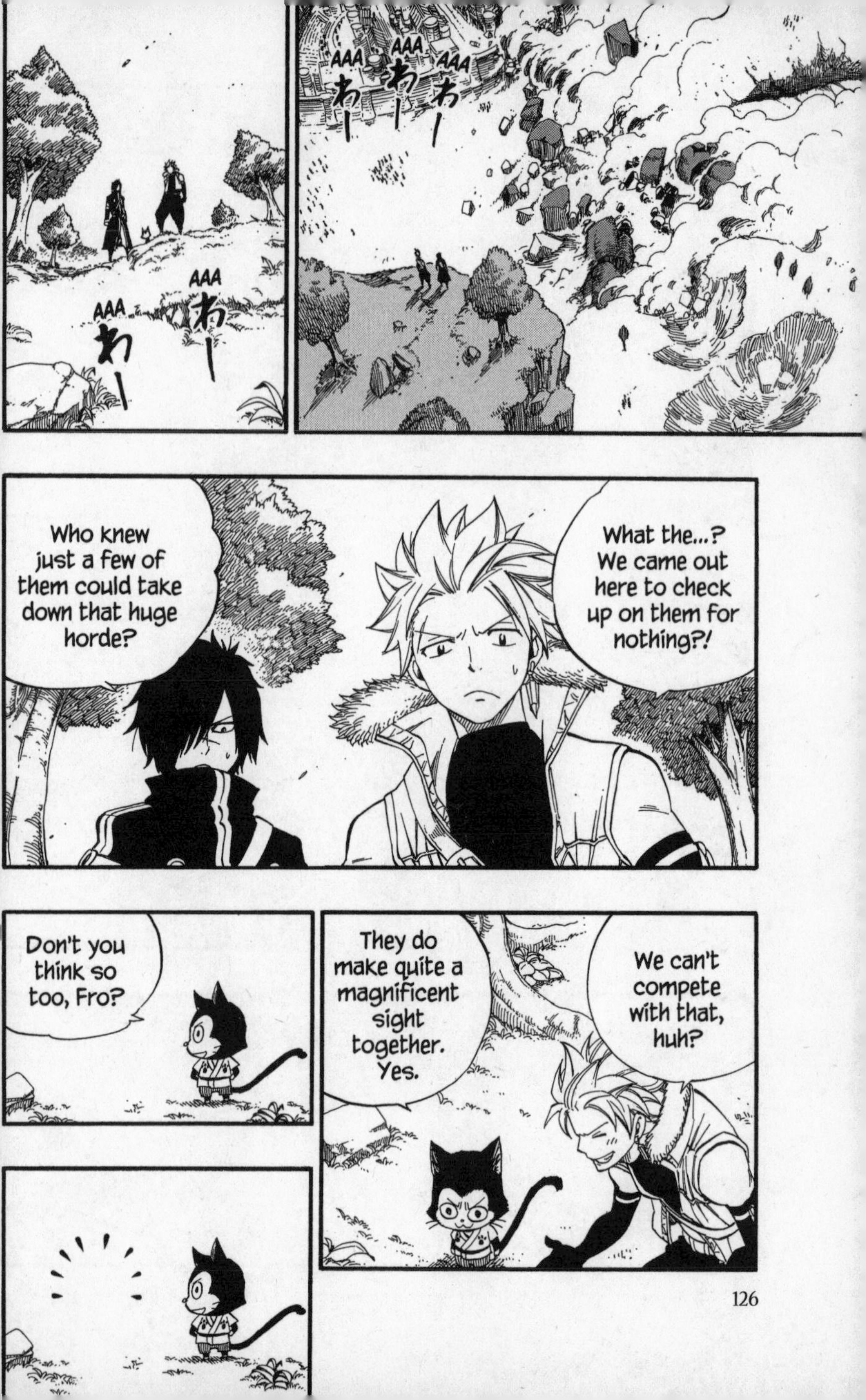
AAA わー
AAA わー
AAA わー
AAA わー
AAA わー
What the...? We came out here to check up on them for nothing?!
Who knew just a few of them could take down that huge horde?
We can't compete with that, huh?
They do make quite a magnificent sight together. Yes.
Don't you think so too, Fro?

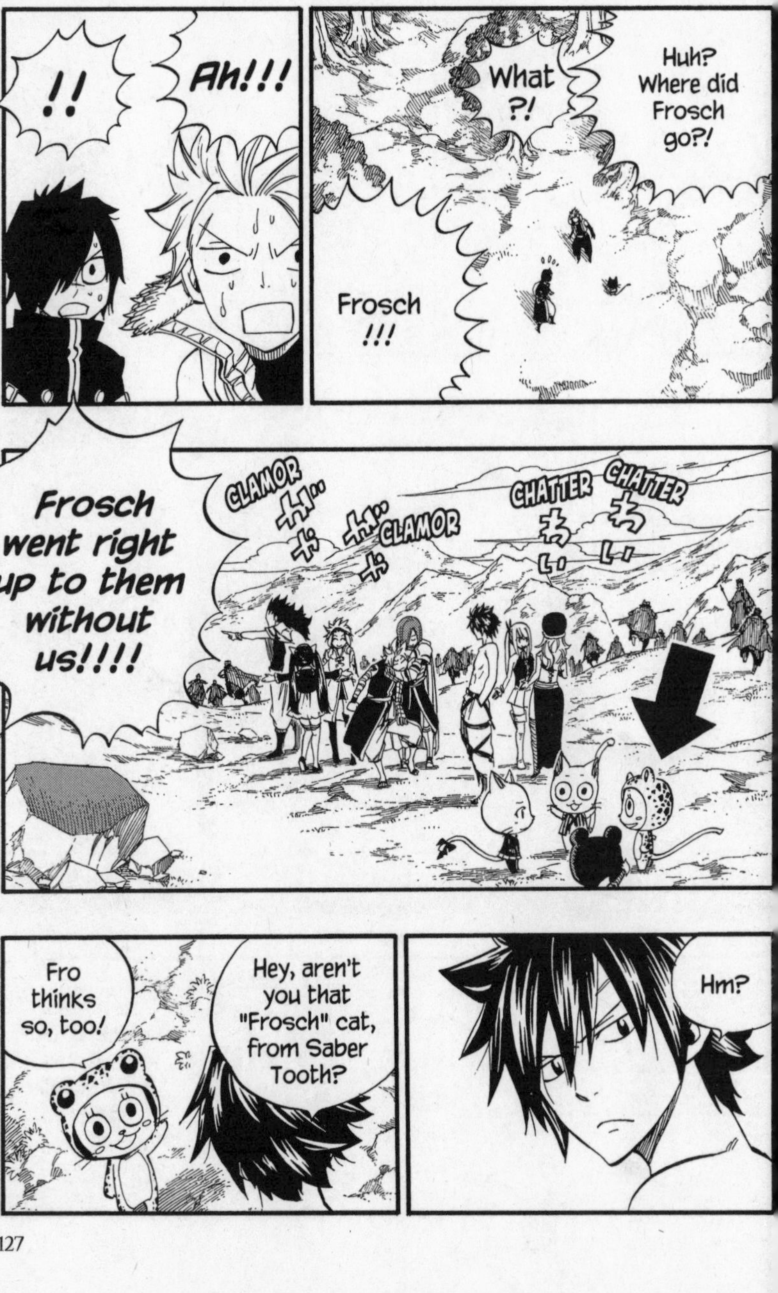
Huh? Where did Frosch go?!
What ?!
Frosch !!!
Ah!!!
!!
CHATTER
CHATTER
CLAMOR
CLAMOR
Frosch went right up to them without us!!!!
Hm?
Hey, aren't you that "Frosch" cat, from Saber Tooth?
Fro thinks so, too!

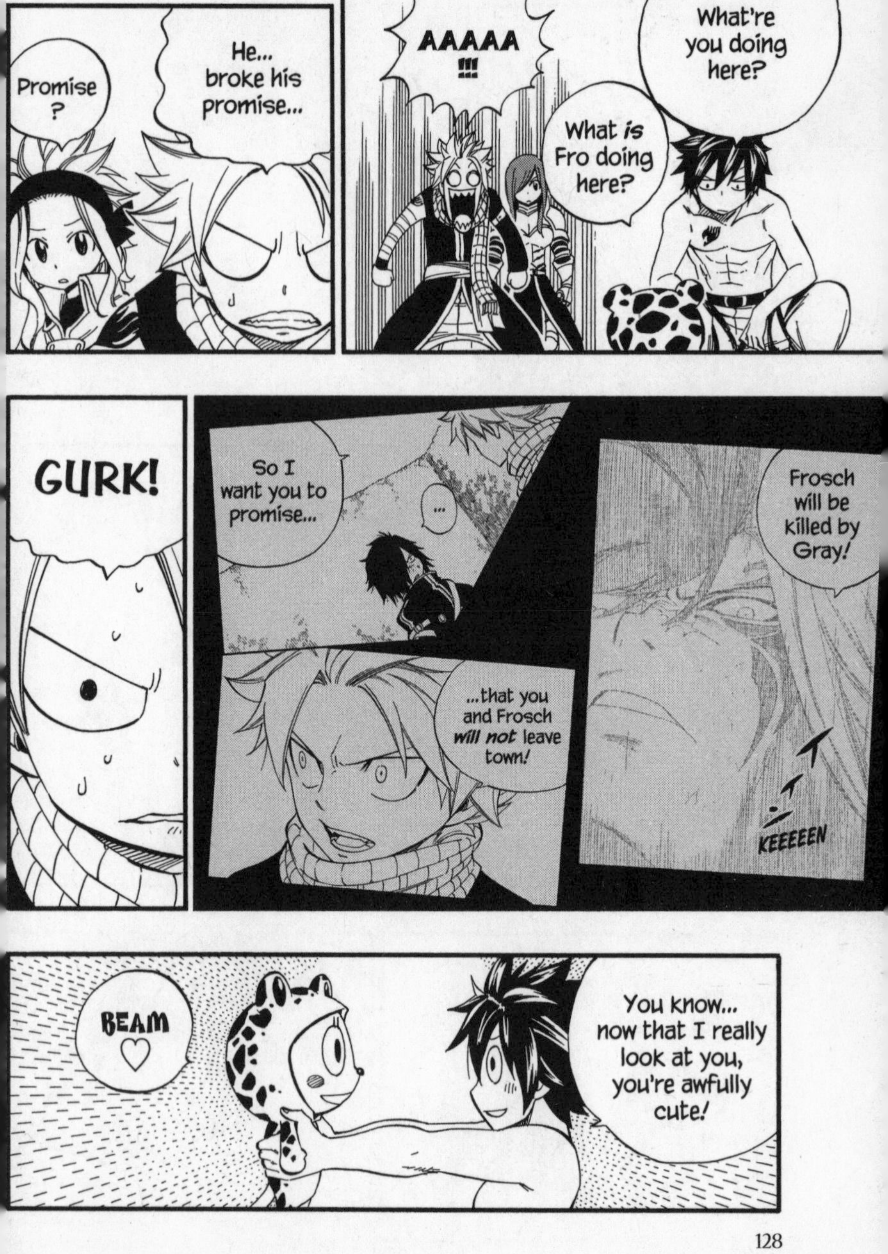
What're you doing here?
What *is* Fro doing here?
AAAAA!!!
He... broke his promise...
Promise?
Frosch will be killed by Gray!
KEEEEEN
So I want you to promise...
...
...that you and Frosch ***will not*** leave town!
GURK!
You know... now that I really look at you, you're awfully cute!
BEAM ♥

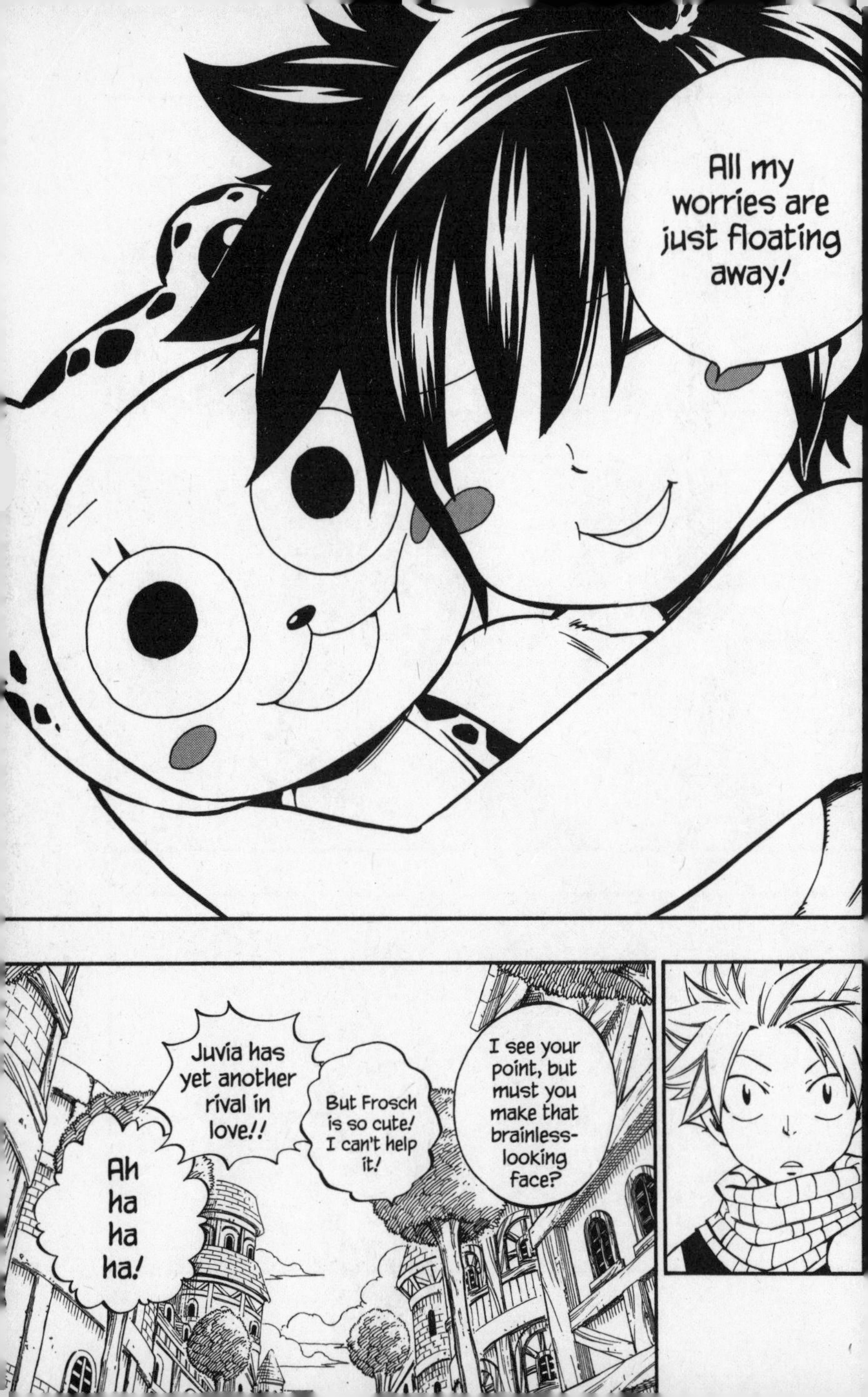
All my worries are just floating away!
I see your point, but must you make that brainless-looking face?
But Frosch is so cute! I can't help it!
Juvia has yet another rival in love!!
Ah ha ha ha!

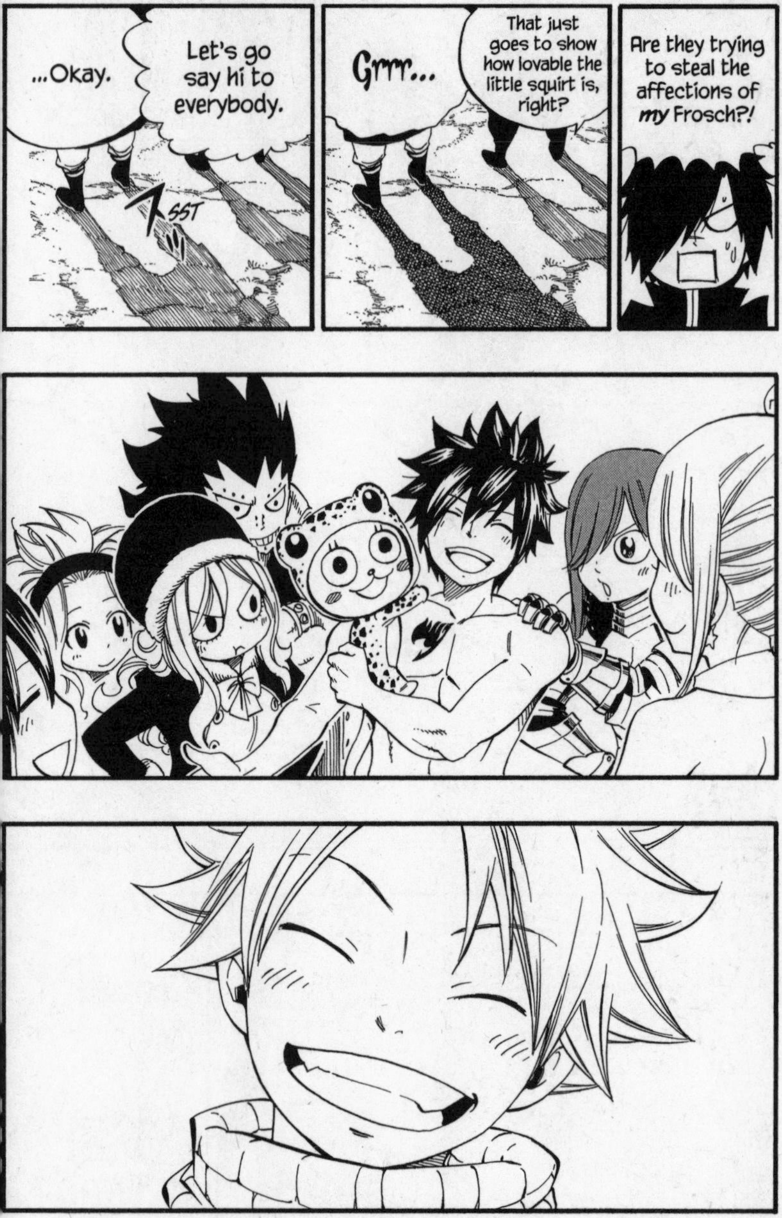
Are they trying to steal the affections of *my* Frosch?!
That just goes to show how lovable the little squirt is, right?
Grrr...
Let's go say hi to everybody.
...Okay.
SST

FAIRY TAIL

フェアリーテイル

Chapter 436: Memoirs

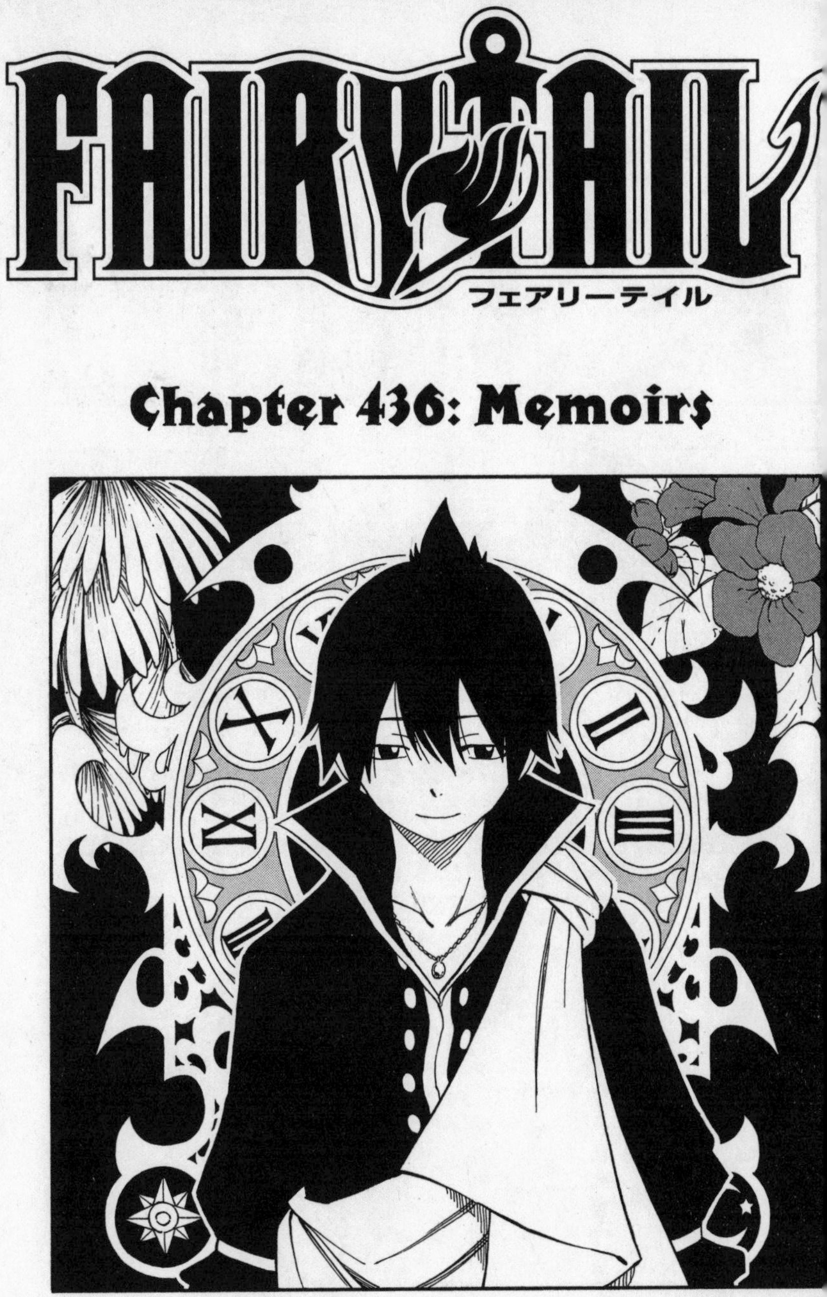

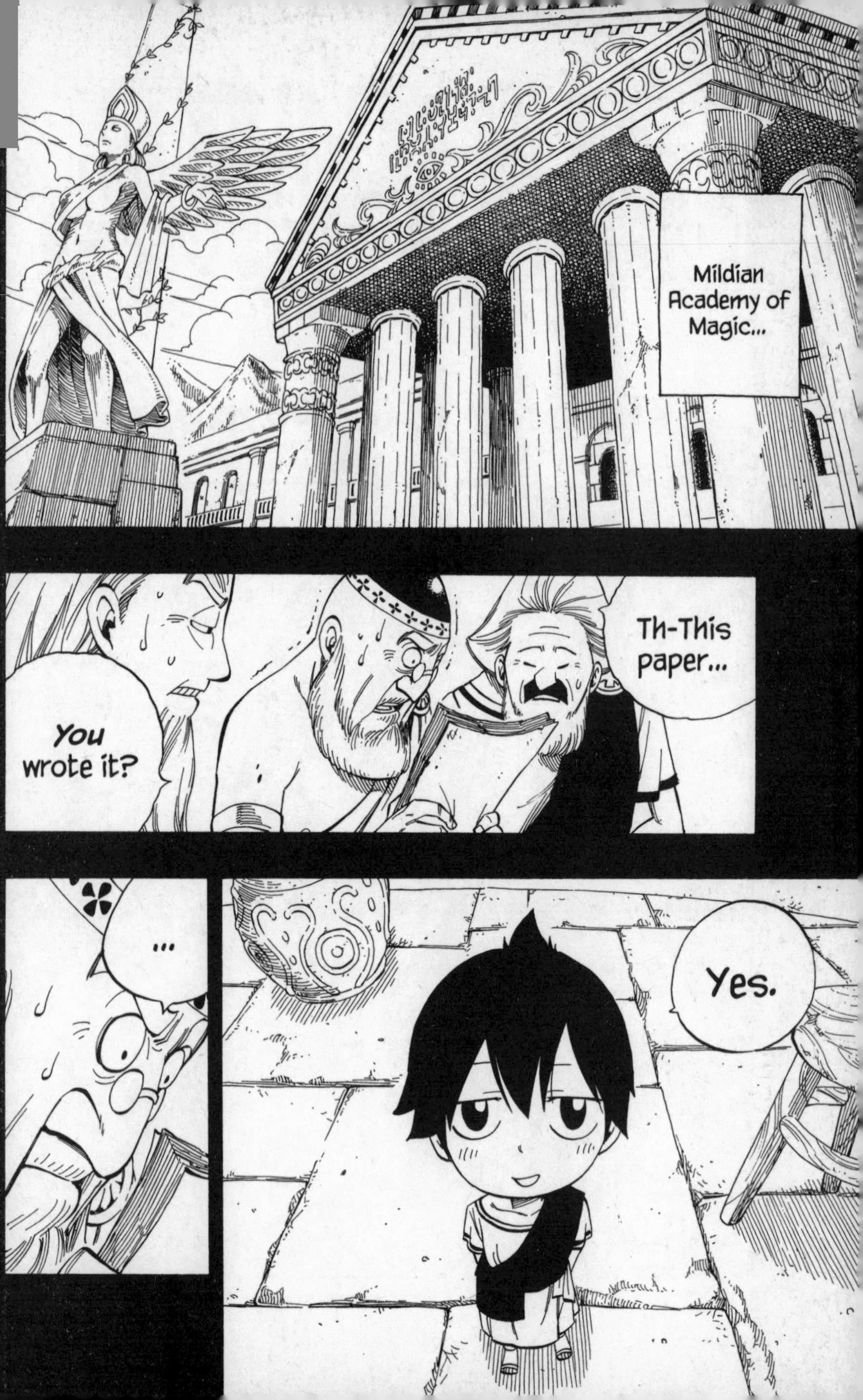
Mildian Academy of Magic...
Th-This paper...
You wrote it?
Yes.
...

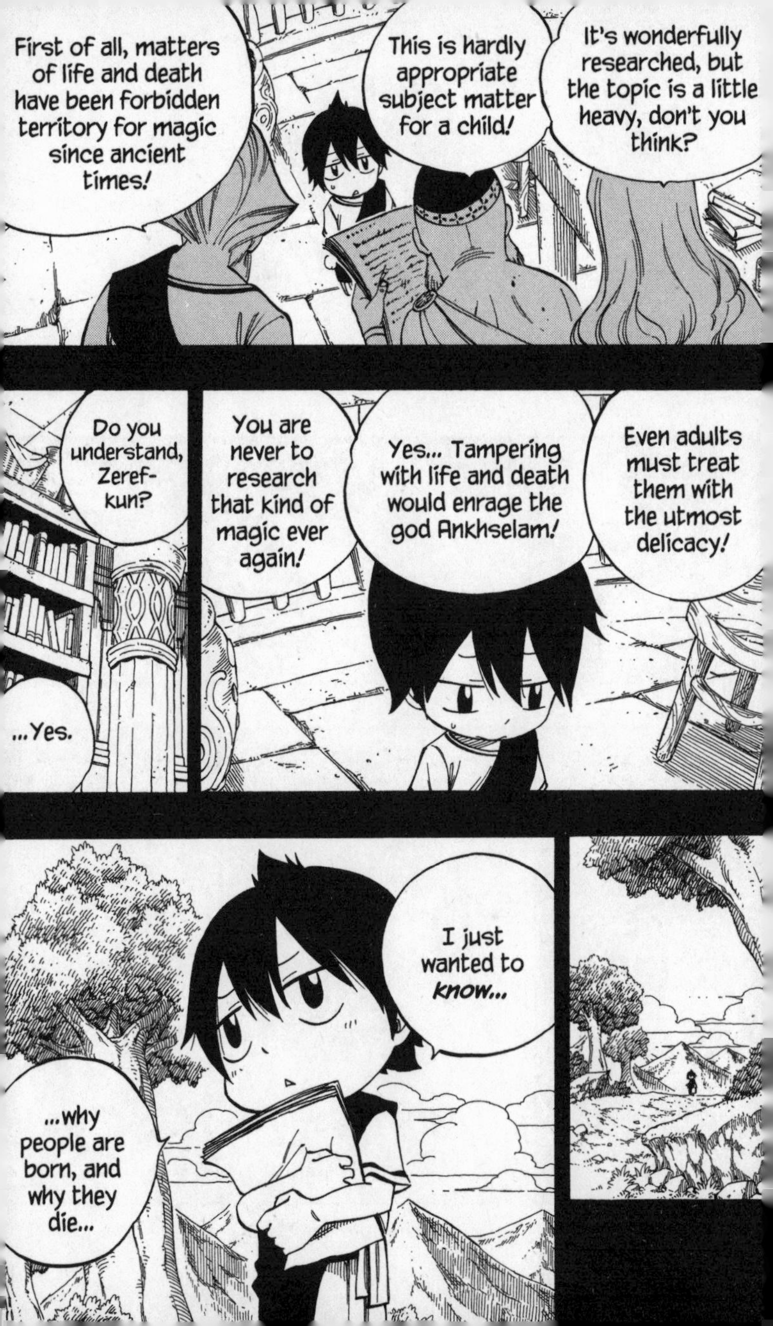
It's wonderfully researched, but the topic is a little heavy, don't you think?
This is hardly appropriate subject matter for a child!
First of all, matters of life and death have been forbidden territory for magic since ancient times!
Even adults must treat them with the utmost delicacy!
Yes... Tampering with life and death would enrage the god Ankhselam!
You are never to research that kind of magic ever again!
Do you understand, Zeref-kun?
...Yes.
I just wanted to *know*...
...why people are born, and why they die...

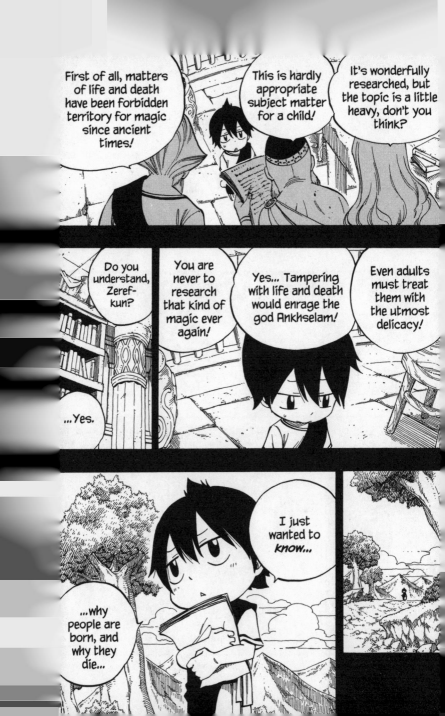

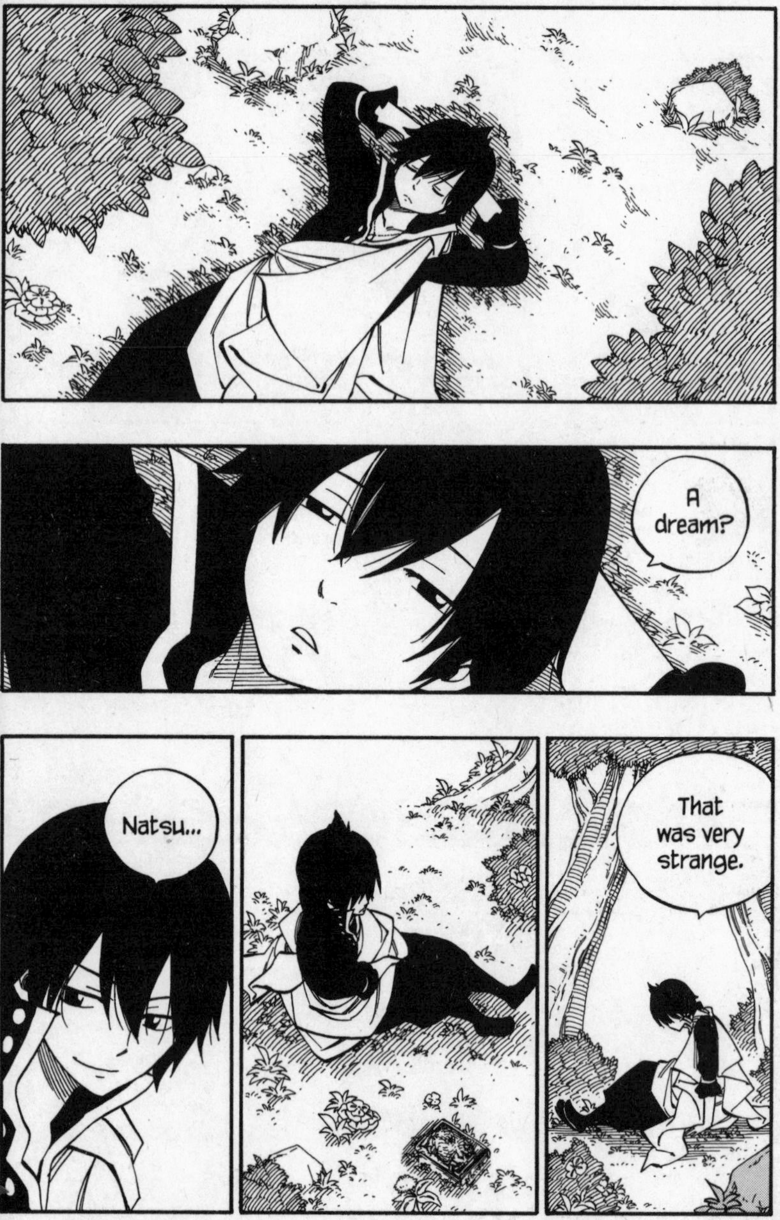
A dream?
That was very strange.
Natsu...

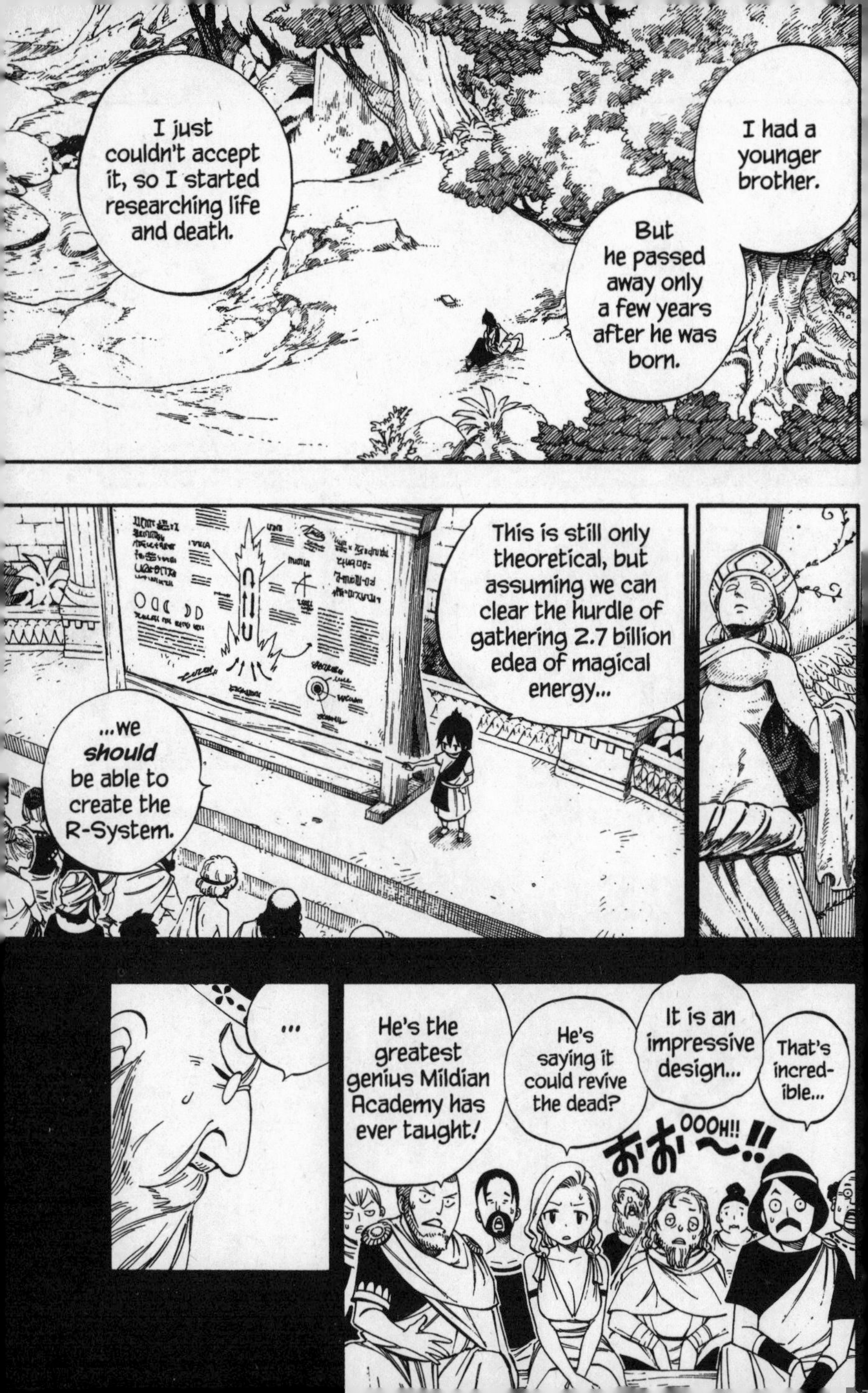
I had a younger brother.
But he passed away only a few years after he was born.
I just couldn't accept it, so I started researching life and death.
This is still only theoretical, but assuming we can clear the hurdle of gathering 2.7 billion edea of magical energy...
...we *should* be able to create the R-System.
That's incred-ible...
It is an impressive design...
おお〜!! OOOH!!
He's saying it could revive the dead?
He's the greatest genius Mildian Academy has ever taught!
...

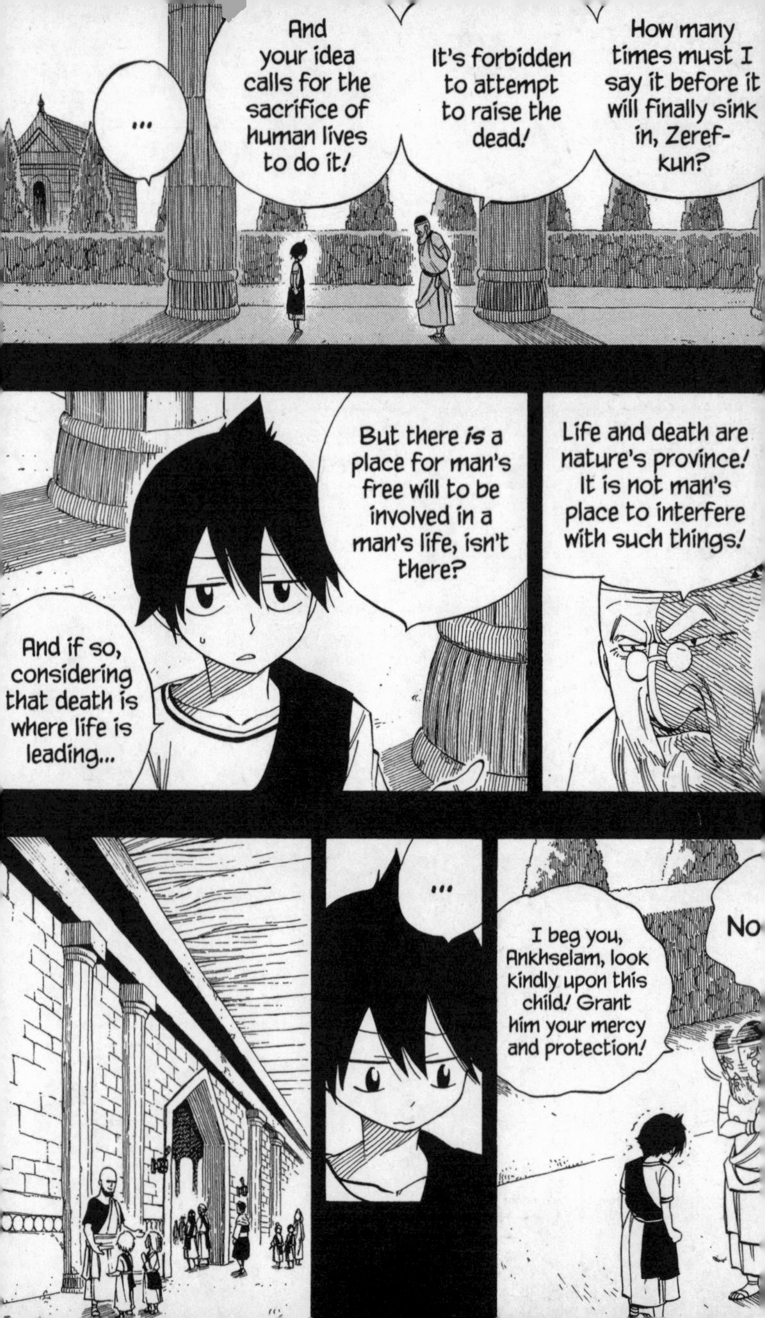
How many times must I say it before it will finally sink in, Zeref-kun?
It's forbidden to attempt to raise the dead!
And your idea calls for the sacrifice of human lives to do it!
...
Life and death are nature's province! It is not man's place to interfere with such things!
But there *is* a place for man's free will to be involved in a man's life, isn't there?
And if so, considering that death is where life is leading...
No
I beg you, Ankhselam, look kindly upon this child! Grant him your mercy and protection!
...

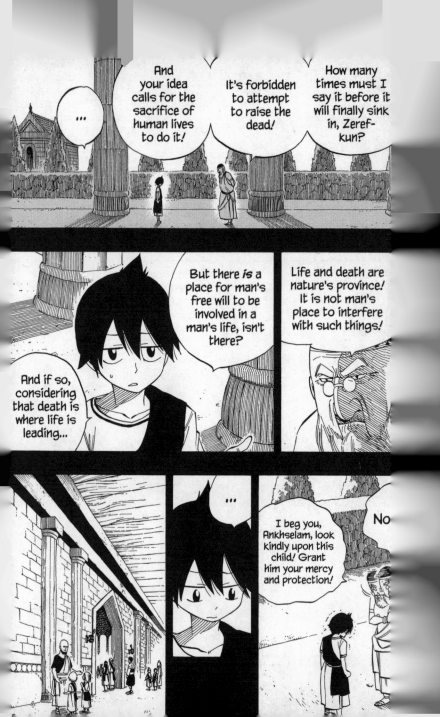

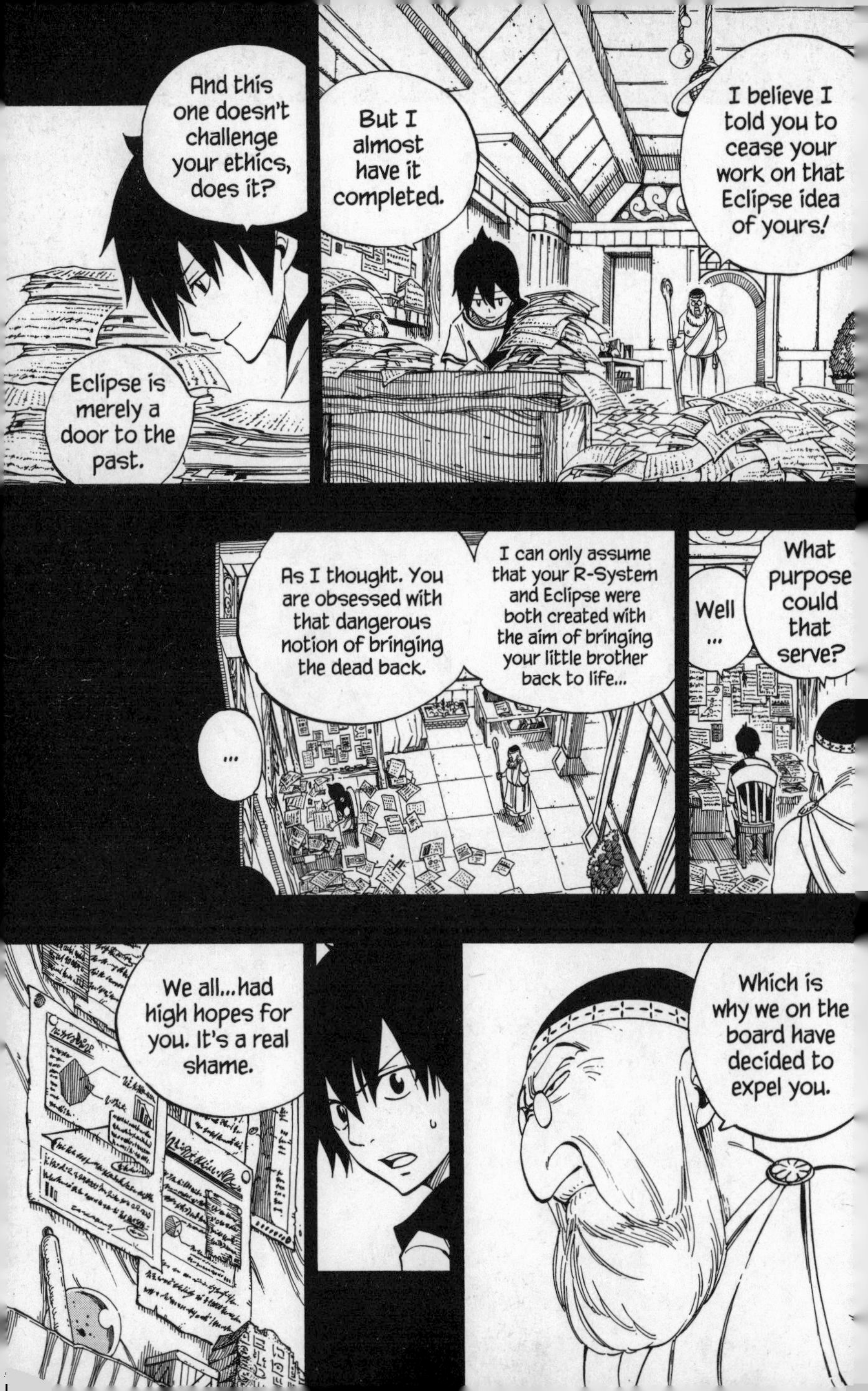
I believe I told you to cease your work on that Eclipse idea of yours!
But I almost have it completed.
And this one doesn't challenge your ethics, does it?
Eclipse is merely a door to the past.
What purpose could that serve?
Well ...
I can only assume that your R-System and Eclipse were both created with the aim of bringing your little brother back to life...
As I thought. You are obsessed with that dangerous notion of bringing the dead back.
...
Which is why we on the board have decided to expel you.
We all...had high hopes for you. It's a real shame.

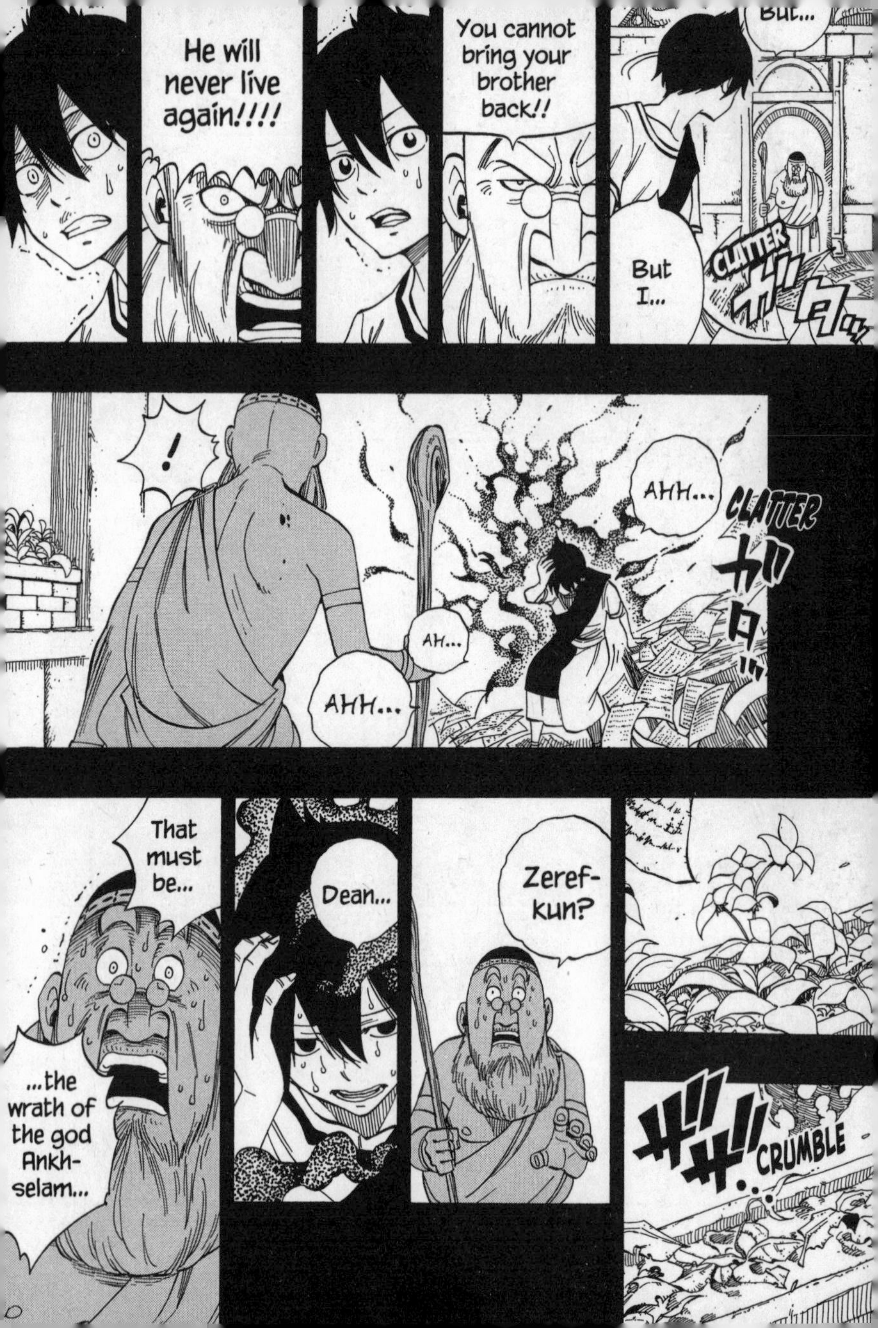
But...
But I...
CLATTER
You cannot bring your brother back!!
He will never live again!!!!
CLATTER
AHH...
!
AH...
AHH...
CRUMBLE
Zeref-kun?
Dean...
That must be...
...the wrath of the god Ankh-selam...

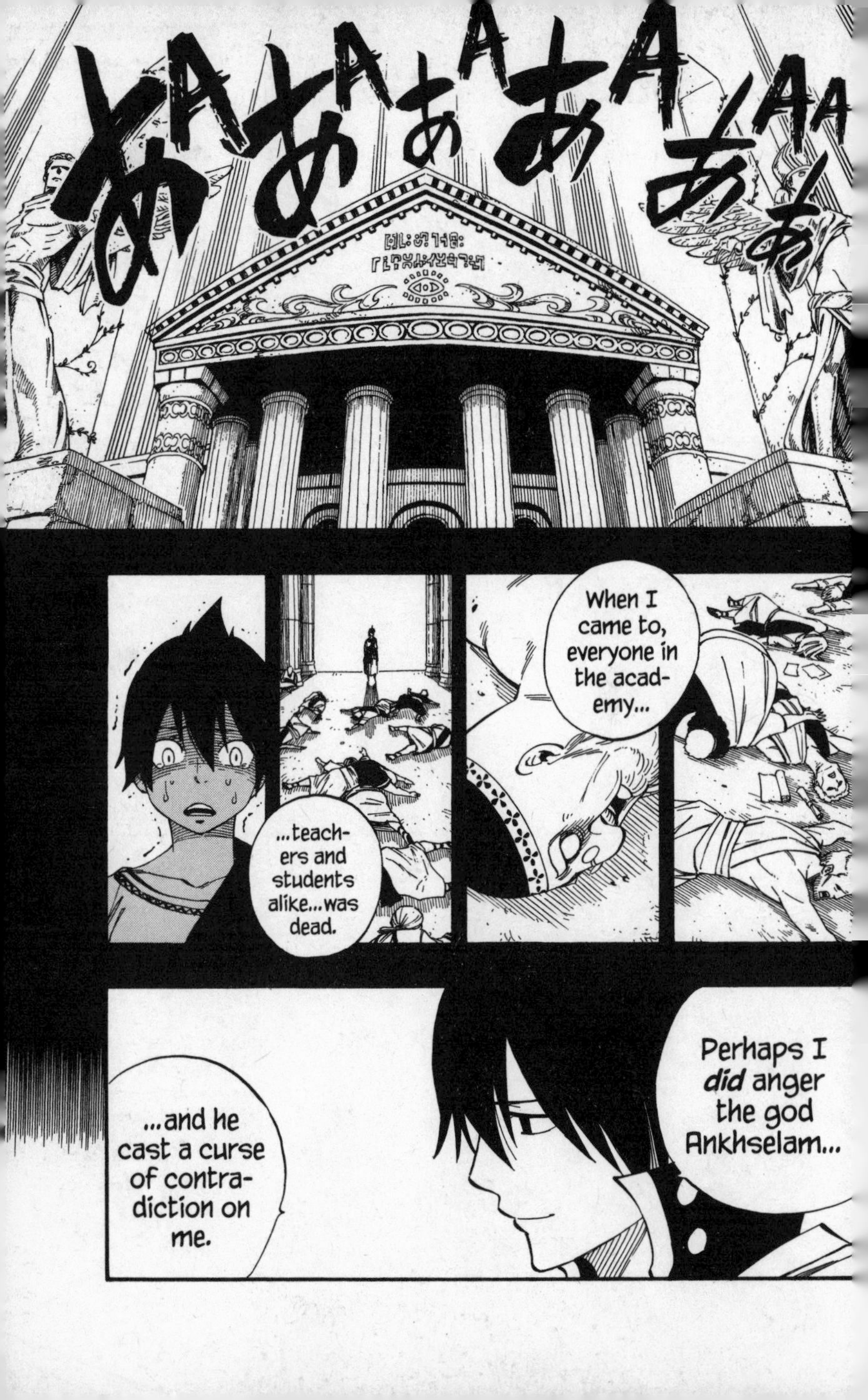
When I came to, everyone in the academy...
...teachers and students alike...was dead.
Perhaps I *did* anger the god Ankhselam...
...and he cast a curse of contradiction on me.

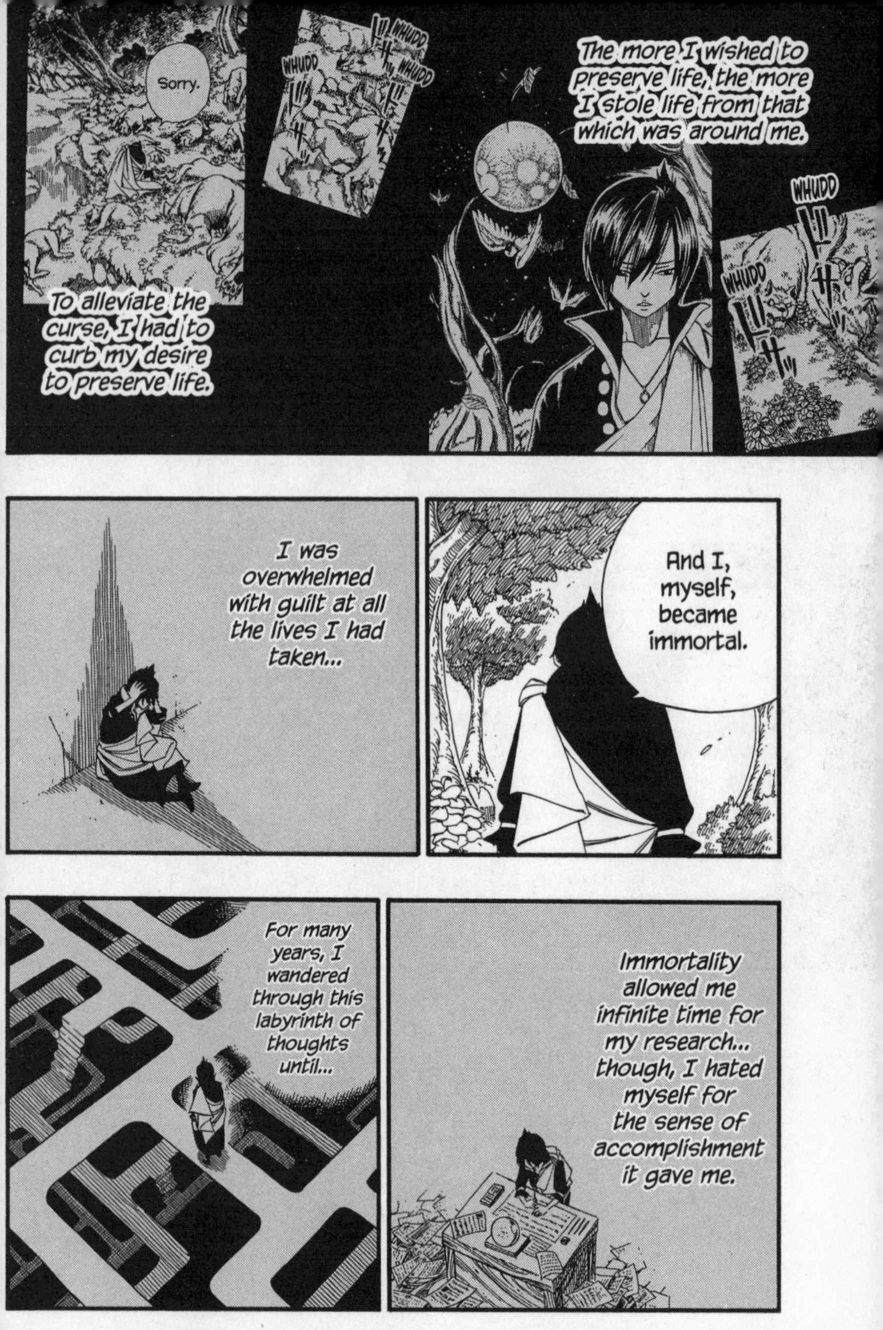
The more I wished to preserve life, the more I stole life from that which was around me.
WHUDD
WHUDD
WHUDD
WHUDD
WHUDD
Sorry.
To alleviate the curse, I had to curb my desire to preserve life.
And I, myself, became immortal.
I was overwhelmed with guilt at all the lives I had taken...
Immortality allowed me infinite time for my research... though, I hated myself for the sense of accomplishment it gave me.
For many years, I wandered through this labyrinth of thoughts until...

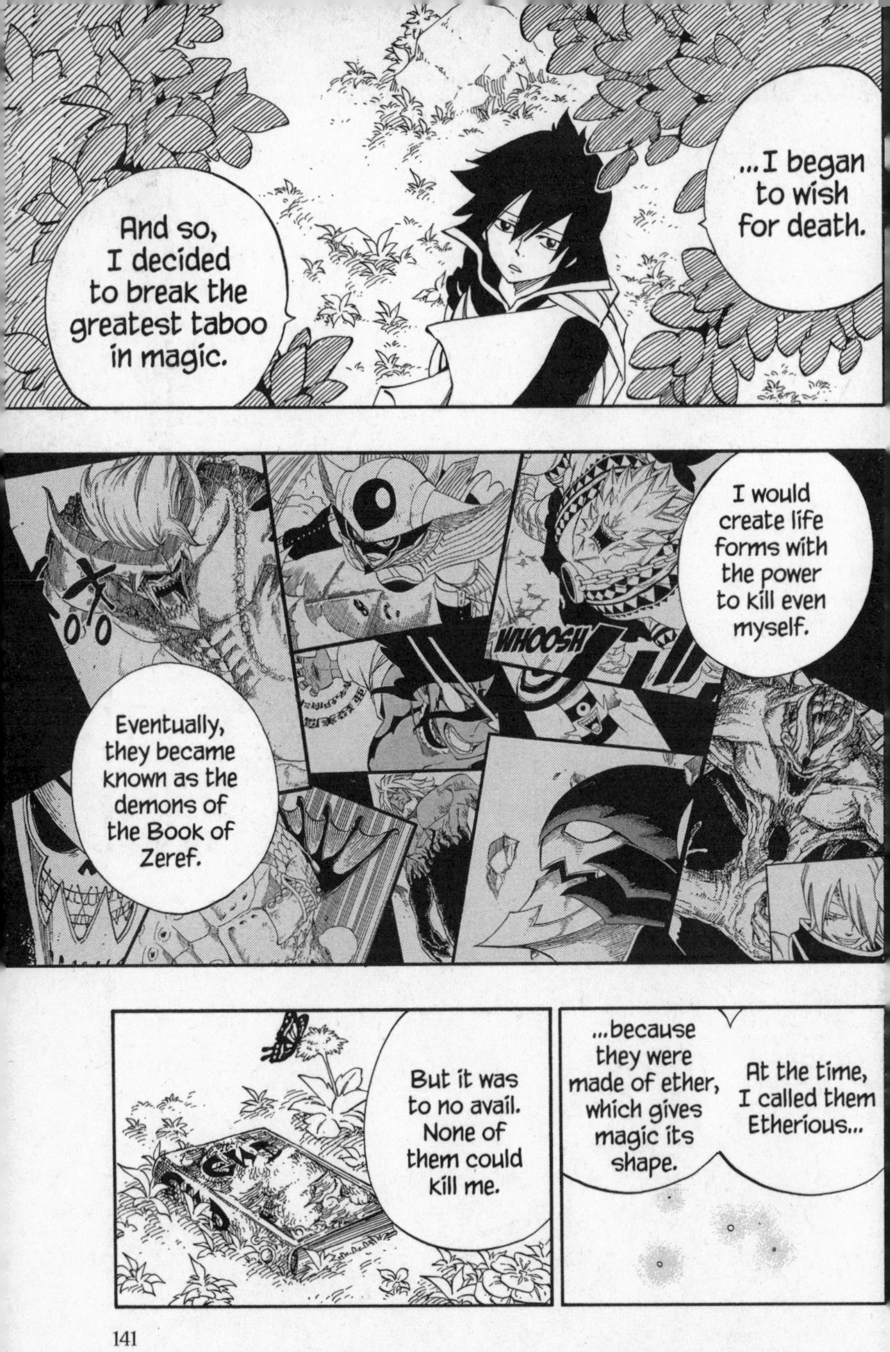
...I began to wish for death.
And so, I decided to break the greatest taboo in magic.
I would create life forms with the power to kill even myself.
WHOOSH
Eventually, they became known as the demons of the Book of Zeref.
At the time, I called them Etherious...
...because they were made of ether, which gives magic its shape.
But it was to no avail. None of them could kill me.

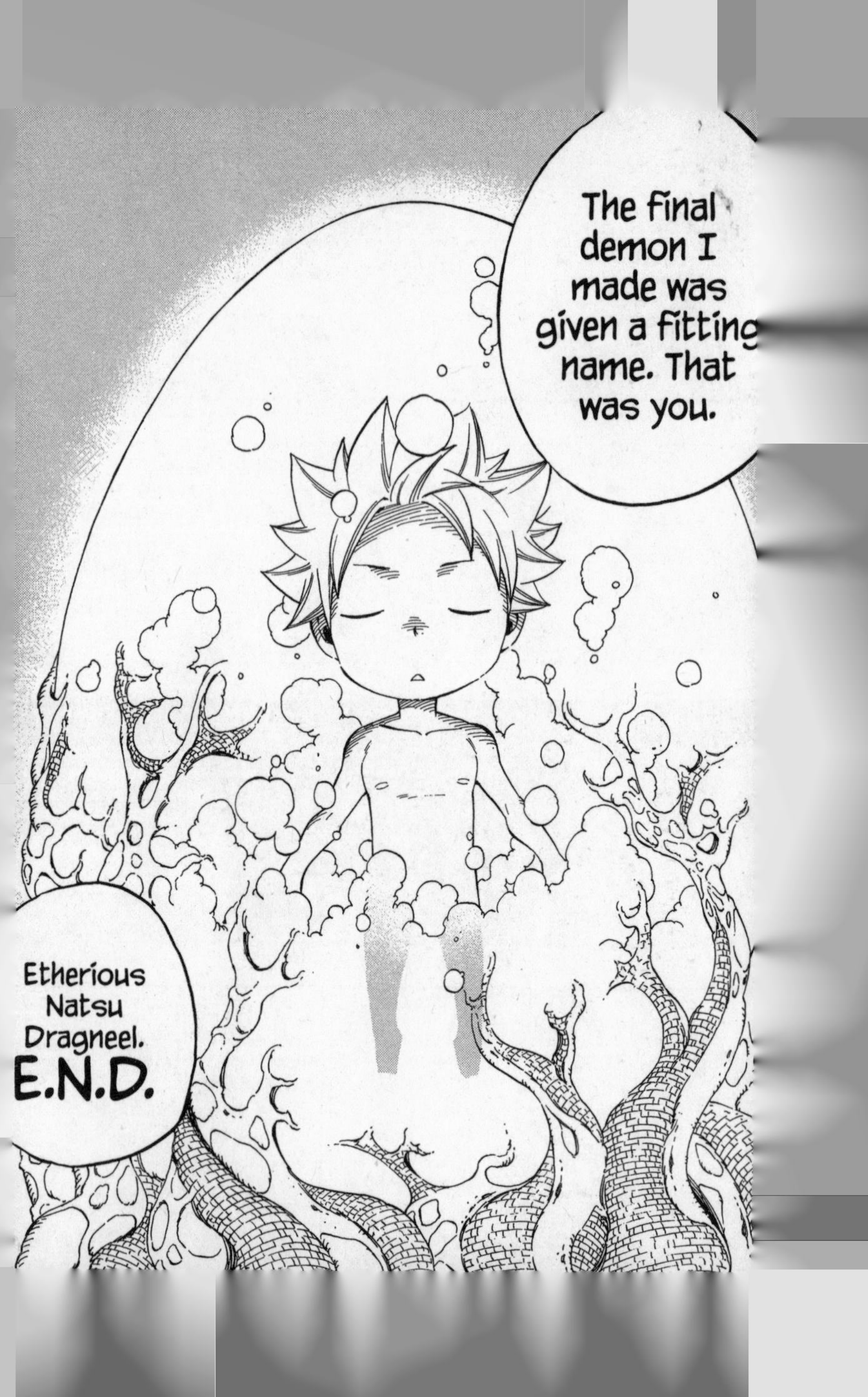
The final demon I made was given a fitting name. That was you.
Etherious Natsu Dragneel. E.N.D.

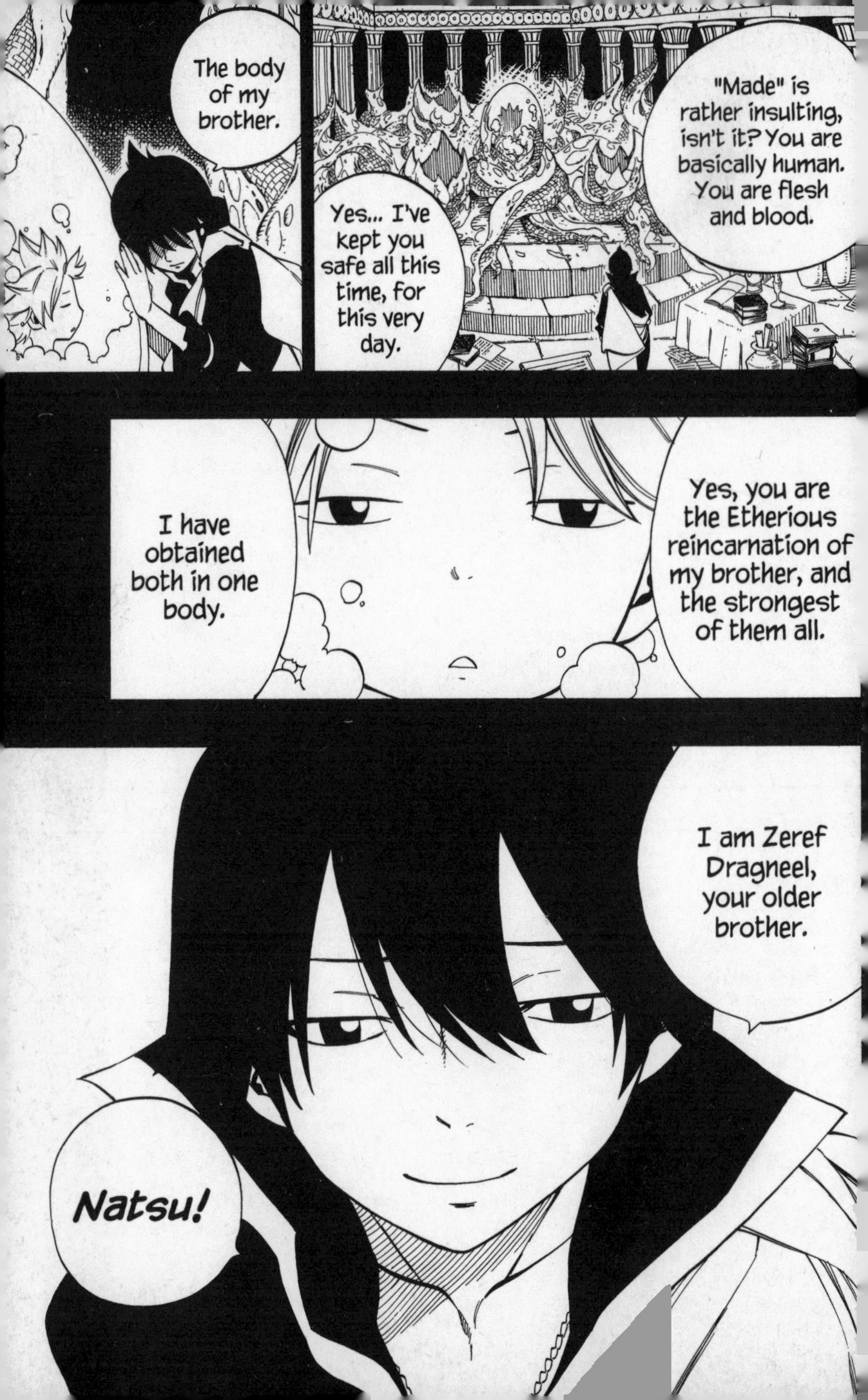
"Made" is rather insulting, isn't it? You are basically human. You are flesh and blood.
Yes... I've kept you safe all this time, for this very day.
The body of my brother.
Yes, you are the Etherious reincarnation of my brother, and the strongest of them all.
I have obtained both in one body.
I am Zeref Dragneel, your older brother.
Natsu!

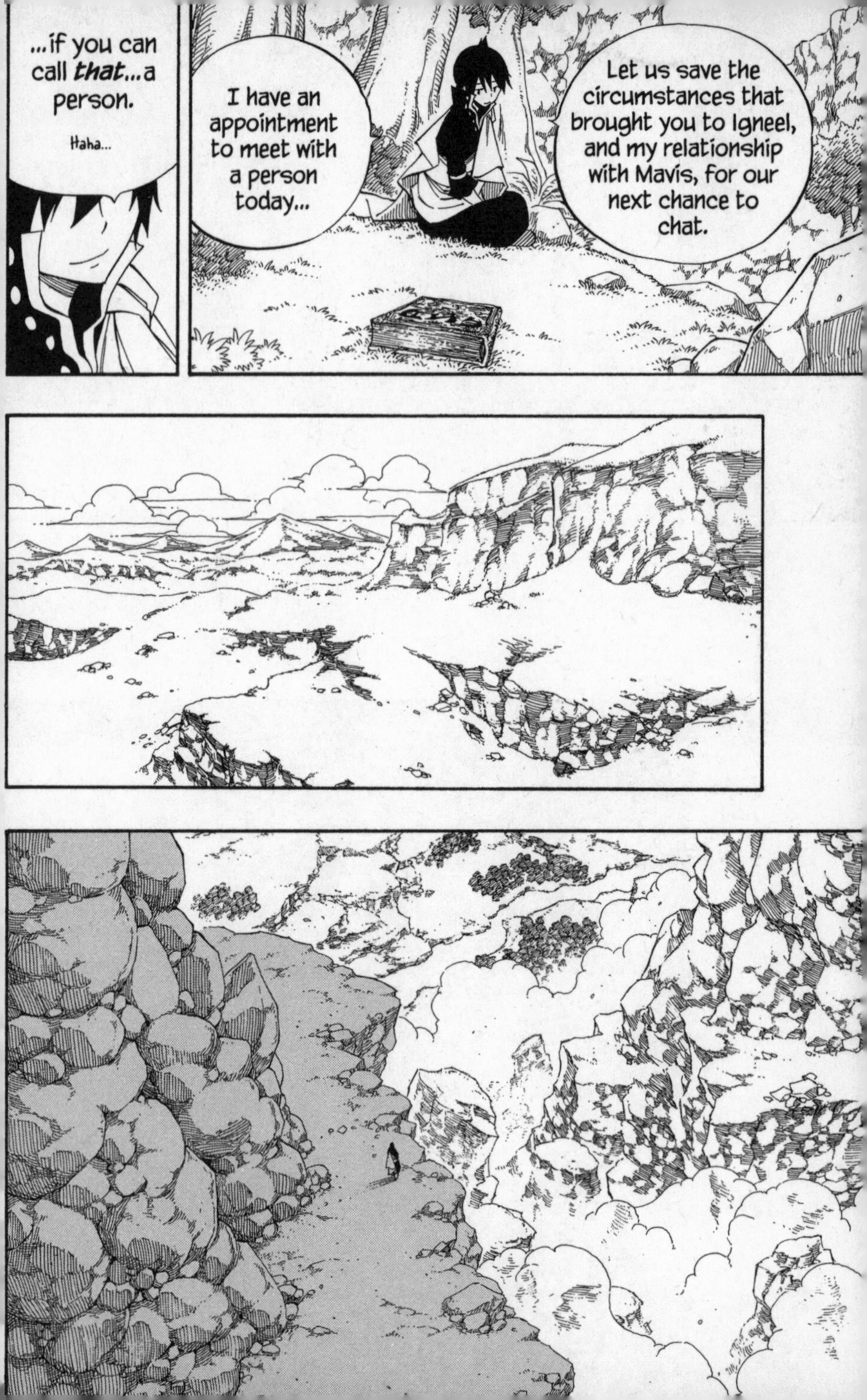
Let us save the circumstances that brought you to Igneel, and my relationship with Mavis, for our next chance to chat.
I have an appointment to meet with a person today...
...if you can call *that*...a person.
Haha...

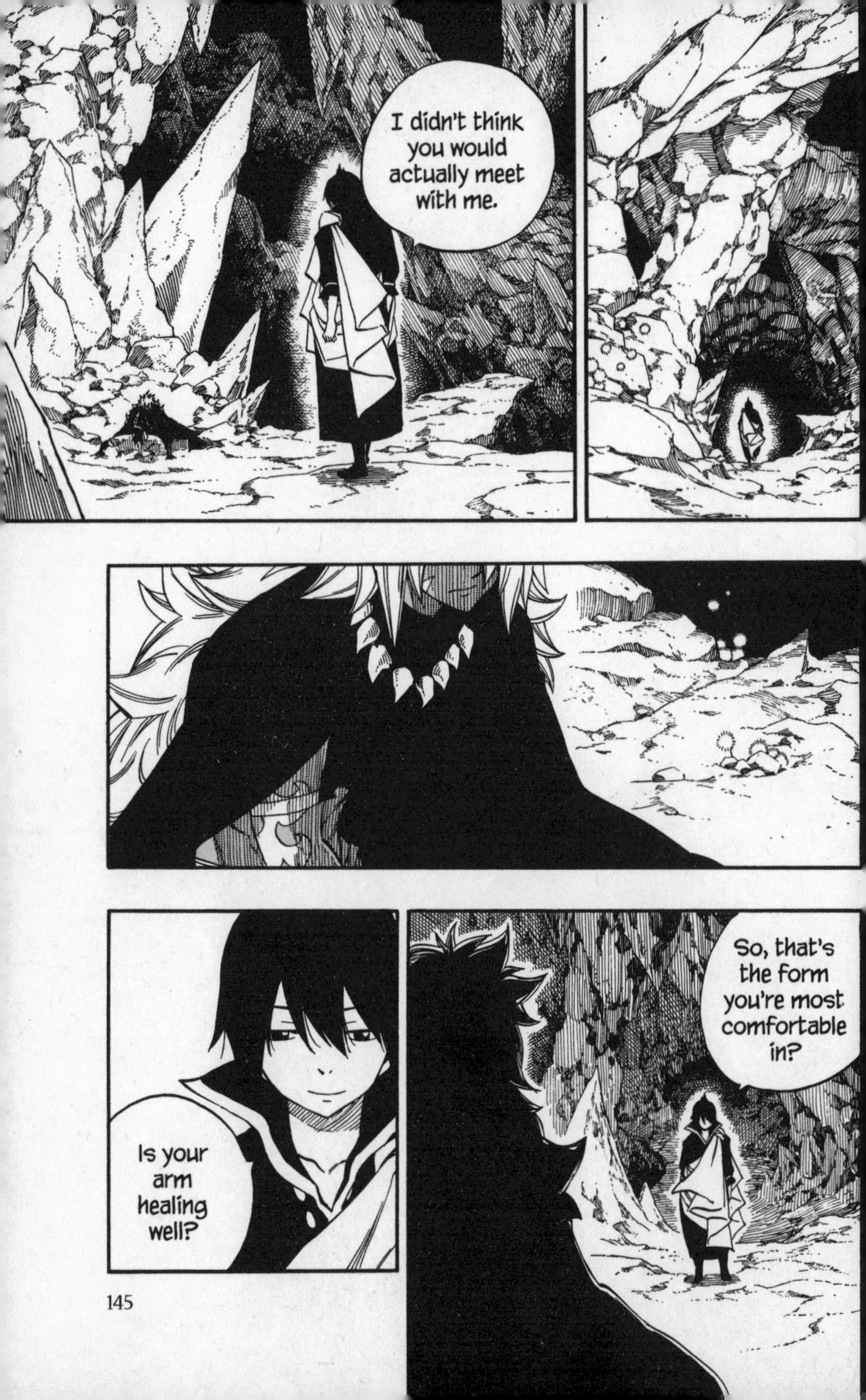
I didn't think you would actually meet with me.
So, that's the form you're most comfortable in?
Is your arm healing well?

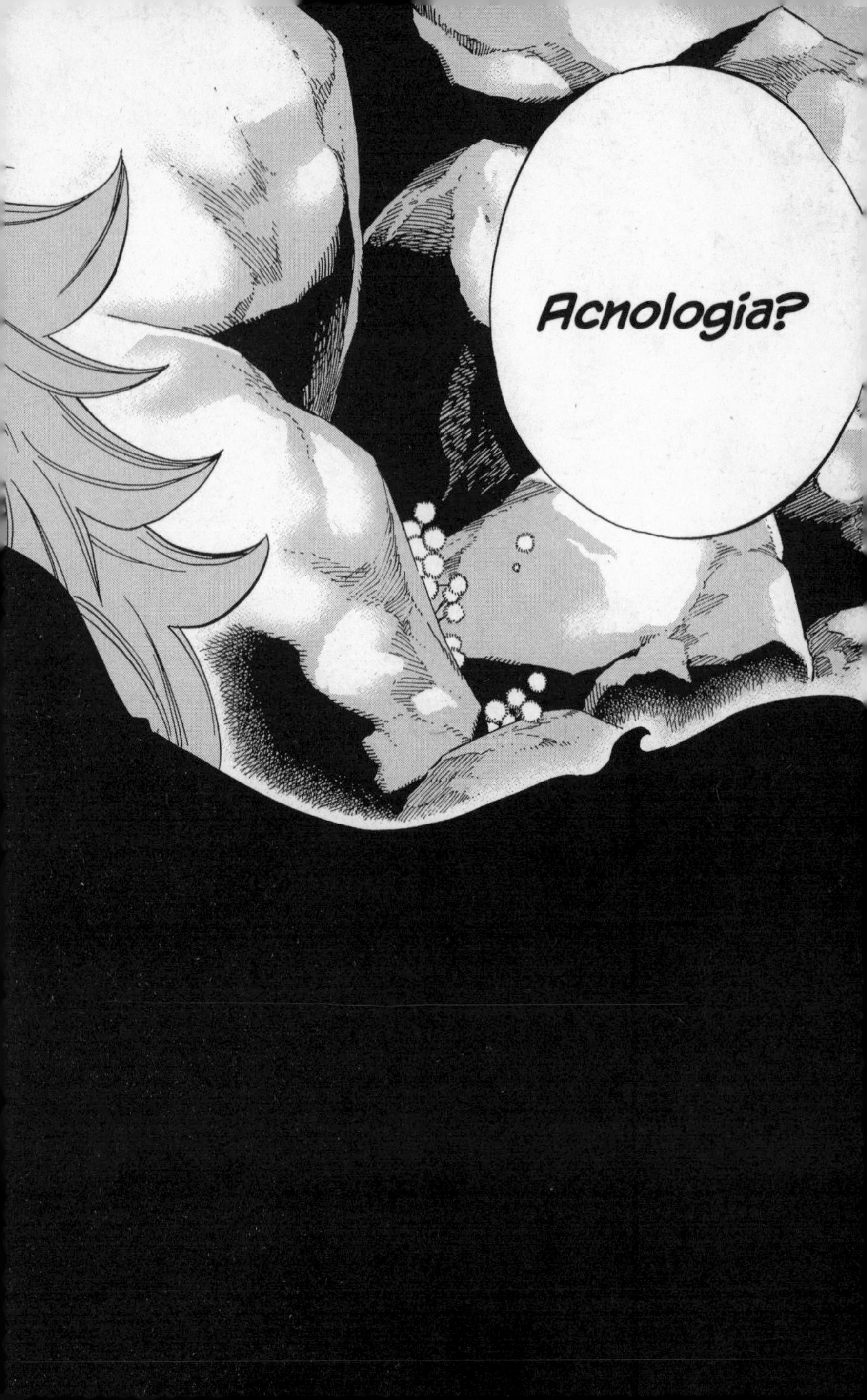
Acnologia?

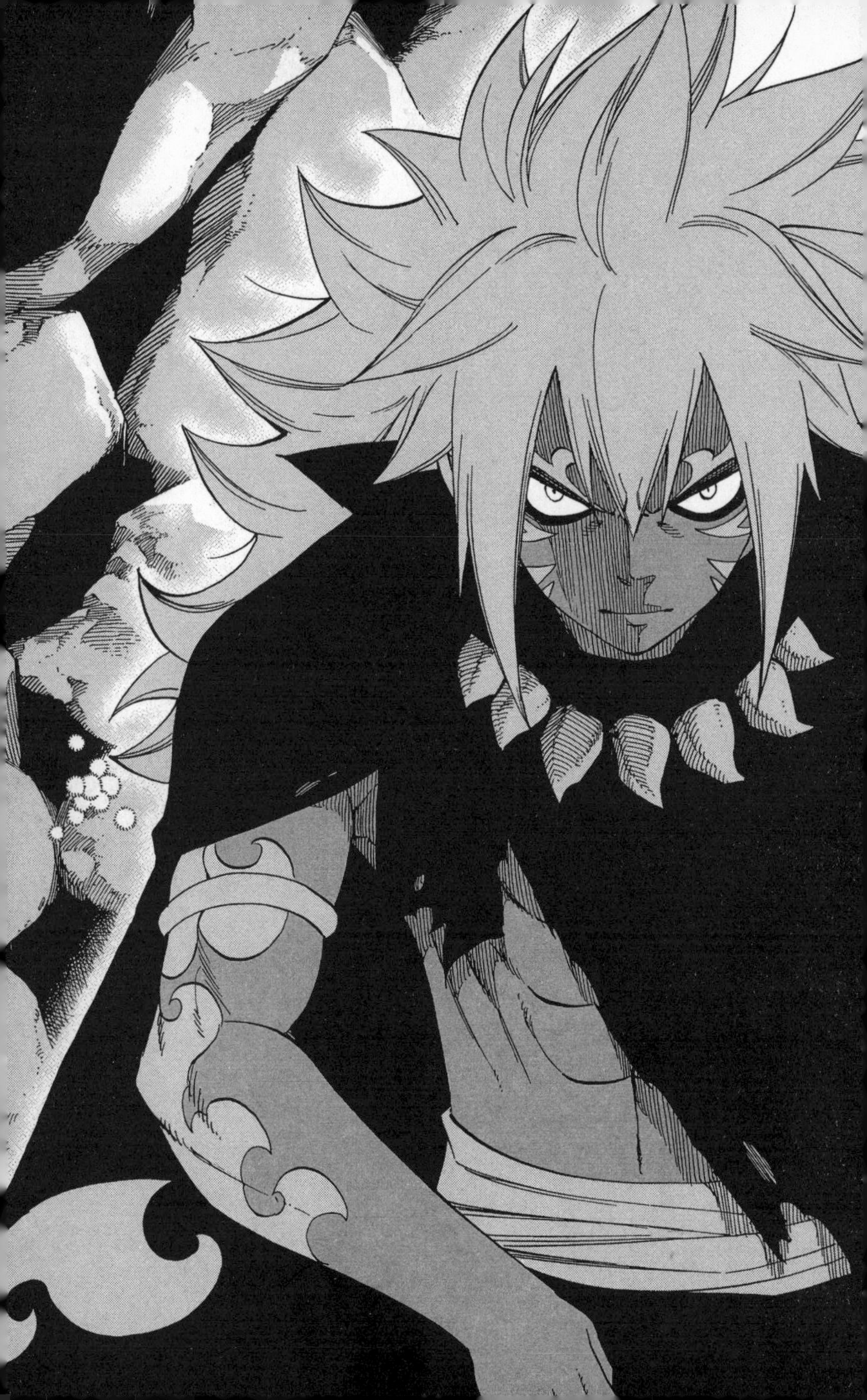

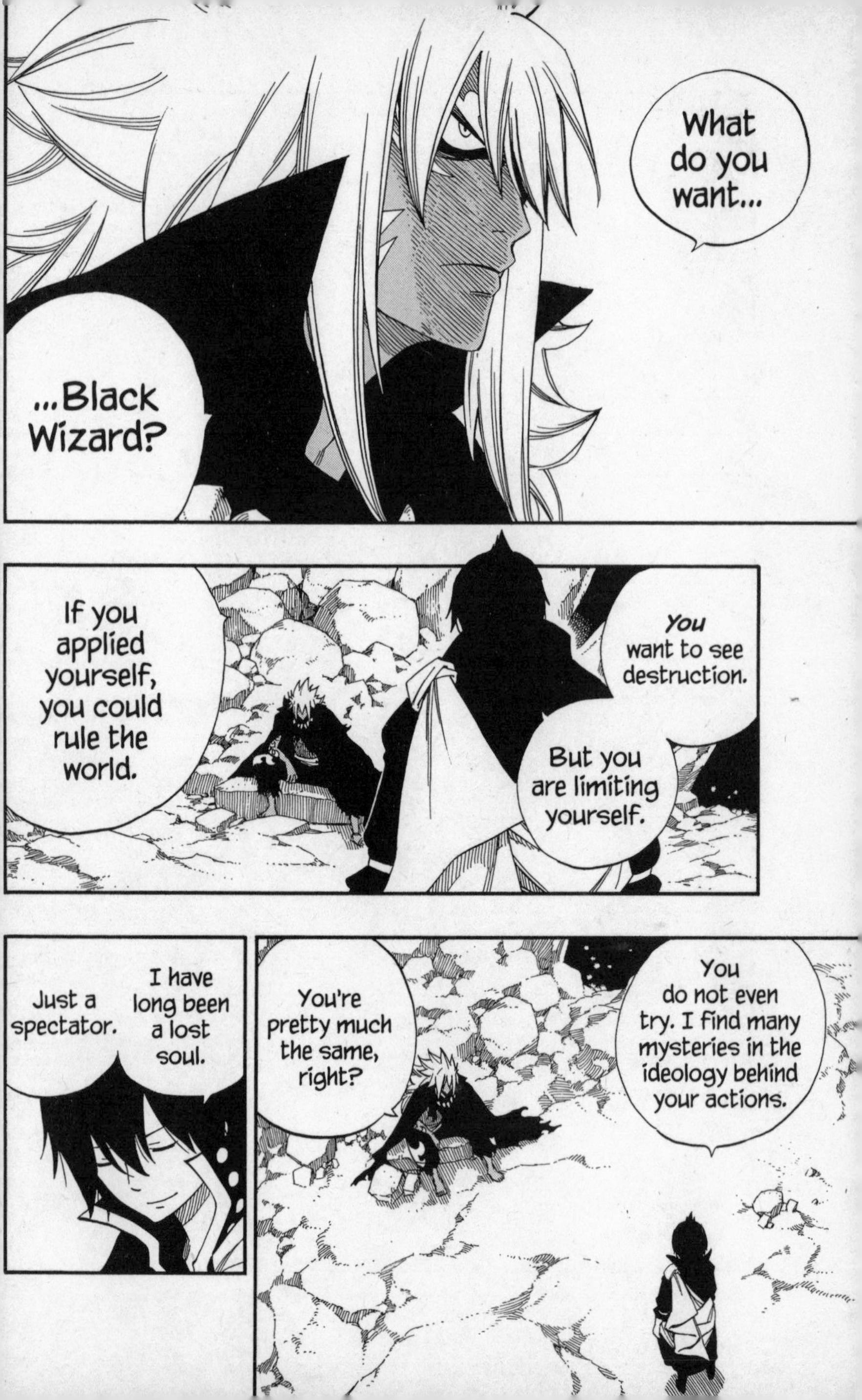
What do you want...
...Black Wizard?
You want to see destruction.
But you are limiting yourself.
If you applied yourself, you could rule the world.
You do not even try. I find many mysteries in the ideology behind your actions.
You're pretty much the same, right?
I have long been a lost soul.
Just a spectator.

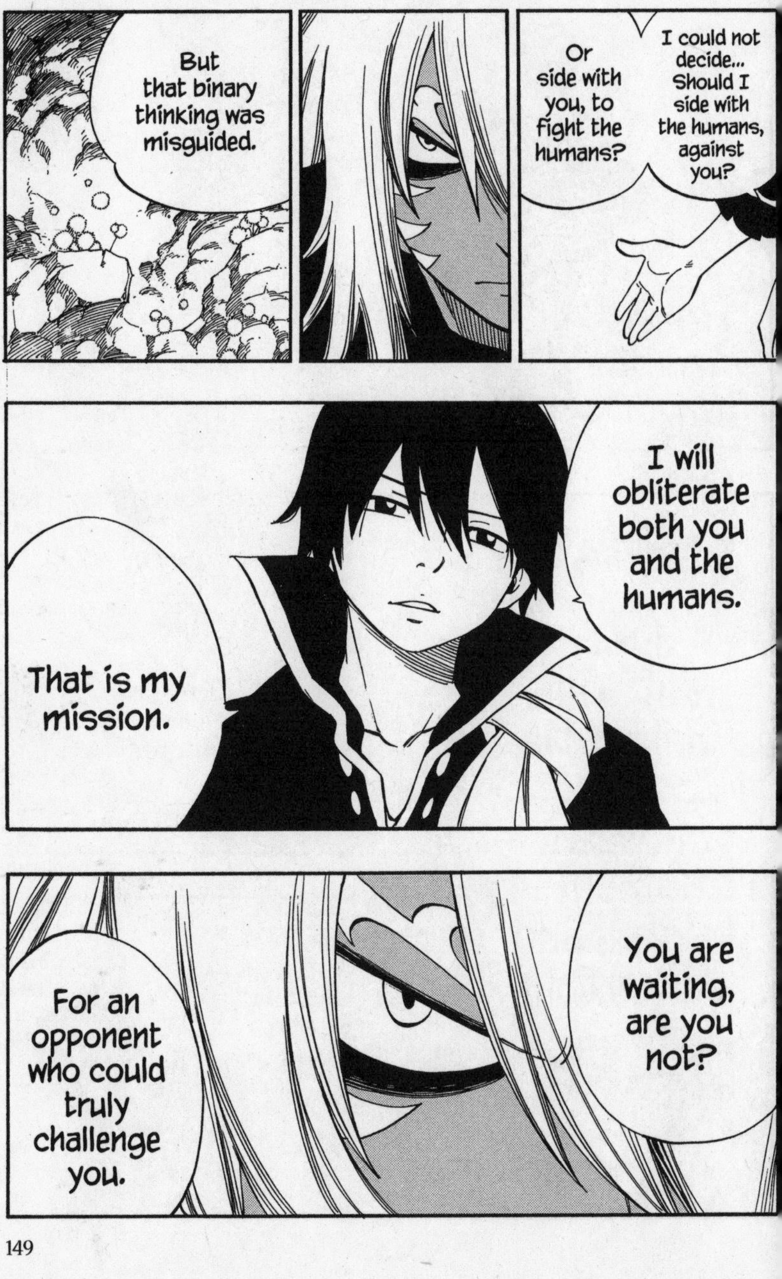
I could not decide... Should I side with the humans, against you?
Or side with you, to fight the humans?
But that binary thinking was misguided.
I will obliterate both you and the humans.
That is my mission.
You are waiting, are you not?
For an opponent who could truly challenge you.

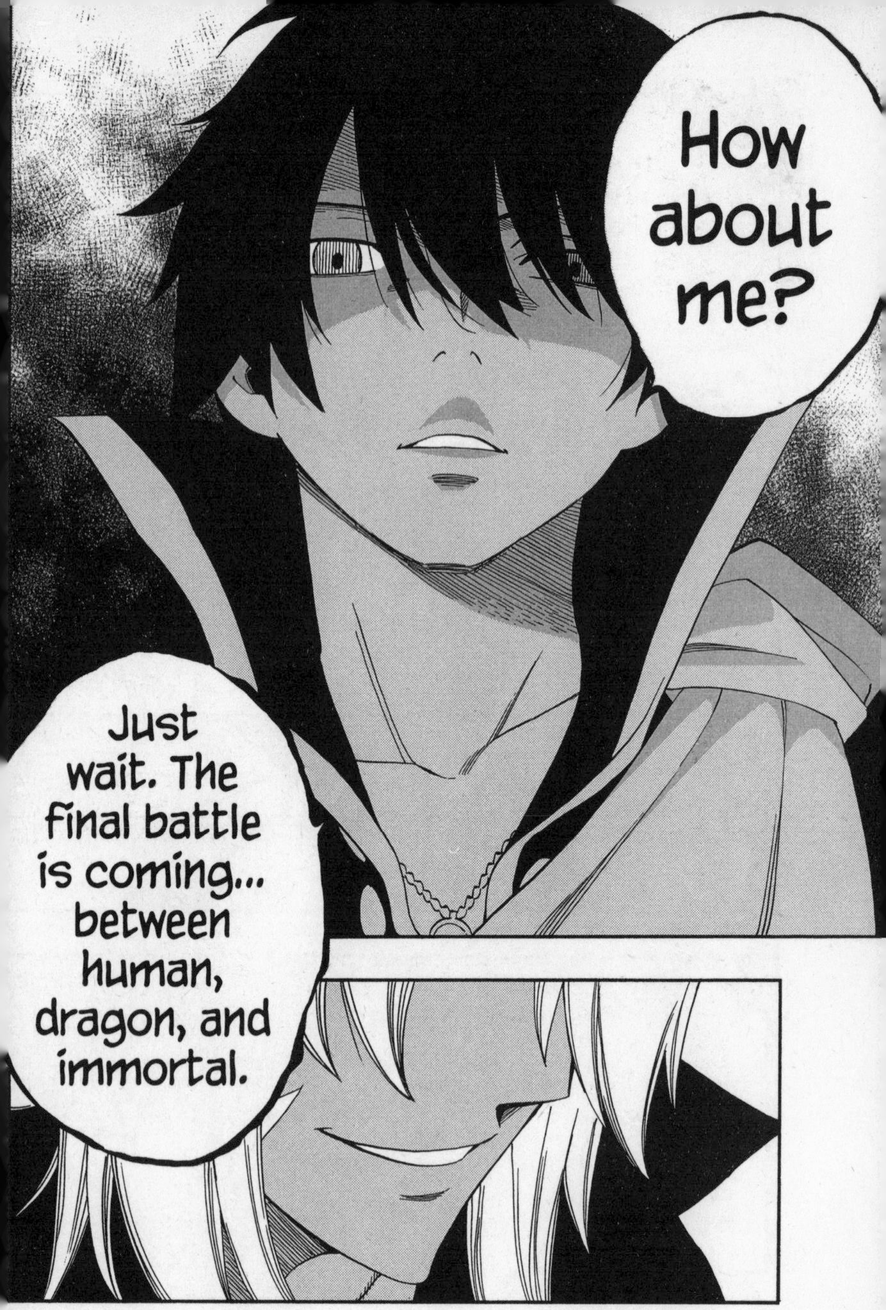
How about me?
Just wait. The final battle is coming... between human, dragon, and immortal.

FAIRY TAIL

フェアリーテイル

Chapter 437: Magnolia

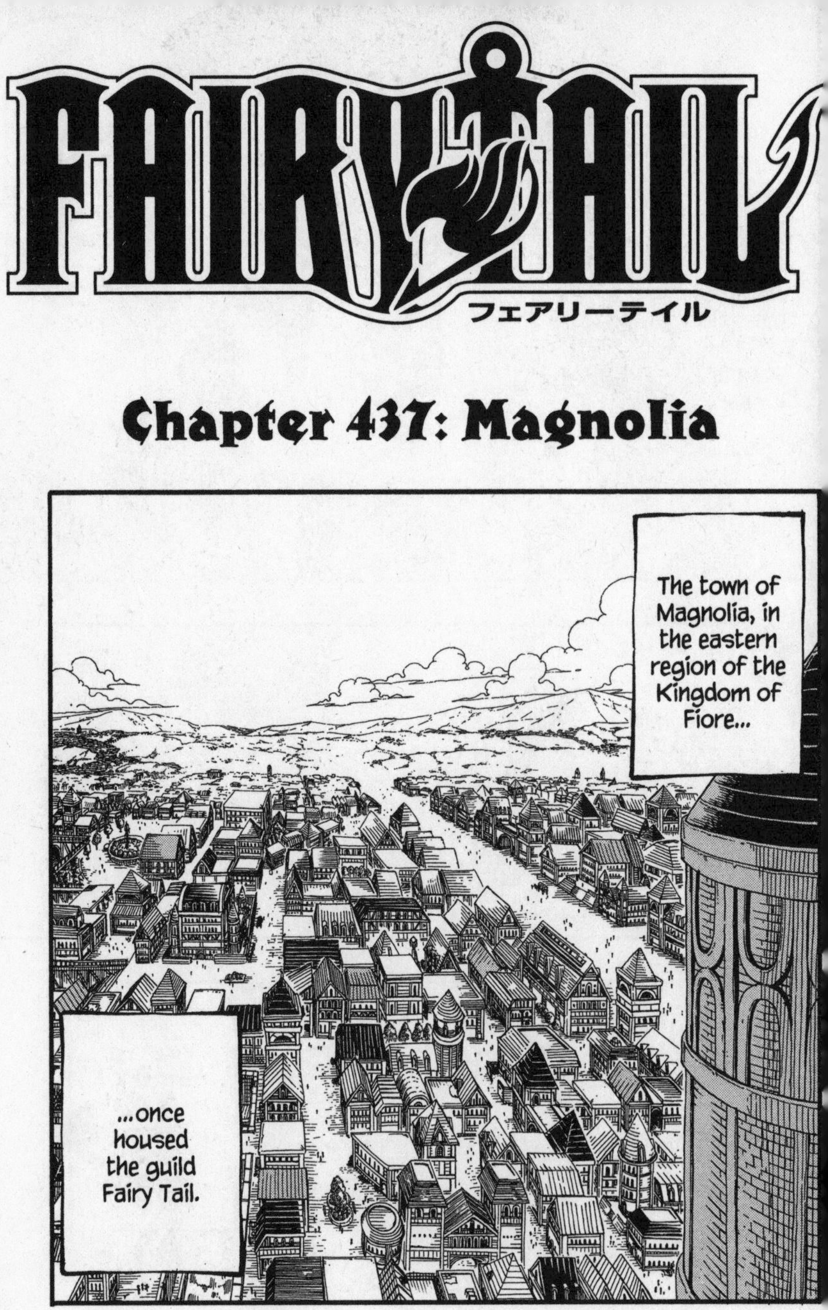
The town of Magnolia, in the eastern region of the Kingdom of Fiore...
...once housed the guild Fairy Tail.

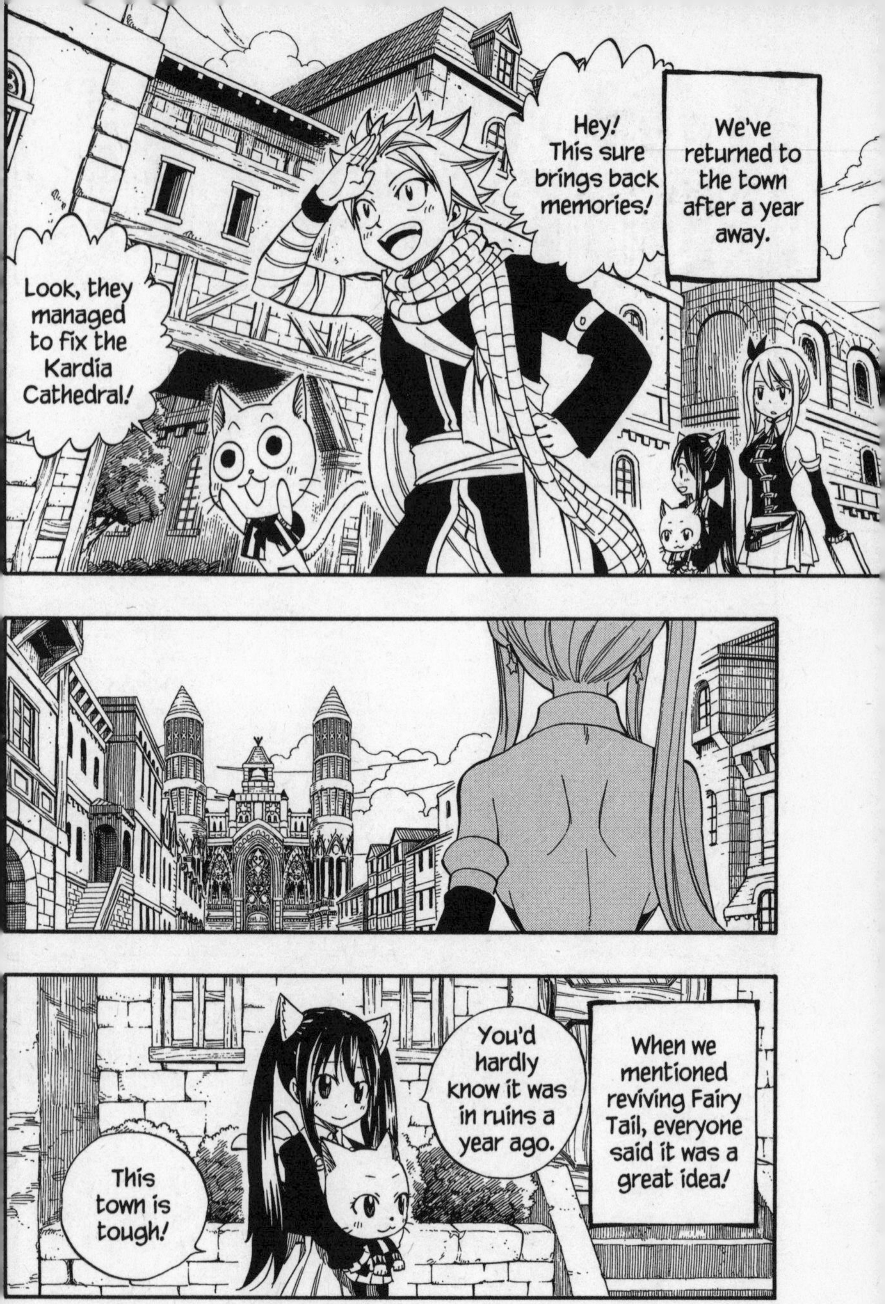
We've returned to the town after a year away.
Hey! This sure brings back memories!
Look, they managed to fix the Kardia Cathedral!
When we mentioned reviving Fairy Tail, everyone said it was a great idea!
You'd hardly know it was in ruins a year ago.
This town is tough!

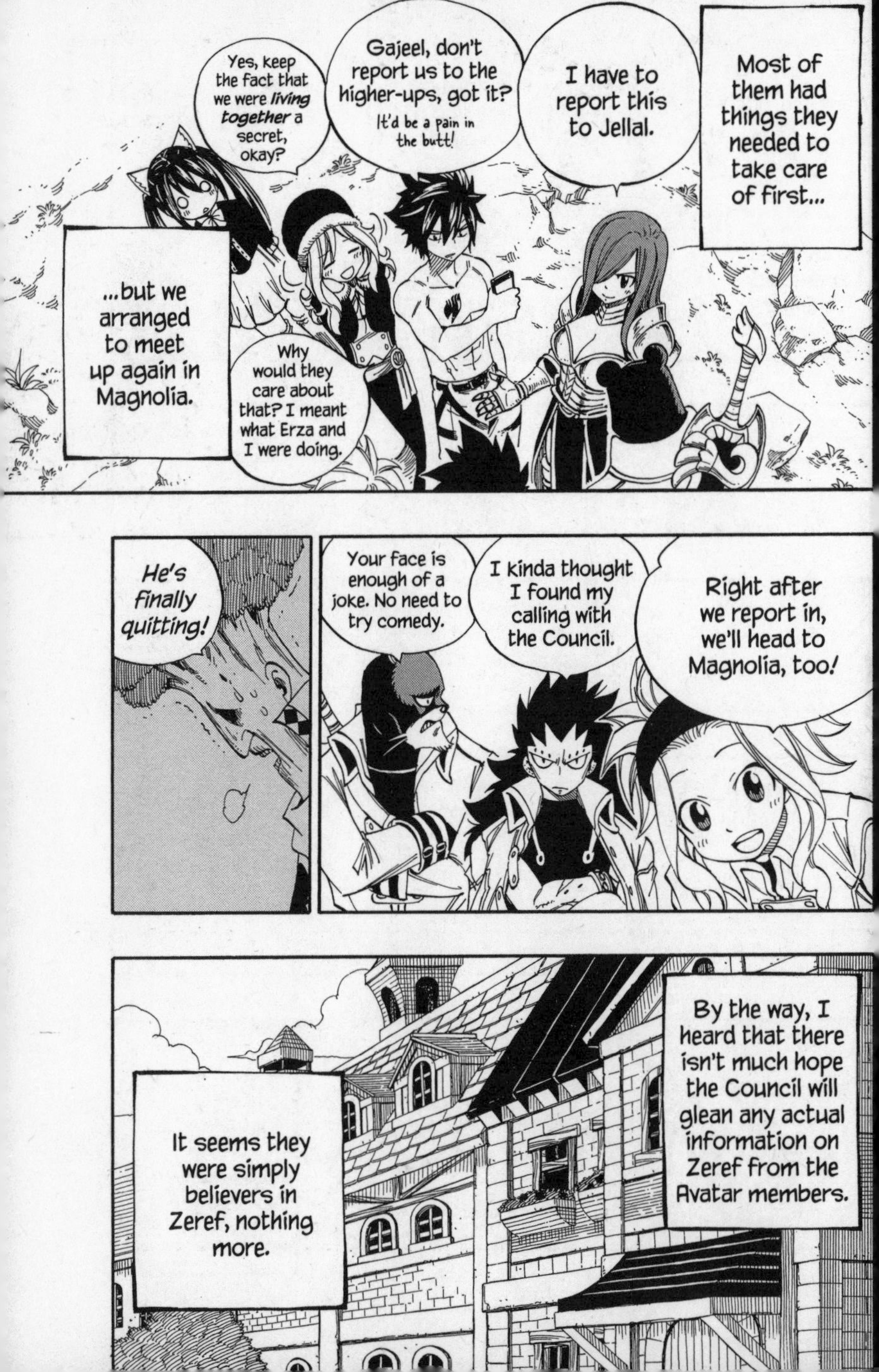
Most of them had things they needed to take care of first...
I have to report this to Jellal.
Gajeel, don't report us to the higher-ups, got it?
It'd be a pain in the butt!
Yes, keep the fact that we were *living together* a secret, okay?
...but we arranged to meet up again in Magnolia.
Why would they care about that? I meant what Erza and I were doing.
Right after we report in, we'll head to Magnolia, too!
I kinda thought I found my calling with the Council.
Your face is enough of a joke. No need to try comedy.
He's finally quitting!
By the way, I heard that there isn't much hope the Council will glean any actual information on Zeref from the Avatar members.
It seems they were simply believers in Zeref, nothing more.

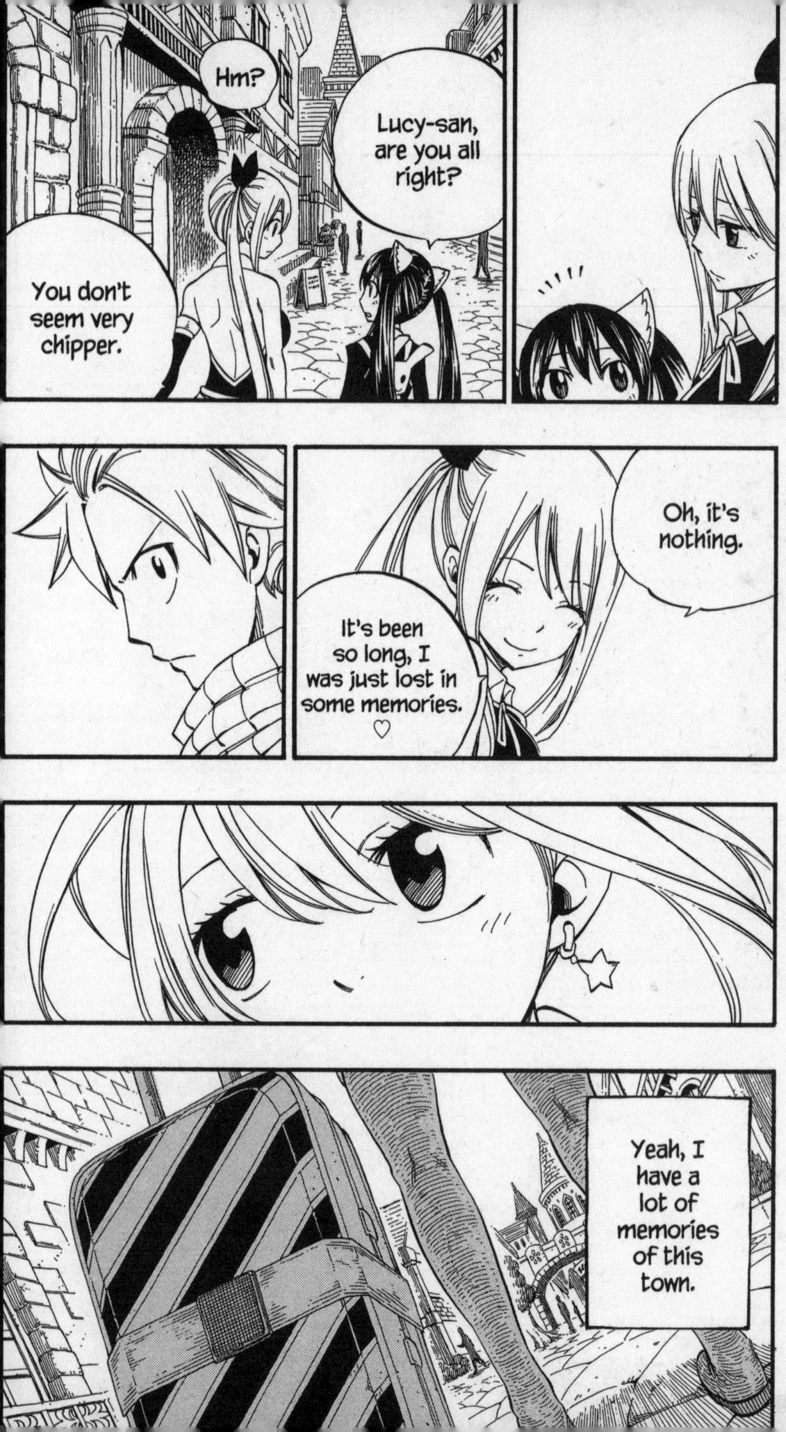
Lucy-san, are you all right?
Hm?
You don't seem very chipper.
Oh, it's nothing.
It's been so long, I was just lost in some memories. ♡
Yeah, I have a lot of memories of this town.

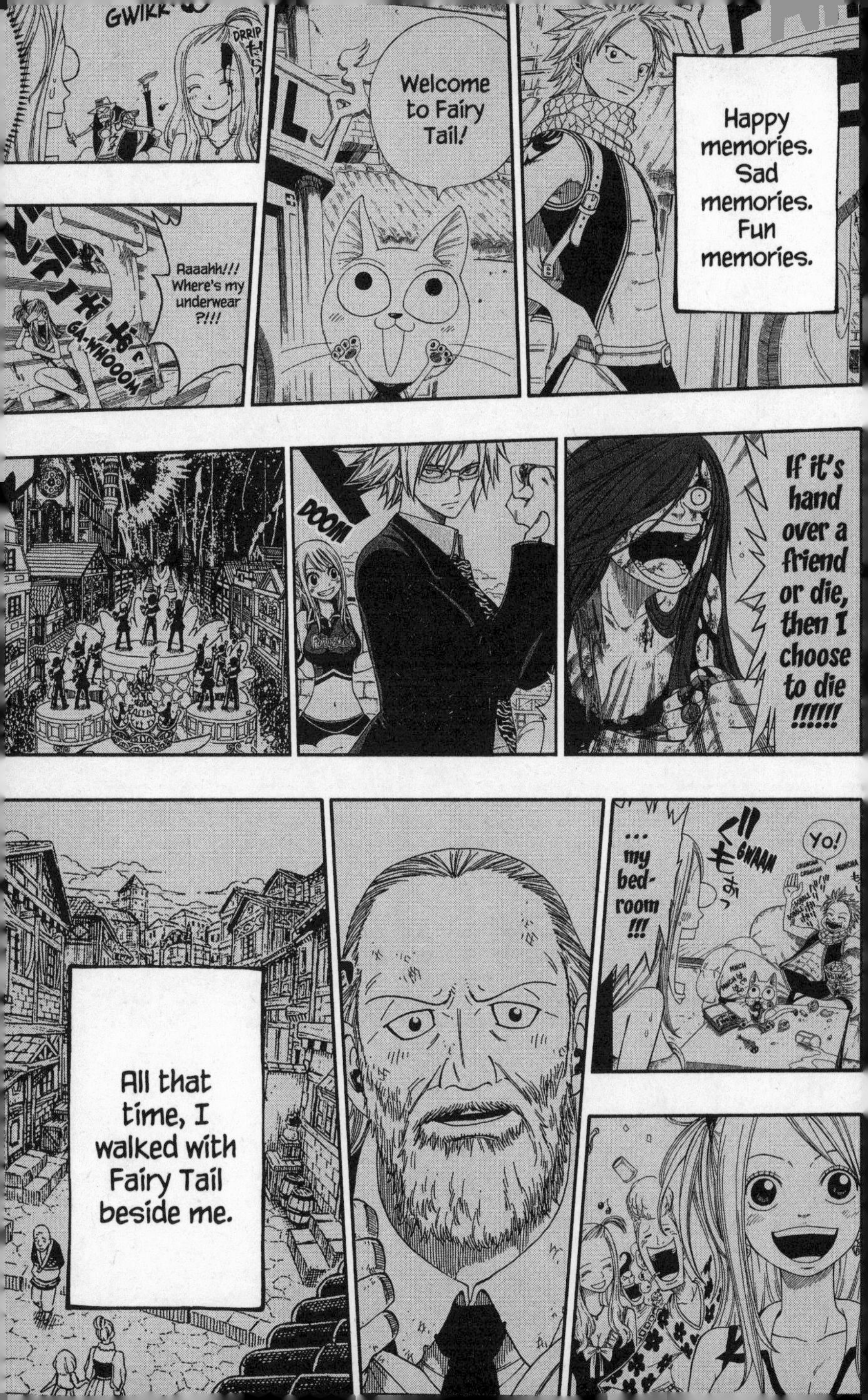
Happy memories. Sad memories. Fun memories.
Welcome to Fairy Tail!
GWIKK
DRRIP
Raaahh!!! Where's my underwear?!!!
GA-WHOOOM
If it's hand over a friend or die, then I choose to die!!!!!!
DOOM
...my bedroom!!!
GNAAN
Yo!
All that time, I walked with Fairy Tail beside me.

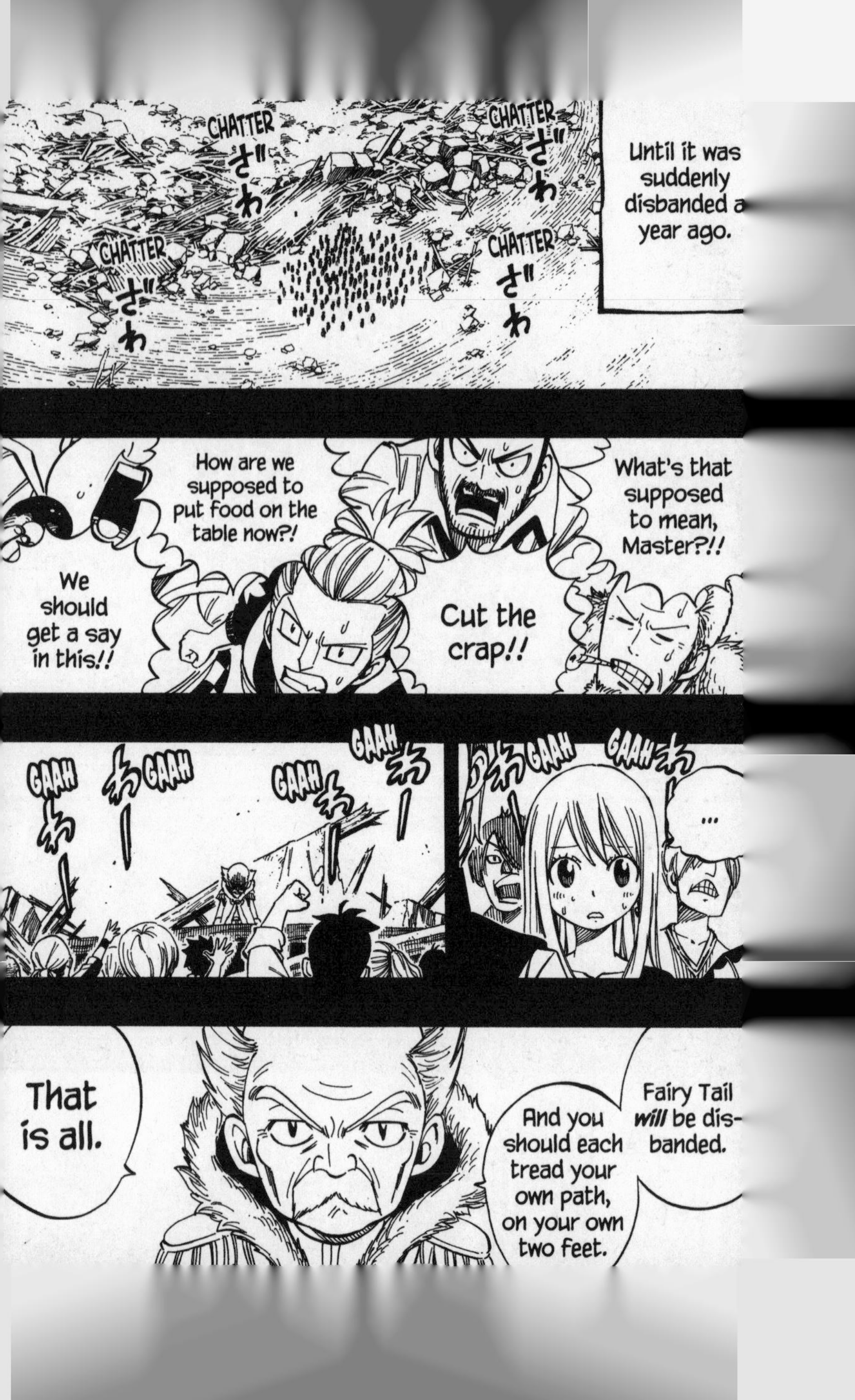
Until it was suddenly disbanded a year ago.
CHATTER
ざわ
CHATTER
ざわ
CHATTER
ざわ
CHATTER
ざわ
What's that supposed to mean, Master?!!
Cut the crap!!
How are we supposed to put food on the table now?!
We should get a say in this!!
GAAH
わ
GAAH
わ
...
GAAH
わー
GAAH
わー
GAAH
わー
GAAH
わー
Fairy Tail *will* be disbanded.
And you should each tread your own path, on your own two feet.
That is all.

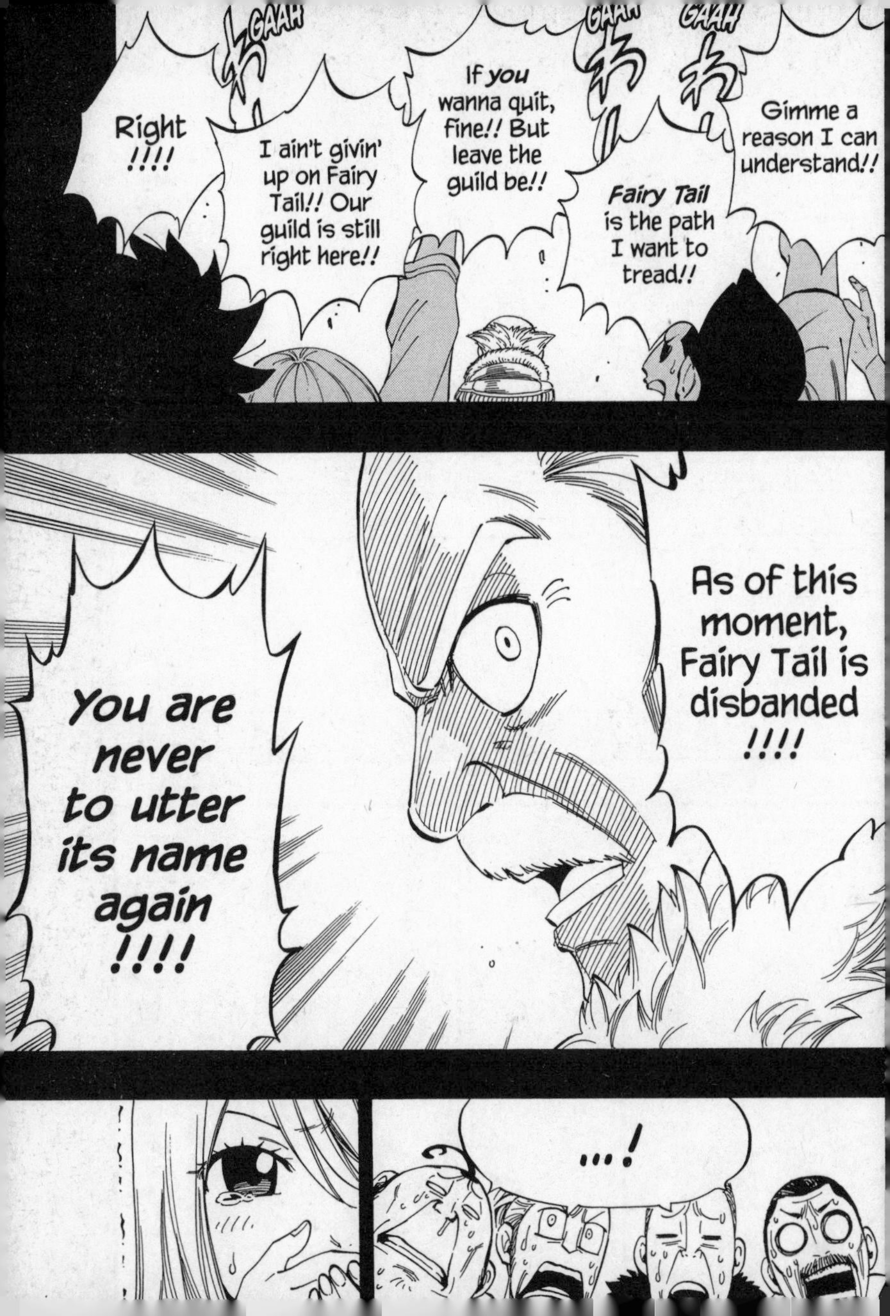
GAAH
GAAH
Gimme a reason I can understand!!
Fairy Tail is the path I want to tread!!
If you wanna quit, fine!! But leave the guild be!!
GAAH
I ain't givin' up on Fairy Tail!! Our guild is still right here!!
Right!!!!
As of this moment, Fairy Tail is disbanded!!!!
You are never to utter its name again!!!!
...!

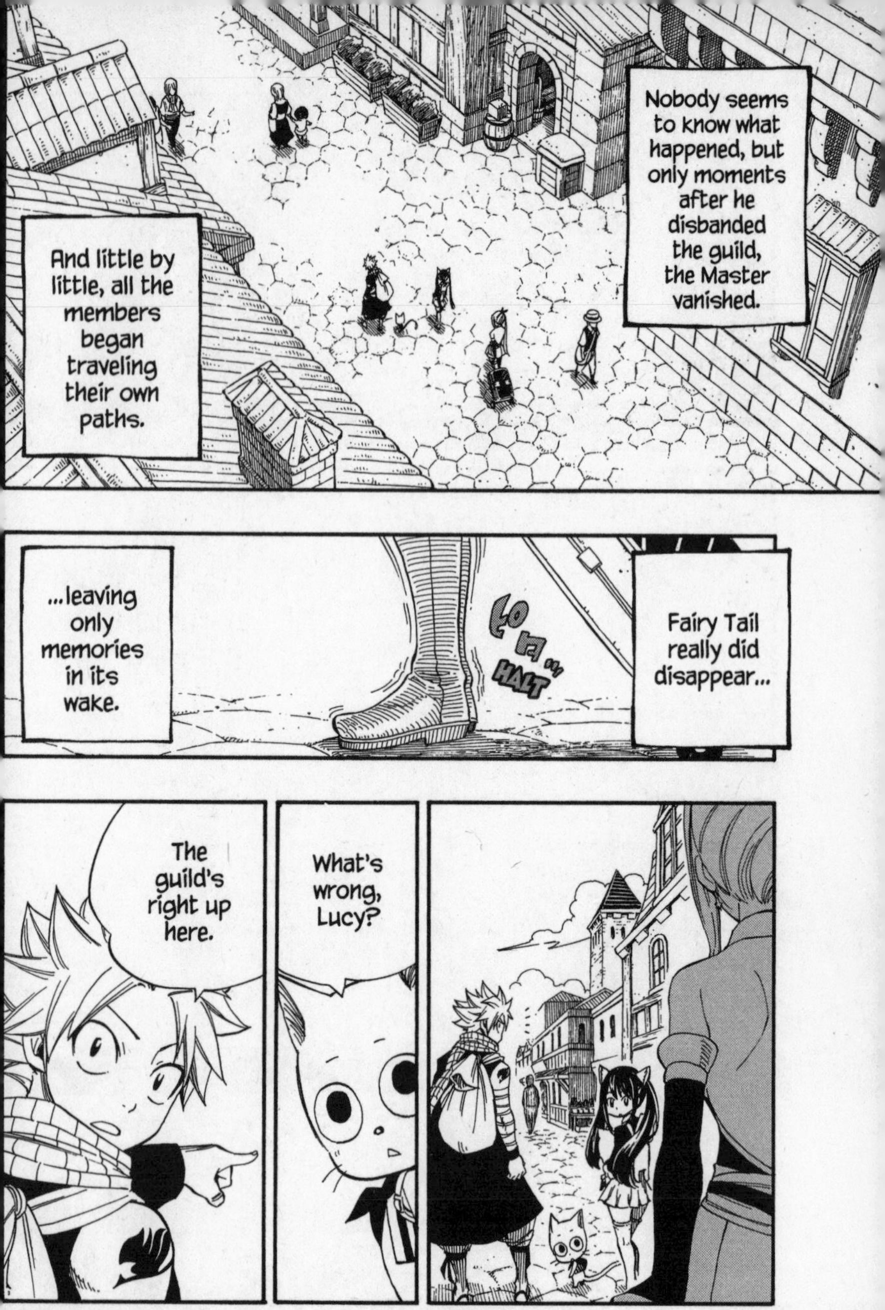

Nobody seems to know what happened, but only moments after he disbanded the guild, the Master vanished.
And little by little, all the members began traveling their own paths.
Fairy Tail really did disappear...
HALT
...leaving only memories in its wake.
What's wrong, Lucy?
The guild's right up here.

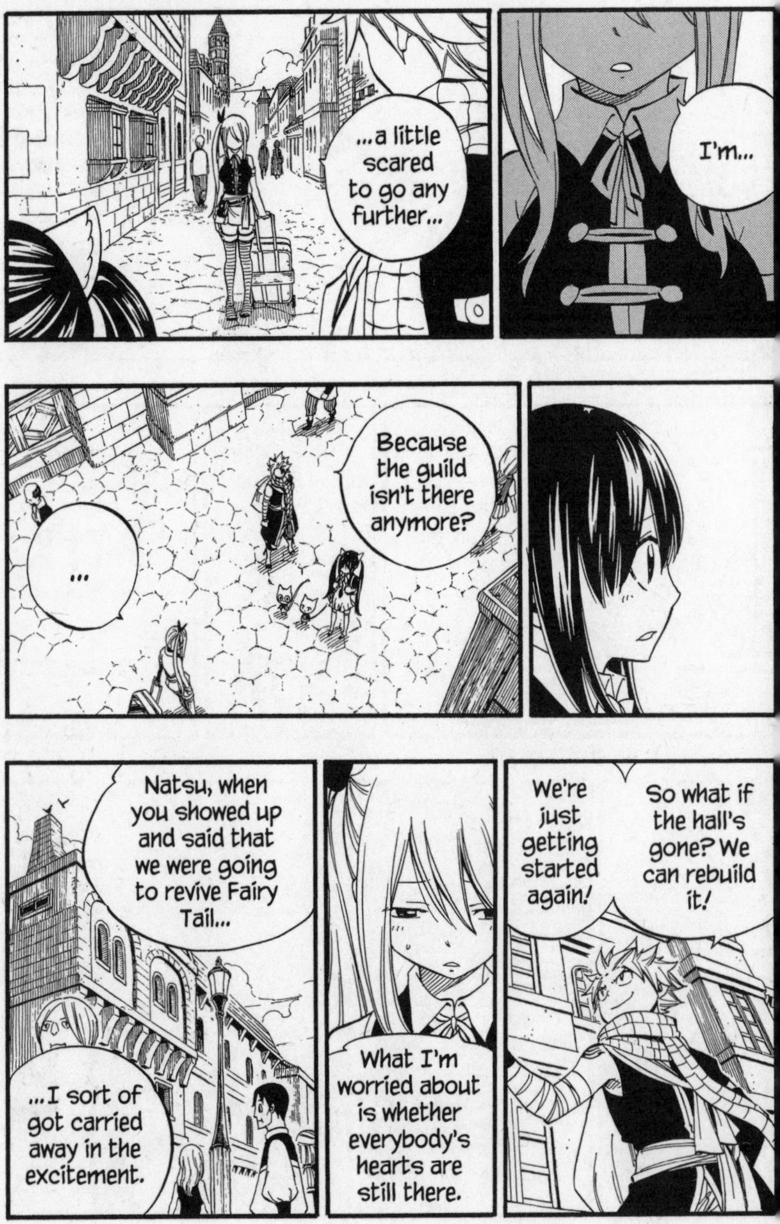
I'm...
...a little scared to go any further...
Because the guild isn't there anymore?
...
So what if the hall's gone? We can rebuild it!
We're just getting started again!
What I'm worried about is whether everybody's hearts are still there.
Natsu, when you showed up and said that we were going to revive Fairy Tail...
...I sort of got carried away in the excitement.

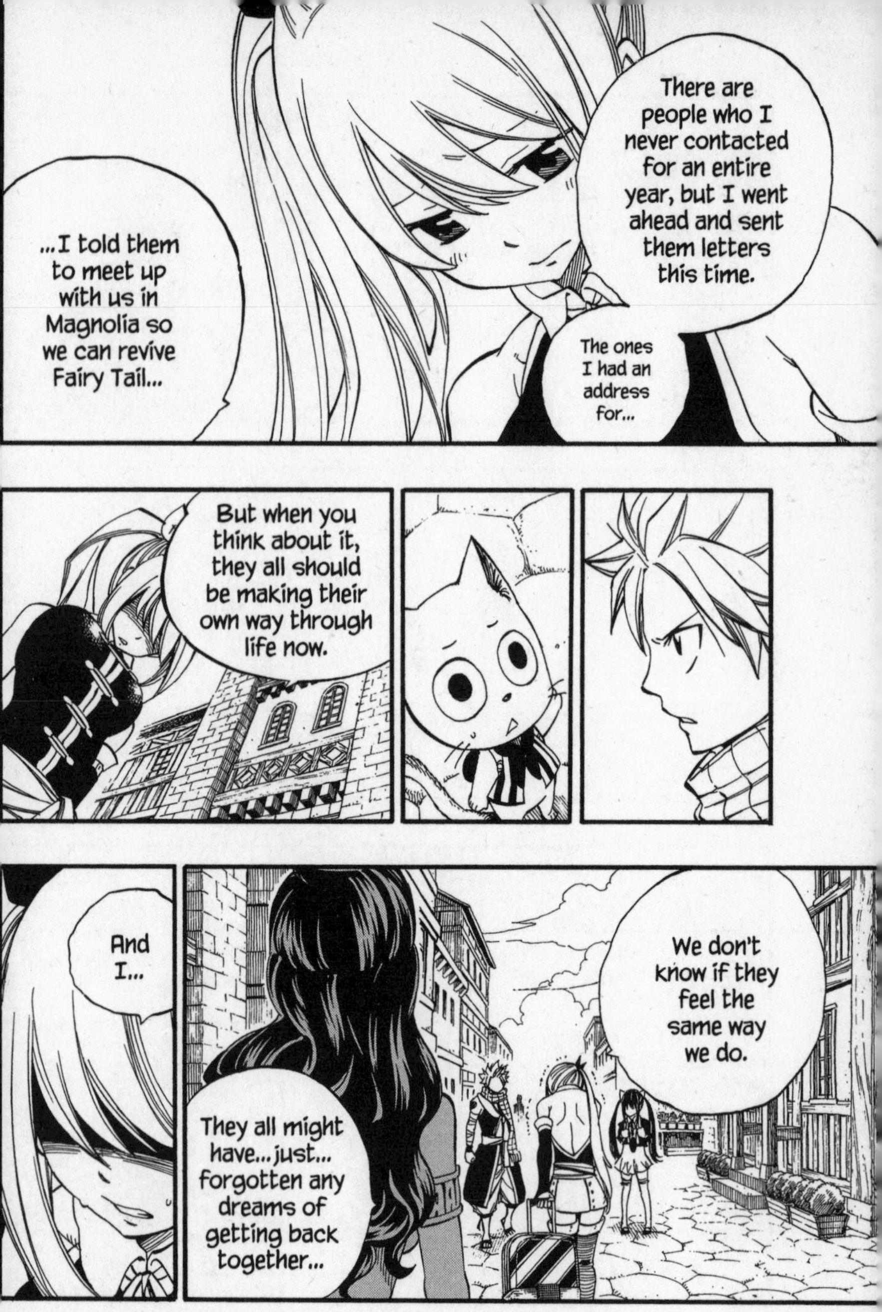
There are people who I never contacted for an entire year, but I went ahead and sent them letters this time.
The ones I had an address for...
...I told them to meet up with us in Magnolia so we can revive Fairy Tail...
But when you think about it, they all should be making their own way through life now.
We don't know if they feel the same way we do.
They all might have...just... forgotten any dreams of getting back together...
And I...

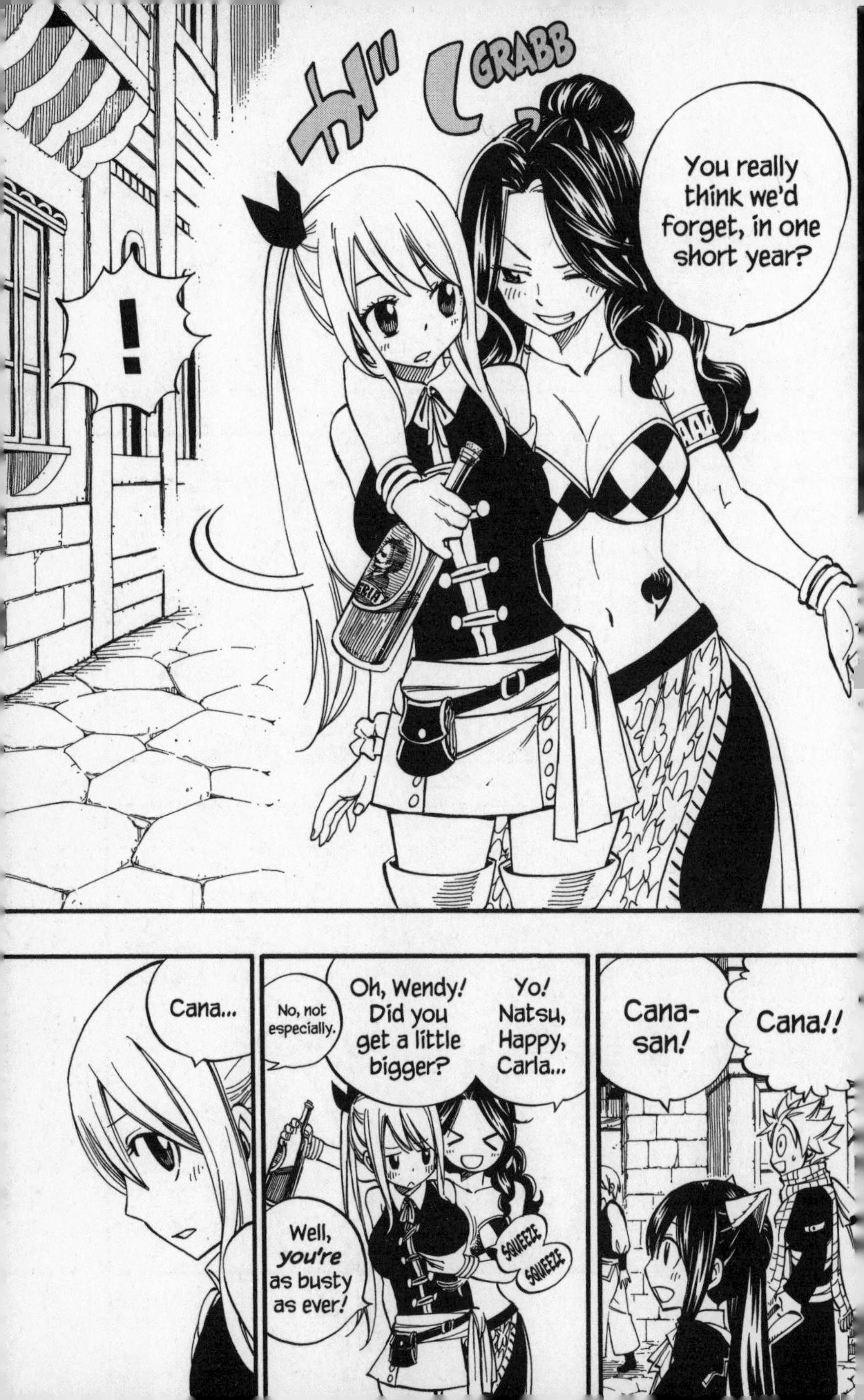
You really think we'd forget, in one short year?
GRABB
!
Cana!!
Cana-san!
Yo! Natsu, Happy, Carla...
Oh, Wendy! Did you get a little bigger?
No, not especially.
SQUEEZE
SQUEEZE
Well, *you're* as busty as ever!
Cana...

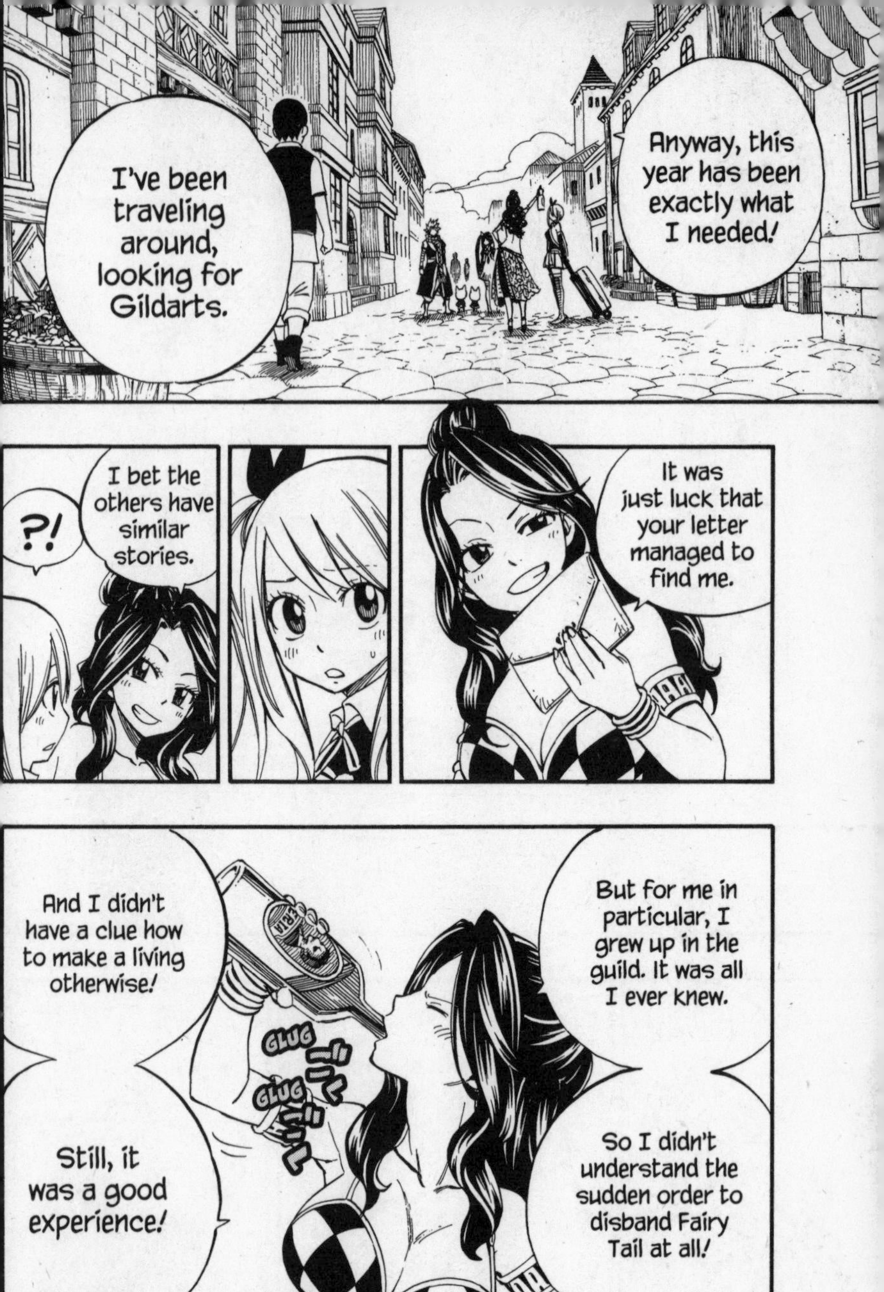
Anyway, this year has been exactly what I needed!
I've been traveling around, looking for Gildarts.
It was just luck that your letter managed to find me.
I bet the others have similar stories.
?!
But for me in particular, I grew up in the guild. It was all I ever knew.
And I didn't have a clue how to make a living otherwise!
GLUG
GLUG
So I didn't understand the sudden order to disband Fairy Tail at all!
Still, it was a good experience!

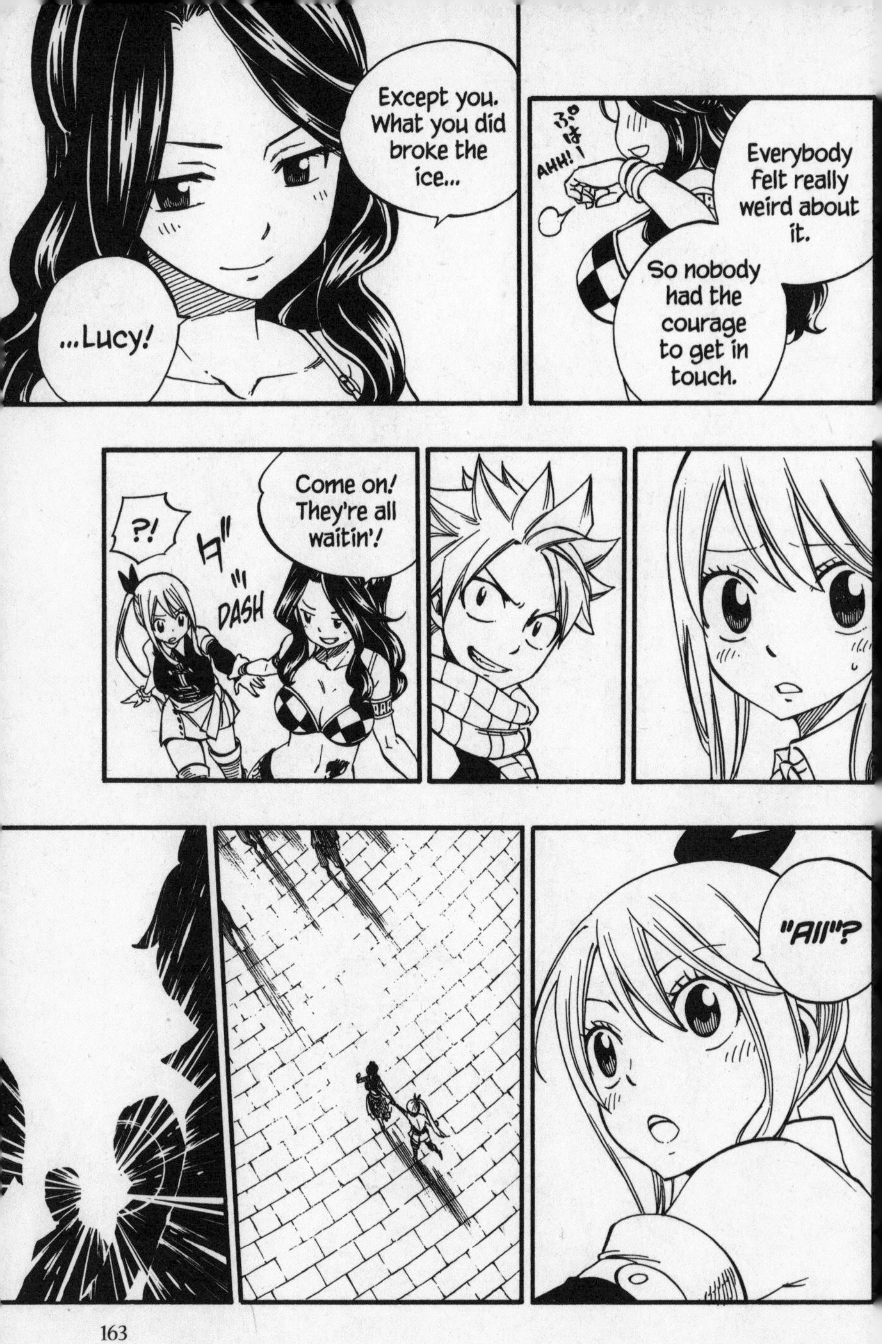
Everybody felt really weird about it.
ぷは AHH!
So nobody had the courage to get in touch.
Except you. What you did broke the ice...
...Lucy!
Come on! They're all waitin'!
ダ DASH
?!
"All"?

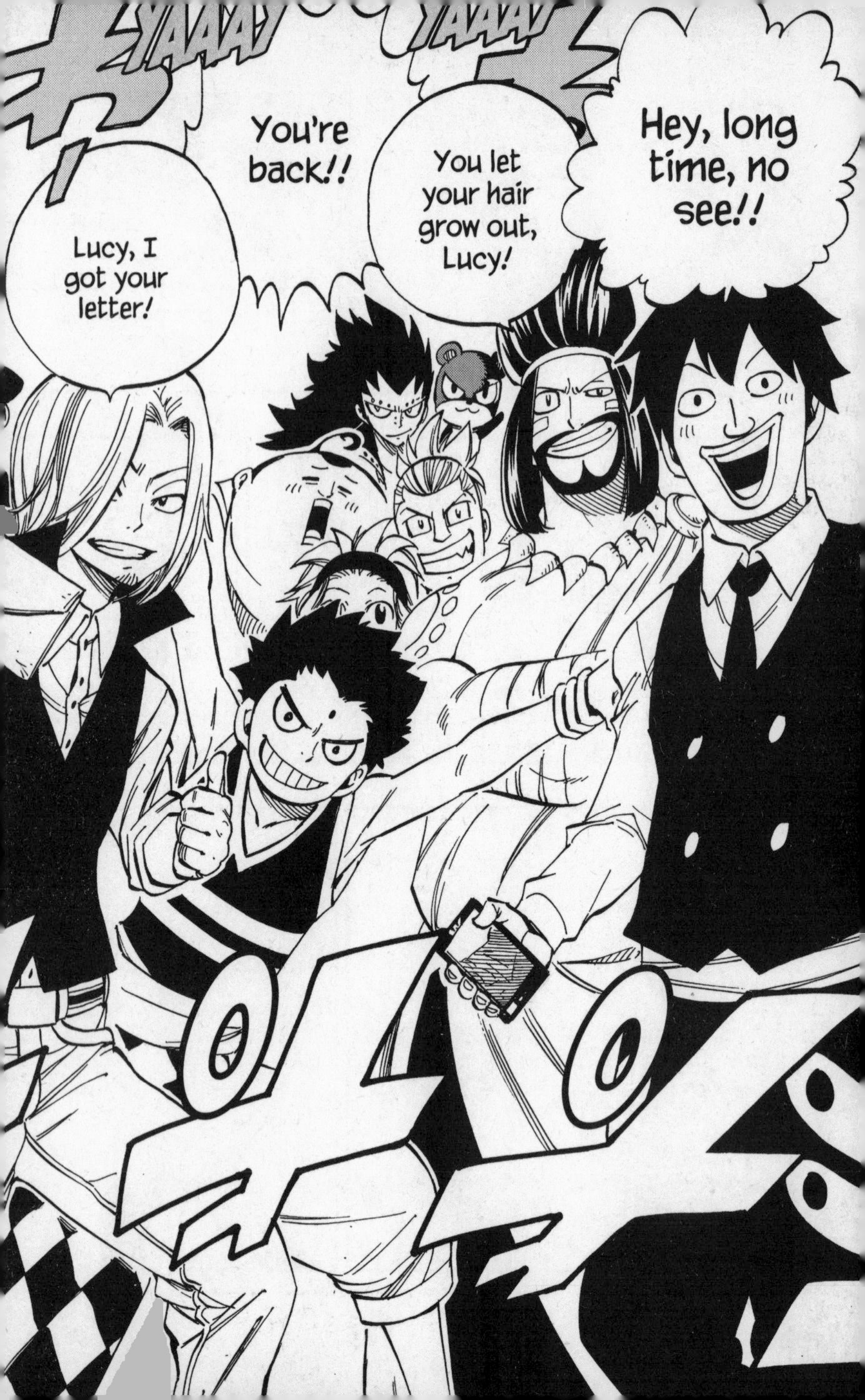
YAAAY
YAAAY
Hey, long time, no see!!
You let your hair grow out, Lucy!
You're back!!
Lucy, I got your letter!

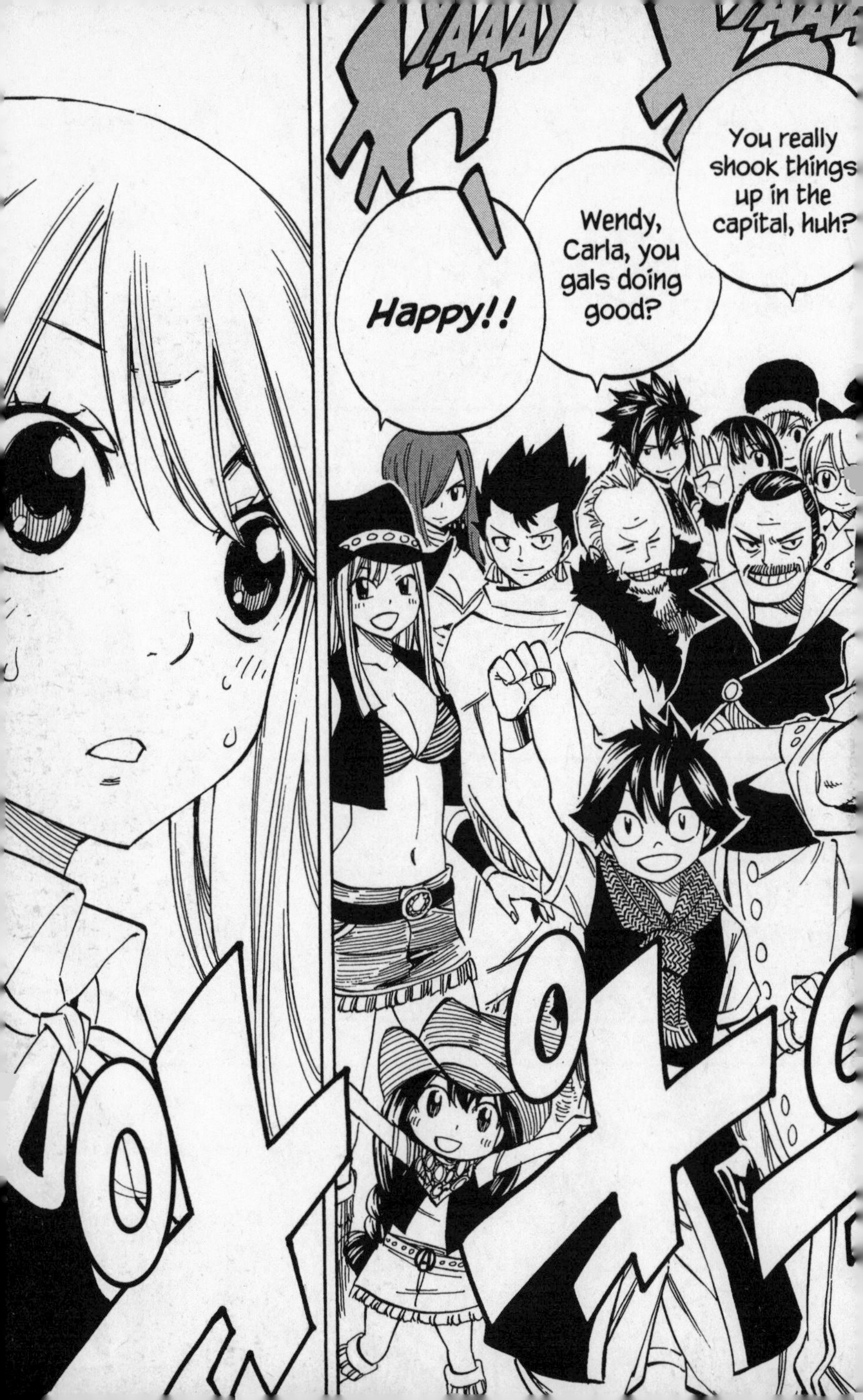
You really shook things up in the capital, huh?
Wendy, Carla, you gals doing good?
Happy!!

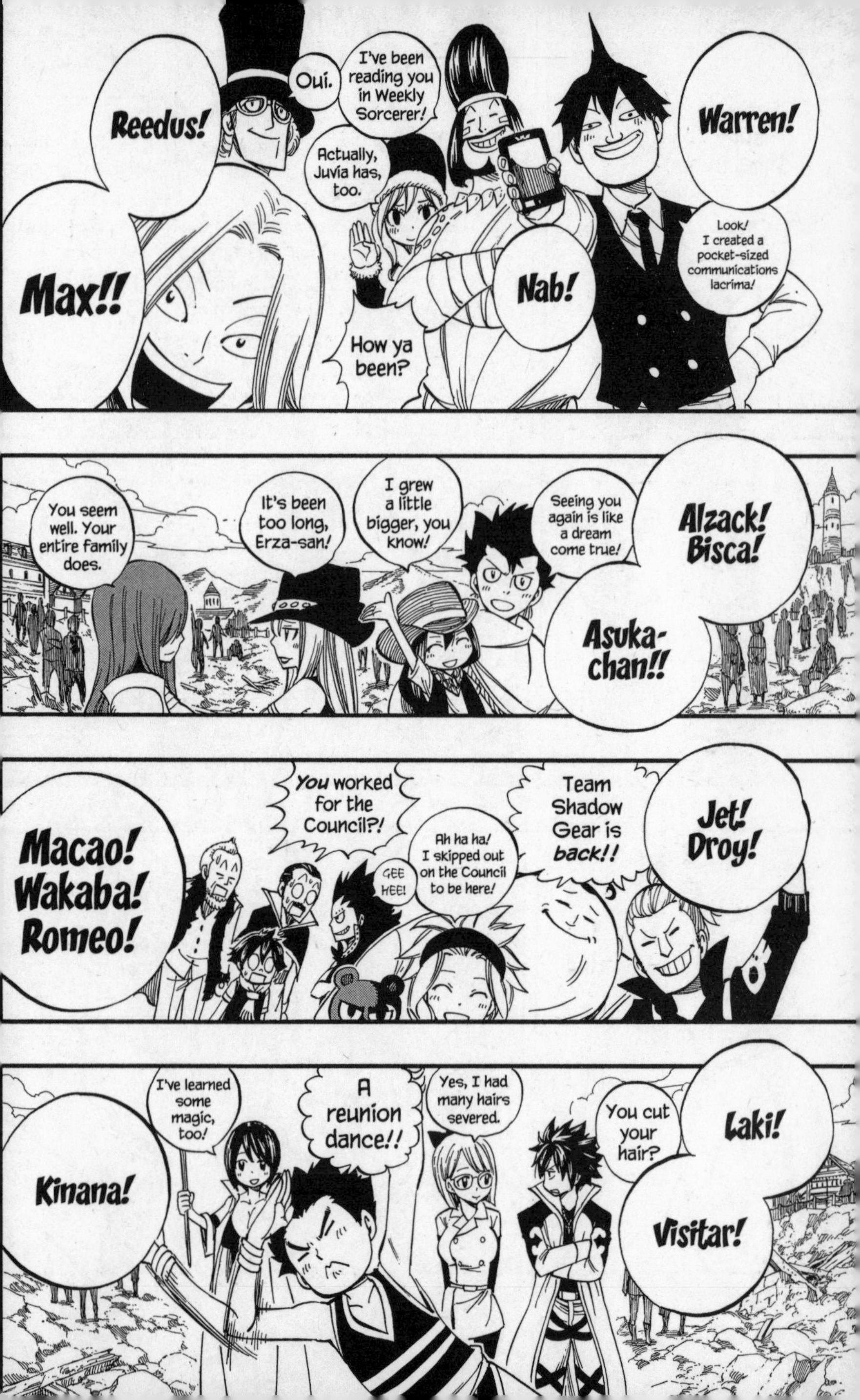
Warren!
Look! I created a pocket-sized communications lacrima!
Nab!
I've been reading you in Weekly Sorcerer!
Oui.
Actually, Juvia has, too.
How ya been?
Reedus!
Max!!
Alzack! Bisca!
Asuka-chan!!
Seeing you again is like a dream come true!
I grew a little bigger, you know!
It's been too long, Erza-san!
You seem well. Your entire family does.
Jet! Droy!
Team Shadow Gear is *back*!!
Ah ha ha! I skipped out on the Council to be here!
You worked for the Council?!
GEE HEE!
Macao! Wakaba! Romeo!
Laki!
Visitar!
You cut your hair?
Yes, I had many hairs severed.
A reunion dance!!
I've learned some magic, too!
Kinana!

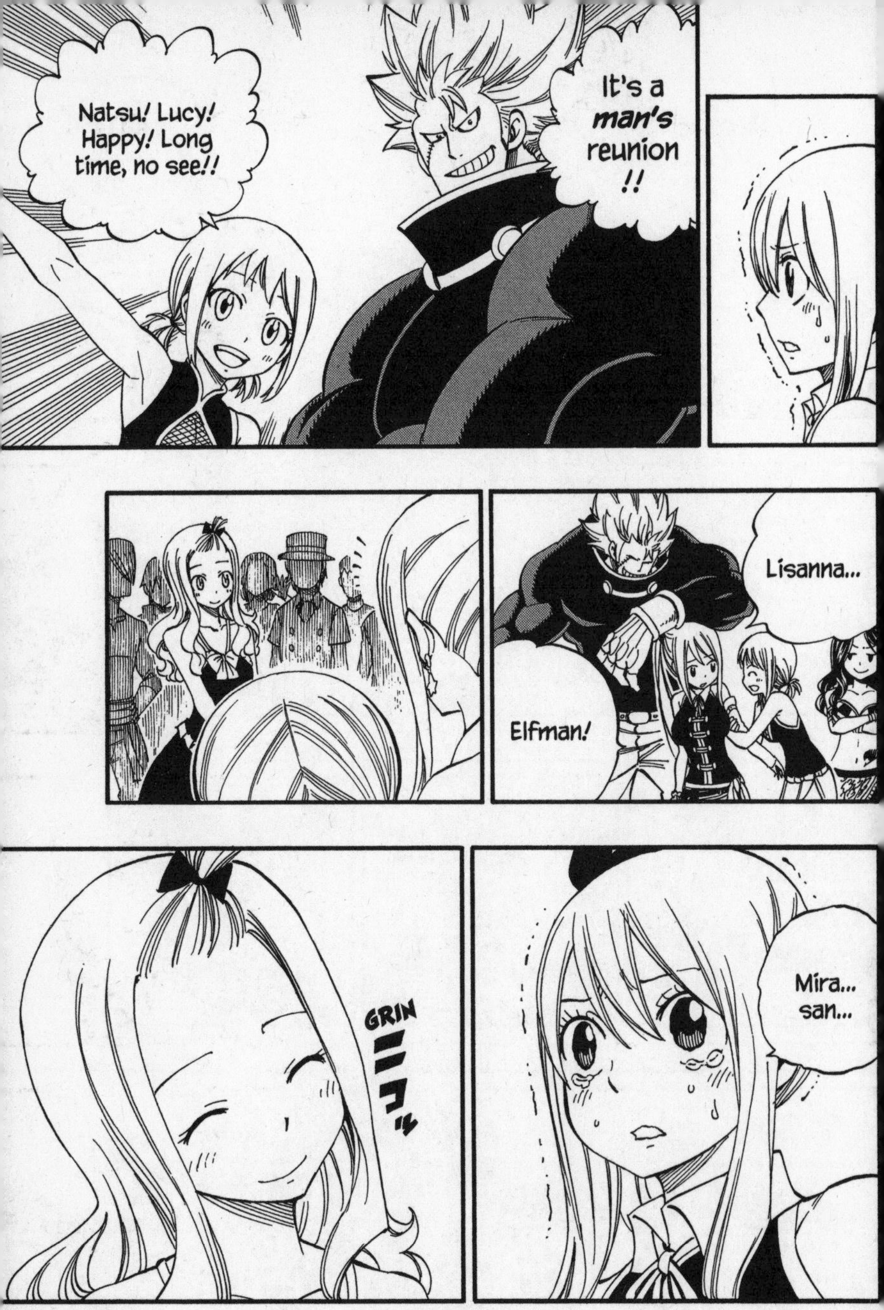
It's a *man's* reunion !!
Natsu! Lucy! Happy! Long time, no see!!
Lisanna...
Elfman!
Mira... san...
GRIN

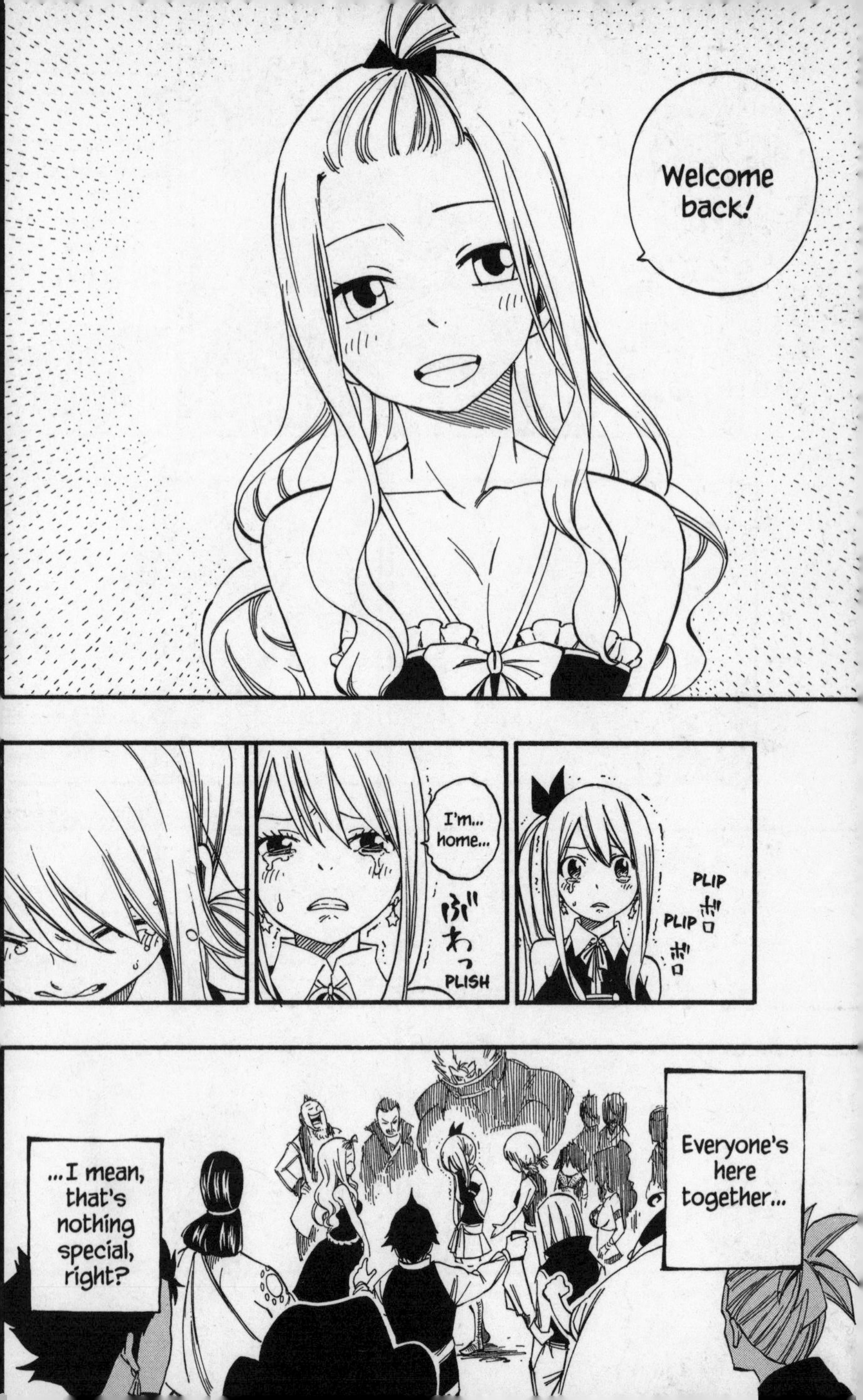

Welcome back!
PLIP
ポロ
PLIP
ポロ
I'm... home...
ぶわっ
PLISH
Everyone's here together...
...I mean, that's nothing special, right?

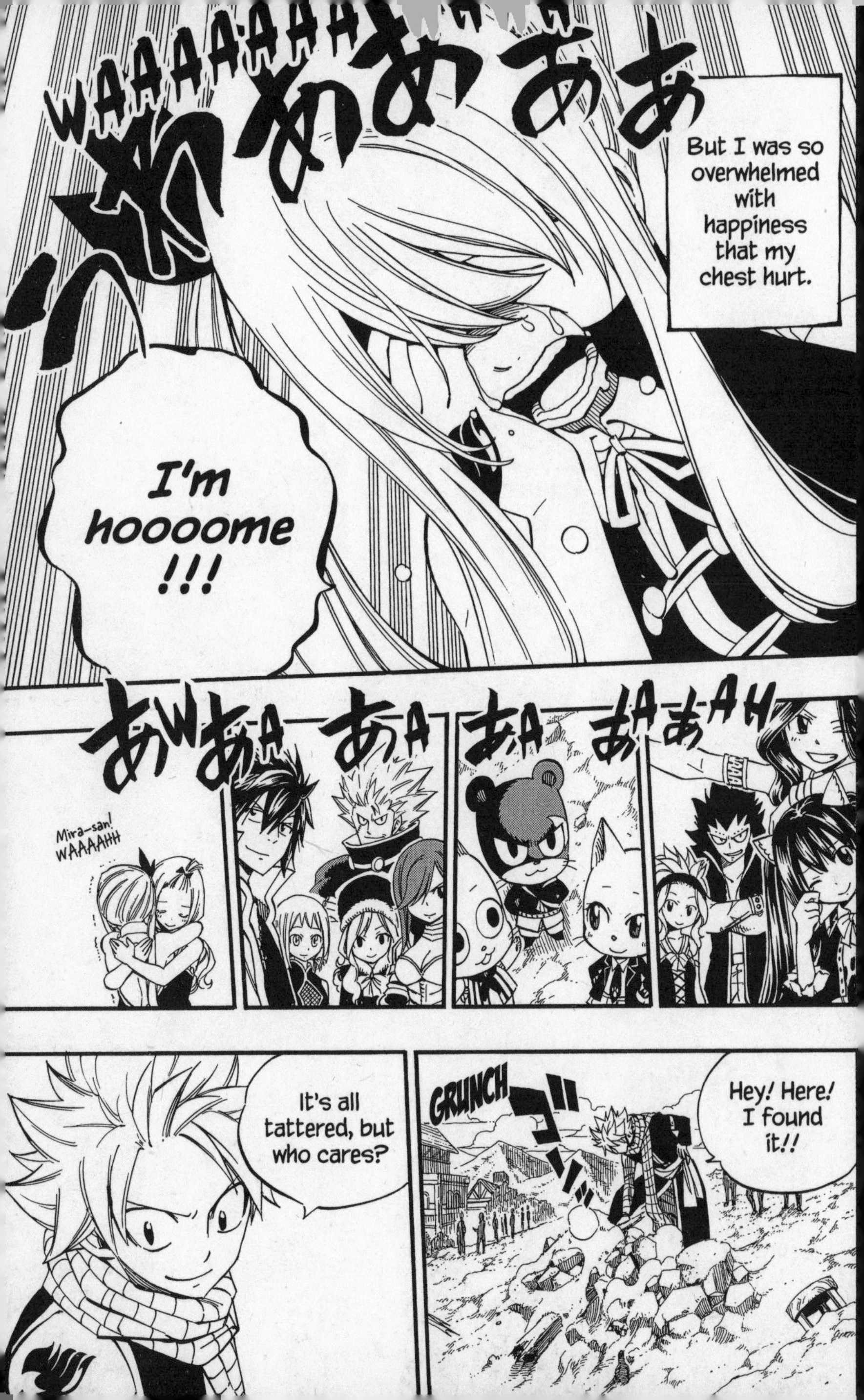
WAAAAAAAH
But I was so overwhelmed with happiness that my chest hurt.
I'm hoooome !!!
WAAAAAH
Mira-san! WAAAAHH
GRUNCH
Hey! Here! I found it!!
It's all tattered, but who cares?

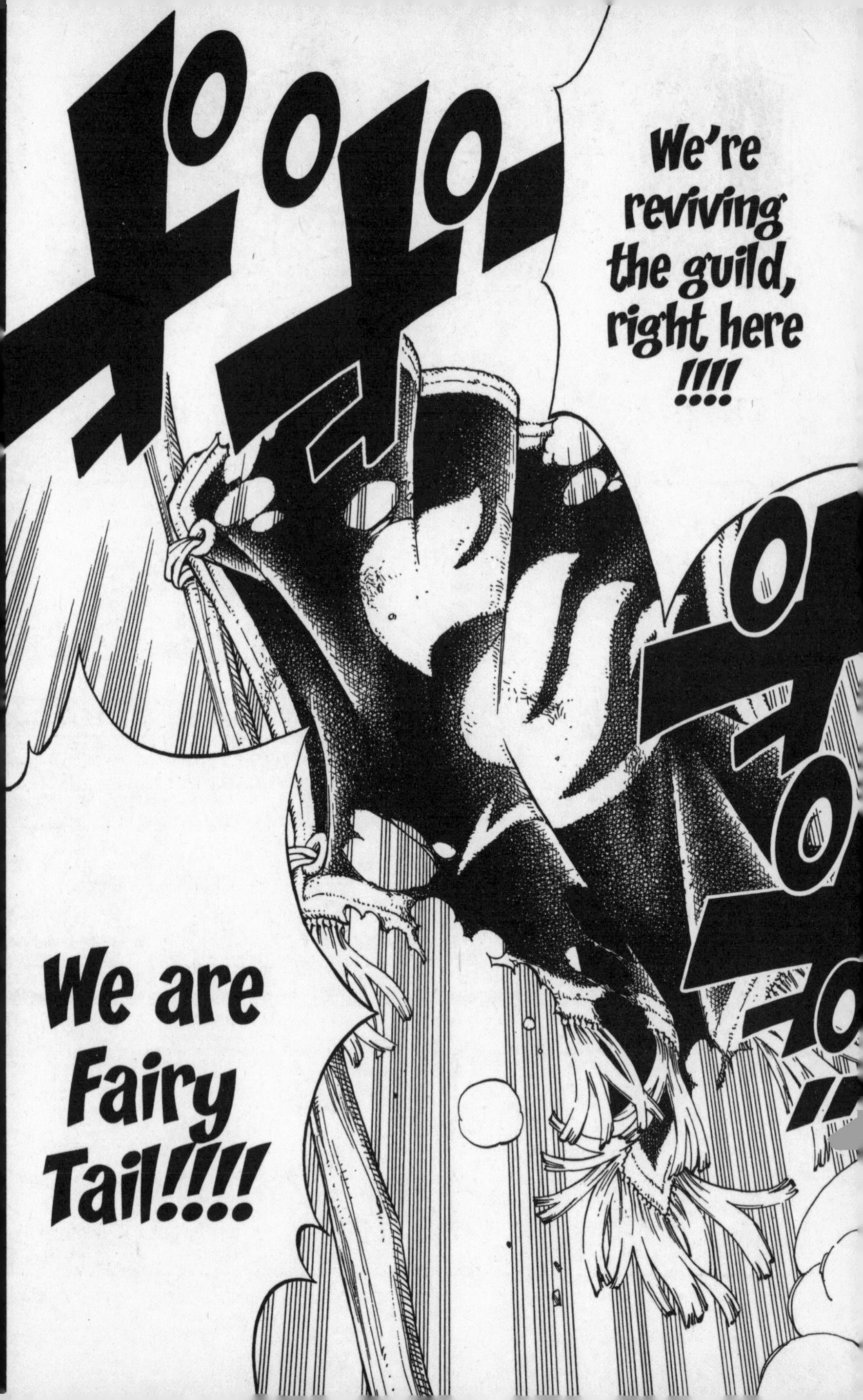
We're reviving the guild, right here!!!!
We are Fairy Tail!!!!

FAIRY TAIL

フェアリーテイル

Chapter 438: The Seventh Guild Master

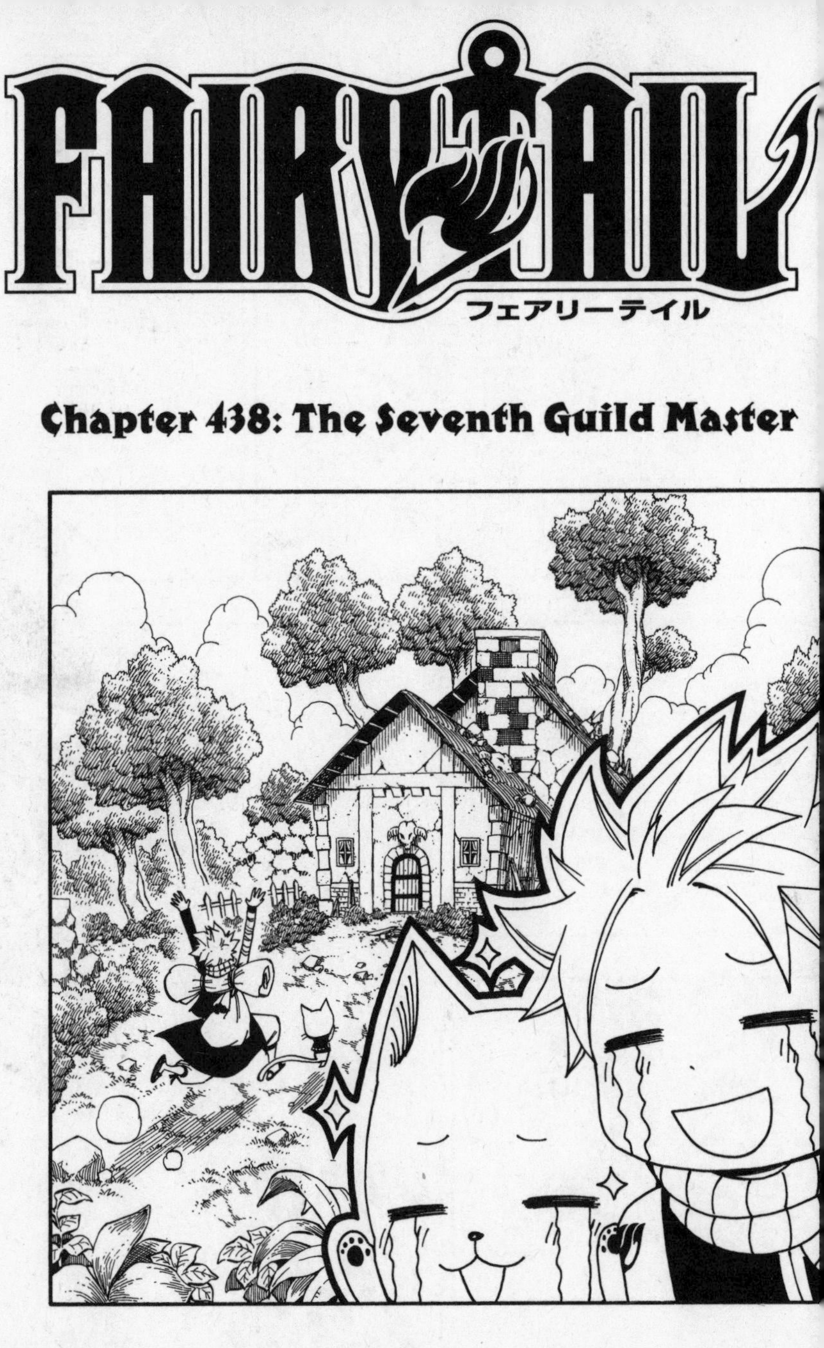

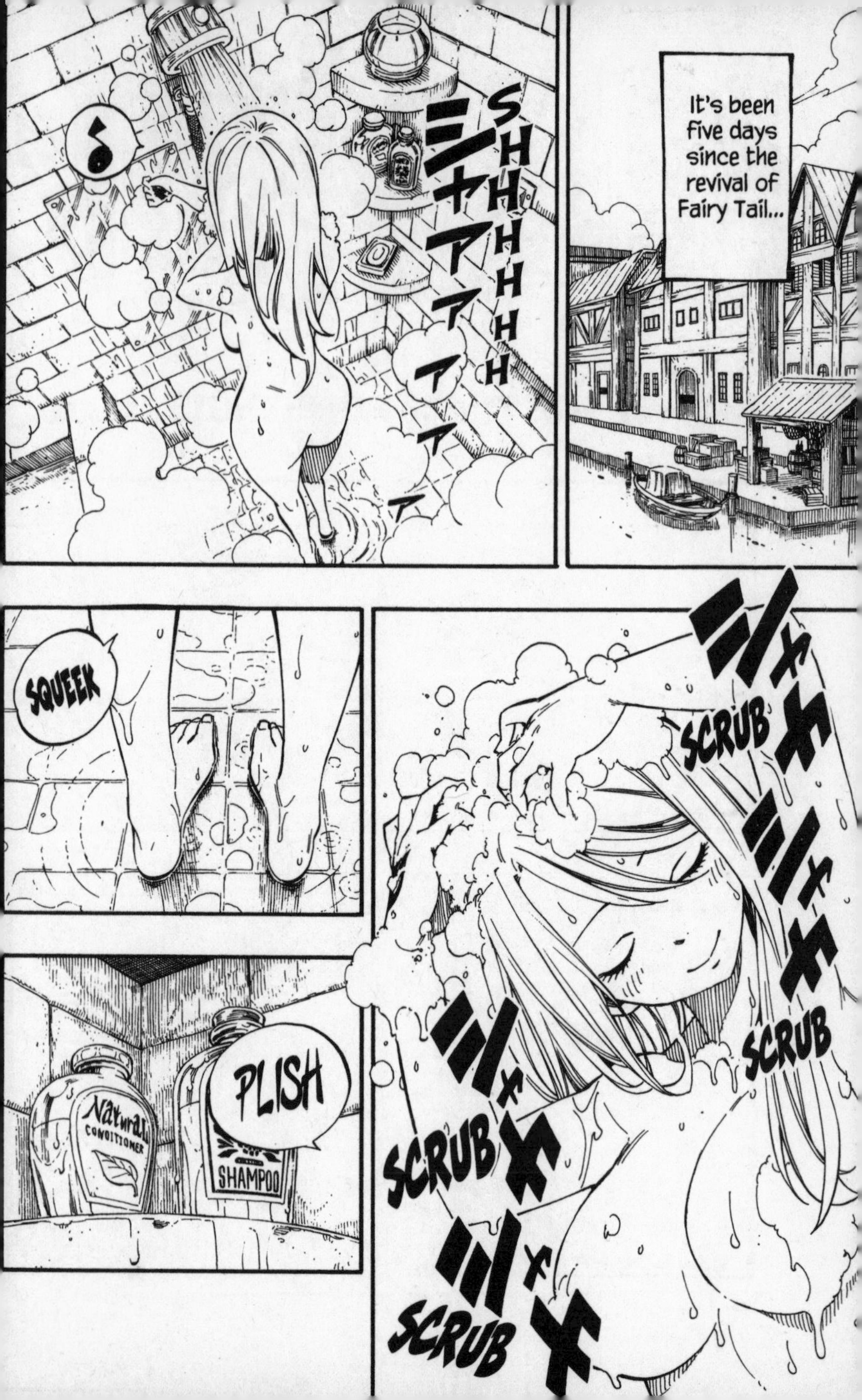

It's been five days since the revival of Fairy Tail...
SHHHHHHH
SCRUB
SCRUB
SCRUB
SCRUB
SQUEEK
PLISH
Natural CONDITIONER
SHAMPOO

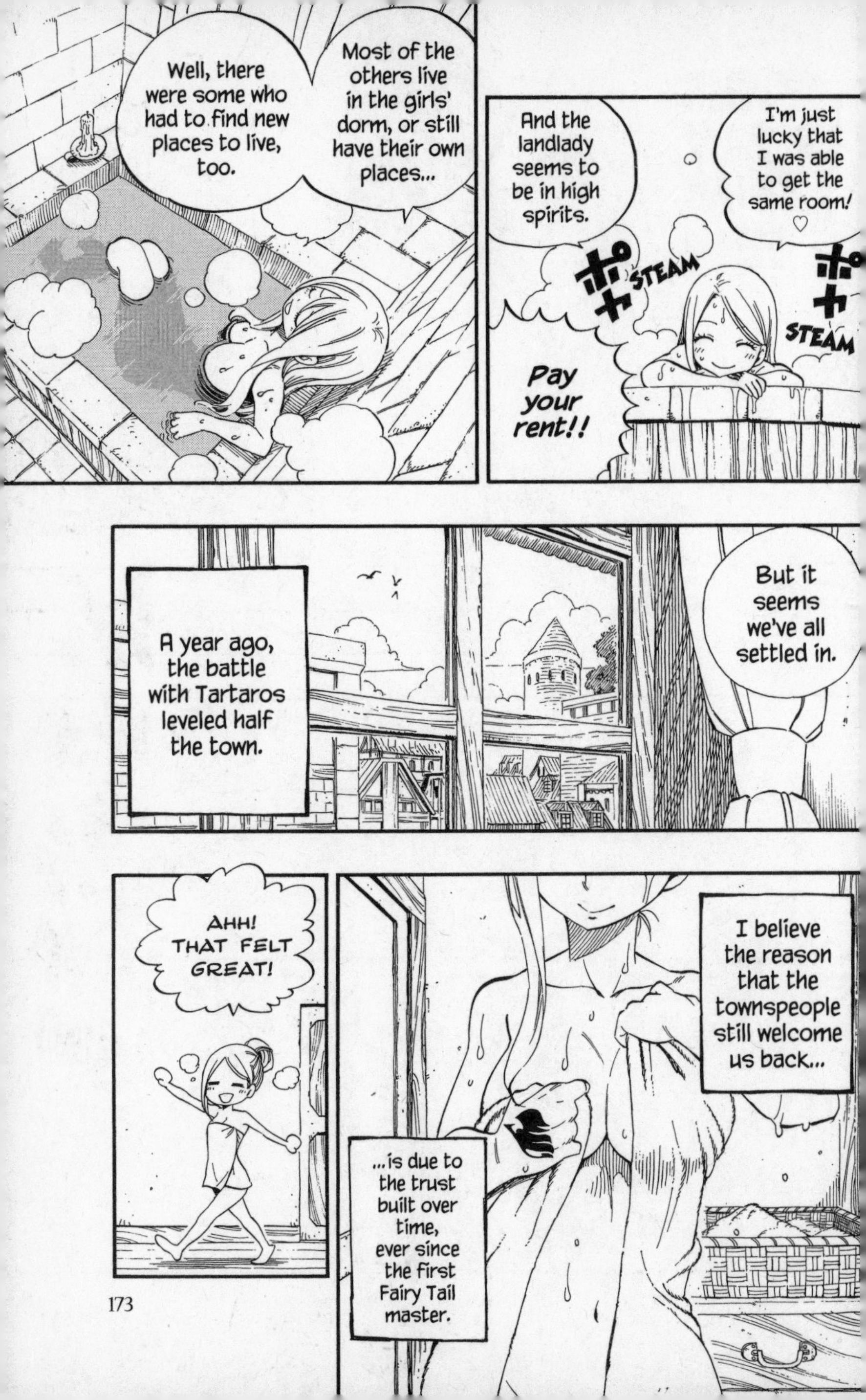

I'm just lucky that I was able to get the same room! ♡
STEAM
STEAM
And the landlady seems to be in high spirits.
Pay your rent!!
Most of the others live in the girls' dorm, or still have their own places...
Well, there were some who had to find new places to live, too.
But it seems we've all settled in.
A year ago, the battle with Tartaros leveled half the town.
I believe the reason that the townspeople still welcome us back...
...is due to the trust built over time, ever since the first Fairy Tail master.
AHH! THAT FELT GREAT!

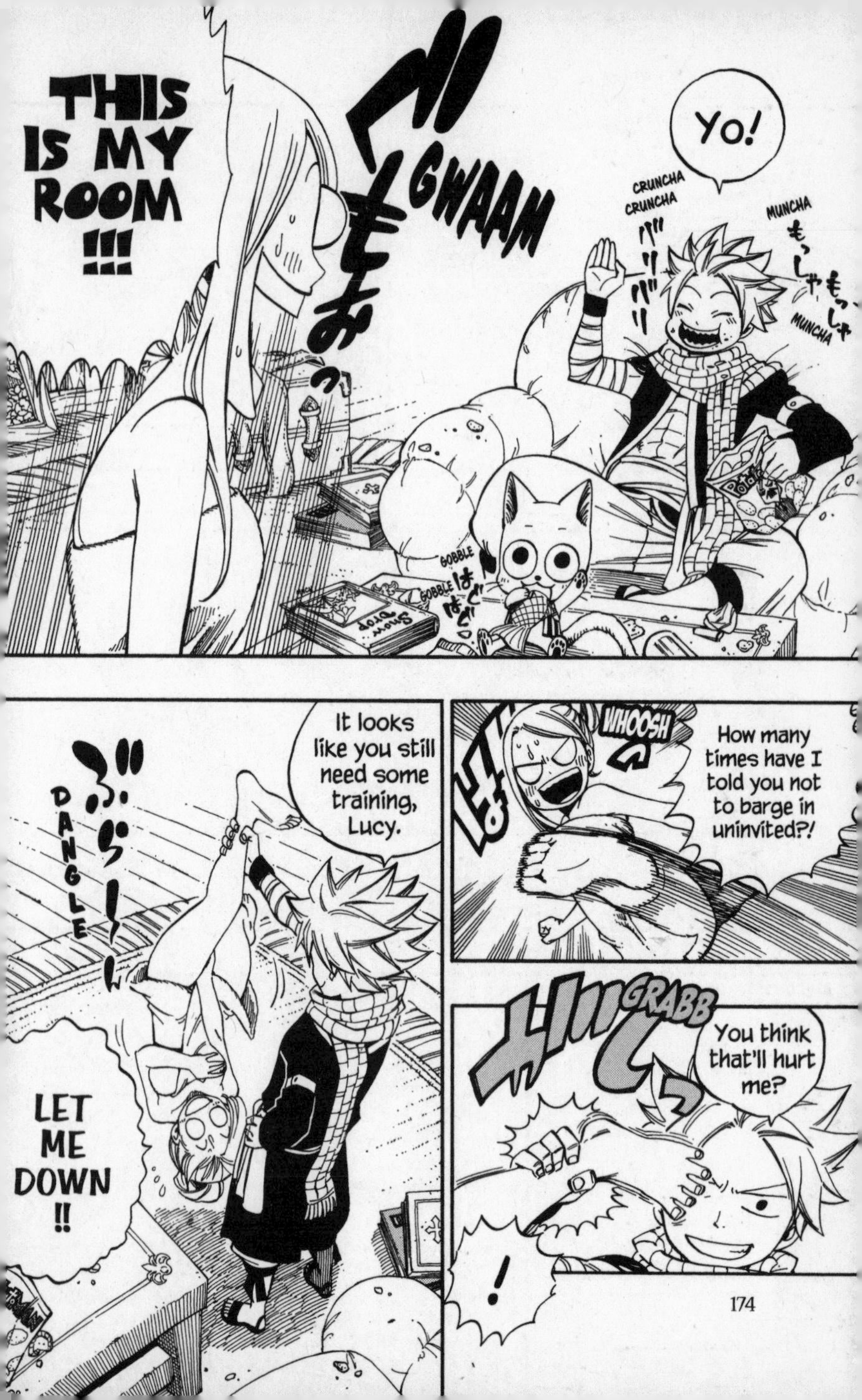
Yo!
MUNCHA
MUNCHA
CRUNCHA
CRUNCHA
GWAAM
THIS IS MY ROOM!!!
GOBBLE
GOBBLE
WHOOSH
How many times have I told you not to barge in uninvited?!
GRABB
You think that'll hurt me?
!
It looks like you still need some training, Lucy.
DANGLE
LET ME DOWN!!

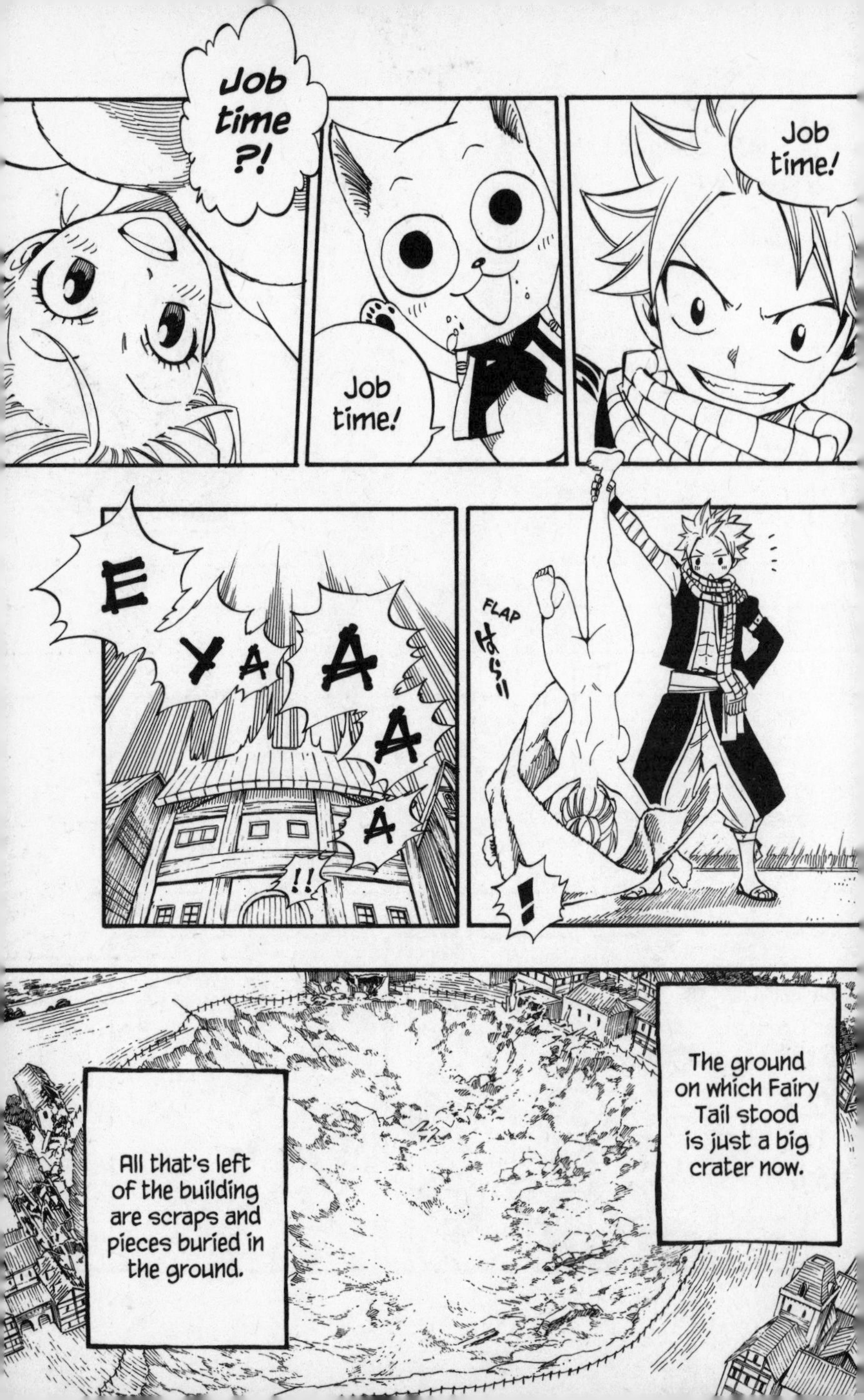
Job time!
Job time!
Job time?!
FLAP
!
E YA A A A A
!!
The ground on which Fairy Tail stood is just a big crater now.
All that's left of the building are scraps and pieces buried in the ground.

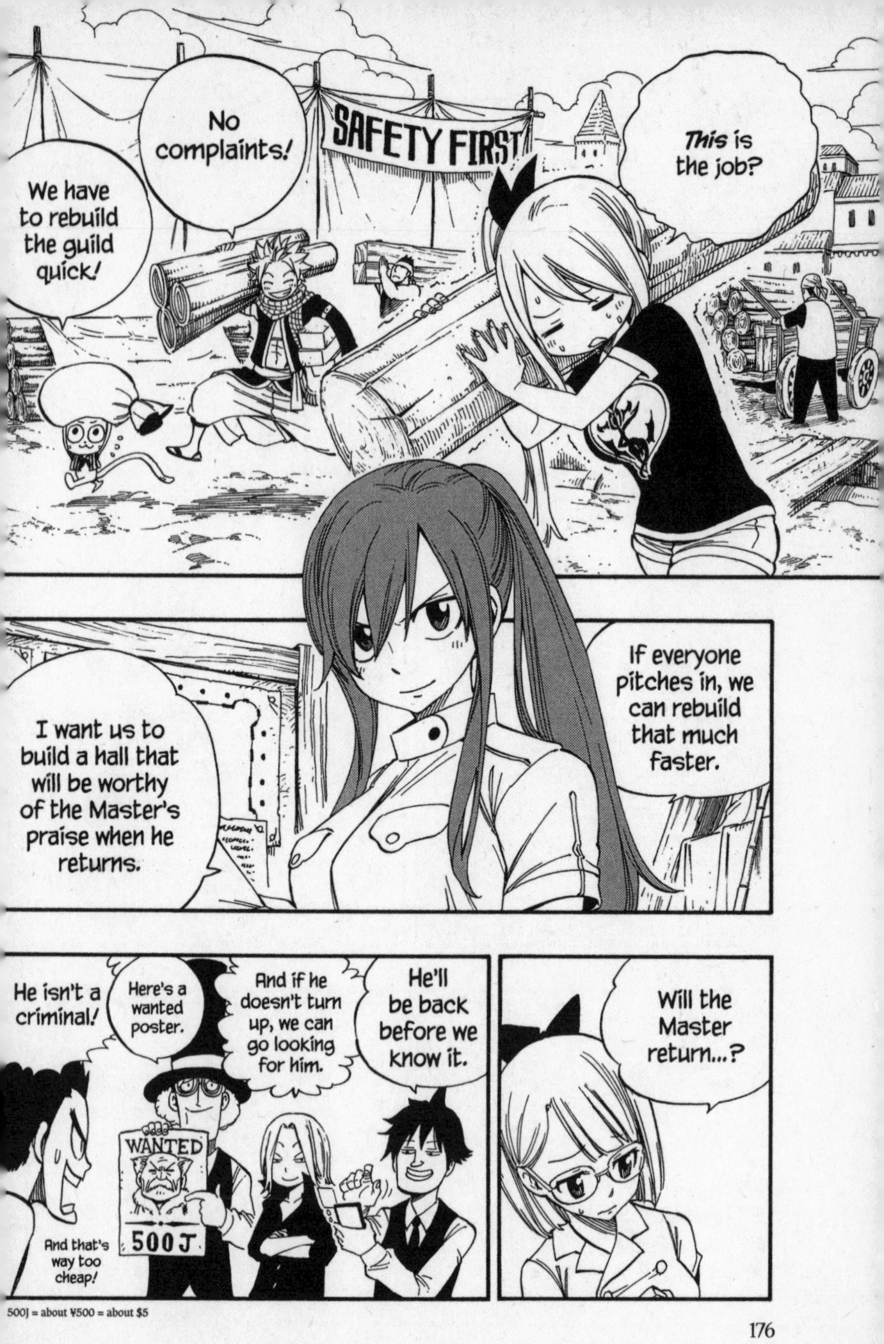

This is the job?
SAFETY FIRST
No complaints!
We have to rebuild the guild quick!
If everyone pitches in, we can rebuild that much faster.
I want us to build a hall that will be worthy of the Master's praise when he returns.
Will the Master return...?
He'll be back before we know it.
And if he doesn't turn up, we can go looking for him.
Here's a wanted poster.
WANTED
500J
He isn't a criminal!
And that's way too cheap!

500J = about ¥500 = about $5

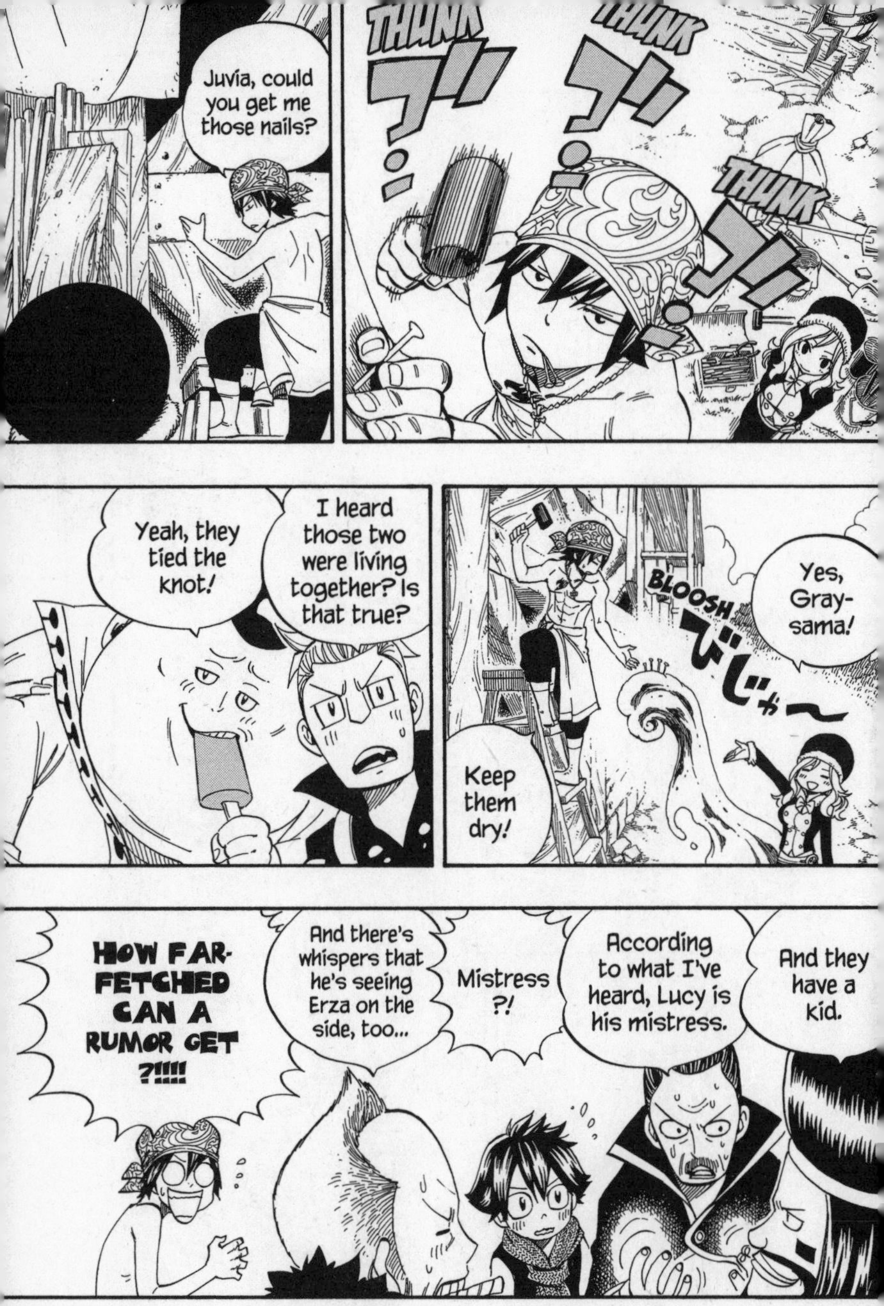
THUNK
THUNK
THUNK
Juvia, could you get me those nails?
Yes, Gray-sama!
BLOOSH
Keep them dry!
I heard those two were living together? Is that true?
Yeah, they tied the knot!
And they have a kid.
According to what I've heard, Lucy is his mistress.
Mistress?!
And there's whispers that he's seeing Erza on the side, too...
HOW FAR-FETCHED CAN A RUMOR GET?!!!!

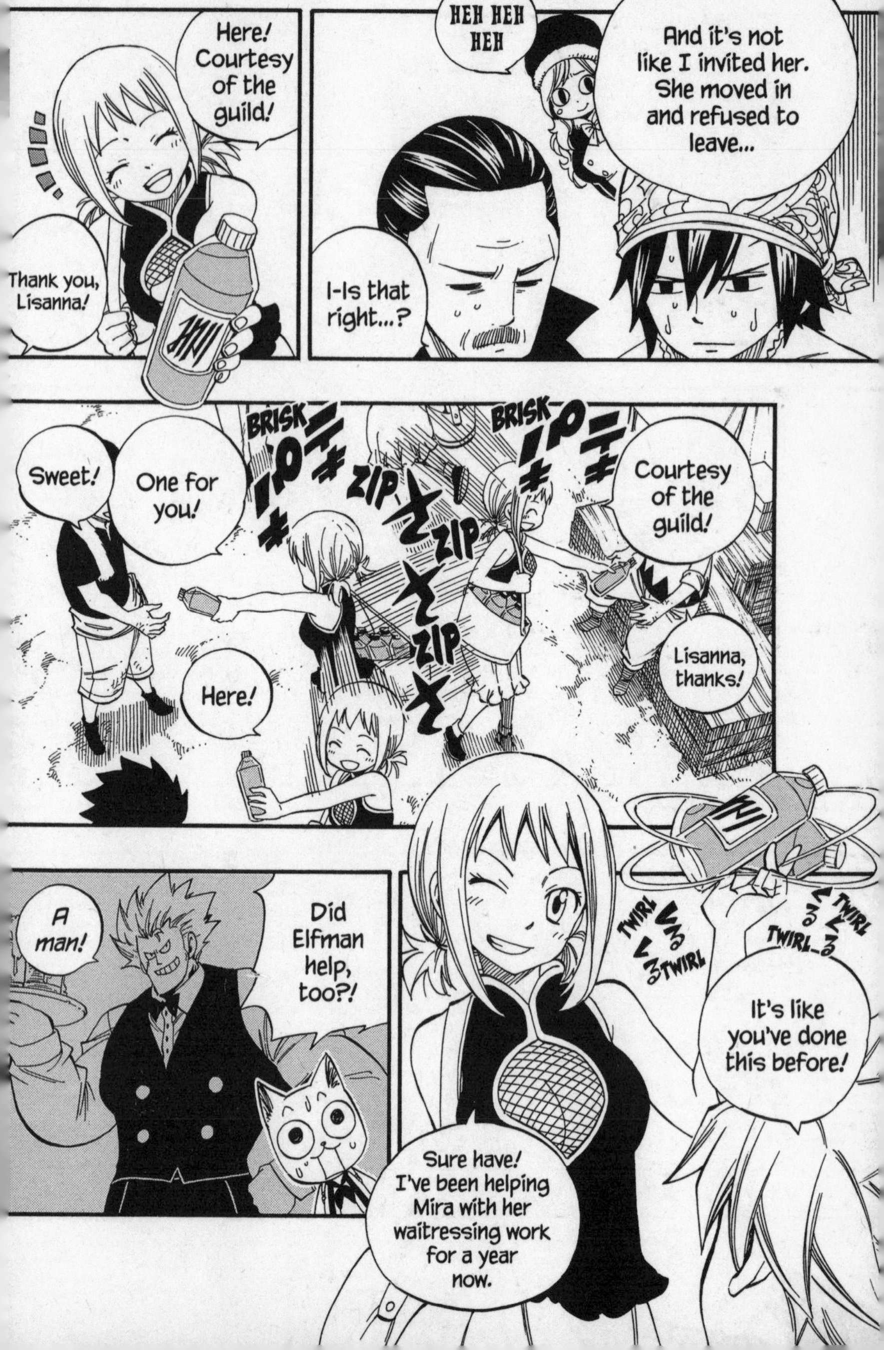
HEH HEH HEH
And it's not like I invited her. She moved in and refused to leave...
I-Is that right...?
Here! Courtesy of the guild!
Thank you, Lisanna!
BRISK
Courtesy of the guild!
Lisanna, thanks!
ZIP
ZIP
ZIP
BRISK
One for you!
Sweet!
Here!
TWIRL
TWIRL
TWIRL
TWIRL
It's like you've done this before!
Sure have! I've been helping Mira with her waitressing work for a year now.
Did Elfman help, too?!
A man!

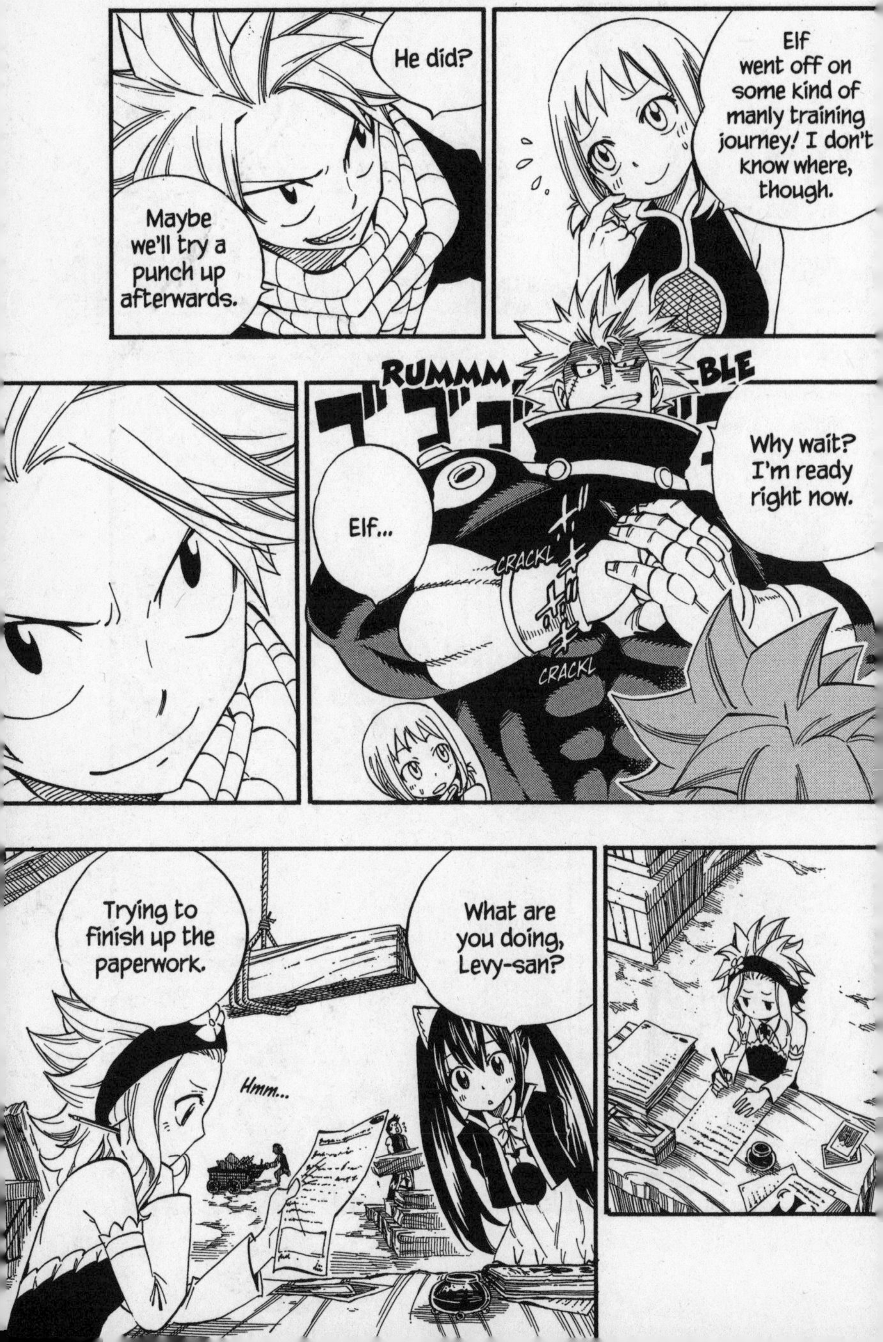
Elf went off on some kind of manly training journey! I don't know where, though.
He did?
Maybe we'll try a punch up afterwards.
RUMMMM
BLE
Why wait? I'm ready right now.
Elf...
CRACKL
CRACKL
What are you doing, Levy-san?
Trying to finish up the paperwork.
Hmm...

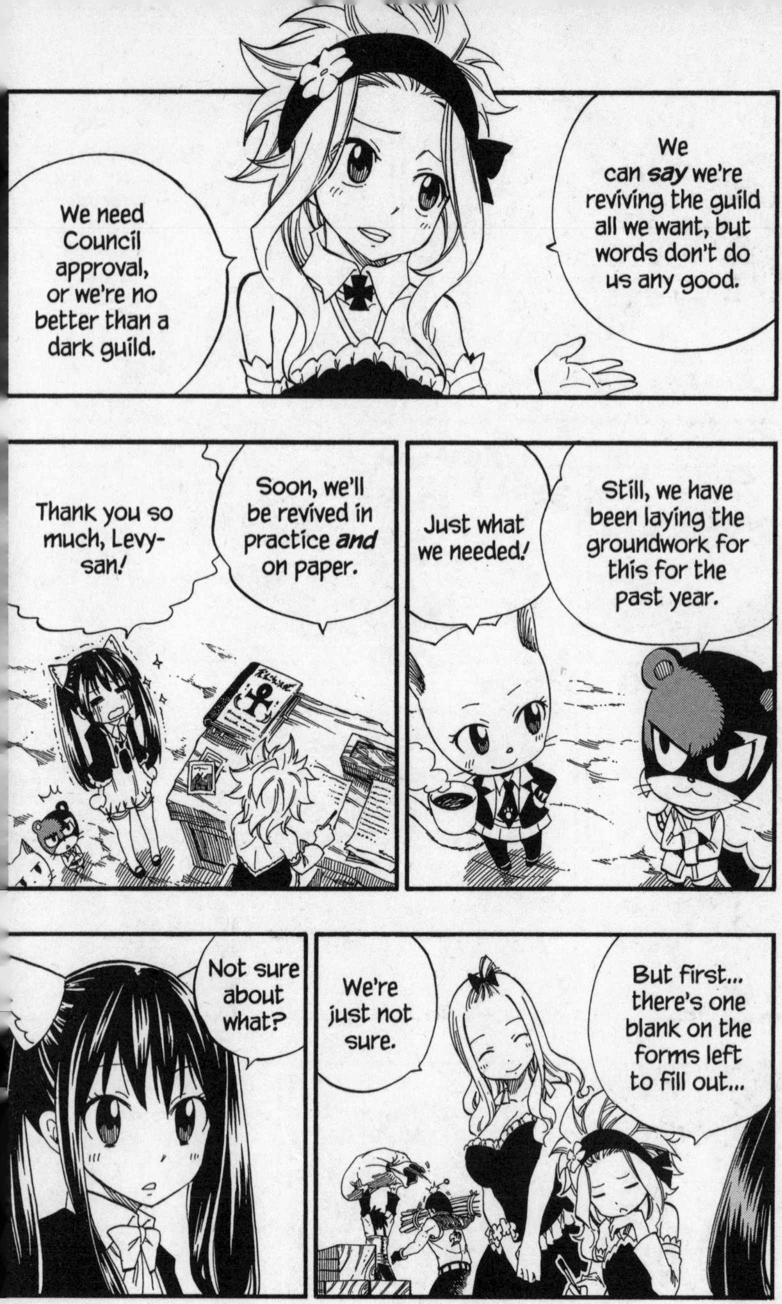
We can *say* we're reviving the guild all we want, but words don't do us any good.
We need Council approval, or we're no better than a dark guild.
Still, we have been laying the groundwork for this for the past year.
Just what we needed!
Soon, we'll be revived in practice *and* on paper.
Thank you so much, Levy-san!
But first... there's one blank on the forms left to fill out...
We're just not sure.
Not sure about what?

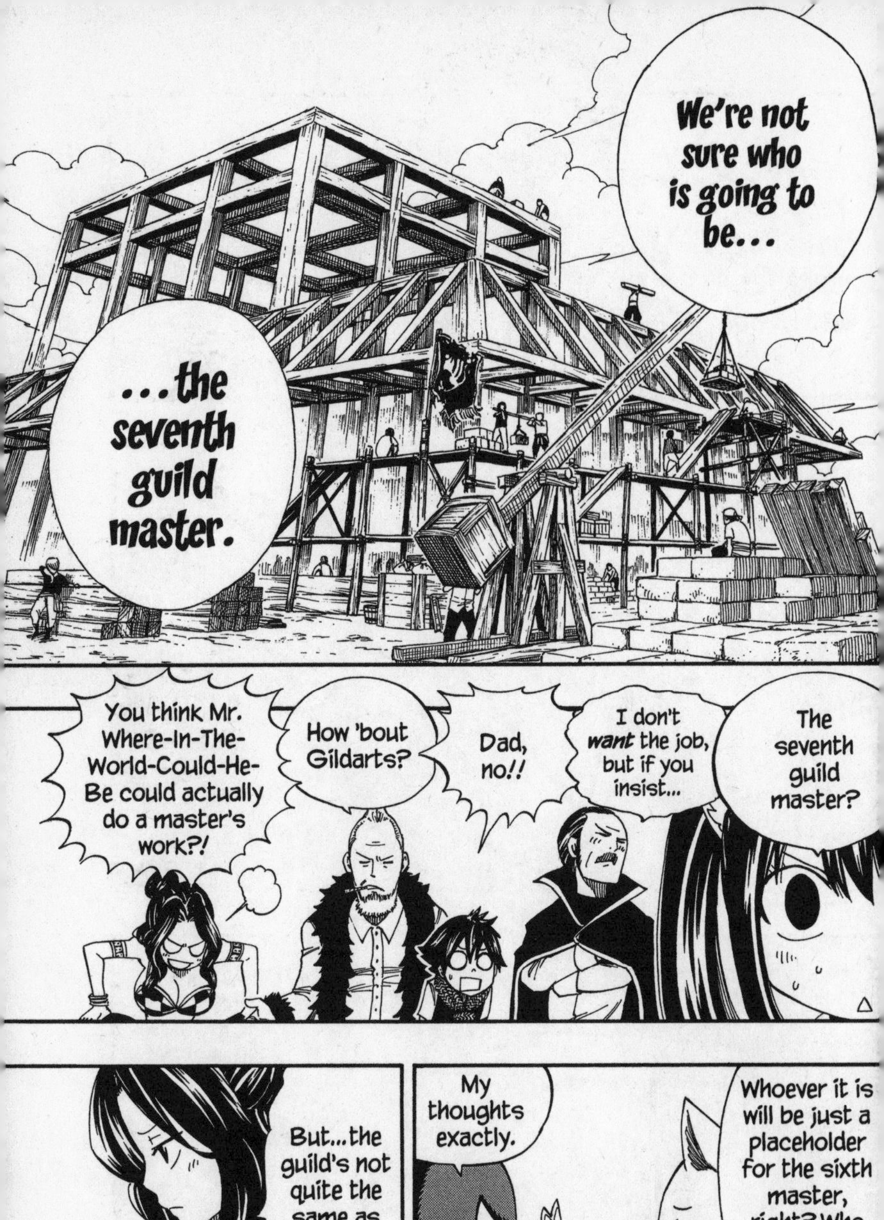
We're not sure who is going to be...
...the seventh guild master.
The seventh guild master?
I don't *want* the job, but if you insist...
Dad, no!!
How 'bout Gildarts?
You think Mr. Where-In-The-World-Could-He-Be could actually do a master's work?!
Whoever it is will be just a placeholder for the sixth master, right? Who cares who it is?
My thoughts exactly.
But...the guild's not quite the same as before.

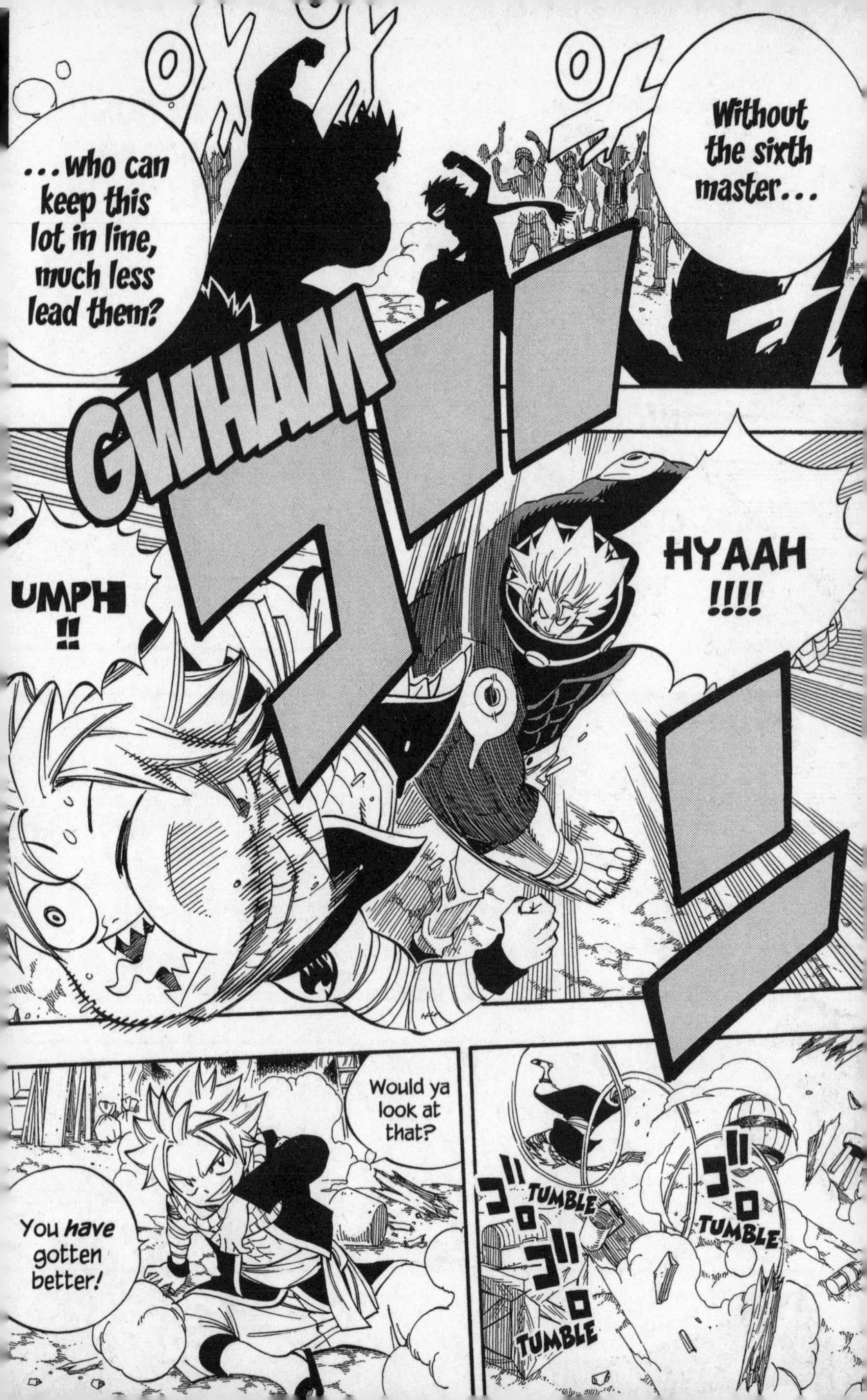

Without the sixth master...
...who can keep this lot in line, much less lead them?
HYAAH !!!!
GWHAM
UMPH !!
TUMBLE
TUMBLE
TUMBLE
Would ya look at that?
You *have* gotten better!

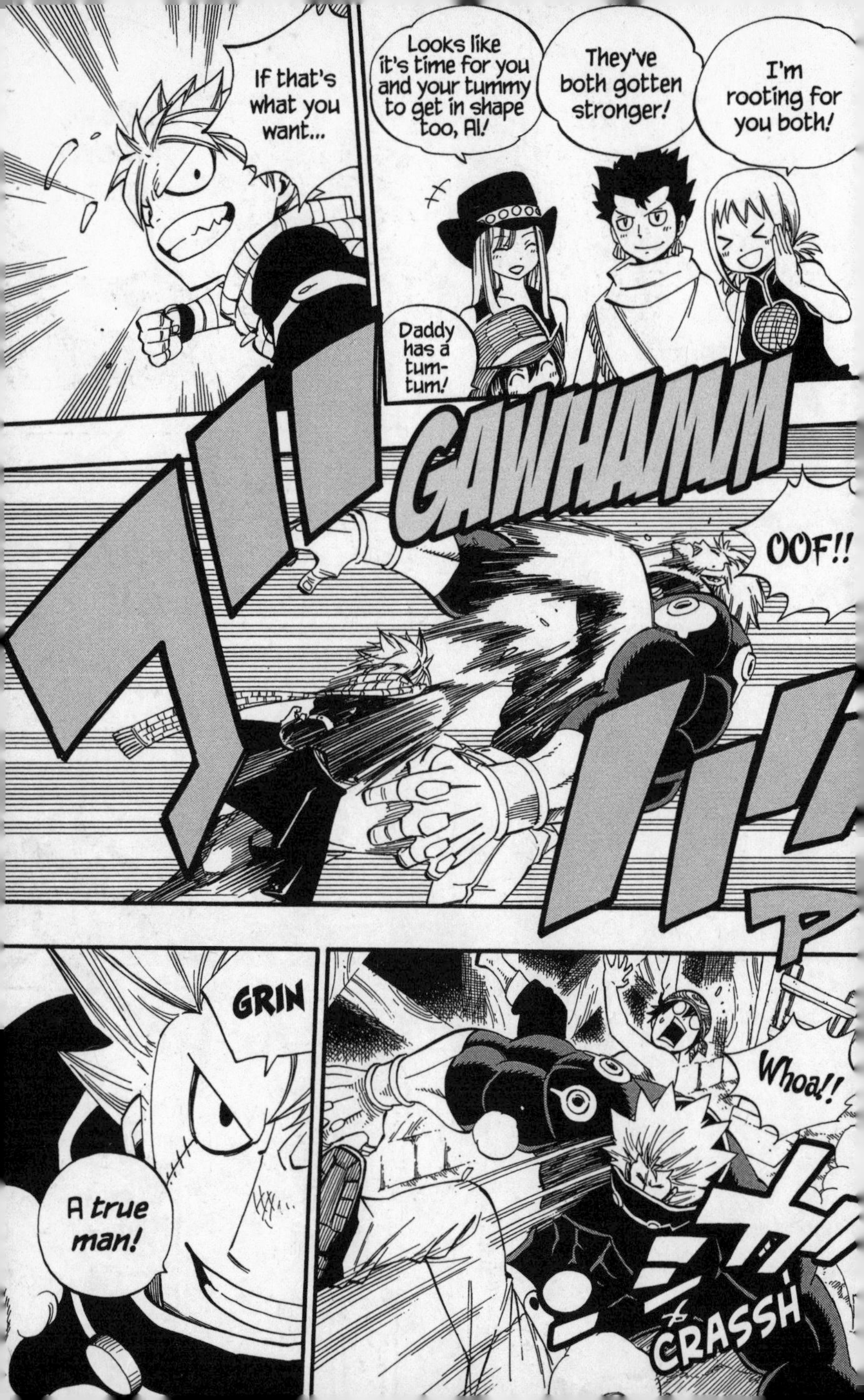
I'm rooting for you both!
They've both gotten stronger!
Looks like it's time for you and your tummy to get in shape too, Al!
Daddy has a tum-tum!
If that's what you want...
GAWHAMM
OOF!!
Whoa!!
CRASSH
GRIN
A true man!

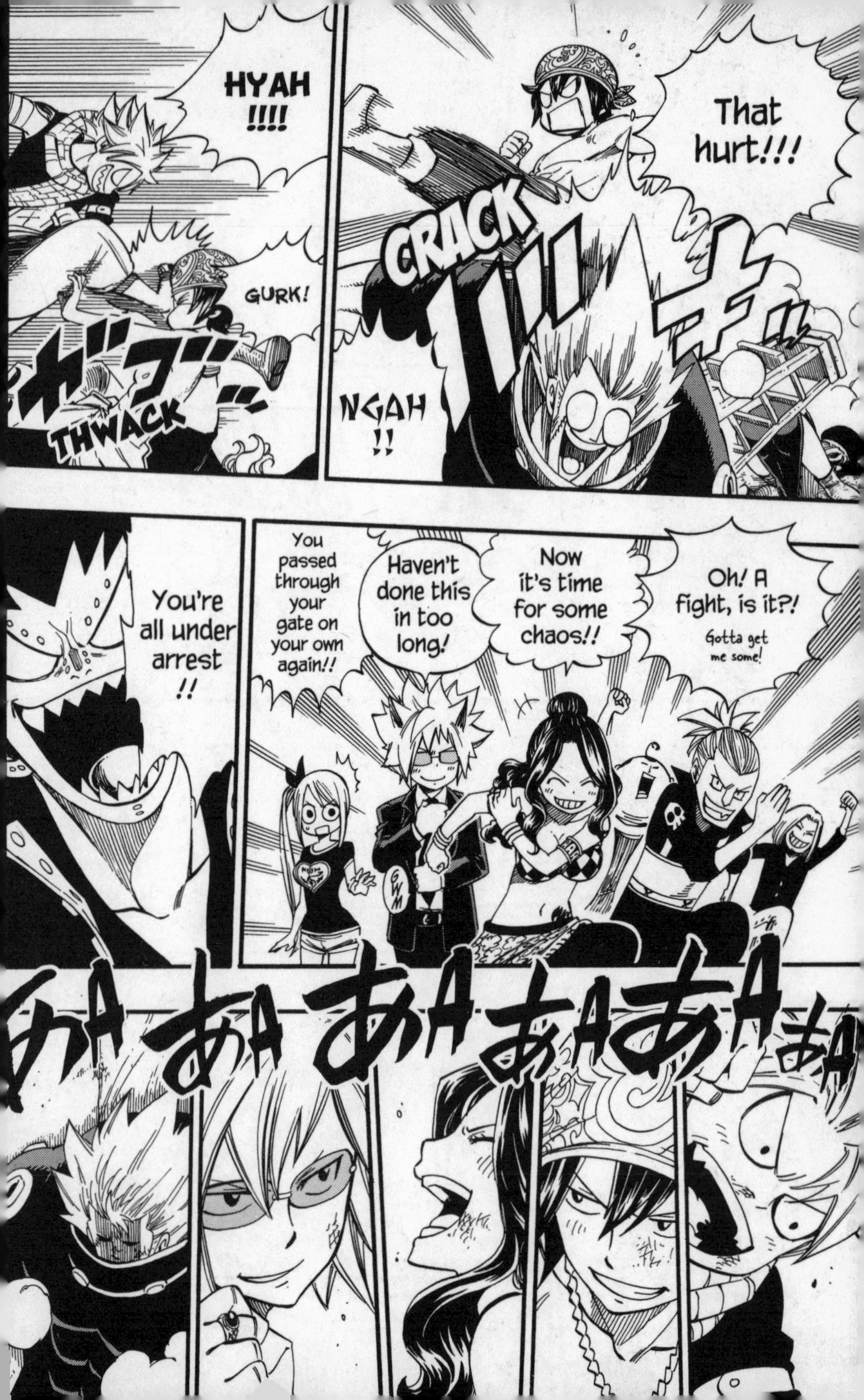
That hurt!!!
CRACK
NGAH!!
HYAH!!!!
GURK!
THWACK
Oh! A fight, is it?!
Gotta get me some!
Now it's time for some chaos!!
Haven't done this in too long!
You passed through your gate on your own again!!
You're all under arrest!!

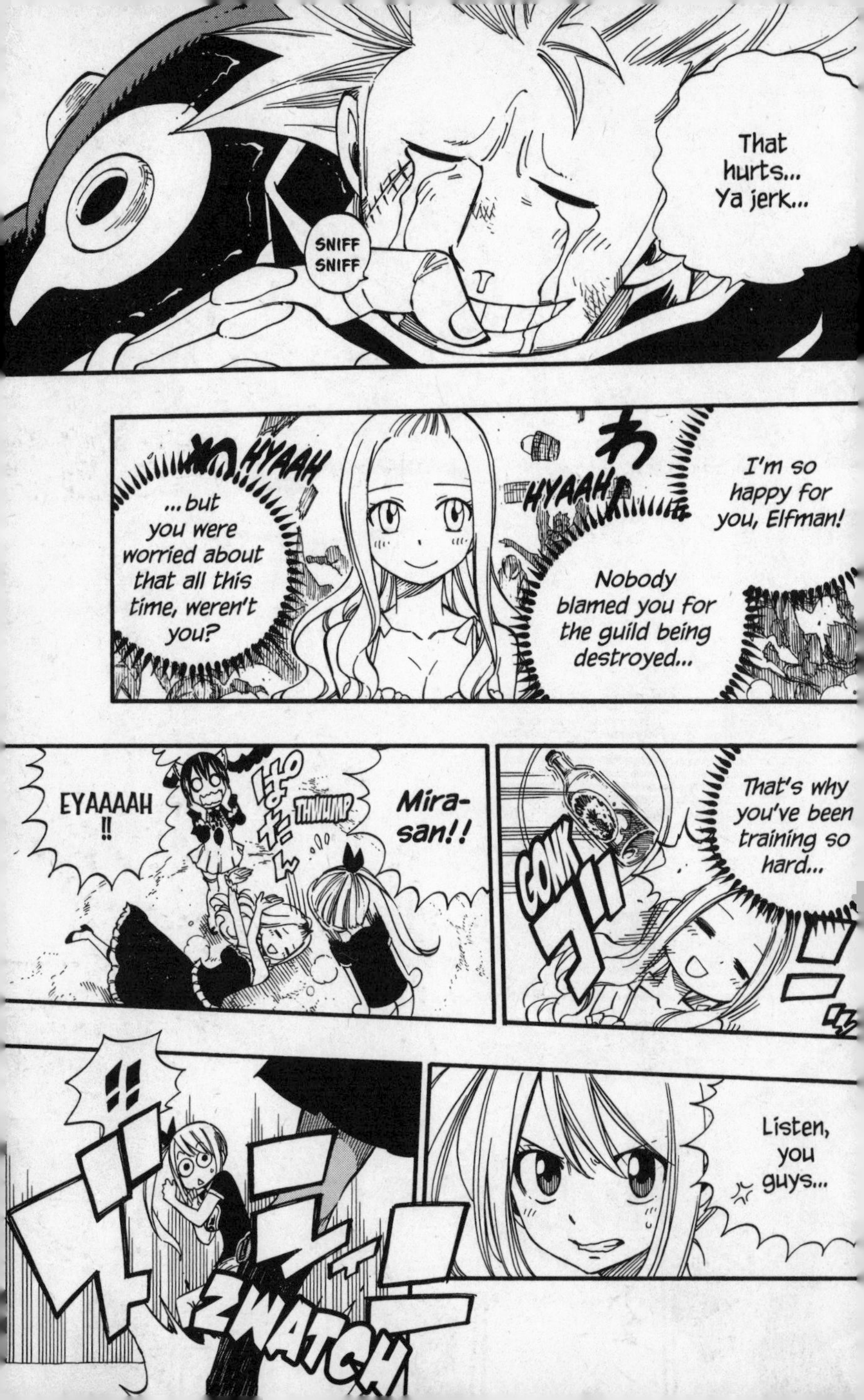
That hurts... Ya jerk...
SNIFF SNIFF
I'm so happy for you, Elfman!
Nobody blamed you for the guild being destroyed...
HYAAAH
...but you were worried about that all this time, weren't you?
HYAAAH
That's why you've been training so hard...
GONK
Mira-san!!
THWUMP
EYAAAAH !!
Listen, you guys...
!!
ZWATCH

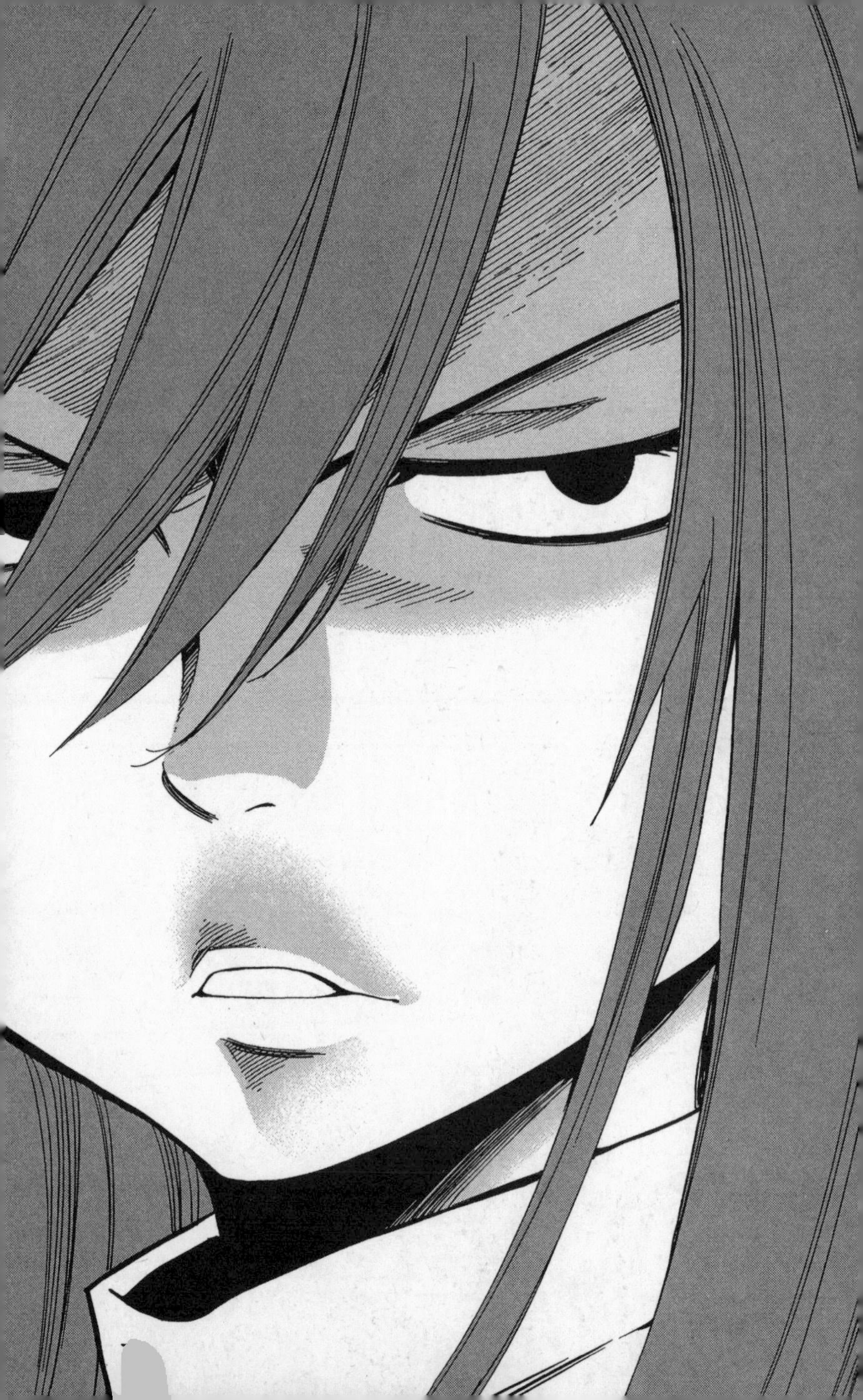

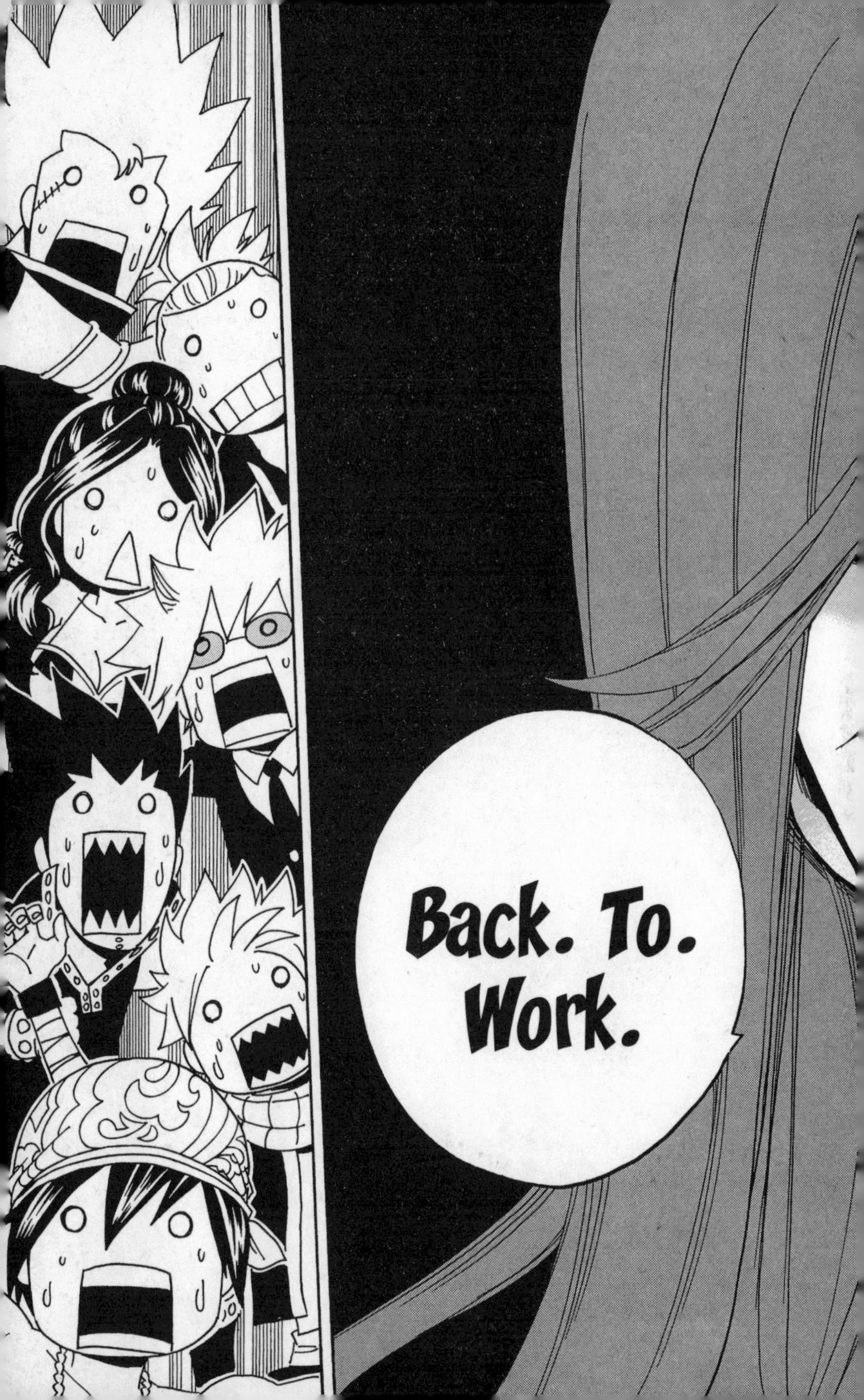
Back. To. Work.

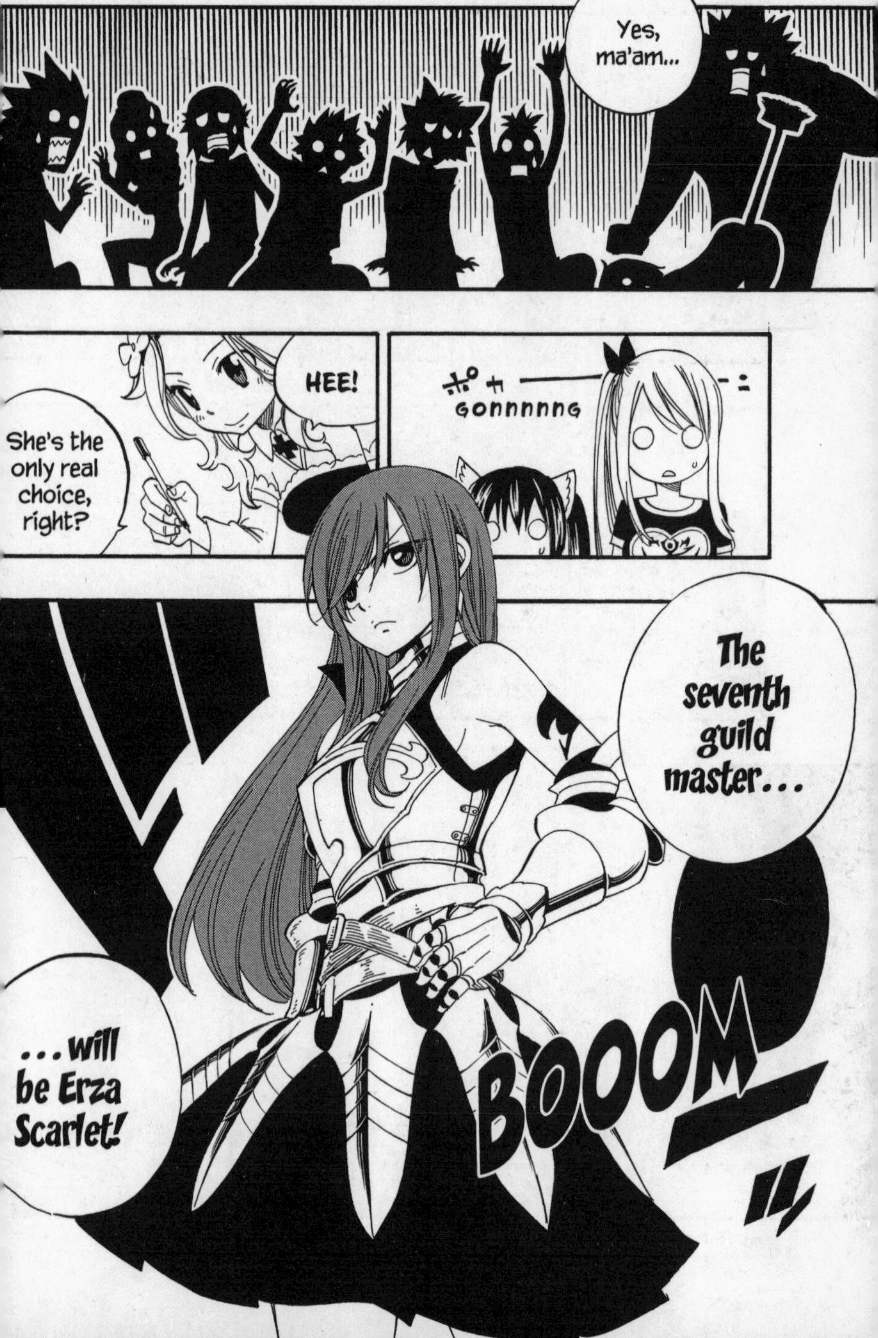
Yes, ma'am...
ポカ
GONNNNNG
HEE!
She's the only real choice, right?
The seventh guild master...
...will be Erza Scarlet!
BOOOM!!

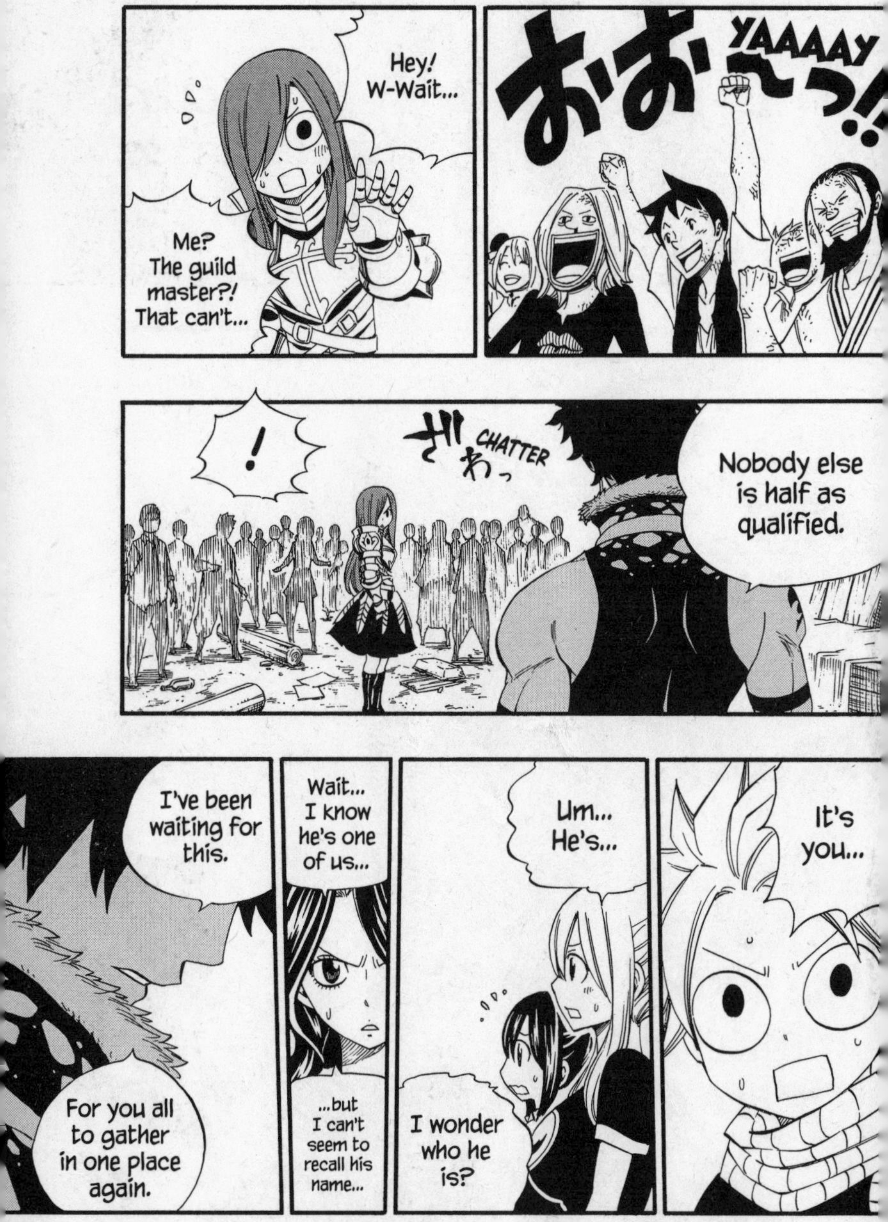
YAAAAY
Hey! W-Wait...
Me? The guild master?! That can't...
Nobody else is half as qualified.
CHATTER
!
It's you...
Um... He's...
I wonder who he is?
Wait... I know he's one of us...
...but I can't seem to recall his name...
I've been waiting for this.
For you all to gather in one place again.

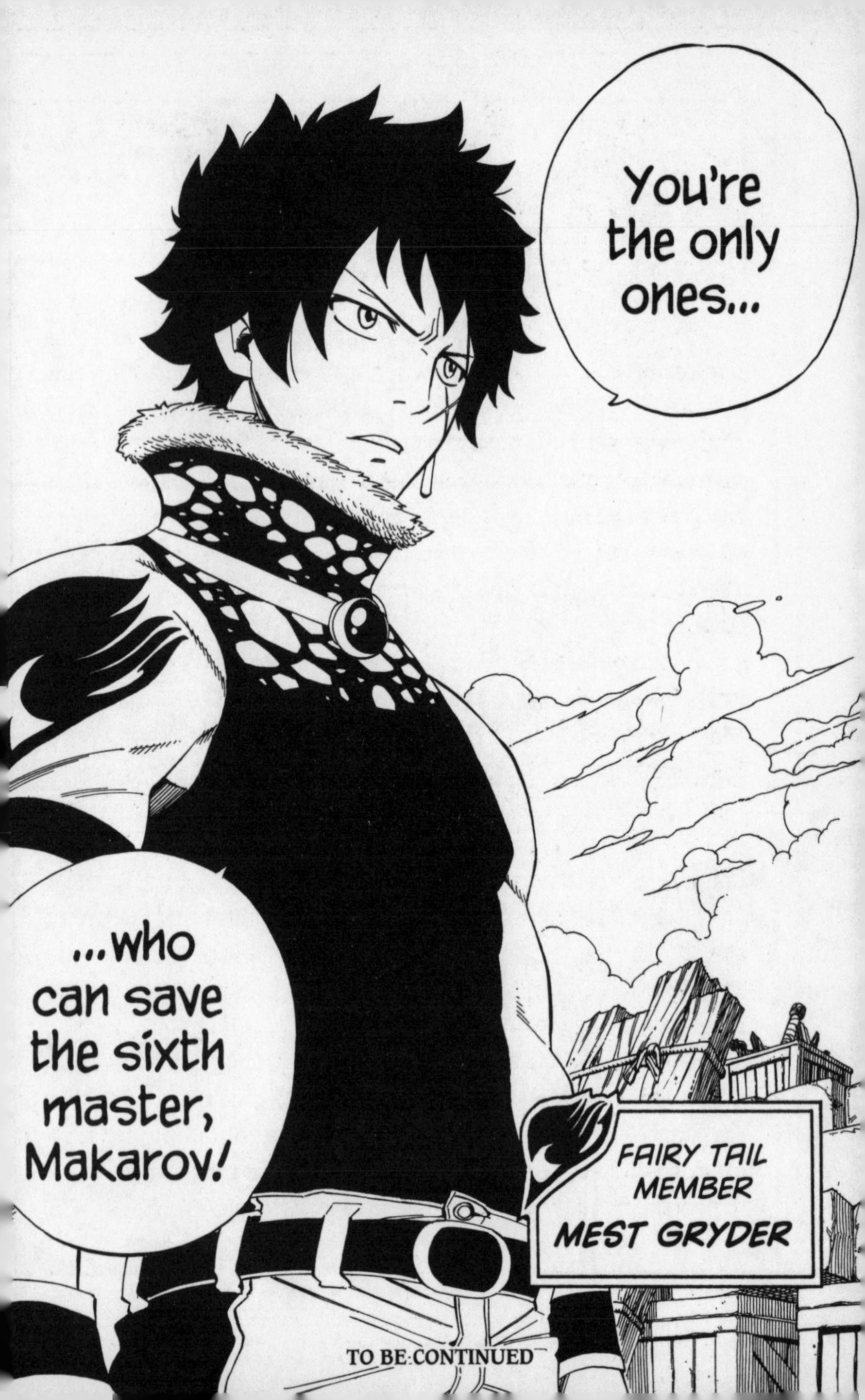
You're the only ones...
...who can save the sixth master, Makarov!
FAIRY TAIL MEMBER
MEST GRYDER
TO BE CONTINUED

あとがき
Afterword

Last time we hit the 50 volume mark!! And just as I was celebrating that, Volume 51 was on me before I knew it. With this volume, all the Fairy Tail members are back together again. I probably could have stretched it out some more, but one of the things that makes FT popular is the quick pace of the plot developments. There are a few guild members that haven't appeared yet, but I hope you're all looking out for how they will find their way back into the story. The number of characters suddenly grew so it's become harder to draw, but the raucous crowd is also part of the fun!

Come to think of it, the other day, I went to a meeting that included a symposium of manga artists, and I received the question, "How long does it take to finish a single page of manga?" Well, the basic answer is, "It depends on the page," but I can explain how some pages take time and how others can be finished quickly.

The quick ones are the ones with few panels and few characters. Say there's a page where Natsu blasts out a burst of fire—a single page with a single drawing. I can finish that one pretty quickly. The pages that take time are the pages with lots of panels and a lot of characters. Also, pages with a high amount of detail (like scenes where an entire town is shown) take up a lot of time, too.

In other words, even though the number of characters within Fairy Tail is huge, you can counterbalance that by limiting the number of characters who appear in a panel and in that way, cut down the amount of time it takes. But since there are so many characters, it really does take time to draw them all.

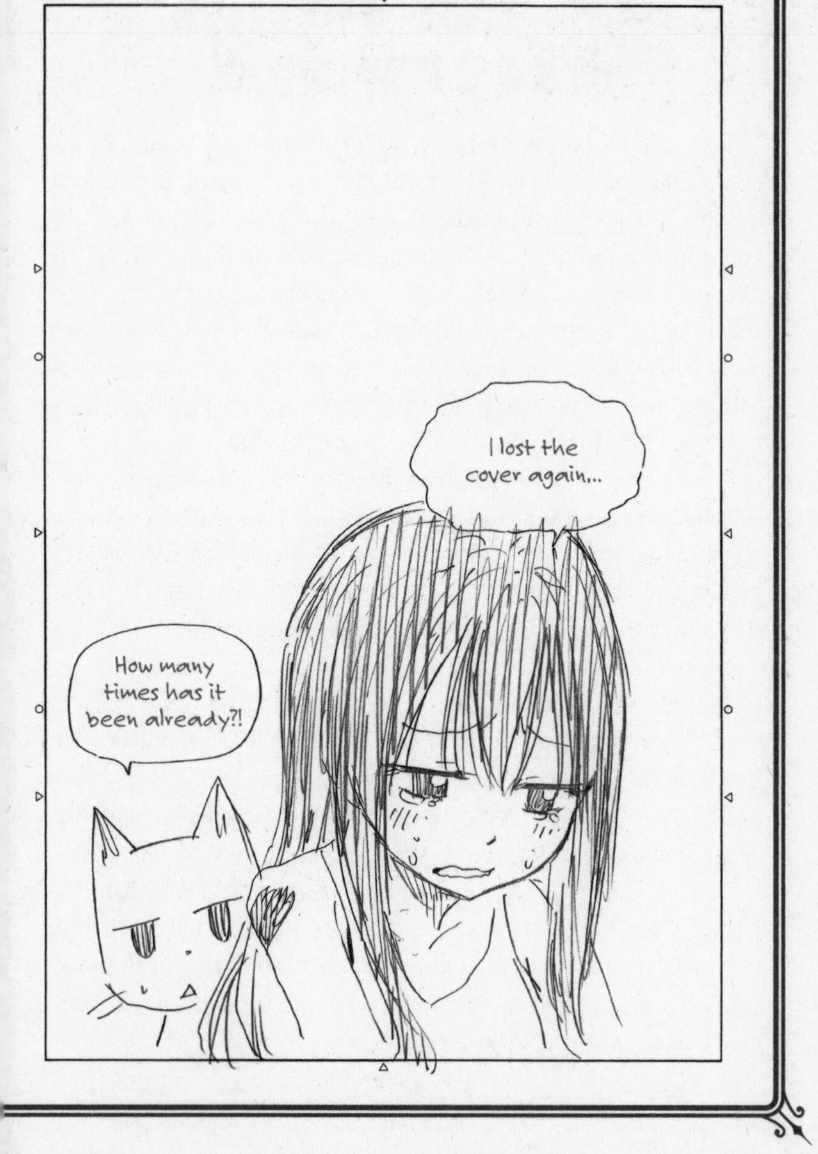
I lost the cover again...
How many times has it been already?!

FAIRY TAIL

フェアリーテイル

51

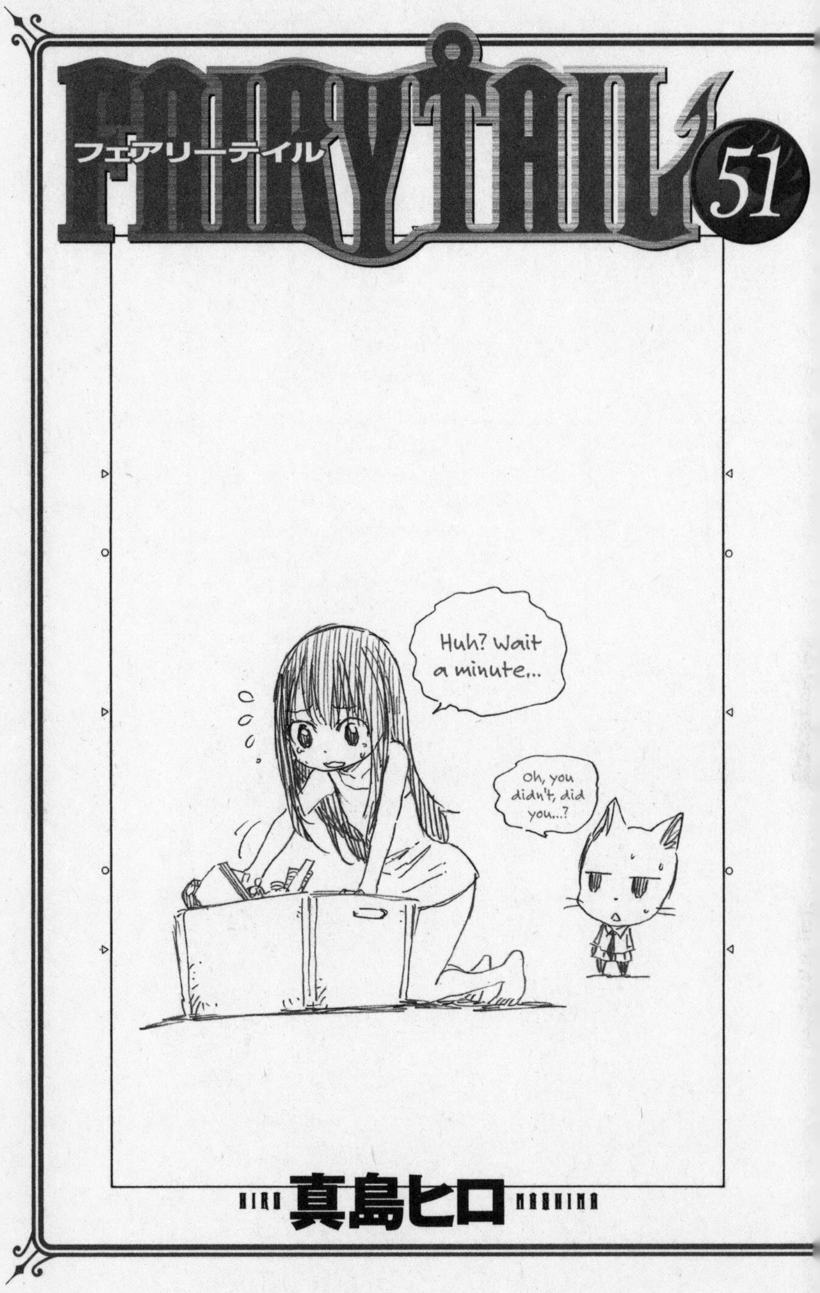
Huh? Wait a minute...
Oh, you didn't, did you...?

真島ヒロ

HIRO MASHIMA

FROM HIRO MASHIMA

Around the time the chapters for this volume were being drawn and published, I went through with a crazy plan to draw two chapters at once, for four issues in a row. It was a lot of work, but I was doing what I loved, so I had fun. Also, the readers of **Weekly Shonen Magazine** seemed to like it, so I thought, "I'm glad I did it." Now, with things gradually escalating in these upcoming volumes, what do you think will happen next?

Original Jacket Design: Hisao Ogawa

Translation Notes:

Japanese is a tricky language for most Westerners, and translation is often more art than science. For your edification and reading pleasure, here are notes on some of the places where we could have gone in a different direction with our translation of the work, or where a Japanese cultural reference is used.

Page 14, Malva

Like most of the towns in the Kingdom of Fiore, Malva is also named after a flower. This one, better known by the English name Mallow, is native to the more tropical regions of Africa, Asia, and Europe. While some are planted as garden flowers, others are thought of as invasive weeds. The color mauve is named after the French word for Malva.

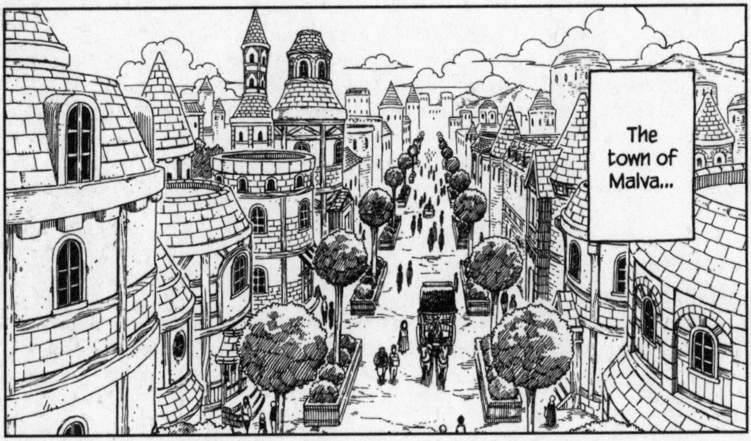
The town of Malva...

Page 85, Eighteen Battle Gods of Yakuma

This isn't the first mention of the Eighteen Battle Gods of Yakuma. Mavis notices that Minerva's power comes from the Eighteen Battle Gods of Yakuma during the Grand Magic Games in Volume 37.

Page 132, Mildian Academy

"Mildian" is a reference to an important village in Hiro Mashima's previous series **Rave Master**, where Mildia was the "Village Carved Out of Time." In **Rave Master**, Mildia is the origin of the Mildian Rave Warriors Games.

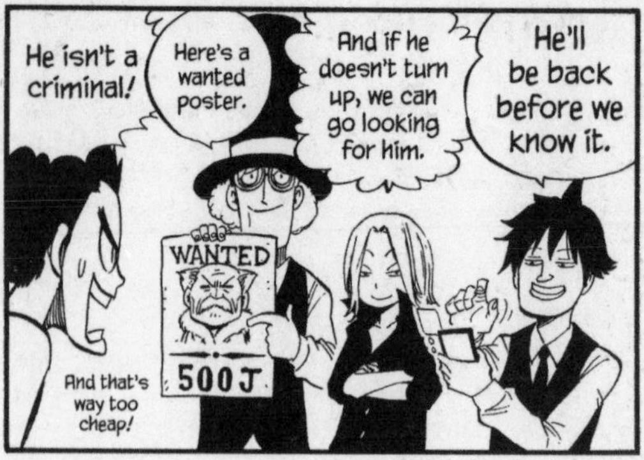
He'll be back before we know it.
And if he doesn't turn up, we can go looking for him.
Here's a wanted poster.
He isn't a criminal!
WANTED
500J
And that's way too cheap!

Page 176, Jewels

\s we noted all the way back in the translation notes for Volume 1, fantasy stories ike to use "intuitive" units of currency for their audience. A fantasy writer in the U.S. night say "100 silver pieces," and make it the equivalent of about $100 worth of goods. apanese fantasy does the same thing, but with yen. In Fairy Tail, if they say 500 jewels, heir audience is supposed to intuit that the price is somewhere around 500 yen. A uick-and-dirty conversion is 100 yen (or in this case, 100 jewels) / $1 USD, so a eward of 500 jewels would be roughly equivalent to a reward of only five bucks.

Page 178, Passing out bottled drinks

here is a tradition of providing water, iced tea, soda, or other beverages for workrs. In previous generations, it was cups of hot tea and crackers during break time. lthough this also happens in Western countries, it isn't as much of a social tradition s it is in Japan.

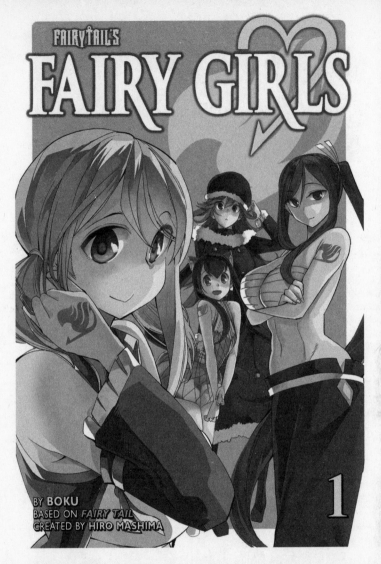

FAIRY TAIL'S
FAIRY GIRLS

1

BY **BOKU**
BASED ON *FAIRY TAIL*
CREATED BY HIRO MASHIMA

In the kingdom of Fiore, wizards are commonplace, but the powerful women of Fairy Tail are each one of a kind! And after fighting their way to the top at the Grand Magic Games, Lucy, Erza, Wendy, and Juvia deserve a vacation. The wizards slip out of the victory celebration to do some sightseeing as a foursome, but where Fairy Tail goes, trouble's never far behind…

We're pleased to present you with a preview of *Fairy Girls*: an all-new series starring the magical ladies of Fairy Tail! Volume 1 available now!

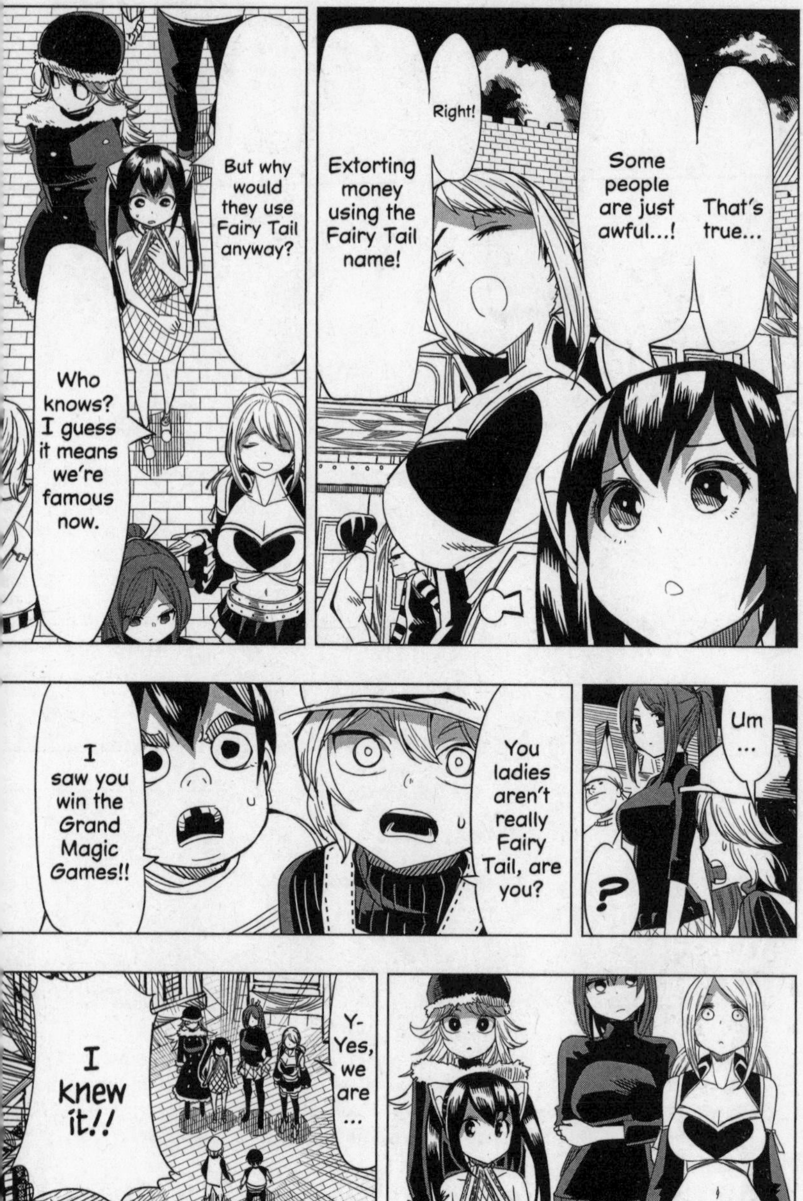

Some people are just awful...!
That's true...
Extorting money using the Fairy Tail name!
Right!
But why would they use Fairy Tail anyway?
Who knows? I guess it means we're famous now.
Um ...
?
You ladies aren't really Fairy Tail, are you?
I saw you win the Grand Magic Games!!
Y-Yes, we are ...
I knew it!!

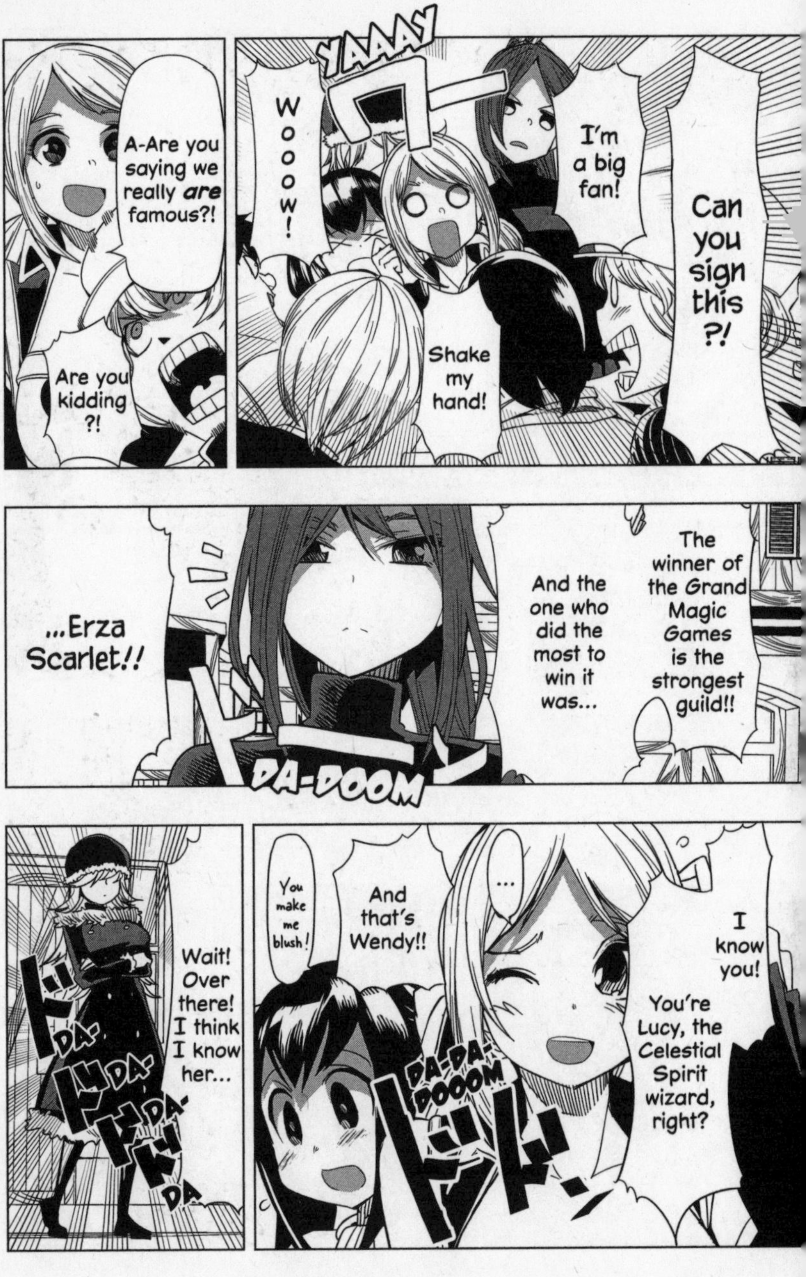
YAAAY
Can you sign this?!
I'm a big fan!
WOOOOW!
Shake my hand!
A-Are you saying we really *are* famous?!
Are you kidding?!
The winner of the Grand Magic Games is the strongest guild!!
And the one who did the most to win it was...
...Erza Scarlet!!
DA-DOOM
I know you!
You're Lucy, the Celestial Spirit wizard, right?
...
And that's Wendy!!
You make me blush!
DA-DA-DOOOM
Wait! Over there! I think I know her...
DA-DA-DA-DA

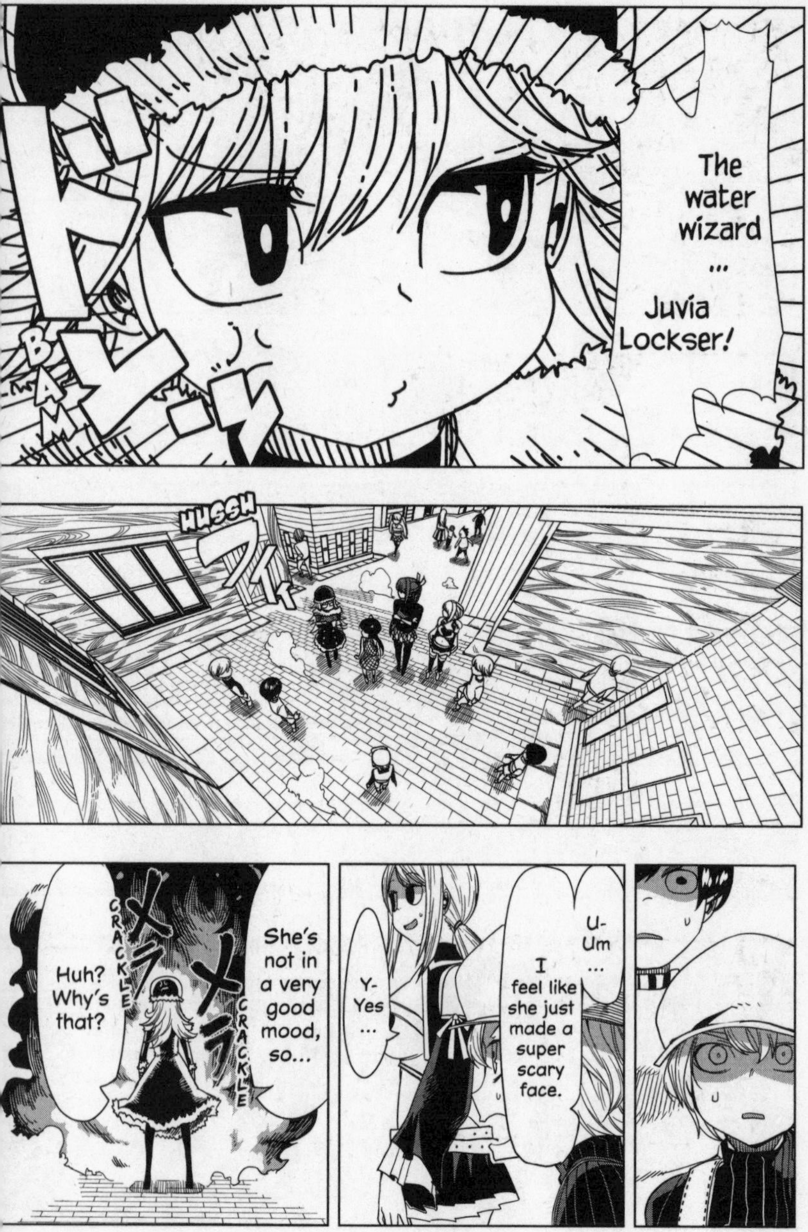
The water wizard ... Juvia Lockser!
BAM
HUSSH
U- Um ...
I feel like she just made a super scary face.
Y- Yes ...
She's not in a very good mood, so...
CRACKLE
CRACKLE
Huh? Why's that?

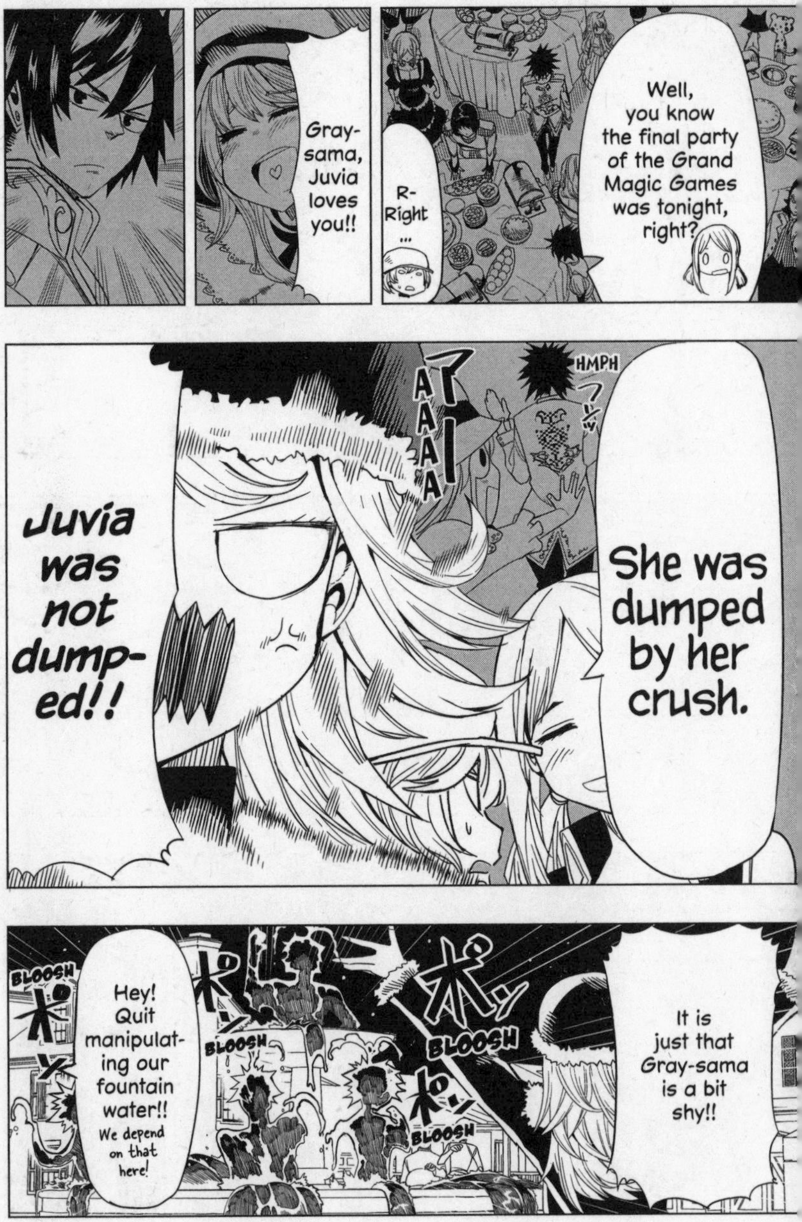
Well, you know the final party of the Grand Magic Games was tonight, right?
R-Right ...
Gray-sama, Juvia loves you!!
She was dumped by her crush.
HMPH
AAAAA
Juvia was not dump-ed!!
It is just that Gray-sama is a bit shy!!
BLOOSH
BLOOSH
BLOOSH
BLOOSH
Hey! Quit manipulat-ing our fountain water!!
We depend on that here!

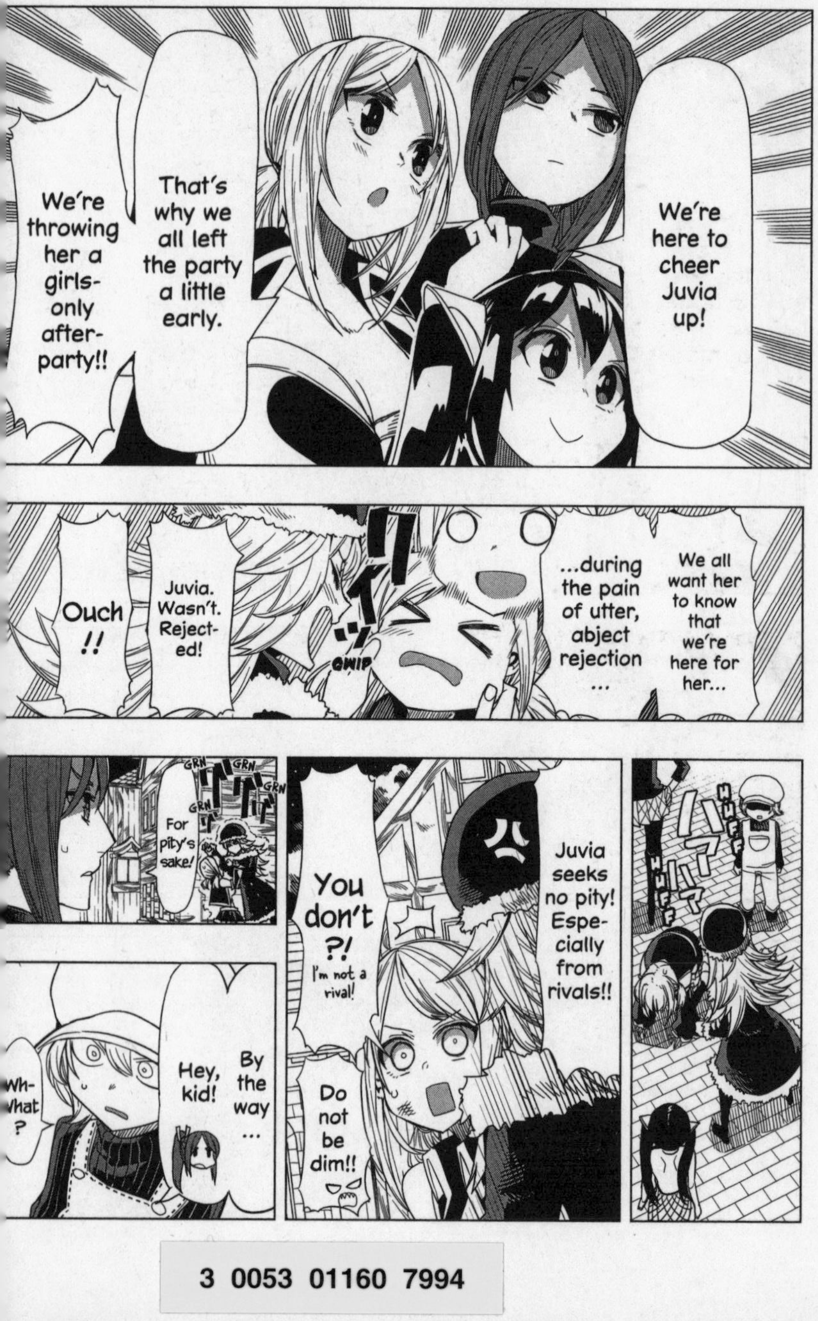
We're here to cheer Juvia up!
That's why we all left the party a little early.
We're throwing her a girls-only after-party!!
We all want her to know that we're here for her...
...during the pain of utter, abject rejection ...
GWIP
Juvia. Wasn't. Rejected!
Ouch !!
HUFF
HUFF
Juvia seeks no pity! Especially from rivals!!
You don't ?!
I'm not a rival!
Do not be dim!!
GRN GRN GRN GRN
For pity's sake!
By the way ...
Hey, kid!
Wh-What ?

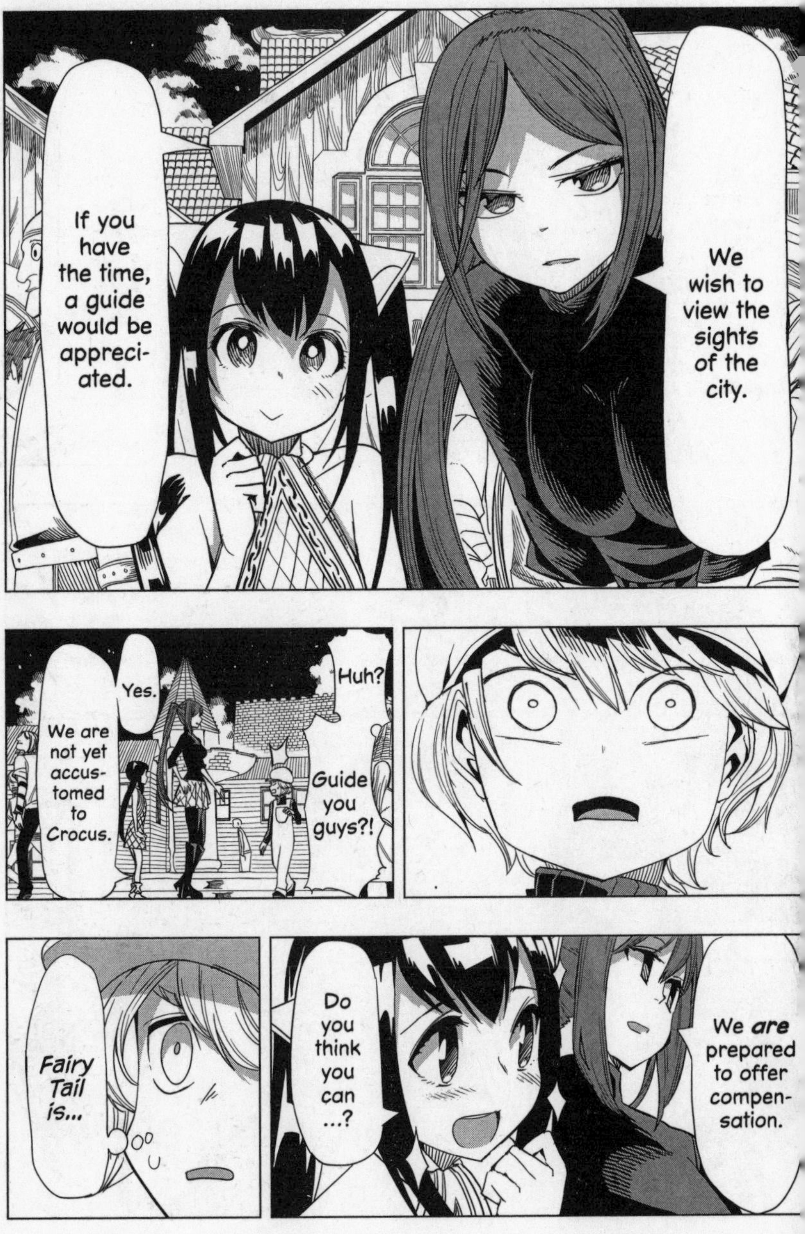
We wish to view the sights of the city.
If you have the time, a guide would be appreciated.
Huh?
Guide you guys?!
Yes.
We are not yet accustomed to Crocus.
We *are* prepared to offer compensation.
Do you think you can ...?
Fairy Tail is...

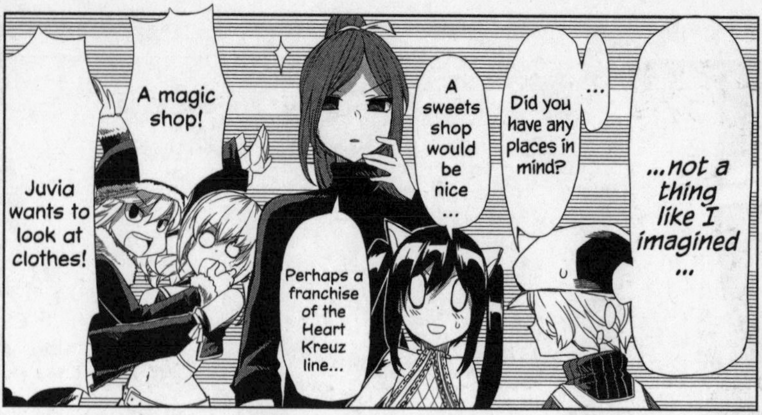
...not a thing like I imagined...
...
Did you have any places in mind?
A sweets shop would be nice...
Perhaps a franchise of the Heart Kreuz line...
A magic shop!
Juvia wants to look at clothes!

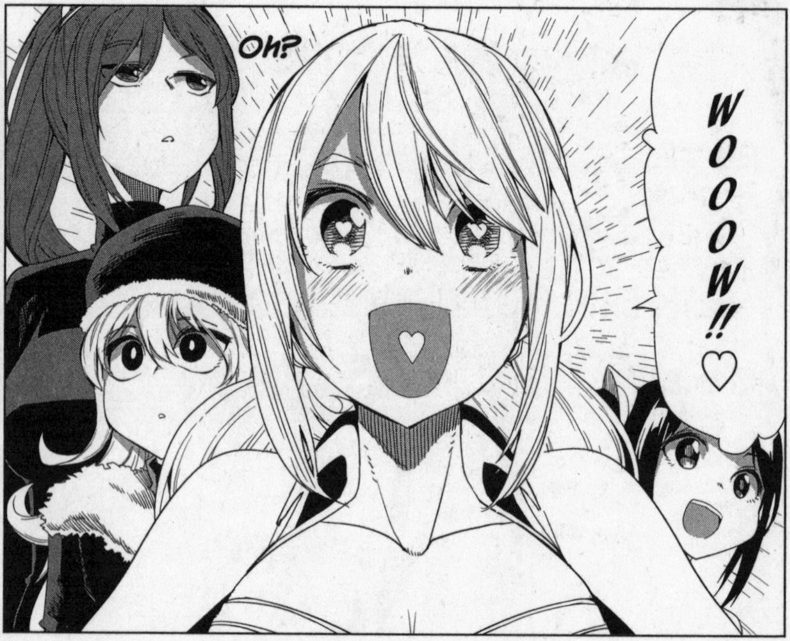
WOOOOW!! ♡
Oh?

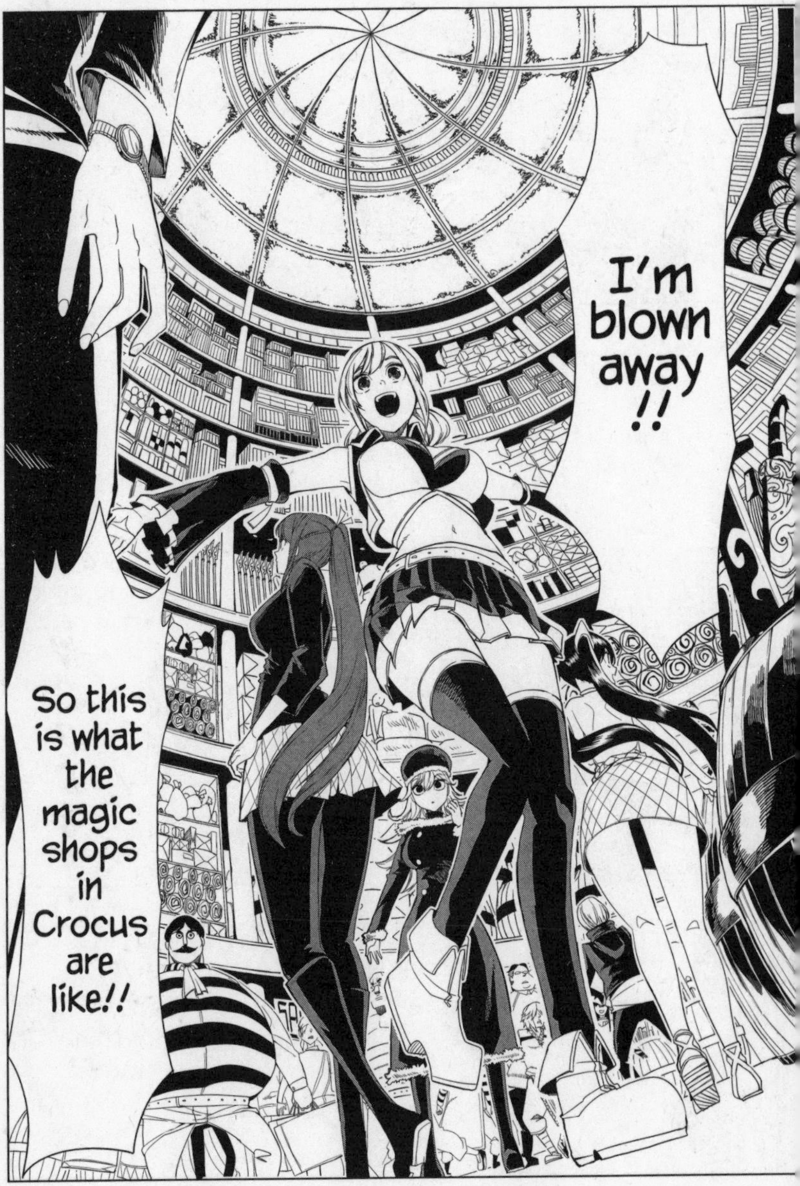
I'm blown away!!
So this is what the magic shops in Crocus are like!!

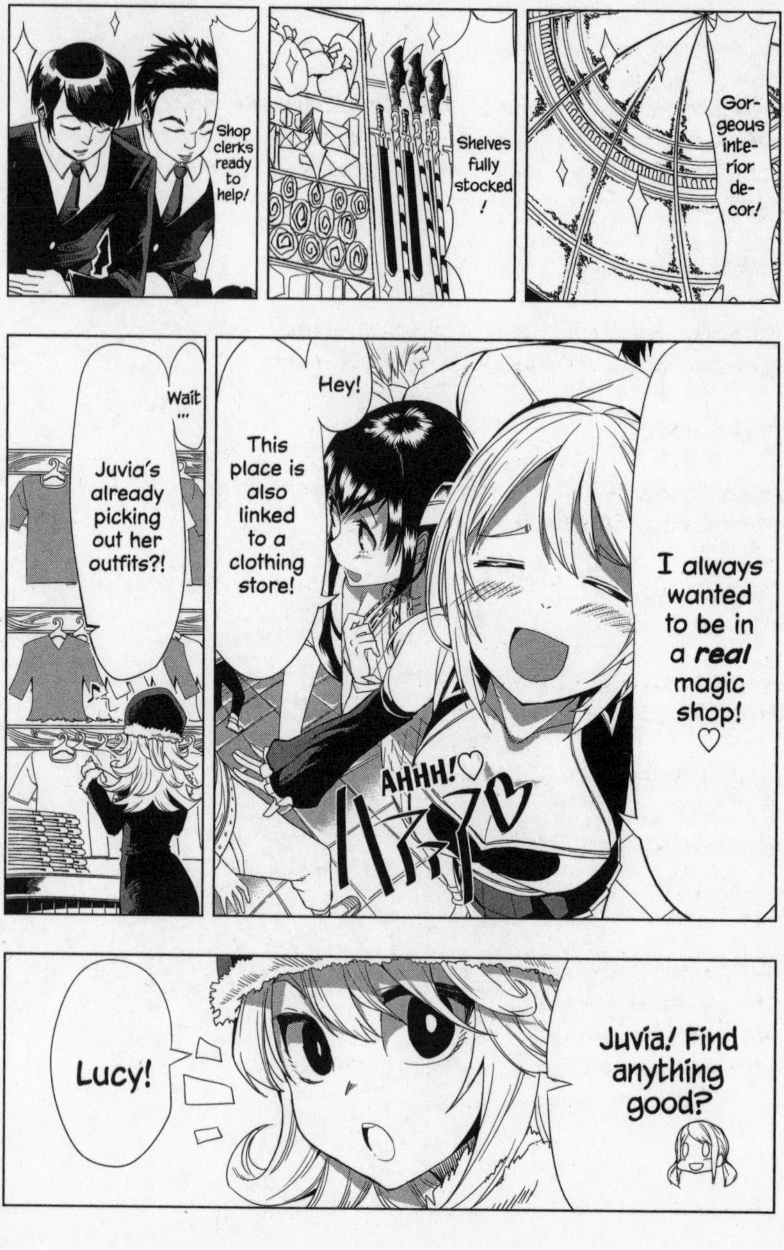
Gor-geous inte-rior de-cor!
Shelves fully stocked!
Shop clerks ready to help!
I always wanted to be in a *real* magic shop! ♡
AHHH! ♡
Hey!
This place is also linked to a clothing store!
Wait ...
Juvia's already picking out her outfits?!
Juvia! Find anything good?
Lucy!

A Kodansha Comics Trade Paperback Original.

Fairy Tail volume 51 copyright © 2015 Hiro Mashima
English translation copyright © 2015 Hiro Mashima

All rights reserved.

Published in the United States by Kodansha Comics, an imprint of Kodansha USA Publishing, LLC, New York.

Publication rights for this English edition arranged through Kodansha Ltd., Tokyo.

First published in Japan in 2015 by Kodansha Ltd., Tokyo
ISBN 978-1-63236-114-1

Printed in the United States of America.

www.kodanshacomics.com

9 8 7 6 5 4 3 2 1

Translation: William Flanagan
Lettering: AndWorld Design
Editing: Haruko Hashimoto
Kodansha Comics edition cover design by Phil Balsman

TOMARE!

止まれ
[STOP!]

You're going the wrong way!

Manga is a completely different type of reading experience.

To start at the *beginning*, go to the *end!*

at's right! Authentic manga is read the traditional Japanese way—
m right to left, exactly the *opposite* of how American books are
d. It's easy to follow: Just go to the other end of the book and read
ch page—and each panel—from right side to left side, starting at
top right. Now you're experiencing manga as it was meant to be!